JAMMU & KASHMIR

A BATTLE OF PERCEPTIONS

JAMMU & KASHMIR
A BATTLE OF PERCEPTIONS

AS Chonker, VSM

Centre for Land Warfare Studies

PENTAGON PRESS LLP

The Centre for Land Warfare Studies (CLAWS), New Delhi, is an autonomous think tank dealing with contemporary issues of national security and conceptual aspects of land warfare, including conventional and sub-conventional conflicts and terrorism. CLAWS conducts research that is futuristic in outlook and policy-oriented in approach.

Centre for Land Warfare Studies
RPSO Complex, Parade Road, Delhi Cantt, New Delhi-110010
Phone: 011-25691308 • Fax: 011-25692347
email: landwarfare@gmail.com • website: www.claws.in

First Published in 2019

ISBN 978-81-941634-4-2

Copyright © Centre for Land Warfare Studies, New Delhi

All rights reserved. No part of this publication may be reproduced, stored in a retrieval system, or transmitted, in any form or by any means, electronic, mechanical, photocopying, recording, or otherwise, without first obtaining written permission of the copyright owner.

The views expressed and suggestions made in the book are solely of the author in his personal capacity and do not have any official endorsement. Attributability of contents lies purely with author.

Published by
PENTAGON PRESS LLP
206, Peacock Lane, Shahpur Jat, New Delhi-110049
Phones: 011-64706243, 26491568
Telefax: 011-26490600
email: rajan@pentagonpress.in
website: www.pentagon-press.com

Printed at Aegean Offset Printers, Greater Noida, U.P.

Contents

	Foreword	*vii*
	Preface	*ix*
	Acknowledgements	*xi*
	Abbreviations	*xiii*
	Executive Summary	*xvii*
1.	Introduction	1
2.	Analysis of Key Internal and External Factors of J&K with Special Reference to Kashmir	10
3.	Systems Analysis	99
4	Psychological Aspects of Kashmir and their Solutions	143
5	SWOT Analysis and Short-Term Strategies	160
6	A Peek into the Future: Scenario-Building Exercise	197
7	Perception Management/Improvement Strategies	290

Appendices and Annexure

Appendix A: Detailed Analysis of the Questionnaire J&K	305
Appendix B: Questionnaire Analysis by Tata Institute of Social Sciences as well as in-House Resources	315
Bibliography	358
Index	360

Foreword

Jammu & Kashmir: A Battle of Perceptions is a net assessment of the current security situation in state. It is a research work initiated by the premier think tank of the Army, i.e., Centre for Land Warfare Studies (CLAWS). Over the years, the Indian Army has borne the brunt of Pakistani designs of proxy war which germinate from a misplaced belief that it can stake claim to this integral part of our country, India. It is but natural that as major stakeholders, the Armed Forces study and understand the underlying currents in the security situation in the state so that remedial and environment-shaping strategies can be worked out to beat nefarious designs.

To this effect, a national level seminar on "Mapping of Perceptions in Jammu & Kashmir – The Way Ahead" was also conducted in August 2018, where renowned authors, academicians, social scientists, leaders of Kashmiri self-help youth groups and generals had discussed the perceptions of the people of the state at length and come to some logical conclusions. Considering the fact that the Kashmir Valley has remained unstable due to proxy war cum cross-border terrorism, the author has focussed on the affected regions. The overwhelming belief of all the participants was clearly indicating that a whole of the government approach needed to be taken so that we could save the state from leaning over the precipice of destruction.

Over the years many authors have recorded the mood of the people and the prevalent conditions in the state, but none have given a road map to positive peace and prosperity in the state. This book has not only compiled the interactions of every possible entity and stakeholder of the state, but also given strategies for the future, especially in the Psychological domain and in shaping of perceptions to achieve lasting peace.

March 2019   Lt Gen (Dr) VK Ahluwalia (Retd)
Director, CLAWS

Preface

Jammu & Kashmir: A Battle of Perceptions has been written at the culmination of a research scholarship undertaken by the Author in Centre for Land Warfare Studies (CLAWS) on the topic of "Perception Management for J&K".

This research study was conceptualized to decipher a complex and contemporary topic, relevant in today's environment, holding immense importance to the Govt of India, State Govt and the Indian Army engaged in combating militancy in the state for last three decades.

It is the culmination of the toil of almost five years starting from a Net Assessment study on the security situation in Kashmir in 2014 at College of Defence Management (CDM), Secunderabad, a premier institute of the Indian Army, followed by an MPhil dissertation on the same subject and a research scholarship on a seat of excellence study sponsored by the Brigade of Guards.

The resolution of the complex Jammu & Kashmir problem cannot be over-emphasised. However, a web of external and political-social-legal-economic factors within the country has created a knotty problem which requires long-term strategising and a whole of the government approach to find solutions that improve the overall security situation and foster peace and prosperity. The study has tapped a vast knowledge bank and experience of various sections of society. Based on these inputs, it has analyzed the perceptions of various actors and has come up with viable strategies for short, medium and long terms.

The author strongly believes that in the coming years, the battle for Jammu and Kashmir will increasingly shift to the cognitive domain and perception management will be the key to success; hence through, this book and the study he has attempted to identify each and every factor playing on the minds of the people of J&K with special reference to Kashmir.

Over the years, many books have been written on the situation in Kashmir, but most of them paint only the not so rosy picture of the state, through the years of turmoil; almost certainly, none give a roadmap with logic for solutions towards achieving peace and prosperity. This book is an attempt towards this end.

Acknowledgements

The book could not have been possible without the express support of Lt Gen Surinder Singh, the Col of the Regt, Brigade of Guards, who selected this contemporary topic for sponsoring it as a Chair of excellence study, and Lt Gen Balraj Nagal (Retd) and Lt Gen VK Ahluwalia (Retd), Directors Centre For Land Warfare Studies (CLAWS), who have constantly provided support and guidance during the research scholarship.

The book could not have been possible but for the in-depth knowledge gained on the subject while working on a Net Assessment Study at College of Defence Management (CDM). The author expresses his gratitude to his project team and the directing staff for the countless hours spent in channelising thoughts.

The author also thanks the staff at Head Quarters Northern Command at Udhampur and 15 Corps at Srinagar for assisting in collecting and analyzing data from the hotbed, as well as Professor Sujata Sriram from the School of Human Ecology, Tata Institute of Social Sciences (TISS), Mumbai, who very graciously accepted to assist in preparing a questionnaire for analysis.

Last but not the least, it is important to thank all the participants of the National Seminar on "Mapping of Perceptions in J&K – The Way Ahead" (conducted by CLAWS in August 2018), including the Chief of Army Staff, who very candidly expressed their opinions and threw light on the current situation in the State.

Abbreviations

Ack	Acknowledge
Amn	Ammunition
Approx	Approximately
AFSPA	Armed Forces Special Powers Act
Art	Article
AIOS	Anti Infiltration Obstacle System
APHC	All Party Hurriyat Conference
BMC	Base Means Capacity
BSF	Border Security Force
CAPF	Central Armed Police Force
Cas	Casualty
CLD	Causal Loop Diagram
CI/CT	Counter Insurgency/Counter Terrorism
COB	Company Operating Base
CISF	Central Industrial Security Force
CPMF	Central Para Military Force
CNP	Comprehensive National Power
Devp	Development
Dte	Directorate
Distt	District
DIA	Defence Intelligence Agency
Emp	Employment
Eqpt	Equipment
Eco	Economy
FATA	Federally Administered Tribal Area
GSDP	Gross State Domestic Product

Govt	Government
GoI	Govt of India
Gps	Groups
Hept	Helicopter
HR	Human Rights
HM	Hizb-ul-Mujahideen
Iden	Identity
ISAF	International Security Assistance Force
Incl	Including
Incr	Increase
IA	Indian Army
ISI	Inter-Services Intelligence
Indl	Individual
IB	International Boundary
Ldr	Leader
LWE	Left Wing Extremism
Loc	Location
MCA	Military Civic Action
MHA	Ministry of Home Affairs
MEA	Ministry of External Affairs
Mov	Move
NC	National Conference
NGOs	Non-Governmental Organisations
NWFP	North West Frontier Force
NLF	National Liberation Front
ORSA	Operational Research and Systems Analysis
OGW	Over-Ground Worker
PLA	People's Liberation Army
PDP	People's Democratic Party
PSA	Public Safety Act
UJC	United Jehadi Council
Posn	Position
Prog	Progress

Proj	Project
PR	Public Relations
Reqd	Required
RF	Reserve Forest
RPF	Revolutionary Peoples Front
Rd	Road
SADO	Search and Destroy Operations
SF	Security Forces (Assam Rifles and Indian Armed Forces)
SAARC	South Asian Association for Regional Cooperation
SE	South East
SE Asia	South East Asia
SEZ	Special Economic Zone
Sq	Square
Str	Strength
Svl	Surveillance
SOG	Special Operations Group
TA	Territorial Army
Trg	Training
TARN	Trans Asian Railway Network
Tpt	Transport
TTP	Tehrik-e-Taliban Pakistan
UG	Underground
ULFA	United Liberation Front of Assam
UNLF	United Nations Liberation Front
UAV	Unmanned Aerial Vehicle
VBIG	Valley-Based Insurgent Groups
Vill	Village
Wpn	Weapon
Wef	With effect from
Wk	Work

Executive Summary

Over the coming decades, India's global influence would look set to rise substantially, as the country becomes an increasingly important economy with an enhanced role to play as a major global power in a multi-polar world. However, internal security issues like the J&K problem, Left Wing Extremism (LWE) and Insurgency in the North-east impede the desired rate of development of our great nation utilising substantial amounts of time and resources in terms of men, material and finances. The state of Jammu and Kashmir has been an integral part of India since 1947. For a permanent solution to the issue at hand, one should be looking at the parameters of reduction in violence and increase in peace which appear suspiciously out of sync with the emerging environment. There are issues such as governance, radicalism, financial conduits to the Separatists, trust between the people and the security forces/other organs of the Central Government, self-esteem and dignity of the Kashmiri people, the degree of connect between the Centre and the State, tourism and other revenue and profit-earning activities which need focussed attention. Hence, if the desired end state to the J&K problem is to seamlessly integrate the state of Jammu and Kashmir with India, the perception of the target population needs to be managed/improved towards the desired end state.

For the above to take place, scientifically it is most important to identify the audiences/elements. This can only be done in case a comprehensive analysis is carried out through a Net Assessment. It is for these reasons that the author amended his research topic to "Perception Management for J&K" from "Perception Management in J&K". While the latter suggests that it is for only internal elements, the former signifies that it is for the complete environment which includes all the audiences (internal, external, affiliated, associated, social, psychological) which are directly or indirectly affecting the emerging situation and the psyche of the people of the state. This book is an attempt at conducting an in-depth analysis of all the internal and external factors affecting the situation in Jammu and Kashmir whether these be the psychological, economic, religious, social, political, administrative, externally influenced factors or the factors affecting the security situation and law and order issues. This book not only provides a look at the current environment but it also tries at taking a peek at the future through scientific analysis. Above all, it provides solutions for the short, mid and long terms at all levels for shaping perceptions and bringing in positive peace to the state of J&K in a logical manner, a feat not often undertaken by contemporary authors.

Key Findings

Some of the key findings of the book are enumerated below:

- **History.**
    - There is a deep connect of the state with the rest of India.
    - The state enjoys a rich syncretic culture and history.
    - 1931 was a crucial year in which politics of the day created a divide in the minds of the Valley.
    - 1932 – Confirmation of Grievances by Glancy commission.
    - US blind eye in wake of Pak Mujahideen adventurism fueled Pakistan's ambition.
    - Rigged Elections 1987 supported the cause for Pakistan.
    - Gawakadal bridge Incident 1990 in which scores of people lost their lives hardened international perceptions.
    - Periods of relative peace and missed opportunities came and went by without an era of positive peace dawning on the state.
- **Youth Bulge.** 70% of the people of the state are under the age of 35 years which becomes an important factor to keep in mind.
- **Unemployment.** The unemployment figures of the state are at 12.3%, much higher than the national average. If extrapolated to the youth of the Kashmir Valley, it simply means that around three and a half hundred thousand youth are unemployed in a small area of the state known as the Kashmir Valley.
- **Lack of Women and Youth Empowerment.** These issues are accentuating the situation at hand.
- **Perceived Regional Disparity.** Perceived disparity in representation, sharing of resources, etc are creating a divide amongst the three distinct regions of the state, i.e., Jammu, Ladakh and Kashmir.
- **Political Deadlock.** The political deadlock between the regional parties and the Central power centres, a lack of a political alternative and years of mis-governance are adding to the uncertainty in the state.

- **AFSPA, a touchy issue all around.** Although the Public Safety Act (PSA) is much more stringent, the focus of attention stays constantly on the Armed Forces Special Powers Act in disturbed areas.
- Subversion of Vernacular Press is a reality.
- Social Media is a game changer.
- Importance of capability building of Police and CAPF.
- Data Analysis of surveys conducted for the book is very insightful.
- Historical Baggage comprises Political, Ethnic and Security turmoil.
- Important to Understand Kashmiri Psyche.
- Organizational and Operational Tools of terror in the state need to studied in detail.
- It is important to deal with the situation as a System.
- No quick fix solutions – will become "Fixes that Fail".
- Jamaat-e-Islami Factor and its attempt at corrosion of the core culture of Kashmiriyat cannot be neglected.
- Tableeghi Jamatis creating the Pull towards increased religious activities.
- Springing of Ahl-e-Hadith Mosques in the Valley are creating the push for the people towards the four sub-schools:
  ❖ Jamait-ul-ahle-Hadith (Puritans).
  ❖ Difai (Ultra-Puritans).
  ❖ Guraba (Religio-political Ultra-Puritans).
  ❖ South-al-Haq (ISISideolgy) where wajib-ul-qatl (eligibility to murder non-believers) is the norm.
- Importance of International Efforts at targeting Ideology through Social and Religious Rehab is coming to the fore and need to be leveraged.
- Importance of the Whole of the Govt Approach to solve the problem cannot be over-emphasized.
- A very complex and dynamic situation. Many important factors at play.
  ❖ Sociological.
  ❖ Psychological.
  ❖ Economic.
  ❖ Religious.
  ❖ Ideological.
  ❖ External.
  ❖ Security related.
  ❖ Political.
  ❖ Administrative.

- Teachers become a very important cog in the wheel. Ideologically inclined teachers are playing havoc with the minds of the youth.
- **Surrender Policy and Rehab.** Correct policies on this front could make the change be felt on the ground.
- Comparison with POK and Development issues becomes a key point.
- Police and CAPF - not only capacity building but image building and best practices towards community policing are also required.
- Pundit Rehab Issue is important to get back the syncretic culture.
- Mindset of Youth for Govt jobs versus Private sector jobs needs to be changed.
- Youth Self-Help Groups are coming to the fore – a Silent Revolution in the making.
- Everything done by the Centre seen as an Agenda by Awaam – Need to tread with caution.
- Through Forecasting techniques one can clearly identify the elements at play in the future.
- Bottom Line – Everything is not Doom and Gloom as being projected by many but in case corrective actions as suggested by this book are not taken, there can only be Doom, doom, doom and gloom, gloom, and gloom after a decade or so.

The Elements/Audiences identified by the Study

People of the State. The people and their Psyche have already been identified as the Centre of Gravity and therefore they need to be given due importance for the purpose of this exercise. Although the Awaam can be treated as one throughout the state, a word of caution however is to deal with the Awaam of the Kashmir Valley, Jammu region and Ladakh region separately also, as is suggested through the system analysis. If the perceptions of the people of Jammu and Ladakh region who consider them culturally different than the people of Kashmir, is not taken into consideration while planning any activity or project in the Valley, there will be a negative feedback from these two areas and the Banihal and Zojila divide will widen.

Mothers, Fathers and Extended Family. The mutually exclusive survey carried amongst the youth of the Valley suggests that 97.6% of the youth impose trust in their families and 80.6% spend their free time with family; hence, this becomes an important audience to address. Currently, the family is playing a benign role in mentoring the youth to follow a path towards prosperity as they themselves are getting influenced by the radicalizing elements in society.

Mothers of Slain Militants. During the course of studying the Psychological aspects in Chapter 4, it came to light that the mothers of slain militants do not grieve in public, but in the privacy and mental comfort of interactions with mental health workers or doctors, they tend to break down and grieve. Theory would suggest that they try to show their resolute and hard-shelled side to the public which creates a false sense of bravado for others to emulate by joining militant organisations. It is extremely important to manage their perceptions and make them accept reality, a sense of loss and unnecessary waste of precious life for a senseless cause. This will go a long way in curbing militancy, and for this there may be a requirement of hiring professional mental health workers and social scientists.

Teachers. Survey suggests that 91.6% of the youths impose trust in teachers. It has also been exposed in the internal scan as well as played out in the scenario-building exercise that the ideologically inclined teachers, who are now entrenched in many schools and have even climbed the stairs of promotions to reach degree colleges of the state, have their own agenda and are creating a negative impact on the psyche of the educated youth of the state, so much so that even when they go to other parts of the country for higher education, they maintain their connect with their ideological Gurus. With a constant and repeated ideological battering, it is just a matter of time that small triggers make them join militancy. Teachers become a major environment-shaping force for the battle of perceptions in Kashmir and need to be perceptually transformed for an extremely positive role for the society.

Religious Teachers/Ulema. In Singapore, RRGs' primary objective was to rehabilitate detained Jemaah Islamiah members and their families through counselling. However, it has since broadened its scope to include misinterpretations promoted by self-radicalised individuals and those in support of ISIS. A similar arrangement could be worked out with the participation of the local religious Ulema in J&K, so that the effect of Radicalisation is reduced/removed through religious counselling. With the advent of the Tableeghi Jamat way of thinking and the mushrooming of Deobandi/Barelvi and Ahl-e-Hadith mosques in the Valley, it becomes imperative to reach out to the religious teachers and manage their perceptions positively so that they in turn can counsel the youth against joining the path of militancy, as Survey suggests that 66% youth impose trust in religious teachers.

OGWs. To fight this most important tool of terrorism and proxy war in the Valley, it is important to categorise them so that separate response strategies can be made for each one of the categories. Although operating as a larger network, the OGWs in Kashmir can be broadly categorised under the following heads (in order to take a de novo look at the issue of OGWs by categorizing them for the sake of strategic communication and perception management/improvement as discussed in Chapter 4 of the book):

- OGWs for Funding & Logistic Support (OGFWLS).
- OGWs providing Ideological & Radicalization Support (OGWIRS).
- OGWs for Recruitment of Terrorists (OGWR).
- OGWs generating negative Perceptions and Sentiment amongst the Awaam (OGWPS).

Trader Community. The trader community in J&K is a highly respected community as due to lack of formal sector facilities, this community has been providing jobs and livelihood to the people of the state. Due to their involvement in trade and businesses, they are generally inclined towards peace and prosperity. Managing their perceptions positively could lead to a sequence of motivating actions which could bring the youth to the path of peace and prosperity and positive contribution to society.

J&K Police. Although a part of the SF, this institution needs to be dealt with as a separate entity. It has been discussed in detail that positive peace can only prevail if the law and order is handled by the J&K police in a community-policing role. For this to materialise, apart from capacity building and police reforms, there is a need for the police to understand its responsibilities to the people by bearing the brunt of sacrifice in the face of adversity and threats to their kin. Overall, there is a requirement for the Police force to exhibit a high degree of propriety and emotional intelligence in dealing with first-time/small-time offenders and thereby protecting them from becoming hardened criminals. It needs no gainsaying that positive perception management and training of Police personnel by trained professionals would go a long way in establishing positive peace in the state.

SF.. The security forces including Army and CAPF need to understand the need to show extreme restraint in the face of difficult situations. There is a need to carry out case study analyses to bring home the point of negative impact on positive peace due to small seemingly inconsequential actions.

Govt Machinery – the Bureaucracy. In order to bear the fruits of corruption-free good governance, the govt machinery has to be motivated to sacrifice their today for the bright tomorrow of their generations to follow. Status quoist perceptions have to be moulded to an interactive state of mind.

The Judiciary. There is a need for the Judiciary to constantly be reminded about the difficult circumstances that the Security forces are operating in J&K and that the justice system within the SF will take care of the aberrations to the generally good and measured behaviour of the troops. In case the Judiciaries perceptions are not addressed in a timely manner, the morale of the troops could get affected in an adverse manner.

Youth Connect Self Help Groups. The municipal and Panchayat elections have brought to the fore many youth connect self-help groups who believe in the cause of peace and prosperity and are daring to change the narrative of a dysfunctional and infiltrated polity to that of positive peace. They have given many candidates in the face of threats by militants. There is a churning of sorts that seems to be going on in Kashmir, a new wave which needs to be supported. If these groups stand up for progress, there will be no turning back for the upward graph of peace and prosperity.

Corporate Houses. Corporates have a perception that no industry can progress in the face of frequent shutdowns and adverse security situation. This perception needs to be amended. Jobs will get a new lease of life in the Valley. They also need to come forward with corporate social responsibility initiatives to support Deradicalization camps and youth connect models being planned out by youth self-help groups.

Local Media. Vernacular newspaper houses need to churn out positive news and correct reporting. Their perceptions are influenced by threats from militants as well as negative influence of the OGWs and agents of ISI from across the LoC. This needs to change to avoid them giving out a constant dose of slow poison to the masses thereby vitiating the already charged environment.

National Media. National newspapers and TV channels need to temper the hatred that they generate amongst the masses against the interests and well-being of a common citizen of Kashmir. The hysteria that they create in mainland

India has a far-reaching negative impact on the minds of the youth of Kashmir further polarizing them.

Fringe Hindutva Elements. Fiery statements of fringe groups affect the psyche of a common man. Ensuring restraint through education of these elements and managing the perception of the media to temper down follow-up debates and headlines in national interest even for a couple of years could be beneficial.

Kashmiri Pandits. The syncretic culture of Kashmir can never be complete without the presence of the Kashmiri Pandits. The desire of the Awaam for their Pandit brothers and sisters is reducing day by day due to the disconnected lives that they live separated by the Pir Panjal. In the recent survey, only 51% youth wanted them to come back to the Valley. It is a matter of time that the society will get completely polarised in the Valley. It is therefore necessary to manage the perceptions of the Kashmiri Pandits, to motivate them or some daredevils amongst them to get back to the land of their forefathers. With adequate security and a liberal investment environment, this feat can be achieved. This could be the turning point in the Battle of Perceptions for Kashmir.

Teachers and Students of Colleges where (including) Kashmiri Youth Study. Quite a large number of Kashmiri students pursue their dreams of education in institutes of excellence outside the state. Of late, there have been disturbing news of Kashmiri youth ending up in clashes with their peers in these colleges due to difference of opinion where they are more often than not branded anti-national. Though it is true that in many instances the Kashmiri youth are also to be blamed for links with anti-national and terror outfits,[1] but there is a need to bend the perceptions of the teachers and the students of these colleges to have a more humane touch towards a particular lot of students who have practically lived their entire lives in a conflict zone. A little accommodative spirit could go a long way of winning the hearts and minds of the students from J&K.

The Separatists. Continuous talks for changing the perceptions of the hardline separatists should be initiated in order to wean them towards the idea of a prosperous Kashmir in the state of J&K under the umbrella of a great and progressing nation India. Indian NGOs and spiritual gurus like Sri Sri Ravi Shankar, the founder of Art of Living Foundation, could be requested to head the effort so that no Agenda politics is seen by this group.

International News Channels. According to the recent survey, 28.23% of the youth were found to be watching international news channels to form opinions and perceptions. There is no way by which the reach of these channels and their foot prints can be reduced. A very workable solution is to make efforts to give youth access to true accounts of current news stories and also commence diplomatic initiatives with the host countries for eradicating fake and needless sensationalization.

The People of Pakistan. Although the people-to-people contact between the two countries has suffered due to policies of no talks till terror is controlled, the concept of multi-track diplomacy suggests that people-to-people contact should continue. The change in perception of the people of Pakistan will finally be a harbinger for peace to prevail in the region.

International Social Media Giants. Social media apps like Facebook, Twitter have to be reined in for allowing anti-India objectionable material on their sites. Their perception that they are invincible due to their global presence needs to be modified to our advantage.

The People of Pakistan-Occupied Kashmir (PoK) including Gilgit-Baltistan. There are very few families who still have relatives who got separated in the J&K war between India and Pakistan in 1948, yet there are many common things including the large number of Kashmiris who crossed the LoC into PoK in the early 1990s when militancy struck J&K. There is exchange of trade, ideas and brides across the LoC and there is a need to address the perceptions of locals on the other side of the LoC. Many parts of J&K are progressing exponentially in terms of infrastructure development which in turn is likely to get investments, development, peace and prosperity. There is a need to force the population across the LoC to constantly compare their standards of living with their counterparts this side so that a quiet revolution to bridge divides starts taking place within the next decade.

Pak Military and ISI. Hard nuts to crack as their perceptions are cast in stone, but a constant effort needs to be placed on record in order to make them realise that it is a zero-sum game that they are playing, and there is only one loser in it, the one who does not have the wherewithal to sustain such activity economically and diplomatically.

Staff at Participant International Organizations and Conferences. Diplomatic offensives to show to the world the collusive support to terrorism that Pak is providing should not be restricted to the UN and a few international agencies. The Perception offensive should be taken to all other relevant Organizations and Conferences in order to create a soft corner for the people of J&K and India's efforts to bring peace and prosperity to the state.

Conclusion

Perception Management/Improvement of the state of J&K, with the Awaam in particular, has been carrying on for past two and half decades, since the Indian Army has made its presence felt for combating militancy. However, it has been restricted to the efforts of the Army and has been carried out in a disjointed manner, with the actions by the Central Govt, actions of the state govt, the Army and other agencies not being in consonance. And this needs to be seen in the light of the perception of the local populace that they have always been persecuted, been at the receiving end. Hence, a sustained, concerted, coordinated, all-inclusive govt approach should be followed which should be long term, with all stakeholders being in sync towards the greater good of the nation in general and the state of J&K in particular. The battle is for the minds of the people of Kashmir, rest of India and the rest of the world. It is quite evident from the writings on the wall and the contents of this book that the battle for Kashmir can only be won by winning the Battle of Perceptions. This book provides a holistic review of every intricate factor that is playing up in Kashmir, and above all solutions and strategies to make it an actual "Paradise on Earth".

CHAPTER 1
Introduction

The Kashmir conflict, which had its genesis at the birth of two nations India and Pakistan, continues to be unresolved to this day, fuelling a bitter conflict lasting over seven decades. This conflict spawned a conventional arms race between the two neighbours which resulted in three major wars with the possibility of many more. Yet at the end of it all, both sides seem no closer to a resolution and Kashmir continues to be the bone of contention with the sunk costs especially in political terms being abhorrent to both sides. The rise of militancy in the late eighties with Pakistan's support has further fortified India's resolve to settle the matter as an internal issue with the Kashmiri people. India insists that the accession of Kashmir to India is final and complete and hence Kashmir is an integral part of India and that all would be well in Kashmir, but for Pakistan's cross-border terrorism. Pakistan, however, insists that Kashmir is a disputed territory and that it is merely providing moral and diplomatic support to an indigenous freedom struggle in Kashmir.

China's position has been shifting since 1950s but for the last decade it has been more or less the same as that of the Western countries which is to see Kashmir as disputed between India and Pakistan. The stapled visa for Kashmiris was an experiment by China that should be understood in the context of India's approach toward the Dalai Lama and Tibetan exiles. China has been clear that it will not accept an independent new state in the region. Actually, it is in China's interest for the dispute to continue and for India and Pakistan to be on loggerheads with each other. This fulfils the primary agenda of preventing any new independent state in the region that may have a domino effect on Uighur Muslims and Tibetans and the secondary agenda of keeping India, the only possible competitor to China in Asia, tied down in South Asia through a permanent rivalry with Pakistan. China will not allow Pakistan to weaken further; one of the reasons is to prevent more Uighur separatists getting radicalized and trained in Pakistani territories and the other of course is the

China-Pakistan Economic Corridor, or CPEC. In all this geopolitical game between China, India and Pakistan, unfortunately the aspirations, dignity and welfare of Kashmiris get crushed.

While the issue of Kashmir appears to be rather simple on the face of it, the multi-dimensional nature of the problem and sheer number of actors, many of them hidden, with stakes of some form or the other have ensured that this problem takes on the character of the proverbial "Gordian knot". In fact, so convoluted is the matter that identifying the problem has itself become a source of angst and hand wringing amongst the disparate populace that makes up the kaleidoscope of Kashmir. All in all, Kashmir appears to a place condemned to have the past repeating itself, over and over again, inflicting untold misery on a people conditioned to suffering by the whimsical currents of history.

While the situation did appear hopeless, much has been done on the ground by both the Centre and the State, chiefly with the help of the Armed Forces to pull the state back from a precipice. After the hectic events of the last three decades, there seems to be a relatively uneasy, very fragile calm which keeps getting disrupted – whether it is a potent for the future or the proverbial "taste of a storm in the future" is too soon to foretell. But Kashmir today is on the cusp of a number of events which will have a direct bearing on its future.

Firstly, the population seems to be tired and intimidated by the senseless acts of violence and is looking forward to a sense of stability and progress. Secondly, the foreign militants have been contained, and the effects of the security forces (SF) and the government in weaning the population away from this path seem to be producing fruit but for sporadic incidents of crowd support during encounters especially after the Burhan Wani encounter. The frequent engineered disruptions during counter-terrorist operations and bye-polls and local youth joining militancy in larger numbers are a cause for concern, and the danger of muddying the waters for narrow political gains is a very real danger. Thirdly, the Hurriyat after furious activity over the last few years seems to be struggling to paper over the differences between its members and present a façade of unity, albeit with indifferent success. Fourthly, on the external side, Pakistan appears to be busy resolving its internal issues – those related to economic issues, internal security and unity, fundamentalism and its relations with Afghanistan. Fifthly, the Pan-Islamisation card and the fate of ISIS hang in balance with the ideology reaching our doorstep in Afghanistan. Lastly, the change of guard at Washington has certainly started having an effect on the unconditional aid being provided to Pakistan and therefore is likely to affect the situation in Kashmir – for better or worse is up in the air for the moment.

The time therefore, appears to be ripe to find and implement a solution to the issue of the troubled state. The solution can never be one which is acceptable to one and all, or acceptable to anyone in all respects but merely one which is acceptable to the largest number of stakeholders in parts or in whole. Selling the solution will be as vital as finding it and hence the issue of Perceptions become extremely vital.

Aim/Research Objective

The aim/objective of the book is to carry out the net assessment of the security situation in the Kashmir Valley, to study the state holistically as a system and through this to formulate perception management/improvement strategies for effective conflict resolution situation in state of J&K in general and Kashmir region in particular.

Present State

The present state of security in the state can be at best narrated as one of unease and mistrust, that is to say that there is a sense of functionality where the security situation in the state is bordering on the line between militancy, law and order situation to completely peaceful in different regions of the state, and yet the governance is struggling. There is an increasing demand by the Awaam to allow them more breathing space, more often than not instigated by inimical elements to the state. The security forces, however, understand the sacrifices that have resulted in this present functional environment and do not want to loosen the grip to allow the Militants to gain lost ground and then go through a tedious process of sanitising the area which may cost more lives and sacrifices. Radicalisation through Wahhabi Islam is a big challenge in the valley; there are 1000 Jamiat-Ahle-Hadith mosques in the Valley, the clergy being from Uttar Pradesh and Bihar but being funded by Pakistan through the Middle East. Increasingly, traditional Sufi Islam is ceding space to a radical brand of Islam in Kashmir. On top of all this, young minds are likely being indoctrinated in schools and Madrasas to become stone-pelters (the maximum being in the school going age of 7–13 years), who when jailed, come in contact with extremist literature, hardcore militants and Over-Ground Workers (OGWs). A new mindset in Kashmir in the younger generation is due to the fact that Kashmiris have been made to sever their relationship with their past through a structured doctrinal Narrative created by Pakistan through radicalisation and this break is being exploited to the maximum as a reinforcing loop by inimical agencies. To say the least, there seems to be a deadlock and all are looking forward to a phased yet definite set of coherent strategies to reach the desired end state and end the cycle of violence.

Desired End State

The desired end state of the J&K situation may be envisioned as "peace and prosperity" in the state, which can be only be achieved if the centre of gravity, that is, the psyche of the Awaam perceives that all their basic needs of physiology, security as well as higher needs of esteem and self-actualisation are met during the process and therefore start supporting national integration.

Perception is the Key to Success

From the desired end state, it is evident that the psyche of the Awaam becomes the centre of all activity. The perception of the Awaam becomes the key to the resolution of this conflict of ideas. Efforts are needed to change the mindset as the hearts will remain where the hearth is. How do we address the higher needs of the Awaam in Maslow's hierarchy of needs, that is, the Esteem need and Self-actualisation need? Although many a study has been carried out on J&K, there is a need to holistically study it as a System. Perceptions are made in the mind and for managing perceptions it is important to study what is actually affecting the psyche of the Awaam today in J&K. Understanding of the comprehensive situation will lead to the derivation of strategies for ensuring peace, progress as well as improving perceptions in J&K which, in turn, would assist us in reaching our above-stated desired end state.

Statement of the Problem

The state of Jammu and Kashmir has been an integral part of India since 1947. However, the people of this state, namely, the Awaam of Kashmir valley have not been able to identify with the nation of India. Issues such as governance, radicalism, financial conduits to the Separatists, trust between the people and the security forces/other organs of the Central Government, self-esteem and dignity of the Kashmiri people, the degree of connect between the Centre and the State, tourism and other revenue and profit-earning activities need greater focus in the coming years. Hence, if the desired end state to the J&K problem is to seamlessly integrate the state of Jammu and Kashmir with India, the perception of the target population needs to be shaped/improved towards the desired end state.

How does this Book Address the knowledge Gap?

From the desired end state, it is evident that the Awaam becomes the centre of all activity. The perception of the Awaam becomes the key to the resolution of this conflict of ideas. How do we address the higher needs of the Awaam in Maslow's hierarchy of needs, i.e., the Esteem need and Self-actualization need? Although many a study and the above literature are available on J&K, there is a need to holistically study it as a System as well as carry out a Net assessment. Perceptions are made in the mind and for managing perceptions it is important to study what is actually affecting the mind of the Awaam today in J&K. Hence this study will connect the critical gap existing in the understanding of the competitive situation through which will arise, the strategies for ensuring peace, progress as well as managing Perceptions in J&K which in turn would assist us in reaching our above stated desired end state.

Conceptual Framework and Relevance of the Concepts

The scope of the book entails the following:

- An environmental scan which includes the analysis of internal and external factors affecting the state of J&K in entirety and identifying the actors on the centre-stage in Kashmir, both external and internal and ascertaining their locus standii as stakeholders in the conflict.
- Examination of the effect of the complex interplay of internal disturbances, rise of religious fundamentalism, army's aspirations, and the desire of the civilian government to establish control on the situation on the LC and infiltration attempts from PoK and utilize these inputs to prepare Causal Loop Diagrams (ORSA technique) and establish strategies for various archetypes. Analyse various strategies being employed over the years for integrating the state.
- Utilise Artificial Intelligence models for simulating trends through the data collected.
- Carry out a holistic System analysis on all relevant domains, namely, **political, military, social, legal and economic, as well as perceptions of local population, Centre-state relations**, etc.
- Carry out an assessment of Psychological aspects affecting the Awaam in Kashmir and providing solutions for the same in line with international efforts dealing with the ISIS ideology.
- Carry out SWOT analysis by deriving relevant factors from the above study for framing short-term strategies.

- Correlate the effect between the aspirations of the Awaam and the situation in the state, especially the changes in the recent years.
- Studying the various strategies derived from the above with respect to the aspect of Perception of various stake holders, primarily the Awaam and deriving strategies and recommendations to improve the perception of not only the populace but also the entities affecting the arrival of positive peace in Kashmir.

Systems Thinking

The Internal Security (IS) situation in the Valley can be analysed by employing the System Dynamics Approach involving the Causal Loop Diagrams (CLD). The IS situation falls under the "complex" and "unitary" cat of System Approach: "Unitary" as the participants (Central and State government, Security Forces and the People of Kashmir) have similar values, beliefs, interests and share a common purpose of achieving "Peace and Prosperity" in the Valley and "Complex" as the situation has a large number of sub-systems that are involved in many more loosely structured interactions, the outcome of which is not pre-determined. In this part, "the IS situation in the Valley" is studied as a whole system. The success of this system lies in the connectedness and inter-relationships of various elements (sub-systems). The dynamics of the systems gives cause-and-effect relationships among the various elements (factors) of the system.

Psychological Aspects Affecting Kashmiris and their Solutions

The study of cause-and-effect relationships will give a vital insight into the behaviour, working and the analysis of this dynamic system through simulation. It will culminate in assessment of Psychological aspects affecting the Awaam in Kashmir and providing solutions for the same in line with international efforts dealing with the ISIS ideology.

SWOT Analysis

Overall SWOT analysis has been carried out for the J&K state. Strength and weaknesses will be identified post BMC (Base, Means and Capacities) analysis. These were then weighted by allocating numerical values for their importance and impact. Accordingly, Threats and opportunities were identified post-analysis of the external scan. These were weighted by giving numerical values for their importance and probability of occurrence.

A Peek into the Future

The book cannot be complete in case we don't have a peek into the future through a Scenario-building exercise which has been completed keeping in mind the latest trends and factors that are likely to affect in the future as drivers of change.

Perception Management/Improvement. Perception management includes all actions used to influence the attitudes and objective reasoning of foreign audiences and consists of Public Diplomacy, Psychological Operations (PSYOPS), Public Information, Deception and Covert Action. The main goal is to influence friends and enemies, provoking them to engage in the behavior that you want. While the exercise of perception management has been carrying on in the Kashmir valley for years, by way of Sadhbhavna and other measures, there needs to be a more focused and concerted approach towards the same which is carried out at all levels over a sustained manner. In 2014, a survey was carried out at the various schools of instruction of the army amongst the officers undergoing courses there and the result was not very encouraging and is tabulated below.

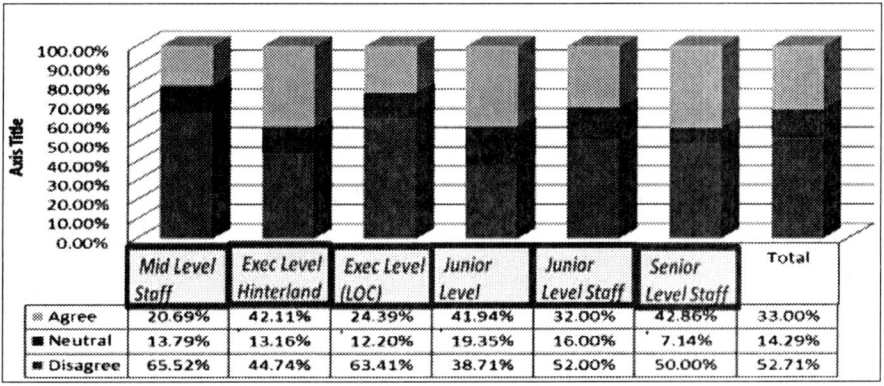

PERCEPTION MANAGEMENT
Perception Management and Media handling is being done effectively by the Army

	Mid Level Staff	Exec Level Hinterland	Exec Level (LOC)	Junior Level	Junior Level Staff	Senior Level Staff	Total
Agree	20.69%	42.11%	24.39%	41.94%	32.00%	42.86%	33.00%
Neutral	13.79%	13.16%	12.20%	19.35%	16.00%	7.14%	14.29%
Disagree	65.52%	44.74%	63.41%	38.71%	52.00%	50.00%	52.71%

Analysis of Data: A major portion of the respondents across the spectrum, almost 52% had opined that perception management and media handling is not being done effectively. A considerable section of senior level decision makers (50%) and mid level officers (65%) also believed about a lack of strategy for perception management and media handling.

It was due to this input that a study on deriving strategies for improvent of perceptions for J&K and not improvement of perceptions in J&K becomes important. To carry out this complex, it is important to study the system as is present today and how it will dynamically play in the years to come. Through this study, we will get a clear perspective about the elements/entities whose perception needs to be managed/improved.

Research Questions

Which are the entities at play in creating the present situation in Kashmir? Which of these are affecting the bringing in of positive peace in Kashmir? What are the short/mid/long-term strategies that need to be put in place to achieve success? How important are perceptions and shaping of the environment and what are the strategies required to do so?

Research Methodology Adopted

Coverage. Net Assessment comprises two words: Net, the consideration of all aspects and perspectives of ours against that of competitor, relevant and significant to the problem at hand, to give a net outcome of a competitive situation. Net Assessment integrates accurate information and intelligence to draw right implications, direct as well as cross. It covers adequate time span of assessment as imperceptibles over a short period can produce large effects when viewed over long term. The study will also include issues holistically that are important but get overlooked. Theresearch methodology that I plan to employ will be as under:

- The ontological position is of Objectivism and the epistemological position is of positivism.
- The Research Strategy is mixed method research with focus on quantitative.
- The Research Design will be Cross-Sectional. I will resort to Stratified Random Sampling.
- In addition, the data collected from past project studies will be made use of.

Methods of Data Collection. The following data has been collected and analysed in the study:

- **Primary Data.** Survey through questionnaires and in-depth interview with experts.
- **Secondary data.** Data pertaining to the governance in the State of J&K as well as data pertaining to military operations in J&K.

Data Analysis. Data Analysis will be conducted by utilizing the MS Excel, Knime, SPSS as well as Artificial Intelligence tools.

Implications of the Study

The J&K conflict spawned an arms race between the two neighbours which resulted in three major wars with the possibility of many more. In a geopolitical game between China, India and Pakistan, unfortunately the aspirations, dignity and welfare of Kashmiris get crushed and if this state continues, it won't be long that an ideological strife crosses the Pir panjal mountain range in to the rest of India; *hence, it is most relevant to be studied.* The book is a result of almost five years of labour starting with a net assessment study on the security situation in J&K as prevalent in 2014, followed by a thesis on a similar subject, i.e., likely future of J&K in terms of the security situation by the author in 2017 and finally a dedicated research on the topic of "Perception Management for J&K", which culminates with the writing of this book. The author thanks his collegues in the net assessment study of 2014, which has become the base for this endeavor. Many books have been written on the Kashmir imbroglio in recent times which have highlighted and analysed the conditions prevalent in their times but none has given solutions which will help tide the situation in favour of a prosperous future. Hence, this book becomes important to the people of India, its neighbours as much to the people of the Indian state of J&K.

CHAPTER 2
Analysis of Key Internal and External Factors of J&K with Special Reference to Kashmir

INTERNAL SCAN

Introduction

Three decades or so earlier, one could safely and securely move about in any remote corner of Jammu and Kashmir even at the dead of night. Any wrong doer would stand isolated, pinned down and duly prosecuted. But today, the Kashmir valley is passing through a critical period. The wrong doer gets lost in the crowd, who later dares to issue even a "press hand-out" justifying the wrong deeds. The polity is in bind, public is not "free" and the situation appears to be calm, but one can feel the tension and suspicion in the air. Backwardness has become reality rather than a perception. Fundamentalism and social insecurity due to omnipresence of multiple terrorist and radical outfits has proliferated the already complex situation in the state. Violence level though has come down due to relentless efforts by all stake holders, but the era of days gone by is still a distant dream. The misperceptions and lack of clear direction amid government agencies and large number of outfits are creating vicious security dilemmas. It appears that as on date Kashmir is standing at a cross road with no one to guide it towards the right path.

Historical Perspective

The word Kashmir is an ancient Sanskrit word which literally means Land of Kashyap Rishi. Kashyap Rishi was one of the Saptarshis, who played a key role in formalizing the ancient Historical Vedic Religion. According to the "Nilmat Puran", the oldest book on Kashmir, in the Satisar (meaning "lake of the Goddess Sati"), a former lake in the Kashmir Valley, lived a demon called Jalodbhava (meaning "born of water"), who tortured and devoured the people, who lived near mountain slopes. Hearing the suffering of the people, Kashyap, a Saraswat Brahmin, came to their rescue. After performing penance for a long time, the saint was blessed, and therefore Lord Vishnu assumed the form of a boar and struck the mountain at Varahamula, boring an opening in it for the water to flow out into the plains below. The lake was drained, the land appeared, and the demon was killed. As a result of the hero's actions, the people named the valley as "Kashyap-Mar", meaning abode of Kashyap, in Sanskrit. The name "Kashmir", in Sanskrit, implies land desiccated from water: "ka" (the water) and "shimeera" (to desiccate). In modern times, the people of Kashmir have shortened the full Sanskrit name into "Kasheer", which is the colloquial Koshur name of the valley, as noted in Aurel Stein's introduction to the Rajatarangini metrical chronicle.

At least 49,000 people have been killed since insurgency began in 1989, according to official estimates. Thousands of Indian soldiers have been killed and it costs billions of rupees to keep the army in Kashmir. The Kashmir conflict continues to be unresolved after more than six decades, fuelling the conventional and nuclear arms race between India and Pakistan and bleeding their economy. Both countries have gone to war on three occasions over Kashmir and the possibility of war between the two countries has become frightening given their nuclear weapon capability.

Kashmir continues to be the bone of contention between India and Pakistan. Each side insists it is right and the other is wrong. India insists that the accession of Kashmir to India is final and complete and hence Kashmir is an integral part of India and that all would be well in Kashmir, but for Pakistan's cross-border terrorism. Pakistan, however, is obsessed that Kashmir is a disputed territory and that it is merely providing moral and diplomatic support for an indigenous freedom struggle in Kashmir. A large number of Kashmiris do not believe that the 1947 accession is final; they insist that Kashmir is a disputed territory and demand self-determination. Indian public is bombarded with the official version of rhetoric on Kashmir, as Pakistanis are bombarded likewise with their version.

Could we objectively revisit this complex issue which continues to exact increasing death toll, as each day passes? All sides cannot be right at once in their claims of absolute moral rectitude, and the truth probably lies somewhere in between.

Important Timelines

- **Ancient Era.** The recorded history of Kashmir, though partially shrouded in myth, extends back nearly three thousand years. Throughout that time Kashmir has been recognized, to a degree matched by few, if any, other areas of South Asia, as a culturally and physically distinct entity. Though subject for brief periods in ancient times to various powers ruling over much of the Indian subcontinent—

notably the Mauryas, Kushanas, Guptas, and Hunas, in that order—Kashmir generally remained, until its incorporation into the Mughal Empire in 1586, an independent state.[1]

- **The Late Classical Period, 6th-7th Centuries CE.** This map depicts the area encompassing Kashmir as it existed in the 6th-7th centuries CE during what might be considered the late Classical period. Over most of the period, Kashmir was a small, independent state. Existing on the periphery of a politically fragmented India, it also

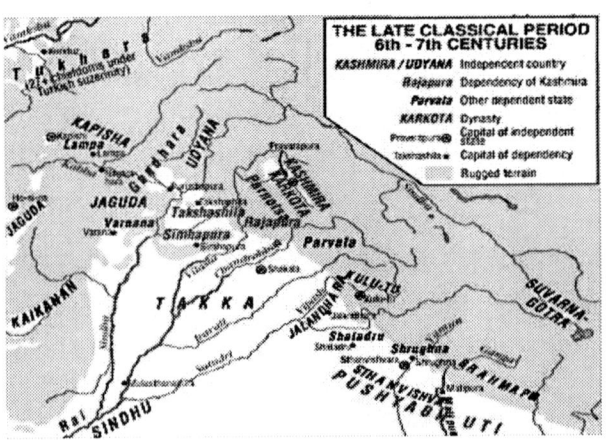

maintained commercial and cultural ties with Central and Southwest Asia. The situation depicted here is that which prevailed shortly before the mercurial imperial expansion of Kashmir in the reign of the Karkota monarch, Lalitaditya (724-761 CE). Following this reign, the state lapsed back into its customary position of relative weakness.

- **The Reign of Sikander "But-shikan" Shah.**[2] Walter Lawrence wrote in 1895 in his book "The Valley of Kashmir" that perhaps the deadliest rule in Kashmir was that of Sikander Shah who ruled Kashmir during the forays of Taimur the lame. The destruction of almost all the ancient temples and previously unheard atrocities were conducted in his reign alongside the spread of Sufi culture from the Central Asian republics.

- **Kashmir Under the Mughals.** The Mughal conquest and annexation of Kashmir in 1586 ended nearly a millennium of continuous Kashmiri independence and ushered in one of several periods during which an external power extended the territory of the political entity known to the outside world as Kashmir to well beyond the actual area of Kashmiri language and culture. Thus, by the death of the Emperor Aurangzeb in 1707, the Mughal Suba (province) of Kashmir was extended to include the greater part of what was later to be incorporated within the Dogra domains. It then included both Ladakh and Baltistan, but the core area of the Dogras, centred on Jammu, remained a part of Lahore Suba.

- **Expansion of Jammu and Kashmir Under the Dogras.** The final period of Kashmiri expansion occurred under the Dogra dynasty of Jammu, which ruled the state from 1846 until the partition of India in 1947. Jammu and Kashmir State is created under the Treaty of Amritsar between the East India Company and Raja Gulab Singh of Jammu who buys Kashmir Valley from the East India Company for Rs. 75,00,000 and adds it to Jammu and Ladakh already under his rule. Kashmir Valley is a Muslim majority region speaking the Kashmiri language and a composite cultural identity called Kashmiriyat

transcending religious barriers; the people are hospitable and engage in Sufi tradition.[3] This century witnessed a remarkable increase in the area and, consequently, in the cultural heterogeneity of the state. This accomplishment was due in large part to military and political assistance from the British Raj without whose imperial protection, the territorial coherence of the state might not have been maintained.

- 1931-46. The movement against the repressive Maharaja Hari Singh begins; it is brutally suppressed by the State forces in July 1931. Rumors of an alleged de-secretion of the Quran by a Hindu Policeman in Jammu led to a series of violent protests which were brutally quelled by the Maharaja's forces which led to the shooting and killing of 21 people in Srinagar on 13 July 1931.[4] However, contradictory claims of the entire incident being orchestrated by the British[5] to put pressure on the Maharaja to give Gilgit-Baltistan to them to counter Russia's push to the south are also rife. The predominantly Muslim population was kept poor, illiterate and was not adequately represented in the State's services. In 1932, Sheikh Mohammed Abdullah ("Sher-i-Kashmir") sets up the All Jammu and Kashmir Muslim Conference to fight for Kashmiri freedom from the Maharaja's rule, which would branch off to become the National Conference (NC) in 1939. The Glancy Commission appointed by the Maharaja publishes a report in April 1932, confirming the grievances of the State's subjects and suggests recommendations providing for adequate representation of Muslims in the State's services. Maharaja accepts these recommendations but delays implementation, leading to another agitation in 1934. Maharaja grants a Constitution providing a Legislative Assembly for the people, but the Assembly turns out to be powerless.[6] In 1946, NC launches the "Quit Kashmir movement" demanding abrogation of the Treaty of Amritsar and restoration of sovereignty to the people of Kashmir. Sheikh Abdullah is arrested.

- **Kashmir Problem is Born.** The Kashmir conflict, which had its genesis in the birth of two nations India and Pakistan, continues to be unresolved to this day, fueling a bitter conflict lasting over seven decades.

- **1947-55.**
  o **1947-49.** Post-independence and formation of India and Pakistan, Kashmir remained non-committal about joining either of the countries. Raiders invaded Kashmir in October 1947 and Mahraja signed the instrument of accession in return of India's assistance to evict them. Thus, commenced the first war over Kashmir between the two nations. India takes the Kashmir problem to the United Nations (UN) Security Council. On 1 Jan 1949, a ceasefire between Indian and Pakistani forces leaves India in control of most of the valley, as well as Jammu and Ladakh, while Pakistan gains control of part of Kashmir including Pakistan-Occupied Kashmir (PoK) and Northern territories. On 5 January 1949, United Nations Commission for India and Pakistan (UNCIP) resolution states that the question of the accession of the State of Jammu and Kashmir to India or Pakistan will be decided through a free and impartial plebiscite. Both countries accept the principle that Pakistan secures the withdrawal of Pakistani intruders followed by withdrawal of Pakistani and Indian forces, as a basis for the formulation of a Truce agreement whose details are to be arrived in future, followed by a plebiscite; however, both countries fail to arrive at a Truce agreement due to differences in interpretation. On 17 October 1949, the Indian Constituent Assembly adopts Article 370 of the Constitution, ensuring a special status and internal autonomy for Jammu and Kashmir, with Indian jurisdiction in Kashmir limited to the three areas agreed in the Instrument of Accession (IOA), namely, defence, foreign affairs and communications.[7]

  o **1950-55.** First post-independence elections are held in J&K in 1951. The UN passes a resolution to the effect that such elections do not substitute a plebiscite. Sheikh Abdullah wins, mostly unopposed.

There are widespread charges of election rigging which continue to plague all the subsequent elections.[8] Sheikh Abdullah drifts from a position of endorsing accession to India in 1947 to insisting on the self-determination of Kashmiris in 1952. In July 1952, he signs Delhi Agreement with the Central government on Centre-State relationships, providing for autonomy of the State within India and of regions within the State. Article 370 is confirmed and the State is allowed to have its own flag. The domination of Kashmir Valley (which has a 95% Muslim majority and accounts for more than 50% of the total population of Indian J&K) and Abdullah's land reforms create discontent in Jammu and Ladakh. An agitation is launched in the Hindu-majority Jammu region against the Delhi Agreement, in favour of full accession with the Indian Union; the movement is withdrawn later, due to pressure from the Centre. Secessionist sentiments in the Valley and communalism in Jammu feed each other. In 1953, the governments of India and Pakistan agree to appoint a Plebiscite Administrator by the end of April 1954. Abdullah procrastinates in confirming the accession of Kashmir to India. In August 1953, Abdullah is dismissed and arrested. Bakshi Ghulam Mohammed is installed in power, who then gets the accession formally ratified in 1954. India would resist plebiscite efforts from then on. Kashmiri activists continue to insist on the promised self-determination.[9]

- **1955-64.** In October 1956, the state Constituent Assembly adopts a constitution for the state declaring it an integral part of the Indian Union. However, in January 1957, UN passes another resolution stating that such actions would not constitute a final disposition of the State. India's Home Minister declares that J&K is an integral part of India and there can be no question of a plebiscite to determine its status afresh. In April 1959, permit system for entry to the State is abolished. In October, the State Constitution is amended to extend jurisdiction of Union Election Commission to the State and bring its High Court at par with courts in the rest of India. Post-1962 Indo-China war, in addition to the illegal occupation of Aksai Chin, 5180 km^2 area is taken over by China at Shaksgam in Northern Areas of Kashmir under Pakistan control. Mass upsurge occurs in Kashmir Valley when the holy relic is found missing from the Hazratbal Shrine in December 1963; the lost relic is recovered on 04 Jan 1964. Sheikh Abdullah is released in April 1964. He reinitiates talks with Pakistan, in an effort to resolve the Kashmir problem, taking into account the wishes of Kashmiris on the behest of Pandit Nehru. Nehru passes away on 27 May and the talks get stranded. Protest demonstrations occur in Kashmir Valley in December against Articles 356 and 357 of the Indian Constitution being extended to the state, by virtue of which the Centre can assume the government of the State and exercise its legislative powers. The special status accorded to the State under Article 370 continues to get eroded over years.[10]

- **1965-1966.** In May 1965, Sheikh Abdullah is arrested on his return to India from Mecca on account of his meeting with the Chinese Prime Minister at Algiers. Angry protests occur in Kashmir Valley; The Plebiscite Front initiates a *satyagraha* for Abdullah's release and many workers are arrested. Pakistan takes advantage of the discontent in the Valley and launches "Operation Gibraltar". An Indo-Pakistan war breaks out which ends in a ceasefire on 23 September. In January 1966, Tashkent Declaration is signed by both countries agreeing to revert to pre-1965 position. Pakistan-supported guerrilla groups in Kashmir increase their activities after the ceasefire. Kashmiri nationalists Amanullah Khan and Maqbool Butt form another Plebiscite Front with an armed wing called the Jammu and Kashmir National Liberation Front (NLF) in PoK, with the objective of freeing Kashmir. Butt crosses into the Valley in June 1966 and engages in clashes with the Indian army. He is arrested and sentenced to death in 1968 but escapes to PoK with help from the local people.[11]

- **1966-1986.** Third Indo-Pak war breaks out in December 1971 resulting in a humiliating defeat for Pakistan and formation of independent Bangladesh. India and Pakistan sign the Simla Agreement in July 1972, which has a clause that the final settlement of Kashmir will be decided bilaterally in the future. The cease-fire line in Kashmir becomes the "Line of Control" (LC) and both sides agree to respect the same. Pakistanis hold India responsible for the dismemberment of their country. In November 1974, Kashmir Accord is signed by G. Parthasarathy for Indira Gandhi and Mirza Afzal Beg for Sheikh Abdullah, who is out of power at that time.[12] The Accord retains Kashmir's special status, but the state is termed as a "constituent unit of the Union of India". Opposition parties and Pakistan condemn the Accord. Abdullah is installed back in power. Later in 1977, he would speak in favour of protecting the autonomy and special status of Kashmir.[13] Maqbool Butt is arrested on his return to the Valley in 1976, Amanullah Khan moves to England and NLF becomes Jammu and Kashmir Liberation Front (JKLF). The USSR invades Afghanistan in 1979. The US and Pakistan are involved in training, recruiting, arming, and unleashing the Mujahideen on Afghanistan. The Mujahideen so recruited would take on the agenda of establishing Islamic rule in Kashmir from the late 1980s.[14] Indian and Pakistani armies engage in clashes in Siachen Glacier, a no-man's land at an altitude of 20,000 ft with extreme weather conditions in 1984, where the cease-fire line had been left undefined by 1972 Simla Agreement. Siachen is perceived to be of strategic importance for access to the Northern Areas as well as the rich water reserves in the form of Glaciers, and the spasmodic clashes would continue through later years, costing thousands of lives and billions of dollars.[15]

- **Geopolitical Upheaval.** The loss of the Soviet forces at the hands of the US supported Mujahideen gave a false sense of resultant adventurism to the ISI handlers. They believed that time was ripe for Kashmir to be taken by employing the now un-employed Mujahideen. The US too turned a blind-eye towards the evil plans of their "most trusted Ally" of the times.

- **1987-1998**
  o Farooq Abdullah won the elections in 1987, which was allegedly rigged. The insurgency in the valley increased in momentum from this point on, given the consistent failure of democracy and limited employment opportunities. The Muslim United Front (MUF) candidate Mohammad Yousuf Shah feels not only cheated in the rigged elections, but also imprisoned and he would later become Syed Salahuddin, chief of militant outfit Hizb-ul-Mujahideen (HM). His election aides called the HAJY group –Abdul Hamid Shaikh, Ashfaq Majid Wani, Javed Ahmed Mir and Mohammed Yasin Malik – would join the JKLF.[16]
  o Amanullah Khan takes refuge in Pakistan, after being deported from England and begins to direct operations across the LoC. Protests begin in the Valley along with anti-India demonstrations, followed by police firing and curfew. End of Soviet occupation of Afghanistan releases a great deal of militant energy and weapons to Kashmir.

Pakistan provides arms and training to both indigenous and foreign militants in Kashmir, thus adding fuel to the smoldering fire of discontent in the valley.

o In **January 1990**, Jagmohan is appointed as the Governor; Farooq Abdullah resigns. On 20 January, an estimated 100 people are killed when a large group of unarmed protesters are fired upon by the Indian troops at the Gawakadal Bridge. With this incident, it becomes an insurgency of the entire population. On **13 February 1990**, Lassa Kaul, director of Srinagar Doordarshan, is killed by the militants for implementing pro-indian media policy. Though the JKLF tries to explain that the killings of Pandits were not communal, it causes a scare among the minority Hindu community. Some warnings in anonymous posters and some unexplained killings of innocent members of the community contribute to an atmosphere of insecurity for the Kashmiri Pandits. Joint reconciliation efforts by members from both Muslim and Pandit communities are actively discouraged by Jagmohan. Most of the estimated 162,500 Hindus in the Valley flee in March 1990.

o From 1990 to 2001, approximately 10,000 Kashmiri youth cross over to Pakistan for training and procurement of arms and join militant groups, JKLF and the pro-Pakistan HM.[17] ISI favours the HM over the secular JKLF and cuts off financing to the JKLF and in some instances provides intelligence to India against JKLF. Since 1995, foreign militant outfits with Islamic agenda such as Lashkar-e-Toiba (LeT) and Harkat-ul-Mujahideen have dominated the militancy in Kashmir, besides the indigenous HM. All of them work under the umbrella of United Jehadi Council (UJC). Though militancy is mainly concentrated in the Valley and is largely non-communal, some militant outfits operate in the Jammu region also and wage a communal campaign. The most serious incident of a communal nature, namely, the murder of sixteen male Hindus in Kishtwar in August 1993 was condemned by the JKLF and the HM.[18] Some militant groups with Islamic agenda have attacked women sporadically for not wearing the veil, which has been condemned by the indigenous militants. The All Parties Hurriyat Conference (APHC) called for foreign militants to leave Kashmir, since they were tarnishing the image of their freedom struggle.[19]

- **1999 till Date.**
  - In **May 1998**, India conducts nuclear tests; Pakistan also responds with nuclear tests. In **June 1998**, Regional Autonomy Committee (RAC) proposes devolution of political power at regional, district, block and panchayats levels and allocation of funds according to an objective and equitable formula. Subsequently, the State Government substitutes the RAC report with its own report recommending the division of the three regions (Ladakh, Kashmir and Jammu) into eight autonomous units on ethnic-religious lines without proposing any devolution of political and economic powers.[20]
  - On 21 February 1999, India and Pakistan sign Lahore Declaration, agreeing to "intensify their efforts to resolve all issues, including the issue of Jammu and Kashmir." In **May 1999**, the Indian Army patrols detect intruders from Pakistan on Kargil ridges in Kashmir. India fights to regain lost territory. The infiltrators are withdrawn by Pakistan in mid-July, following Washington Agreement with US. War between India and Pakistan becomes more frightening given the nuclear weaponry possessed by both countries and Kashmir remains the underlying flashpoint.
  - In **March 2000**, around the time of US President Clinton's visit to India, unidentified gunmen gun down 36 Sikhs at Chittisinghpora. In **June 2000**, the State Autonomy Committee (SAC) Report is discussed and an autonomy resolution is adopted in the J&K Assembly. The SAC Report recommends restoration of Article 370 to pre-1953 status with Indian jurisdiction limited to defence, foreign affairs and communications. However, the Indian Cabinet rejects the autonomy recommendation in July. In **November 2000**, India announces a unilateral ceasefire in Kashmir[21] which continues through May 2001. APHC welcomes the ceasefire but states that the ceasefire will not be effective unless it is supplemented with unconditional dialogues to resolve the Kashmir dispute and an end to human right violations. HM declares an unilateral ceasefire in July 2001 which is withdrawn only two weeks later, following India's refusal to include Pakistan in any trilateral talks over the Kashmir dispute proposed by the militants.
  - In **July 2001**, India and Pakistan fail to arrive at a joint agreement at Agra Summit, given the deadlock on Kashmir. Following the

terrorist attacks on the Indian Parliament on 13 December 2001, India threatened to attack Pakistan by building up massive troops along the border. After months of diplomacy, troops are withdrawn on either side.

- On **21 May 2001**, Abdul Ghani Lone, a moderate Hurriyat leader is assassinated by unidentified gunmen. Mirwaiz Maulvi Farooq had been assassinated by unidentified gunmen exactly 12 years back. On both occasions, India blamed Pakistan-sponsored militants while Kashmiris blamed Indian-sponsored renegades. Unless an impartial investigation is carried out, it is not possible to ascertain these claims in such attacks by unidentified gunmen who could be either separatist militants or renegades. There have been numerous attacks on Hindus by unidentified gunmen including 2003 Nadimarg, and 2006 Doda massacres. India blames it on foreign militants and Kashmiris blame it on renegade militants used by Indian security forces. The State assembly elections held in 2002, 2008 and 2014 have been relatively free and fair but the voters turned out in large numbers more to improve local governance than to signal their support for Indian rule in Kashmir.[22]
- Huge anti-India protests were held against the transfer of land to SASB (shrine board), which was an outside state organization, as it was perceived as a direct violation of Article 370 of the Indian constitution. In May 2009, there were huge protests against rape and murder of two young women in Shopian village. It was followed by huge uprising in 2010 as an aftermath to alleged killings of five villagers on LC in Machil.[23] What followed was a series of mass protests and beginning of the agitational dimension of the conflict. However, mature handling of the situation by the state with Army remaining in the background kept it in the realms of Law & Order issue, thereby blunting the secessionist's agenda. There is relative calm in the years that followed with increasing demand for AFSPA to be removed at least in some districts of J&K as a start.
- The whole nation pouring in relief during the floods in the Kashmir Valley in 2014 creates a sense of belonging in the alienated communities in the Kashmir Valley.
- Poster boys and tech savvy misguided elements are lured by Pakistan-sponsored agencies and Burhan Wani is born as a figure.
- In July 2016, Burhan Wani is killed in an encounter and agitational

dynamics return to the Kashmir valley with a vengeance. Disticts of South Kashmir, namely, Kulgam, Budgam, Pulwama, Shopiyan and Anantnag see rise in militant activities which is responded to by the security forces.
o BJP withdraws its support to the coalition at the helm of affairs with PDP and Governor's rule was established in the state for the eighth time since it acceded to India.

Geospatial Base

Introduction. Perched securely among the lofty snow-sprinkled mighty Himalayan mountain chain, the emerald blue skies peeping through the chinks of the clouds, the tall chinar trees swaying to the rhythm of the gusts of wind, all condense into a kindly smile, forming the lovely state of Jammu and Kashmir. It is located in the northern part of the Indian sub-continent in the vicinity of the Karakoram and western mountain ranges. It falls in the great northwestern complex of the Himalayan Ranges with marked relief variation, snow-capped summits, antecedent drainage, complex geological structure and rich temperate flora and fauna.[24]

Geography. Although the terrain of Jammu and Kashmir is highly diversified, only a small portion of its total area of approximately 85,000 square miles (220,000 square km) is well suited to human settlement. Of particular note is the fertile Valley of Kashmir, a valley roughly 80 miles long and up to 35 miles wide (130 × 55 km) astride the upper Jhelum River. This densely settled and surpassingly beautiful area lies at an average elevation of approximately 5,500 ft (1,675 m). The Valley comprises the core of Kashmir proper. It supports an economy based on tourism, handicraft industries and intensive agriculture. Two other favorable areas are of note: the foothills of the Himalayas, together with a narrow strip of the adjoining plain, in southern Jammu; and the northwestern extension of that region, comprising the greater part of PoK. These mainly agricultural areas are all relatively well-watered and, where not cleared for cultivation, support rich stands of mainly coniferous forest. Between southern Jammu and PoK on the one hand and the Valley on the other is the Pir Panjal mountain range, which, despite its rugged nature, supports a moderately dense and partially migratory population dependent on largely terraced agriculture, pastoralism, and forestry. Through these mountains must pass the overland traffic connecting the Valley with the plains of India. In the immediate aftermath of the partition of the state in 1947-48, this traffic was

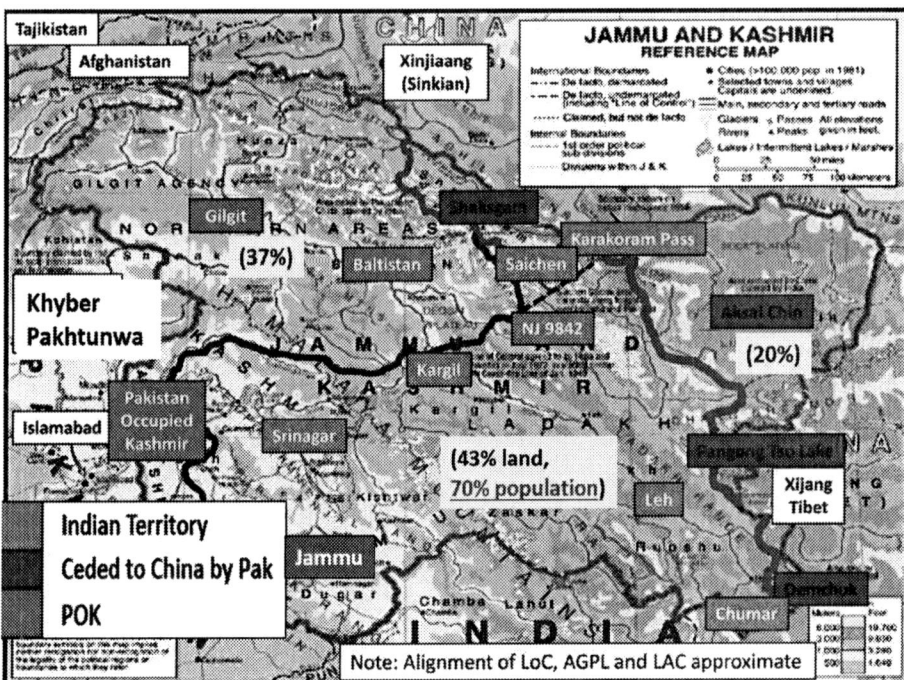

funneled through the Banihal Pass, which, at an elevation of 9,290 ft (2,830 m), was often closed by winter snows. This problem has been mitigated, however, though not entirely eliminated, by the construction of the Jawaharlal Nehru Tunnel at a significantly lower elevation, and by increasing reliance on air transportation. A much easier and formerly much more heavily utilized route to and from the Valley ran through the Baramula gap by which the Jhelum River flows to what are now PoK and Pakistan. Along the NE flank of the Valley runs the main range of the Himalayas. This enormous mountain chain extends from the eastern border region of the North-West Frontier Province of Pakistan southeastward to and well beyond the southern border of Jammu and Kashmir. Forested on their windward southwestern flanks, the Himalayas present a dramatically different, largely barren, aspect to the northeast. There the terrain gives way to the high, arid regions of Pakistan-occupied Baltistan, administered as a part of the Northern Areas, and Ladakh. These two thinly populated regions, comprising well over half the total area of the state, form a western extension of the Plateau of Tibet and are compartmentalized by a series of mountain ranges, generally paralleling the main crest of the Himalayas. An even more barren area, further to the northeast, is known as the Aksai-Chin (White Stone Desert), which is held by China since the 1960s.

State of Jammu and Kashmir comprises three regions, namely, Kashmir, Jammu and Ladakh. The State is further divided into 22 districts, 2 in Ladakh, 10 each in Jammu and Kashmir. The number of Tehsils and CD Blocks are 82 and 142, respectively. There are as many as 6,652 villages and 68 urban areas besides 7 urban agglomerations.

Climate. Climate exerts a profound influence on the inhabitants of any region. Their social, cultural, economic and other aspects of life are directly or indirectly governed by climate. The climate of the state ranges from the burning and the scorching heat of the plains of (Jammu Division) to the snow-capped heights of Gulmarg (Kashmir) and the mud peak of Mount Godwin Austin (Ladakh) 21,265 feet above sea level, the second highest in the world. Considering the overall distribution of climatic elements, four units become obvious:

- The windward (Jammu region).
- The leeward (Ladakh region).
- The high-altitude Kashmir (Himadri, Pir Panjal).
- The Kashmir valley.

The climate of the valley of Kashmir has its own peculiarities. The seasons are marked with sudden change and the climate can be divided into six seasons of two months each.[25]

Seasons of Kashmir Valley

Season	Dates	Local Terms
Spring	16 March to 15 May	Sont
Summer	16 May to 15 July	Retkol (Grishm)
Rainy	16 July to 15 Sep	Waharat
Autumn	16 Sep to 15 Nov	Harud
Winter	16 Nov to 15 Jan	Wandah
Ice Cold	16 Jan 15 March	Shishur

Physiography. The territory of the state is divided into seven physiographic zones closely associated with the structural components of the western Himalayas. These include:

- **The Plains.** The plains of the Jammu region are characterized by interlocking sandy alluvial fans that have been deposited during the Pleistocene age by the streams flowing from the foothills and by a much-dissected pediment (eroded bedrock surface) covered by loams and loess (fine deposits of silt).

- **The Foothills.** Rising from 2,000 to 7,000 ft, the foothills form the outer and inner zones.
- **The Lesser Himalayas.** Composed of Permo-Carboniferous volcanic rocks of granite, gneisses, quartz and slates, the Pir Panjal constitutes the first mountain rampart comprising the western-most part of the Lesser Himalayas.[26]

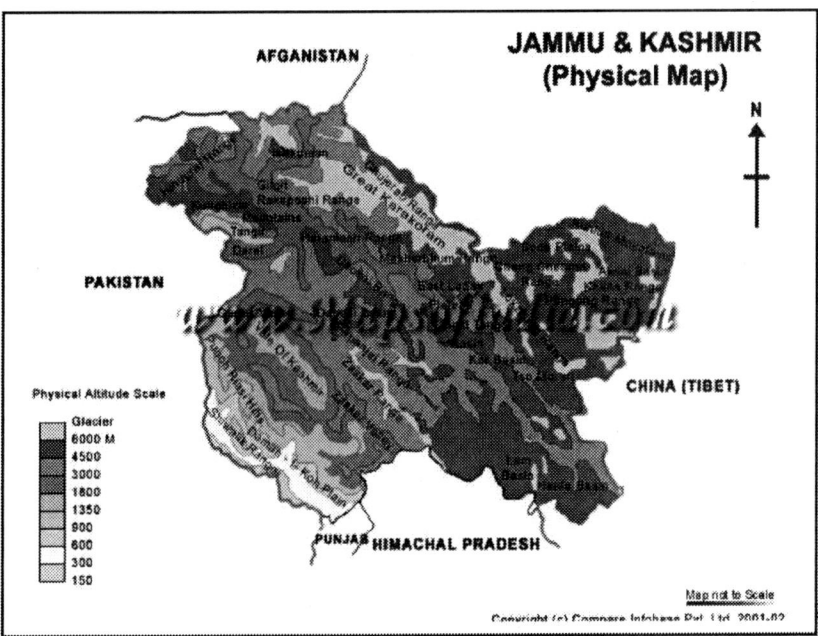

- **The Greater Himalayas.** This contains ranges reaching more than 20,013 ft (6,100 m) in altitude. These ranges act as a climatic divide and stop the cold wind coming from Central Asia.
- **Valley of Kashmir.** Between the Pir Panjal and the western end of the Great Himalayan ranges lies a deep asymmetrical basin called the Valley of Kashmir.
- **The Upper Indus Valley.** The valley of the upper Indus river follows the geological strike (structural trend) westwards from the Tibetan border to the point in the Pakistani sector where it rounds the great mountainous mass of Nanga Parbat to run southwards in deep gorges cut across the strike. In its upper reaches, gravel terraces flank the river; each tributary builds an alluvial fan out into the main valley. The town of Leh stands on such a fan, 11,483 ft (3,500 m) above sea level.
- **The Karakoram Range.** The Karakoram region contains some of the

world's highest peaks. As the altitude rises very much and majestic peaks appear, K_2 (Godwin Austin) the second highest peak in the world (28,264 ft or 8,615 m) occupies the most important position.

Demographic Base

Jammu and Kashmir has a Muslim majority population. As per 2011 census, though Islam is practised by about 67% of the population of the state and by 97% of the population of the Kashmir valley, the state has large communities of Buddhists, Hindus (inclusive of Megh Bhagats) and Sikhs. In Jammu, Hindus constitute 65% of the population, Muslims 31% and Sikhs, 4%. In Ladakh, Buddhists constitute about 46% of the population, the remaining being Muslims. The people of Ladakh are of Indo-Tibetan origin, while the southern area of Jammu includes many communities tracing their ancestry to the nearby Indian states. In totality, the Muslims constitute 67% of the population, the Hindus about 30%, the Buddhists 1%, and the Sikhs 2% of the population. Buddhists, Hindus, Sikhs and a few Christian, Jain, and Zoroastrian communities were once natives and made up a vast majority of the whole Kashmir province, but because of economic changes, riots, political tension, military involvement, and foreign extremists resulted in vast majority of the followers of these religions to settle in the growing and advancing neighbouring regions and major cities in India over the years. Hindu pandits were specifically affected in this region due to their status in the local society. Approximately 95% of the total population of 160,000 to 170,000 of Kashmiri Pandits, (*i.e.,* approximately 150,000-160,000) left the Kashmir Valley in 1990 as militancy engulfed the state and are settled as internally displaced people in Jammu, Delhi and other parts of the country due to the ongoing violence.

Population Data as per 2011 Census

	2011	2001
Approximate Population	1.25 Crores	1.01 Crore
Actual Population	12,541,302	10,143,700
Male	6,640,662	5,360,926
Female	5,900,640	4,782,774
Population Growth	23.64%	29.04%
Percantage of Total Population	1.04%	0.99%
Sex Ratio	889	900
Child Sex Ratio	862	964
Density/km^2	56	46
Total Child Population (0-6 age)	2,018,905	1,485,803
Male Population (0-6 age)	1,084,355	765,394
Female Population (0-6 age)	934,550	720,409

	2011	2001
Literacy	67.16 %	55.52 %
Male Literacy	76.75 %	66.60 %
Female Literacy	49.12 %	42.22 %
Total Literate	7,067,233	4,807,286
Male Literate	4,264,671	3,060,628
Female Literate	2,802,562	1,746,658

Region-wise Population of State as per 2011 Census

Name	Area (km²)	Population 2001 Census	Population 2011 Census
Jammu Division	26,293	4,430,191	5,350,811
Kashmir Valley Division	15,948	5,476,970	6,907,622
Ladakh Division	59,146	236,539	290,492
	101,387	10,143,700	12,548,925

Percentage Distribution of Population

Division	Area	Population	Muslim	Hindu	Sikh	Buddhist and other
Kashmir	15.73%	53.9%	97.16%	1.84%	0.88%	0.11%
Jammu	25.93%	43.7%	30.69%	65.23%	3.57%	0.51%
Ladakh	58.33%	2.3%	47.40%	6.22%	–	45.87%
Jammu and Kashmir	100%	100%	66.97%	29.63%	2.03%	1.36%

The Kashmir Valley is dominated by ethnic Kashmiris, who have largely driven the Azadi campaign. Non-Kashmiri Muslim ethnic groups (Paharis, Sheenas, Gujjars and Bakarwalas), who dominate areas along the Line of Control, have remained indifferent to the separatist campaign. Jammu province region though has a 70:30 Hindu-Muslim ratio, parts of the region were hit by militants, but violence has ebbed there, along with the Valley. Dogras (67%) are the single largest group in the multi-ethnic region of Jammu living with Punjabis, Paharis, Bakerwals and Gujjars. Ladakh is the largest region in the state with over 200,000 people. Its two districts are Leh (77% Buddhist) and Kargil (80% Muslim population). Union territory status has been the key demand of Leh Buddhists for many years.

Youth Bulge. The number of officially registered unemployed youth rose from 4,47,653 to 5,97,332 between Nov 2009 and Dec 2010. Today, over 70% of Jammu and Kashmir's population is estimated to be under 35. According to the Mercy Corps findings from an extensive research effort conducted across

10 districts of Kashmir Valley to analyze and understand key factors that are critical to boosting youth entrepreneurship, which was also presented to the state government: "with right investment and support, Kashmir's youth bulge could eventually yield a demographic dividend in terms of increased productivity and economic growth." "Kashmir's burgeoning youth population is an untapped asset and represents a potential opportunity for the positive economic and social change. Large percentages of Kashmir's youth are potential entrepreneurs. Kashmiri youth are highly resilient, educated and motivated but currently lack skills needed to compete in the 21st century and face acute scarcity of employment opportunities in both the public and private sector."

Education. J&K govt provides compulsory and free education upto Elementary Level under SSA. It includes opening/upgration of schools for Elementary Education, 100% enrollment of children in Educational Institutions and providing of Infrastructure facilities; 79 Kasturba Gandhi Balika Vidayalayas (KGBVs) are functional in the state. The Education Department provides free-of-cost text books and mid-day meals upto 8th class. Strengthening of Secondary and Higher Secondary Education Institutes under Rashtriya Madyamik Shiksha Abhiyan (RMSA) has also been a priority of the state govt.

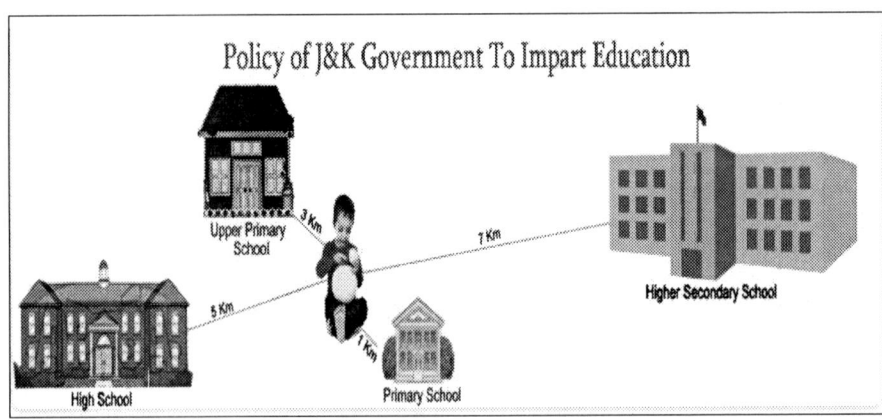

The snapshot from the official website of J&K Education Department clearly amplifies their focus. The various education indexes of the state are tabulated below.

State Education Profile

Population	12,548,926
Percentage of Male Population	53.94%
Percentage of Female Population	46.89%
Literacy Rate	68.74%
Male Literacy Rate	78.26%
Female Literacy Rate	58.01%
Female Population	47.16%
Urban Literacy Rate	68.75%
Rural Literacy Rate	53.61%
All India Average Literacy Rate	74.04%
Number of Primary Schools	14171
Number of Upper Primary Schools	6665
Number of High Schools	1194
Number of Higher Secondary Schools	597
Number of Sainik Schools	02
District Institute of Education (DIETs)	22
State Institute of Education (SIEs)	02
Number of KGBVs	79

Literacy Scenario (Census 2011)

S.No.	District	Male	Female	Total
01	Jammu	89.77%	77.41%	83.98%
02	Srinagar	78.01%	63.47%	71.21%
03	Rajouri	78.38%	57.20%	68.54%
04	Ganderbal	70.74%	47.62%	59.99%
05	Doda	80.36%	50.34%	65.97%
06	Kargil	86.73%	58.05%	74.49%
07	Poonch	81.04%	54.80%	68.69%
08	Leh	89.39%	64.52%	80.48%
09	Kathua	81.40%	64.56%	73.50%
10	Baramulla	77.35%	55.01%	66.93%
11	Samba	89.76%	74.39%	82.48%
12	Budgam	68.18%	46.60%	57.98%
13	Kishtwar	71.75%	44.13%	58.54%
14	Kupwara	77.10%	54.79%	66.92%
15	Udhampur	79.93%	58.22%	69.90%
16	Anantnag	74.13%	54.15%	64.32%
17	Shopian	71.86%	52.77%	62.49%
18	Reasi	69.93%	47.55%	59.42%
19	Ramban	71.97%	40.04%	56.90%
20	Bandipora	68.41%	46.24%	57.82%
21	Pulwama	75.41%	53.81%	65.00%
22	Kulgam	70.59%	49.74%	60.35%

Enrolment in Schools. Enrolment in Government Schools increased from 14.50 lacs in 2004 to 19.50 lacs in 2009-10. No of Out of School Children (OOSC) was reduced from 3.76 lacs in 2002-03 to 0.39 lacs in 2009-10.[27]

Higher Education. J&K Higher Education Department is the controlling authority for all the Higher Education Institutions of the State. It has seven Universities and numerous Government and Non-Government Colleges to look after. There has been a gradual increase in the number of governmnet colleges and enrollment over the years. The graphs below highlight the same.[28]

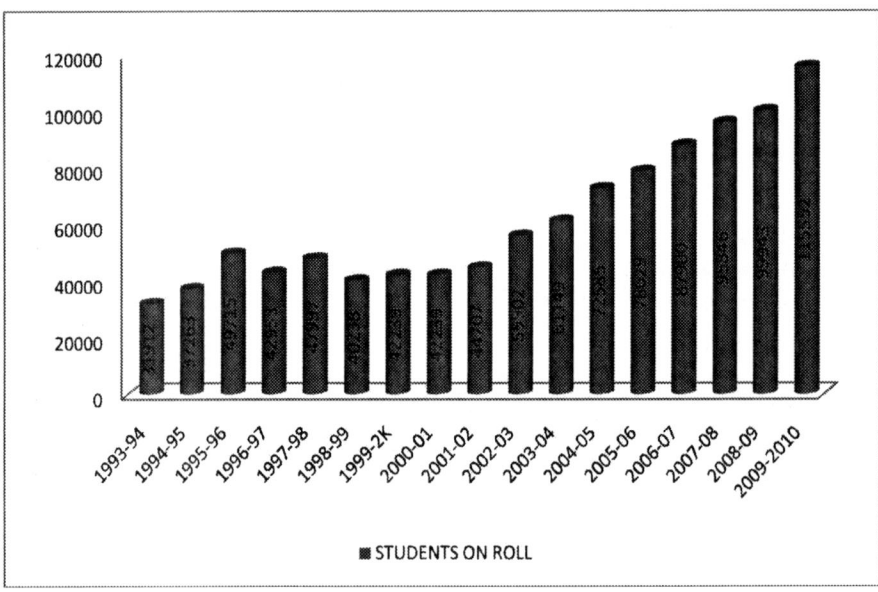

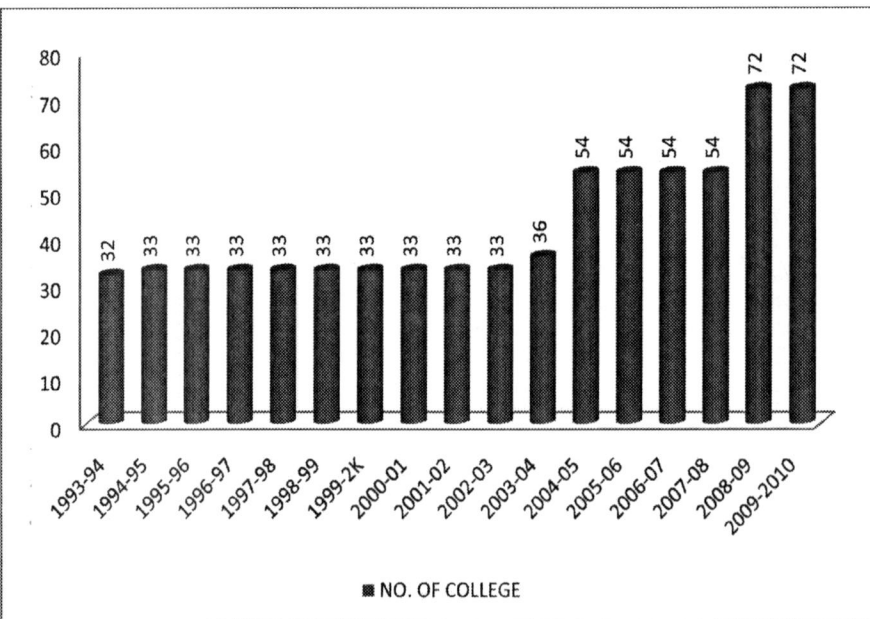

District-wise breakdown of government colleges in the state is as under.

	Jammu			Kashmir			Ladakh	
S. No.	District	No. of Colleges	S. No.	District	No. of Colleges	S. No.	District	No. of Colleges
1	Jammu	12	11	Srinagar	8	21	Leh	2
2	Kathua	7	12	Baramulla	8	22	Kargil	2
3	Udhampur	3	13	Anantnag	7			
4	Rajouri	6	14	Budgam	5			
5	Poonch	3	15	Pulwama	4			
6	Doda	4	16	Kupwara	5			
7	Reasi	3	17	Ganderbal	2			
8	Kishtwar	3	18	Kulgam	3			
9	Ramban	3	19	Shopian	1			
10	Samba	1	20	Bandipora	3			
	Total	45		Total	46		Total	4

Initiatives. New market-friendly and job-oriented subject combinations have been introduced in newly established colleges. Government College of Engineering and Technology, Jammu, has become a full-fledged Engineering College. UGC has sanctioned sufficient grants for development under XI Plan to state colleges. Four mini campuses have been setup in J&K under UGC funding. A total of 144 B. Ed. colleges are functioning in the state imparting technical education to local and outside state students.

Details of private colleges are as follows:

Jammu Division		Kashmir Division	
B. Ed.	75	B. Ed.	67
M. Ed.	3	M. Ed.	
Degree College	16	Degree College	
PG Course	1	PG Course	2
BCA	30	BCA	5
MCA	4	MCA	
BBA	27	BBA	4
MBA	5	MBA	
Law	7	Law	
PGDCA	4	PGDCA	
PGDBM		PGDBM	

Women Empowerment. In a state like Jammu and Kashmir where a huge population of women is unemployed and another significant section consists of widows and half widows, the importance of women's economic independence for their overall dignity and even survival is brought out by the fact that there is a linkage between the physical survival of women and their entry into the workforce. The main barriers to women empowerment are as follows:

- Violence against women.
- Lack of decision-making authority.
- Lack of participation in political affairs.
- Poor and low status of women.
- Lack of education.
- Lack of awareness.
- Inadequate and unorganized health care delivery system.
- Under/unemployment leading to poverty.

Programmes for Women's Economic Empowerment. Taking cognizance of women empowerment as one of the main focused area, the J&K government has launched various schemes for self-employment of the women. The Jammu and Kashmir State Women Development Corporation (JKWDC) established in the year 1991 is the channelizing agency for implementation of the schemes for social and economic upliftment of the women living below the poverty line. Few of the JKWDC schemes which are benefitting women are as follows:

- **Empowering Skilled Young Women Scheme (ESW).** It forms a part of Sher-i-Kashmir Employment and Welfare Programme. Women entrepreneurs belonging to different districts of the state can establish gainful income-generating units on a nominal interest rate of 6% on select trades of readymade garments, aromatic medicinal plants, boutique, fashion designing, cosmetic shop, DTP, medical health care, mushroom cultivation and floriculture/agriculture etc.
- **Swayam Sidha.** This scheme is meant for economic empowerment of women by framing Self-Help Groups. The centre government provides 100% grant in aids for implementation of the scheme.
- **Social Welfare Department.** The J&K Social Welfare Department is also implementing various schemes for development of women which include "Development of Vocational Skills" and "Lady Vocational Training Centres". Females in the age group of 15 to 35 years are imparted trainings in various crafts through Social Welfare Training Centres. At present, there are 150 Social Welfare Centres which are engaged in imparting training to women folk. The inmates are being provided training for 11 months and are being provided stipend of Rs 100 per month. Apart from this, there are four ladies' vocational training

centres in the State, one each at Jammu, Srinagar, Kargil and Leh. In these centres, besides imparting advanced trainings in various crafts, training in stenography is also imparted.[29]

Empowerment of Youth. Empowerment of youth and women, besides panchayati raj institutions, in Jammu and Kashmir is the top priority of the Centre and the State Government. **Skill Empowerment and Employment in J&K (SEE J&K)** is a project to provide options and opportunities to all youth in J&K, ranging from school dropouts to college educated, to select training program for salaried or self- employment as per their interest. The placements will be in the private sector, both within and outside J&K.[30]

- Himayat is a part of the SEE scheme of the Prime Minister's Office (PMO) recommended by the Rangarajan Committee. Ministry of Rural Development (MoRD) acts as the nodal agency for the project. Himayat has its focus on bridging the gap between the industry requirements and the skill set of the youth, so that more employment opportunities can be generated. Himayat, meaning support, intends to benefit the youth of Jammu and Kashmir with an employment-linked skills training program. The project envisages to train and place over 100,000 youths of J&K in the next five years. The skill training is to be imparted for multiple sectors like items, retail, hospitality etc. Salient features are as follows:[31]
    o The implementation of Himayat is being done by private companies or NGOs. The scheme aims to target 100,000 youth in 5 years.
    o Training centres have been developed at the block level where youth will be trained.
    o Support will be available for trainees after training and during placement as well.
    o However, even after five years, the scheme had not been able to take off in the right earnest. One look at the project status as of Jan 2014 presents a very discouraging picture. Only 5,833[32] candidates have successfully completed training against the target of 100,000, out of which 15% candidates have either dropped out or not opted for a placement.
- **Udaan.** Under the Special Industry Initiative of the Prime Minister, the National Skills Development Corporation (NSDC) and Ministry of Home Affairs have been mandated to work with the corporate sector in bringing about a positive change in the employment and skills space

of Jammu and Kashmir. The Special Industry Initiative, known as "Udaan", targets the youth of J&K, specifically graduates and postgraduates, who are seeking global and local opportunities. Udaan thereby aims to provide skills to 40,000 youth over a period of 5 years in high-growth sectors. Udaan has two objectives:

- o To provide exposure to the graduates and postgraduates of Jammu and Kashmir to the best of corporate India.
- o To provide corporate India with exposure to the rich talent pool available in the state.
- o Implementation of this scheme is also not very successful. Though the commitment from industries and corporate partners is available, attracting the youth to undergo training remains a major challenge.

Udaan Milestones as on 01 Nov 2013[33]

Corporate partnered with Udaan	42
Commitment for 5 Years	59,133
Youth Joined Udaan Training Programme	1,953
Candidate Undergoing Training	1,212
Registered Candidate	27,694

Human Development Index. Human Development Index, HDI, makes use of four parameters for measuring and ranking countries/states according to their social and economic development which includes the Life Expectancy at Birth, Expected Years of Schooling, Mean Years of Schooling and Gross National/State Income per Capita. **HDI** scores ranges from 0 to 1, with 1 being the best possible score to attain. At present, the overall average **HDI** Score of India is 0.547. Below provided is a list of Indian States and Indian Union Territories along with their respective **HDI** scores.[34]

HDI of Indian States

States	HDI Rank	HDI
Andhra Pradesh	20	0.473
Arunachal Pradesh	15	0.617
Assam	22	0.444
Bihar	28	0.367
Chhattisgarh	23	0.358
Goa	3	0.617
Gujarat	14	0.527
Haryana	11	0.552
Himachal Pradesh	8	0.652
Jammu and Kashmir	17	0.529
Jharkhand	24	0.376
Karnataka	18	0.519

States	HDI Rank	HDI
Kerala	1	0.921
Madhya Pradesh	26	0.375
Maharashtra	6	0.689
Manipur	5	0.707
Meghalaya	19	0.585
Mizoram	2	0.790
Nagaland	4	0.770
Orissa (now Odisha)	27	0.362
Punjab	9	0.605
Rajasthan	21	0.434
Sikkim	7	0.684
Tamil Nadu	10	0.570
Tripura	16	0.608
Uttar Pradesh	25	0.380
Uttarakhand	13	0.490
West Bengal	12	0.492

HDI of Indian Union Territories

Union Territories	HDI Rank	HDI
Andaman and Nicobar Islands	4	0.766
Chandigarh	1	0.892
Dadra and Nagar Haveli	7	0.618
Daman and Diu	5	0.754
Delhi	3	0.750
Lakshadweep	2	0.796
Pondicherry	6	0.748

HDI of J&K at 0.527 is just below the national average of 0.541. However, J&K's ranking of 17/24 among states and UTs doesn't paint the true picture of poverty index of the state.

Poverty Analysis. The Poverty figures thrown up by the Planning Commission on the basis of data collected by the NSSO through its socio-economic surveys in respect of Jammu and Kashmir State was a matter of debate and controversy in the State. The estimates have shown a phenomenal decrease during the period from 1993-94 to 1999-2000.

Psychological Aspects

- **Kashmiriyat.**
    - **Origin.** Kashmir has historically been an important centre for Hinduism and Buddhism. Islam was introduced in the medieval centuries, and Sikhism also spread to the region under the rule of the Sikh Empire in the early 19th century.[35] Kashmir has a significant place in the mythology and history of all four religions. The region

is home to many legendary Hindu and Buddhist monuments and institutions. The Hazratbal shrine houses a relic that is believed to be the hair of Muhammad, the prophet of Islam. In his journeys seeking religious enlightenment, Guru Nanak travelled to Kashmir. Although the process was initiated by the likes of Bulleh Shah and Shah Hamadani in the 14th Century, *Kashmiriyat* per se is believed to have developed under the rule of Muslim governor Zain-ul-Abedin and the Mughal emperor Akbar, both of whom gave equal protection, importance and patronage to Kashmir's different religious communities.[36]

o **Philosophy.** Kashmir's existence is characterised by its insular Himalayan geography, harsh winter climate and isolation in economic and political terms. The region has also seen political turmoil and foreign invasions. *Kashmiriyat* is believed to be an expression of solidarity, resilience and patriotism **regardless of religious differences**. It is believed to embody an ethos of harmony and a determination of survival of the people and their heritage. To many Kashmiris, *Kashmiriyat* **demanded religious and social harmony and brotherhood**.[37] It has been strongly influenced by Kashmir Shaivism, Buddhism and Sufism, carrying a long-standing conviction that any and every religion will lead to the same divine goal. However, the impact and importance of *Kashmiriyat* has been concentrated in the Vale of Kashmir only, which is the real historical Kashmir. The farther regions of Gilgit, Baltistan, Jammu and Ladakh have not been influenced by this philosophy, as these regions are not Kashmiri in terms of culture, language or ethnicity.

o **Challenges.** The culture and ethos of *Kashmiriyat* was greatly eroded at the onset of the Kashmir conflict, when the region was claimed and divided during the Indo-Pakistani War of 1947. In the political debate on sovereignty over Kashmir, many interpret *Kashmiriyat* as nationalism and an expression for political independence from both Pakistan and India. The onset of militancy in Kashmir from 1989 has led to the exodus of almost all Hindus from Kashmir and violent attacks against the remaining communities of Hindus and Sikhs, further eroding the fabric of *Kashmiriyat*. Amidst the wider dispute between India and Pakistan, there are also political demands for the separation of the territories of Ladakh and Jammu from the Kashmir valley. Conscious efforts to revive *Kashmiriyat* have been made by various communities of Muslims and Hindus through united opposition to violence in the state.[38] Efforts to promote *Kashmiriyat* through cultural activities, social programmes and literature have increased throughout Jammu and Kashmir and amongst expatriate Kashmiri communities. In 2007 poll conducted by the Centre for the Study of Developing Societies in New Delhi, 84% of people in Srinagar wanted to see the return of Kashmiri Pandits.[39]

- **Sufism.** The most remarkable event of the partition in our history, however, is the fact that Kashmir's Muslims stayed secular in this hour of their gravest trial.[40] It was no mean thing, for them, unlike even their brethren in Mirpur and Poonch, not to speak of other parts of the country, to hear horrendous stories of communal carnage involving millions of Hindus and Muslims and remain utterly unaffected.[41] Instead of giving in to the deadly and rampant communal virus, Kashmiri Muslims waited for and welcomed Indian troops, 70 years ago, to help them in their fight against Pakistani Muslim tribal raiders. Kashmir has been in the grip of militant separatism for years now. A small Muslim-majority region, i.e., Kashmir Valley has been seeking to secede from a Hindu-majority country. This is bound to create an incorrect impression of communalism and obscurantism rampant in that state. And yet, barring the misdeeds of isolated groups, largely funded from abroad, the masses of people remain secular. Nothing could demonstrate this better than the fact that ordinary Kashmiri Muslims are even today eagerly awaiting the return of their Pandit brothers and sisters who had left the valley at the height of militancy. It has surprised many observers that, contrary to the general experience of communal rioting in most parts of the sub-continent, Kashmiri Muslims have been looking after the homes and hearths of their migrated Kashmiri Pandit brothers for years in the fond hope that one day there would be peace and they would be able to return.[42] The demolition of the Babri Masjid at Ayodhya was followed by the demolition of numerous Hindu temples in the Muslim Bangladesh and Pakistan, but temples in Kashmir, as very dramatically demonstrated by *India Today's* video-magazine, remained safe from the effects of Islamic frenzy seen elsewhere in the sub-continent,[43] contrary to the claims made by vested interests. Where from does this deep commitment to secularism, to a composite Hindu-Muslim culture emanate? What is the source of this deep connection with India? Why is Kashmiriyat so important to the Kashmiri Muslim? The answer lies in the eclectic and syncretic nature of the Kashmiri Muslims' philosophy of life,[44] their spiritual beliefs.[45] It is the impact of Sufi and *Rishi* visions of Islam that have helped one synthesise the teachings of Prophet Mohammad with the teachings of earlier sages of Hinduism, Buddhism and Jainism. While elsewhere in the sub-continent, too, people have maintained their pre-Islamic beliefs, it is in Kashmir alone that one finds them claiming their ancient Indian, particularly Vedic and Buddhist heritage consciously.[46]

- The explanation for spread of Sufism perhaps lies in the history of the spread of Islam in this region. Definite historical facts that would account for the extraordinarily large number of conversions that took place in Kashmir are not available, as Sir Thomas Arnold points out in his highly regarded book *Preaching of Islam*. But whatever scanty information is available leads us to attribute this surprising phenomenon to a long and continuous missionary movement carried out by Sufi saints, Pirs, Faqirs, Dervishes and Ulema. The Islamic missionary entered the valley at a time when, in the words of W. R. Lawrence (*The Valley of Kashmir*), it "was a country of drunkards and gamblers." Such an atmosphere is very much suited for the spread of a new philosophy or religion. The Mughal rule provided further impetus to the spread of Islam, as many learned ulema and mystics arrived in the valley during this period. The process continued during the Afghan rule (1752-1819) as well. Thus, the process that had been started by a simple faqir called Bulbul Shah (1301-1320 in Kashmir)[47] was continued by a volley of saints and mystics, *Rishis* and faqirs, ulema and learned men like Shah Hamdani[48] (1371-1383 in Kashmir). No generals like Mohammad bin Qasim or warriors like Shahab-ud-Deen or conquerors like Mahmud were involved. No wonder the colour of Islam in the valley is still so deeply mystical and deeply respectful of other religions. It is extremely depressing to see people with such mystical traditions living in such violent times. It is difficult to see Kashmir living permanently in the grip of obscurantism and fundamentalism.[49]

- **Spread of Fundamentalism.** Militancy has dramatically transformed Sufism- and Kashmiriyat-influenced people of Kashmir into a fractured and radically influenced society which in turn has given rise to religious fundamentalism. This has affected all aspects of the society including Kashmiri institutions such as political parties, government and non-government organisations, militant groups, educational institutions, self-help groups and many other such organisations within and outside Kashmir Valley.[50] Rise of fundamentalism also signifies a transformation in the mindset of Kashmiri people from being an accommodative and a tolerant society to a more static, traditional and conservative society which is not averse to use of violence and advocates extremist outlook. Fundamentalist mindset has brought to fore many terrorist institutions such as Hizb-ul-Mujahideen, Harkat-ul-Ansar, Jaish-e-Mohhamad, Harkat-ul-Mujahideen, Lashkar-e-Toiba etc (fully conceptualised and supported by Pakistan) and secessionist groups such as Mutahida Jehad Council (a conglomerate of Pakistani Jehadi Groups), Jammu and Kashmir Liberation Front, APHC (propped and supported by Pakistan), Dukhtaran-e-Milat (a soft terrorist group supported by Pakistan) etc. One critical area expected to be exploited by such fundamentalist organisations is leveraging of the institution of "madrasas" to their advantage.[51]

In spite of the progress with respect to education and literacy, the Islamic education in Kashmir remains in focus. Islamic education in Jammu and Kashmir encompasses various madrasas and Islamic institutions. The curriculum involves 80% emphasis on religious studies, while 20% time is devoted on other subjects. These include the schools which are run by religious trusts like Salafia, Falhan-e-Alam (Jamaat-e-Islami, or JEI) and are affiliated to the State Board of Education.

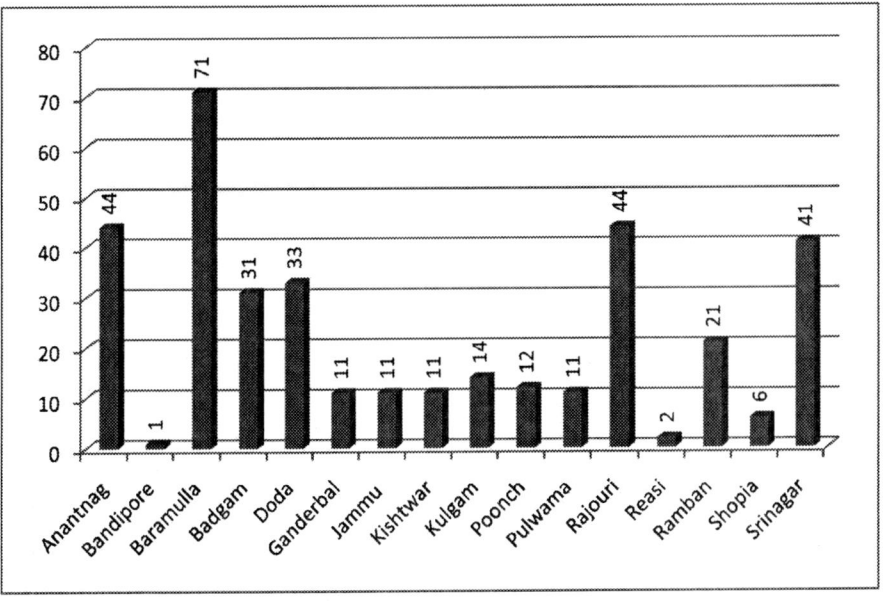

MADRASAS SUPPORTED BY GOVERNMENT IN J&K[52]

Slowly but steadily, Islamic schools and madrasas have gained importance amongst the valley population. As madrasas focus on the Islamic identity, they weaken the concept of Kashmiriat. Many of the madrasas, which are affiliated to Salafia Trust, JEI and Deobandi School of thought, are focusing on establishing orthodox Islam thought and practices which in turn erode the core values of Sufism. Shariah traditions as advocated by orthodox Islam, advocate shunning of local traditions such as shrine worship and advocate strict "Purdah" by women. Reducing the influence of Shia maulvis is another motivating factor for the fundamentalists. There is no direct evidence of involvement of madrasas in anti-national militancy. However, products of these institutions do nurture anti-establishment feeling. Some of the maulvis have been investigated by the state police for alleged links with terrorist organisations. Since maulvis are held in high esteem, it may be possible for them to indoctrinate the students of madrasas into the ways of militancy. If influenced by the communal and anti-national forces, the institution of madrasas is being exploited by the hardliners for leveraging the cause of fundamentalism.

All Parties Hurriyat Conference

Formation. APHC is a political front formed as an alliance of 26 political, social and religious organizations in Kashmir. It was formed for achieving the right of self-determination according to UN Security Council Resolution 47. "Hurriyat" in Koshur (as well as in Arabic, Urdu and Persian, from which the word is taken) means "liberty." The origins of the Hurriyat are traced to the 1993 phase of the Kashmir militancy. The initial euphoria of "armed struggle" had subsided in the light of counter-insurgency operations launched by the Indian security forces. The JKLF with its pro-independence ideology had been marginalised and replaced by a network of Islamist extremist outfits controlled by the Inter-Services Intelligence (ISI), Pakistan's external intelligence agency. Parallel to this, Pakistan was aggressively pursuing an agenda to portray its proxy war against India as an indigenous uprising against Indian sovereignty and internationalise the Kashmir issue. It was in this context that the Hurriyat was formed on 09 March 1993 as an umbrella body for all over-ground secessionist organisations. Since the international community frowned upon the resort to violence by non-state actors, the Hurriyat was an ideal platform to promote the Kashmiri secessionist cause.

Ideology and Role. According to the Hurriyat Conference, Jammu and Kashmir is a disputed territory and "India's control" on it is not justified. It supports the Pakistani claim that Kashmir is the "unfinished agenda of Partition" and needs to be solved "as per the aspirations of the people of Jammu and Kashmir." The APHC perceives itself to be the sole representative of the Kashmiri people, a claim that has so far been endorsed explicitly only by Pakistan. The outfit's primary role has been to project a negative image of counter-insurgency operations in Jammu and Kashmir and to mobilise public opinion against the Indian security forces. The alliance has consistently followed up local allegations of security force excesses, and in several documented cases, allegedly distorted facts to suit its propaganda.

Split. Till as late as January 2014, there were two factions of the Hurriyat Conference led by Mirwaiz (a hereditary title of one of Kashmir's important religious seats, and also head priest of the Jamia Masjid in Srinagar) Umar Farooq and Syed Ali Shah Geelani. The Mirwaiz-led group, also referred to as the "moderate faction" along with non-Hurriyat leaders like Yasin Malik undertook, during 02 to 16 June 2005, the first formal visit of Kashmiri separatists to Pakistan-occupied Kashmir (PoK) and subsequently, though unsanctioned by Indian authorities, to Pakistan. Internal fissures within the Hurriyat Conference had culminated in a formal split on September 7, 2003, with at least 12 of its 26 constituents breaking away from the moderate faction under the leadership of SAS Geelani, a pro-Pakistani hardliner leader of Jamaat-e-Islami (JEI). It was named the Tehreek-e-Hurriyat Jammu and Kashmir. The Geelani faction reportedly has 16 constituents. In January 2014, three senior separatist leaders, Shabir Ahmad Shah, Azam Inquillabi and Naeem Ahmad Khan, of the moderate group of the APHC have formally parted ways with it, challenging the leadership of Mirwaiz Umar Farooq.[53]

Views on Right to Self-determination. Hurriyat led by Shabir Shah, Nayeem Khan and Azam Inquillabi as well as Syed Ali Geelani demands Right to Self-determination as per UN Security Council Resolution 47. Hurriyat led by Mirwaiz Umar Farooq is unclear on the Right to Self-determination with Abdul Ghani Bhat repeatedly stating that the UN resolutions for Right to Self-determination are dead. These views go against the Constitution of Hurriyat Conference and are viewed by common Kashmiris as disempowerment of their rights. Bhat's views have snowballed into a major controversy and are one of the main reasons for the alienation of the Hurriyat conference from the common people.[54]

Pakistan's Role. Pakistan has been making efforts to unite the two factions of Hurriyat Conferences to present a united platform for separatist groups in Kashmir.[55] In order to put pressure on separatists for unity in Kashmir, Pakistan even closed down one of the offices of the Hurriyat Conference in Islamabad last year. Since then, the two factions are operating from same office in Islamabad, with Yusuf Naseem, representative of Mirwaiz faction of the Hurriyat Conference and Ghulam Mohammad Safi, representing Geelani faction of Hurriyat Conference, issuing statements jointly signed by them. In Kashmir valley after Pakistan failed to unite the two Hurriyat factions, it was mulling formation of a Coordination Committee of two factions of Hurriyat Conference. But instead of uniting two factions, one more division in Hurriyat Conference took place. This is likely to be a major setback for the Hurriyat as well as Pakistan's efforts. Since the formation of Government by Nawaz Sharif, Pakistan Government has thrown its weight behind hardline Hurriyat Conference leader Syed Ali Shah Geelani. Earlier when Pervez Musharraf was in power in Pakistan, he had thrown his weight behind Mirwaiz and the People's Party-led Government followed the suit.[56]

People's Perception. Awaam is getting more and more disillusioned and APHC is losing its sway in the valley. As per general perception, lack of ability to lead people led to this factionalism and the difference in these pro-freedom leaders adversely affected the united cause. The meaningless basis of identity crisis parted them from the public too. The recent split in Hurriyat Conference (M) has on one hand disappointed the people of Kashmir and on the other has let the cat out of the bag. Kashmiris are demanding accountability from these leaders who claim to be representing the mass aspiration.[57] Geelani's age is also an issue of concern with no formidable leader to step in his shoes.

J&K Economy

Jammu and Kashmir state with its varied and diversified geographic, agro-climate and topographic features poses peculiar and unique problems of development. The Gross State Domestic Product (GSDP) at constant (2011-12) prices for the year 2017-18 is estimated at Rs. 109136.52 crore, as against the estimate of Rs. 100597.57 crore for 2016-17, indicating growth of 8.49% during 2017-18. At current prices, GSDP for 2017-18 is estimated to be Rs. 140886.76 crore as against the estimate of Rs. 126230.91 crore for 2016-17, showing an increase of 11.61% during the year. The projected estimates for the year 2018-19 at constant (2011-12) prices and current prices of GSDP are Rs. 116637.44 crore and Rs. 157383.77 crore. The estimate of State Income (i.e., Net State Income) at constant (2011-12) prices for 2017-18 is Rs. 90902.60 crore, as against the estimate of Rs 83717.39 crore for 2016-17, suggesting a rise of 8.58% during 2017-18. At current prices, the State Income for 2017-18 is estimated at Rs. 119294.71 crore as compared to the estimate of Rs. 106326.40 crore for 2016-17, showing a rise of 12.20% during the year.[58]

Based on the figures mentioned above the Government may claim that the economy of the state has been on the upswing but a detailed scrutiny of the revenue generation lets the cat out of the bag. The state's economy is heavily dependent upon the grants from the centre, the central funded schemes and the security forces deployed in the state.

Important Economic Sectors

Agriculture. Agriculture as we know plays a very prominent role for the development of economy of J&K State. Around 70% of the population in the State gets livelihood directly or indirectly from the Agriculture and allied Sectors. Paddy is the main crop of Kashmir, followed by maize, oilseeds, pulses, vegetables, fodder and wheat. In Jammu region, wheat is the prominent crop followed by maize, paddy, pulses, oilseeds, fodder, vegetables and other crops while in Ladakh, barley is the major cereal crop followed by wheat. State also has the honour of being amongst the world's few places where quality saffron is cultivated. Pampore tehsil of district Pulwama is famous for its high-grade saffron. Saffron is also grown, though on a limited scale, in Kishtwar district of Jammu region.

Horticulture. Horticulture plays an important role in the foreign exchange earnings. The state is abounding in crops like Apple, Almond, Mango, Walnut, Cherry, Apricot, Plum, Kiwi, Litchi, Olive, Citrus, etc. which have a high commercial value. A high growth in the horticulture sector can contribute to the generation of gainful and permanent employment to a sizeable number of people. Potential for bringing additional area under Walnut is enormous. As per preliminary estimates, about 0.50 lakh hectares are still available on which walnut cultivation can be undertaken successfully. This will help to create green cover in hilly areas and conserve soil from erosion, besides, providing high-value wood for wood carving industry, as well as walnuts for export purposes.

Fruit Sector. Area under Fruits in J&K State has increased from 2.95 lakh hectares in 2007-08 to 3.38 lakh hectares in 2016-17. The production has increased from 16.36 lakh MTs in 2007-08 to 22.35 lakh MTs in 2016-17.[59] Export of fruit outside the State has occupied a prominent place in trade of the State, but it is showing a fluctuating trend over the years. The total quantity exported ending November 2013-14 is 7.20 lakh MTs.

Animal Husbandry. Estimated livestock Population of the state, as per the latest available integrated sample survey (2011-12), is 160.407 lakh. The milk production for the year 2016-17 has reached to 2356.658 thousand metric tones in the State.[60] The total wool production estimated for the state was 73.819 lakh kg. Under Poultry Development programme of the State, 12.21 lakh hatching eggs and 5.31 lakh Day Old chicks were produced during the year 2016-17. Meat production registered a growth from 308.986 lakh kg to 322.781 lakh kg in the year 2016-17 over the previous year resulting into 4.47% growth.

Forest. Jammu and Kashmir has a total forest cover of 20,230 sq km (20.23 lakh hectares) accounting for 19.95% of the total geographical area of 101,387 sq km on this side of line of control. Forests cover 48% of the total geographical area of the State (excluding Ladakh region) which is above the national average of 24.47%. It is, however, less than the norm of National Forest Policy, 1988, which provides forest cover of one third of total geographical area (20% for plains and 66% for hilly areas).

Floriculture. Floriculture sector has been identified as a focus segment and accorded a top priority. Income of farmers from flower cultivation has seen a phenomenonal jump due to the ever-growing demand for flowers in domestic and international markets. The Government has taken several measures to promote this activity. It is catalytic for uplifting the economic condition of the small and marginal farmers of the State. Under Commercial Floriculture, the scope of the employment has also been expanded to a large extent. Progressive growers are also showing a keen interest in diversification of floriculture crops, as there is bright horizon in the sphere of floriculture sector.

Industrial Policy. A comprehensive Industrial Policy came into being in 2004 which facilitated provision of incentives to attract private sector investment for the industry in a big way. The incentives are aimed at overcoming the constraints of remoteness, poor connectivity, high transportation cost and erratic power supply faced by the Industry. It focuses on private sector industrialization in backward blocks of the State and modernization of the existing units. Prior to State incentives, the Central Government in 2002 announced its Package of Incentives which has been extended for further five years up to 15 July, 2017, on its expiry of the 10-year period in July 2012. The State Government notified and issued new Industrial Policy 2016. The Policy envisages to attract substantial investment especially in high-potential areas of food processing, leather, pharmaceuticals, wood-based sports goods/bats/willow wicker, high-grade raw silk, woollen fabrics, computer/electronics and information technology. The Policy anticipates creating a new land bank of 20,000 kanals across the state with emphasis on locations outside the urban areas and envisages attracting an investment of Rs. 20,000 crore over the period of next ten years.[61] Therefore, two sets of incentives are available to the entrepreneurs: one from the Centre Government and the other from the State Government. Infrastructure development serves as an engine for industrial development and calls for continuous attention of the Government. Inspite of all these, investment in the state is negligible mainly due to the security situation and land policies.

Handicraft. Handicraft activities occupy an important position in the economic structure of J&K State. Being environment friendly, these activities are best suited to the state as they are more labour intensive and less capital intensive in nature, therefore having scope for employment generation at a large scale. The Kashmir handicraft products have earned worldwide fame for their attractive designs, functional utility and high-quality craftsmanship. In absence of other manufacturing industries in the state, handicrafts remained a key economic activity from time immemorial. The artistic imagination and craftsmanship of the Artisans, reflected through a wide range of products, has delighted the connoisseurs world over for centuries. Crafts like shawls, crewel, namdha, chain stitch, wood carving, papier-mâché, costume jewellery, kani shawls and the carpets hold a significant share in the overall production and export of the State. Silken carpets in particular constitute a specialty having no parallel in quality and design at a national level and, therefore, occupy an important position in the international market. The handicraft sector of the state has great contribution towards foreign exchange earnings to the state and country in particular.

Information Technology. Information Technology sector, identified as one of the thrust areas, is growing in the state at a healthy pace. Information Technology has proved to be a very effective tool in the development of a society and become the driving force in the growth of economies across the globe. Recognizing the IT sector as a major tool for fostering state's economy, various initiatives have been/are being taken up by the State Government to strengthen this sector.

Tourism

During the year 2017, till October 10.5 lakh tourists visited Kashmir valley, 2.59 lakh tourists visited Ladakh, 57.39 lakhs devotees visited Mata Vaishno Devi Ji and 2.59 lakh Amar Nath Ji Holy Cave.[62] Tourism is not only a growth engine but also an export growth engine and employment generator. The sector has a capacity to create large-scale employment both direct and indirect, for diverse sections of society from the most specialized to unspecialized work force. J&K has a great promise for the development of tourism in view of its inherent potential. J&K is a premier as well as established tourist destination in the country. Kashmir valley in the lap of Himalayas has many internationally acclaimed tourist destinations. The lush green tourist resorts of Gulmarg, Pahalgam, Yousmarg, Kokernag and golden meadows of Sonamarg have remained an attraction for the centuries. Hospitality and Tourism are in fact part of the valley's tradition, culture, and now more importantly, economy. Jammu region is attracting a large number of pilgrim tourists and the important destination has been the Mata Vaishno Devi Shrine. The other places are Shiv Khori, Sukhrala Mata and Shahdra Sharief. Newly identified and emerging destinations in Jammu are Bhaderwah, Rajouri and Poonch. The Ladakh region has been a much sought-after destination especially for the foreign tourists. The region is like a slice of desert high up in the Himalayas, complete with salt water as well as fresh water lakes, sand dunes and camels. Its monasteries, some of which are very famous like Hemis Gompa, the Lama-Buddhist Culture, the beautiful paintings, sculptures and ancient books preserved in the monasteries are an additional source of attraction to the tourists.

Energy. Energy is one of the key drivers of the economy. J&K is richly endowed with vast water resources having hydel power potential of more than 20,000 MW capacity. Energy generation in 2014-15, 2015-16, and 2016-17 has been recorded as 39887.17 MUs, 40302.88 MUs and 48662.06 MUs respectively, recording an increase by 21.99% from 2014-15 to 2016-17.[63] Owing to Indus Water treaty, the state has to choose less economic designs of Hydel projects. Another area of concern has been the transmission and distribution losses which are very high in the state than at the National level.

Infrastructure. The Jammu-Srinagar Highway is the only lifeline that connects the state to the rest of the country. The government has taken the initiative of creating an alternate highway via Shopian-Bufliaz popularly known as Mughal Road. The construction of this road is presently going on in full swing and the project being constructed under the Prime Minister's Reconstruction Plan (PMRP) is expected to be completed this year. This will provide much needed mobility facility to the people. The railway network is a recognized mode of communication, which has started making its presence felt. This was realized through commissioning of Banihal-Baramulla Rail link. The rail connectivity under Udhampur-Banihal section is the final missing link. This connectivity scenario has rendered the State dependent on road connectivity for common mode of commutation.

Regional Disparity. One of the most astonishing facts about J&K's economy is the disparity in distribution of economy among the three regions. The table below is self-explanatory.

	Jammu	Kashmir	Ladakh
Population	62 Lakh	58 Lakh	2 Lakh
Area	25.96%	15.67%	58.37%
Villages	3,614	2,029	242
Lok Sabha Seats	2	3	1
Vidhan Sabha Seats	36	47	4
Jobs in Secretariat	10% (approx)	90% (approx)	–
Revenue Generation	70% (approx)	30% (approx)	–
Funds given by Govt.	30% (approx)	70% (approx)	–
Education Fund	30% (approx)	70% (approx)	–
Electricity Supply	23 Mega Watt	350 Mega Watt	–

Politics and Governance

Political Importance. The state of Jammu and Kashmir has acquired since the 19th century a unique geo-political status in the Indian sub-continent. It has contiguous boundaries with Russia, Afghanistan, Pakistan, China and Tibet that deserve constant vigil and as such it has made the State very important, geographically, politically, economically and from the military point of view. Jammu and Kashmir state acceded to the Indian Union in 1947 after the partition. Before the partition in 1947, The English rulers of India took away Gilgit in 1946 from the Maharaja of Jammu and Kashmir on lease for thirty years so that they could check the advancement of Russia towards India.

Constitutional Framework. The state of Jammu and Kashmir retains a special status within the union government of India. Unlike the rest of the states, which are bound by the Indian constitution, Jammu and Kashmir follows a modified version of that constitution—as delineated in the Constitution (Application to Jammu and Kashmir) Order, 1954—which affirms the integrity of the state within the Republic of India. The union government has direct legislative powers in matters of defence, foreign policy, and communications within the state and has indirect influence in matters of citizenship, Supreme Court jurisdiction, and emergency powers. Under the constitution of Jammu and Kashmir, the governor, who is head of state, is appointed by the president of India and is aided and advised by an elected chief minister and a council of ministers.

Jammu and Kashmir is the only state in India which enjoys special autonomy under Article 370 of the Constitution of India, according to which no law enacted by the Parliament of India, except for laws in the field of defence, communication and foreign policy, will be extendable in Jammu and Kashmir unless it is ratified by the state legislature of Jammu and Kashmir.

Subsequently, jurisdiction of the Supreme Court of India over Jammu and Kashmir has been extended. Jammu and Kashmir is the only Indian state that has its own official flag and constitution, and Indians from other states cannot purchase land or property in the state. Designed by the then ruling NC, the flag of Jammu and Kashmir features a plough on a red background symbolising labour; it replaced the Maharaja's state flag. The three stripes represent the three distinct administrative divisions of the state, namely Jammu, Valley of Kashmir, and Ladakh. Since 1990, the Armed Forces Act, which gives special powers to the Indian security forces, has been enforced in Jammu and Kashmir.

Political Deadlock. J&K is a unique state and has been on politically volatile right from independence. Reason for four Indo-Pak conflicts, the state has been in turmoil for the last 25 years. The ethnic divide as enumerated in para 71 above substantiates the feeling of alienation in other two regions. With NC's domination fading away, and emergence of PDP in the Kashmir's politics and BJP in the Jammu region, the 2002 elections ushered in the era of collation politics in the state. The composition of the 2014 assembly is also a testimony to the same. The compulsions of collation and regional aspirations will always be a hindrance in good governance and solution to the deadlock.

A school of thought in the state is of the view that the prime cause of failure to break the deadlock in the State is that all suggested solutions are based on the misguided notion that the 2,000 square kilometers Kashmir Valley represents the entire State of Jammu and Kashmir, that the political aspirations of all the people in the State are identical or nearly identical and that the contradictions among them, if any, can be easily reconciled. None of these formulations enjoys any universal support in Jammu, Kashmir and Ladakh. The two prime factors are:

- The State of Jammu and Kashmir houses a number of religious and ethnic groups.
- The political aspirations and needs of the people of Jammu and Ladakh – who constitute almost half of the State's population and inhabit about 90% of the State's land area – and Kashmiri Pandits and Muslims are conflicting.[64]

Centre-State Relations. The relationship between the Govt of India and J&K has been like a roller coaster ride. However, the downs will outnumber the ups hands down. The history of this blow hot–blow cold marriage of convenience has been amply highlighted in the beginning. Few of the significant issues are further elaborated in the succeeding paragraphs.

Article 370 – the Raison d'être

The Instrument of Accession of Jammu and Kashmir to India was signed by the Maharaja Hari Singh in October 1947 and a special status was given to the State through the Article 370 in October, 1949. The wordings of Article 370 and its title "Temporary provisions with respect to the State of Jammu and Kashmir" are both significant as they imply that it was designed as a temporary or provisional arrangement. Thus, among the main aims of granting a special status were:

- To ensure the Kashmiris that their distinct identity would be preserved.
- To placate the Muslims of the Valley who were feeling uncertain over their future.

Why was Article 370 inserted in the Constitution? Or as the great poet and thinker, Maulana Hasrat Mohini, asked in the Constituent Assembly on October 17, 1949, "Why this discrimination please?" The answer was given by Nehru's confidant, the wise but misunderstood, Thanjavur Brahmin, Gopalaswami Ayyangar (Minister without portfolio in the first Union Cabinet, a former Diwan to Maharajah Hari Singh of Jammu and Kashmir, and the principal drafter of Article 370). Ayyangar argued that for a variety of reasons Kashmir, unlike other princely states, was not yet ripe for integration. India had been at war with Pakistan over Jammu and Kashmir and while there was a ceasefire, the conditions were still "unusual and abnormal." Part of the State's territory was in the hands of "rebels and enemies."[65]

370 Governs Centre-State Relations

The Article essentially governs centre-state relations pertaining to J&K. Centre-state relations and issues of regional balance within States are similarly dealt with in the case of Gujarat, Maharashtra, Andhra Pradesh, Assam, Sikkim, Manipur, Nagaland, Tripura, Meghalaya, Arunachal etc in Article 371-A to I and Schedules 5 and 6. Kashmir, in this sense, is not uniquely treated. When objections were raised in the Constituent Assembly regarding the inclusion of Article, an assurance was given by the framers of the Constitution that it would get eroded gradually. This happened to some extent during the premiership of Bakshi Ghulam Mohmmad, but it was not taken to its logical conclusion. So, stating the Article as the root cause of all the trouble over J&K and in the fear of demand for a plebiscite, some political parties have been demanding abrogation of the Article. They also believe that this Article has encouraged the secessionist elements in other part of the country. In December 1964, Articles 356 and 357 were extended to the state.

What does it Entail?

Article 370 specifies that except for Defence, Foreign Affairs, Finance and Communications (matters specified in the instrument of accession), the Indian Parliament needs the State Government's concurrence for applying all other laws. Thus, the state's residents lived under a separate set of laws, including those related to citizenship, ownership of property, and fundamental rights, as compared to other Indians. Jammu and Kashmir is the only state in India which enjoys special autonomy under Article 370 of the Constitution of India, according to which no law enacted by the Parliament of India, except for laws in the field of defence, communication and foreign policy, will be extendable in Jammu and Kashmir unless it is ratified by the state legislature of Jammu and Kashmir. Subsequently, jurisdiction of the Supreme Court of India over Jammu and Kashmir has been extended. Now the question arises, how can we amend Article 370 when the Constituent Assembly of the state no longer exists? Or whether it can be amended at all? Some jurists say it can be amended by an amendment act under Article 368 of the Constitution and the amendment extended under Article 370(1). But it is still a moot question.

Arguments

Equally valid arguments are forwarded by those in favour of and those against its abrogation.

- Those in favour argue that it has created certain psychological barriers and the root cause of all the problems in J&K. Article 370 encourages secessionist activities within J&K and other parts of the country. They say, at the time of enactment, it was a temporary arrangement which was supposed to erode gradually. They also argue that it acts as a constant reminder to the Muslims of J&K that they have still to merge with the country.
- Those against its abrogation argue that Abrogation will have serious consequences. It will encourage secessionists to demand plebiscite which will lead to internationalization of the issue of J&K. They further argue that the contention of Article giving rise to secessionist activities is baseless as states like Assam and Punjab, which don't have any special status have experienced such problems. It would not only constitute a violation of the solemn undertaking given by India through the instrument of accession, but would also give unnecessary misgivings in the minds of the people of J&K, making the issue more sensitive.

SAC

In March 2000, around the time of US President Clinton's visit to India, unidentified gunmen gun down 36 Sikhs at Chittisinghpora. In **June 2000**, the State Autonomy Committee (SAC) Report is discussed and an autonomy resolution is adopted in the J&K Assembly. The SAC Report recommends restoration of Article 370 to pre-1953 status with Indian jurisdiction limited to defence, foreign affairs and communications. However, the Indian Cabinet rejects the autonomy recommendation in July 2000.

Working Groups

It is notable to mention here that Prime Minister Dr Manmohan Singh, during his first tenure, had set up five working groups on confidence building in Jammu and Kashmir on May 25, 2006, at the end of the second round-table conference in Srinagar. Headed by Justice (Retd) Sagheer Ahmed, working group on centre-state relations held first meeting at New Delhi on 12 December 2006 (NC abstained from this meet), second at Jammu on 03 February 2007 and third at New Delhi on 29 March 2007. The group last met for two days on 02 September 2007 again at New Delhi but failed to come up with recommendations as members were seen to be pulling in too many directions. The other four working groups on Strengthening Relations Across LoC (Line of Control dividing Kashmir between India and Pakistan), Confidence Building Measures Across Segments of Society in the state, Economic Development of Jammu and Kashmir and Ensuring Good Governance submitted their recommendations to the PM in the third round-table conference on 25 April 2007.

The 196-page report alongwith 400 pages of annexures and a small booklet of recommendations though addressed to Prime Minister Manmohan Singh was strangely presented to Chief Minister of Jammu and Kashmir Omar Abdullah on 23 December 2009 in Jammu by the chairman of the working group Justice (Retd) Sagheer Ahmed through its Secretary Ajit Kumar. This inexplicable act of the working group set off a political row for and against autonomy. NC talking advantage of the controversy went on to strengthen the fictional impression that its edited proposal of "Greater Autonomy" had been accepted and recommended by working group (WG) as the only possible way of restructuring centre-state relationships. However, contents of report and annexure appended with it tell a contrasting story to what was made public about autonomy plan through an official handout released by Jammu and Kashmir government. The relevant recommendation of WG however says that the autonomy plan of NC, PDP's self-rule be discussed alongwith other proposals opposing both these prepositions. Few of the major issues highlighted in the report are as under:

- Referring to recommendations of Gajendragadkar Commission, the group has maintained that it is for the people of Jammu and Kashmir to decide how long to continue Article 370 in its present form and when to make it permanent or abrogate it forever.
- The report has asked the central government to address the issue of scrapping Article 356 and appraise the Jammu and Kashmir government about reasons for non-abrogation of this article which in any case has subjective value.
- Another striking feature of Justice Sagheer Ahmed WG report is that it has found nothing improper or objectionable in the process of application of central laws to Jammu and Kashmir from 1954 till date which in political parlance is dubbed as "slaughter of autonomy." Referring to NC's position on "Erosion of Autonomy," Justice Sagheer's panel upholds the view that the central provisions have been applied under prescribed procedure and with duly elected state governments

in position from time to time. In procedural terms, it appears that these measures had the sanction and approval of state government of corresponding period which in turn represented the will of people.
- The report had rejected the BJP's demand of "delimitation of constituencies." It also emphasized thar "Integrity of Jammu and Kashmir has to be maintained at all cost" and did not support demand for giving UT status to Ladakh.

The Bone of Contention

Demand for "Greater Autonomy or Self-Rule" has been the major bone of contention between the centre and state governments. Various attempts were made by the state to attain the same from the Shiekh Abdullah's days. He had also instituted two separate commissions to recommend viable solution to the issue. In any case, the cabinet never came to see much less consider any of these reports by the time Sheikh expired in September 1982. Justice Sagheer writes, "It is not clear what happened to these two reports; whether they were placed before the Cabinet or the House and discussed; and, if so, what decision was taken and which Report was accepted arid which rejected. The last nail in the coffin on the issue of erosion of autonomy was the unanimous resolution of state legislature, with former Chief Minister Farooq Abdullah led NC having 2/3 rd majority in both the houses of state legislature, sponsoring the resolution for the restoration of autonomy to the state of Jammu and Kashmir. The BJP led National Democratic Alliance (NDA) which was ruling at the Centre and of which National Conference was a component summarily rejected the resolution."

Political parties in J&K have been utilizing Article 370 in swaying public opinion to their advantage from time to time. So much so that huge anti-India protests were even held against the transfer of land to SASB (shrine board), which was an outside state organization, as it was perceived as a direct violation of article 370 of the Indian constitution.

Special Status and Alienation. People in the valley feel that Article 370 of Indian constitution as applicable to J&K should continue while groups like Kashmiri Pandits feel that J&K should become federal state in the Union of India like all other states.

Observation of the Hon'ble Supreme Court. The Supreme Court said on 03 April 2018 that Article 370 of the Constitution which gives special status to Jammu and Kashmir is not a temporary provision. The apex court said that in its earlier verdict of 2017 in the SARFESI case, it has been already held that Article 370 was "not a temporary provision."[66] The top court was hearing an appeal filed by petitioner Kumari Vijayalakshmi Jha, against the Delhi High Court's April 11, 2017, order.

Out of the Box. Special situations often require out of the box thinking. Why don't we exploit the lease clause by creating three SEZ type areas in South, Central and North Kashmir Valley with large land on lease. Create them as Srinagar Cantt type economic development areas, co-located with Army operational bases, having KV schools, police and CRPF training institutes, Kashmiri Pandits rehab camps etc and ensure these SEZ are comprehensive and self-sustaining for private companies with adequate security. Make these as hubs for PPP model with industries of software, handloom, handicraft, agriculture etc within this all-encompassing area. It could turn out to be a win-win situation for all.

Armed Forces Special Powers Act (AFSPA). AFSPA has been the biggest thorn in the centre-state relations[67] in the recent past. The longstanding demand of separatists, their supporters and some political parties has been to repeal the AFPSA altogether. However, the Chief Minister of J&K has propounded the idea of a partial revocation from certain areas of the state. Echoing public sentiment, its votaries repeatedly blast the Act as "draconian" in nature and the Army's misuse of the Act to perpetrate human rights violations and excesses. Public sentiment and those swaying with it often term the AFSPA as illegal and unconstitutional.

A perusal of the various powers available to the police in J&K under the provisions of the Criminal Penal Code vis-à-vis those available to the Armed Forces under the AFSPA would reveal that the police authorities still enjoy more encompassing and wider powers relating to arrest, search, seizure, summoning of witnesses and preventive detention than the powers enjoyed by the Armed Forces.[68] In October 2010, the Chief of the Army Staff, in an interview to the Raj Chengappa, Editor-in-Chief, *The Tribune*, categorically stated, "The AFSPA is an enabling provision and Act passed by the Parliament. It assists the Armed Forces in dealing with special situations." The Central Government vide Article 355 of the Constitution of India is duty bound to protect every state not only against external aggression but also internal disturbances and to ensure that every state is governed in accordance with the provisions of the Indian Constitution. It is also an established fact that the judiciary is the custodian of the Constitution. An independent judicial system performs better than any other agency to maintain equilibrium between the liberty of the individual and the powers of the State. It is in this context that the Honourable Supreme Court of India has upheld the constitutional validity of the AFSPA. The Court further observed that the instructions issued by military authorities in the form of "Dos and Dont's" while acting under the AFSPA are to be treated as binding and are required to be followed by the Armed Forces. By analysing the issue of safeguard further, it would transpire that the protection envisaged is for only those persons who act in good faith in discharge of their official duties and not otherwise. Acting in good faith would mean to act without any malice. The protection under Section 7 would not be available to a member of the security forces who commits acts which constitute criminal offences not in the discharge of his official duties even in the areas which have been declared as "disturbed."

Repeal or Retain AFSPA? Should the Act be repealed based on the supposed "normalcy?" There is no doubt that 2017 has been relatively peaceful as compared to 2016 after the Burhan Wani incident. Year 2011 had been a year sans massive protests; it has seen an increased influx of tourists and yatris and by and large, the violence levels have been at an all time low. But so was 2009 relatively peaceful after the Amarnath Shrine Board Agitation in 2008. Similarly, just when normalcy appeared to be returning in 1999, Pakistan hit us with Kargil. Goes to show that one swallow definitely does not make a summer. The current situation in the Valley raises serious security concerns. Section 3(b) of the AFSPA states that "activities directed towards disclaiming or questioning the sovereignty and territorial integrity of India or bringing about cession of a part of the territory of India or secession of a part of the territory of India from the Union or causing insult to the Indian National Flag, the Indian National Anthem and the Constitution of India" are reason for an area being declared as "disturbed" by the Governor of the State or by the Centre. Thus, the act comes into play only when there is a major crisis at hand. The act is extremely important for operations in the valley particularly so in the wake of people having greater access and knowledge of their legal rights through propaganda and social media. The lack of such an act would have dangerous legal implications particularly due to the propensity of the people to leverage the lack of legal protection to arm twist the armed forces.

J&K Interlocutors Report on Review of AFSPA. The interlocutors' report on Jammu and Kashmir has recommended review of the AFSPA in the state and said the Defence Ministry needs to consider how to respond "positively" to the issue. The 176-page report of the interlocutors – Dileep Padgaonkar, Radha Kumar and MM Ansari – also suggested decrease in the presence of security forces from residential areas and vacation of properties used by them to pave way for locals to carry out socio-economic activities. The report sought amendments in the Public Safety Act (PSA) which gives sweeping powers to security forces to detain people on grounds of propagating or attempting to create feelings of enmity or hatred or disharmony in the state. The group's impression is that AFSPA is more the symbol of a problem than its cause. But symbols are important for peace processes, and thus the Ministry of Defence needs to consider how to respond positively to this issue rather than negatively. "Security arrangements, especially in relation to the Disturbed Areas Act (DA) designation, need to be reviewed and a decision taken on AFSPA. The PSA should be amended," the report recommended. It suggested improvements in police-community relations and rationalisation of security installations through reducing their spread to a few strategic locations and creating mobile units for rapid response. However, no action has been taken on the report till date.

Media

Media is the fourth pillar of democracy. However, it needs to fulfill their professional responsibilities with utmost care and sensitiveness. They have a huge responsibility towards the society and it is the duty of media to play their role in an active and responsible manner. The Press in the valley was at the mercy of the militants in the nineties. Correspondents of national dailies who tried to be objective were beaten up and driven out of Kashmir. Any journalist, who does not report the utterances of the various militant outfits, almost all of it propaganda, had to face their wrath. There has been an improvement in the situation in the new millennium. The national press more or less has been objective and truthful in its reports but the same can't be said about the vernacular press.

Subversion of Vernacular Press. The vernacular press in the Valley is the focus of attention of the militant groups. Facing the gun, it has little choice except to publish distorted and exaggerated stories. Stringers controlled by the militants put out colorful and doctored reports which are a travesty of the truth. The people in the Valley who would rather believe what is printed in the local press rather than the news put out by All India Radio and Doordarshan get worked up by the provocative militant-inspired writings and often come out in the streets to stage protest demonstrations. The foreign media which often have a problem understanding the nuances and background then project the demonstrations as a reflection of the spontaneous support of the people for the militants and secession. This is the chain reaction sought to be achieved. The diabolical hand of Pakistan is behind this orchestrated campaign against India. Disinformation, false reports and rumors are floated by militants and these are forced on the local media.

Electronic Media. Proliferation of electronic media has brought in a new dimension. The breaking news culture and need for sensational reporting to remain relevant has added new challenges for both the government and the security forces. Freedom of press without much thought to responsibility has many a time resulted in avoidable crisis situation for the authorities. Any attempt to place a curb or restriction on this media has always evoked huge criticism.

Social Media. Violent clashes in Kashmir remain highly visible on the Internet, where youth are using social media to continue to air their grievances and advance their cause. "Social media is a paradigm shifter in terms of the tools available to protestors in Kashmir. They no longer need to take illegal measures to protest straight away. Rather, Facebook, Twitter, and the like, have allowed them space to share information, plan protests, and raise awareness in completely legal ways." Violent protests against Security Forces are hardly a new occurrence in the valley. Jammu and Kashmir has experienced similar types of domestic uprisings since 1989. However, the protests in the aftermath of Machil incident in 2010 saw the emergence of social media as the most powerful tool. The deaths in SF actions during the protests have prompted young protestors, mostly teenage boys, to go viral with online videos that capture the security forces' role in these deaths and blogs publicize their "rock throwing" campaigns. Youth also see the Internet as a way to make visible what is happening in Kashmir to the international community. But many observers believe that these videos will ignite more violence rather than remedy the problem, because the videos and photos keep alive and resonant a memory that feeds continued unrest. The string of violent protests after the Burhan Wani incident and showcasing these on social media has not helped the cause in any way. The advent of social networking technology is a major challenge one has to deal with in today's environment not only in J&K but everywhere else as well.

Jamaat-e-Islami - The Movement[69]

As a part of the BMC analysis, it is important to understand the effect of neo-fundamentalism on the dynamics in J&K. Early in the 20th century, Kashmir saw the emergence of the religious neo-fundamentalist movement that was to lay the foundation for the rise of the Jamaat-e-Islami. **From the outset, education was a core part of this programme** as it was an instrument in the minds of the religious right. In 1899, Mirwaiz Rasul Shah – whose grandnephew and clerical heir is today the APHC chief – started the Anjuman Nusrat ul-Islam (Society for the Victory of Islam). It aimed not only to give Kashmir's nascent middle class modern scientific education but also eradicate folk Islam and create a religion-centred political consciousness. The Anjuman funded the creation of the Islamiya High School in 1905. Rasul Shah's successor, Mirwaiz Ahmadullah, went on to set up the Oriental College in Srinagar. In turn, Ahmadullah's successor, Mirwaiz Yusuf Shah, set up Kashmir's first printing press, and used the two magazines it published to rally against what he saw as heretical practices embedded in Kashmiri folk Islam. Perhaps the most important voice of the neo-fundamentalist movement was the Jamaat-e-Islami, and drawing on Mirwaiz Rasul Shah's early efforts, it went on to create an educational empire.Another important character in the power game, Tarabali was born into a family long-linked to Kashmiri Sufism. Tarabali had come to despise the faith of his parents, seeing it as the cause of the political weakness of the people of Kashmir. Early in his life, he encountered the work of the seminal Islamist ideologue, Maulana Abul Ala Mawdudi, through the Islamist journal Tarjuman al-Quran. Tarabali also despised the socialism of Jammu and Kashmir's most important political figure, Sheikh Mohammad Abdullah. Having started his career as a teacher at the Islamiya High School, Tarabali went on to work at government-run educational institutions at Chrar-e-Sharif, Baramulla and Shopian. Before he left government service to devote himself full time to Jamaat-e-Islami work, Tarabali had succeeded in recruiting dozens of young men from elite Pir caste families. Most were from Baramulla, Shopian, Srinagar, and Pulwama — the very areas which have seen a number of clashes between police and stone-throwing mobs. "Islam, for them," scholar Yoginder Sikand has noted in his seminal study of the Jamaat-e-Islami, "was a call for political assertion in a context of perceived Muslim powerlessness."Among the young who joined the Jamaat was Syed Ali Shah Geelani — now the patriarch of Kashmir's Islamist movement. Geelani, like Tarabali and many other Jamaat leaders, started his adult life as a schoolteacher. He first worked at the government-run primary school in Srinagar's Pather Masjid area, and then at the Rainawari high school. Many teachers at the Rainawari school, interestingly, went on to become influential figures in the Jamaat-e-Islami.

From the outset, the Jamaat understood the centrality of education to its political project. According to the account of Pakistani scholar Tahir Amin, Jamaat schools were intended to prepare the ground for a "silent revolution." The Jamaat believed, Mr. Sikand has written, "that a carefully planned Indian conspiracy was at work to destroy the Islamic identity of the Kashmiris, through Hinduizing the school syllabus and spreading immorality and vice among the youth. Not long after independence, the Jamaat set up the first of what would become a network of schools in Srinagar's Nawab Bazaar, with five students and one teacher. Many of the students, Pakistani scholar Alifuddin Turabi has recorded in an essay on the contribution of educational institutions to the Kashmiri secessionist movement, went on to play a key role in the jihad that began in 1989. During the Emergency, Sheikh Abdullah cracked down on the Jamaat. Some 125 schools run by it, with over 550 teachers and 25,000 students, were banned. So were another 1,000 evening schools run by the organisation, which reached out to an estimated 50,000 boys and girls. In one speech, **Abdullah described the Jamaat schools as "the real source for spreading communal poison.** But Jammu and Kashmir's crackdown on the Jamaat proved short-lived. In 1977, the party founded the Falah-i-Aam trust and charged the Doda-based Islamist activist Saadullah Tantray with reviving its school network. The Jamaat also formed a student wing, the Islami Jamaat-e-Tulaba (IJT). Helped by Saudi Arabia-based Islamist organisations, the IJT soon grew into a powerful force in schools and universities. In 1979, the IJT was granted membership of the World Organisation of Muslim Youth, a controversial Saudi-funded body which financed many Islamist groups that later turned to terrorism. The next year, the IJT organised a conference in Srinagar which was attended by dignitaries from across West Asia, including the Imam of the mosques of Mecca and Medina, Abdullah bin-Sabil. By the end of the decade, the IJT had formally committed itself to an armed struggle against the Indian state. Its president, Sheikh Tajamul Husain – now a mid-ranking leader of the secessionist movement – told journalists in Srinagar that Kashmiris did not consider themselves Indian, and that the forces stationed there were an "army of occupation." Mr. Husain also called for the establishment of an Islamic state. A year later, in 1981, he reiterated his call to his followers to "throw out" the Indian "occupation." In 1990, as the jihad in Jammu and Kashmir gathered momentum, the state cracked down on the Jamaat-e-Islami once more. The party was banned, and the Falah-i-Aam schools were shut down. Promises were made that the teachers would be brought into the State school system. However, fearful that the Falah-i-Aam teachers would misuse their position to spread the Jamaat message, successive governments went slow.

Militancy/Terrorism

Introduction. The genesis of the conflict and growth of armed struggle has been discussed in detailed in the Historical Perspective section. Militancy has been major fuel for discord between India and Pakistan since the 1980s. Attacks in the region began to increase in scale and intensity following the Soviet invasion of Afghanistan, when foreign insurgents flooded the region to join the Afghan Mujahadeen. The majority Muslim region has its own local militant groups, but most of the recent Kashmir and Kashmir-based terrorism has been the work of foreign Islamists who seek to claim the region for Pakistan. A spate of Islamist cross-border attacks into Indian-held territory, the December 2001 storming of the Indian parliament in New Delhi, and the 2008 Mumbai attacks have all reinforced Kashmir's standing as the significant bone of contention between India and Pakistan. Both states have nuclear weapons, making Kashmir one of the world's most dangerous flashpoints.

Origin of Conflict. For Pakistan, incorporating the majority Muslim province of Kashmir is a basic national aspiration bound up in its identity as an Islamic state. Islamabad's official line on Kashmir, which the United States echoed as recently as June 2009, is that incorporation into either India or Pakistan must be determined by Kashmiris. Meanwhile, India sees the province as vital to its identity as a secular, multiethnic state. Movements for an independent Kashmiri state, such as the Kashmir Freedom Movement and the JKLF, also exist and have many supporters. India and Pakistan fought two wars over the region in 1947 and 1965, and a limited conflict in 1999. At least 50,000 people have died in political violence in Kashmir since 1989. Though flare-ups have occurred on both sides of the line, violence in Kashmir has decreased dramatically. The South Asia Terrorism Portal reports that 2008 also marks the first time civilian casualties have been under one hundred since 1990.

Major Terrorist Groups. There are numerous terrorist groups which have operated or are operating in the state. As of now Hizbul Muzahideen a local outfit and three Islamist groups are active in Kashmir as foreign terrorist organizations: Harakat ul-Mujahideen, Jaish-e-Mohammed, and Lashkar-e-Toiba. The first group has been listed for years, and the other two were added after the December 2001 Indian parliament attack. All three groups have attracted Pakistani members as well as Afghan and Arab veterans who fought the 1980s Soviet occupation of Afghanistan.

- **Hizb-ul-Mujahideen (HM).** Of the terrorist outfits currently operating in Jammu and Kashmir (J&K), the Hizb-ul-Mujahideen (HM) is the one of the largest, with a cadre base drawn from indigenous and foreign sources. It is one of the most important terrorist outfits in terms of its effectiveness in perpetrating violence across the State at regular intervals. The Hizb-ul-Mujahideen stands for the integration of J&K with Pakistan. Since its inception, the HM has also campaigned for the Islamisation of Kashmir. Headquartered at Muzaffarabad in PoK, the Hizb-ul-Mujahideen with an estimated cadre strength of at least 1500, is presently headed by Syed Salahuddin. The HM has its own news agency, Kashmir Press International, and a women's wing, Banat-ul-Islam. The Hizb reportedly has a substantial support base in the Kashmir Valley and in the Doda, Rajouri, Poonch districts and parts of Udhampur district in the Jammu region.

- **Harakat ul-Mujahideen (HuM).** The Harkat-ul-Mujahideen (HuM), a Pakistan-based terrorist outfit, has been in existence twice in the history of that country's involvement in cross-border terrorism. In the interim between the two phases, it continued to exist, but under the name of the Harkat-ul-Ansar (HuA). While the first renaming was an outcome of a reorganisation effected by the Inter-Services Intelligence (ISI), Pakistan's external intelligence agency, among its various sponsored terrorist outfits in Jammu and Kashmir (J&K), the second renaming was necessitated by a US proscription of the outfit. Based first in Pakistan and then in Afghanistan, it has several hundred-armed supporters in Pakistan and Kashmir. The group is responsible for the December 1999 hijacking of an Indian airliner and numerous attacks on Indian troops and civilians in Kashmir. The HuM's operational capabilities had been severely curtailed by the formation of the Jaish-e-Mohammed (JeM) by Masood Azhar, immediately after his release. News reports from Pakistan suggested that the JeM had weaned away several HuM cadre and other resources. Subsequently, only isolated instances have been reported from J&K where cadres of the HuM have been involved.

- **Jaish-e-Mohammed (JeM).** It was founded in 2000 by Maulana

Masood Azhar, a Pakistani cleric. The group seeks to incorporate Kashmir into the state of Pakistan and has openly declared war on the United States. JEM has carried out attacks on Indian targets, the Pakistani government, and various sectarian minority groups within Pakistan. Acts of terrorism attributed to the group include the 2001 attack on the Indian Parliament and a series of assaults in 2002 on Christian sites in Pakistan. The outfit is closely linked, through the Binoria Madrassah in Karachi, with the former Taliban regime of Afghanistan and Al Qaeda. JeM chief, Masood Azhar was released by Indian authorities in Kandahar and has reportedly met Taliban and Al Qaeda leaders in Afghanistan on various occasions. The JeM is also reported to have links with Sunni terrorist outfits operating in Pakistan such as the Sipah-e-Sahaba Pakistan (SSP) and Lashkar-e-Jhangvi (LeJ).

- **Lashkar-e-Toiba (LeT).** Active since 1993, was formed as the military wing of the well-funded Pakistani Islamist organization Markaz-ad-Dawa-wal-Irshad. The group, one of the largest and most proficient of the Kashmir-based terrorist groups, has claimed responsibility for a number of high-profile attacks in Jammu and Kashmir, as well as within India. Over the last several years, the group has split into two factions, al-Mansurin and al-Nasirin. There is wide speculation that LeT was responsible for the July 11, 2006 string of bombings on Mumbai's commuter railroad, though a spokesman for the group denied any involvement. The LeT was also responsible for coordinating the 2008 Mumbai attacks. The Lashkar-e-Toiba does not believe in democracy and nationalism. According to its ideology, it is the duty of every "Momin" to protect and defend the interests of Muslims all over the world where Muslims are under the rule of non-Muslim in the democratic system. It has, thus chosen the path of Jihad as the suited means to achieve its goal. Cadres are drawn from the Wahabi school of thought. The LeT has consistently advocated the use of force and vowed that it would plant the "flag of Islam" in Washington, Tel Aviv and New Delhi. The outfit's headquarters (200 acres) is located at Muridke, 30 kms from Lahore, which was built with contributions and donations from the Middle East, with Saudi Arabia being the biggest benefactor. Hafiz Muhammad Saeed is the Amir (chief) of Lashkar-e-Toiba.

The Pakistan Connection. ISI has been arming, training, and providing logistical support to militants in Kashmir. Pakistan denies any ongoing collaboration between the ISI and militants, stressing a change of course after September 11, 2001. After the December 2001 attack on India's parliament, former Pakistani President Pervez Musharraf promised to crack down on terrorist groups active in Kashmir and purge ISI officials with ties to these groups. However, the Indian government implied the ISI's involvement in a July 2008 attack on the Indian embassy in Kabul, and again in the November 2008 attacks in Mumbai. But some experts believe the relationship between the Pakistani military and some Kashmiri groups has turned with the rise of militancy within Pakistan. Shuja Nawaz, author of *Crossed Swords: Pakistan, its Army, and the Wars Within*, says the ISI "has certainly lost control" of Kashmiri militant groups. According to Nawaz, some of the groups trained by the ISI to fuel insurgency in Kashmir have been implicated in bombings and attacks within Pakistan, therefore making them army targets.

The Al Qaeda Connection. Many terrorists active in Kashmir received training in the same *madrasas*, or Muslim seminaries, where Taliban and Al Qaeda fighters studied, and some received military training at camps in Taliban-ruled Afghanistan. Leaders of some of these terror groups also have Al Qaeda connections. The long-time leader of the Harakat ul-Mujahideen group, Fazlur Rehman Khalil, signed Al Qaeda's 1998 declaration of holy war, which called on Muslims to attack all Americans and their allies. Maulana Masood Azhar, who founded the Jaish-e-Mohammed organization, traveled to Afghanistan several times to meet Osama bin Laden. Azhar's group is suspected of receiving funding from Al Qaeda. In 2006, Al Qaeda claimed to have established a wing in Kashmir.

Funding of Groups. The terrorist funding in J&K is taking place through number of channels. Few significant ones are discussed below:

- **Direct Funding.** It is funded mainly by the ISI in which the terrorists bring the money with them across the border. It sometimes includes counterfeit currency too, but it is not playing a major role in funding of the groups. On the contrary instead of earning goodwill, it has generated more hostility on the part of local population.
- **Hawala.** Hawala route is being used by ISI as well as Islamic Fundamentalist groups based in Middle East. Legitimate businesses are being used as fronts to deliver money to J&K terrorist organisations.

- **Remittances from Abroad.** Legal remittances, to the educational institutions as well as travel agencies conducting Haj tours, in which there is an element of overinvoicing or cancellations are other sources of funding.
- **Pakistan High Commission.** A lot of money is being given directly to the terrorists by the Pakistan High Commission. There are instances when some Hurriyat leaders have acted as courier for the same.
- **Nepal Route.** Nepal route is the most preferred one by the top leadership. It can easily be carried from Pakistan to Nepal by air, from Nepal due to no restriction on movement to India, this money easily finds it way into the hands of terror groups.
- **Extortion; Sympathizer's Contribution.** Extortion from the locals especially from corrupt elements also is a major constituent of terrorist funding. Quite a few sympathizers, especially in the valley, contribute to the terrorist kitty.
- **J&K Bank.** J&K Bank has also played a dubious role in channelizing terrorist funding in the state.[70]
- **Narcotics.** Due to squeeze in international funding, very little is available with Pakistan to fund the proxy war in J&K. As per reports, Pakistan is extensively using funds generated through illegal drug trade to support this agenda. Pak narcotic smugglers, who are controlled by ISI, are reportedly getting 2.5 billion dollars from illegal narcotic trade.
- To sum up, on a conservative estimate, the terrorist funding in Kashmir is estimated to be approximately 250 crores[71] with a major chunk coming from Pakistan. Pakistan doesn't mind it, considering the expenditure India has to incur to neutralize it.

Current State. Despite a resumption of formal peace talks between India and Pakistan in 2004, militant attacks continue to hinder progress towards a sustainable deal on Kashmir. After New Delhi and Islamabad agreed to launch a landmark bus service in February 2005 across the LC, militants vowed to target the service. In April of the same year, one bus survived a grenade attack. Talks were effectively put on hold in 2008 after India accused the ISI and Pakistani authorities of being complicit in the Mumbai attacks. 2003-04 has been a watershed year in the fight against terrorism for the Armed Forces. Construction of Anti Infiltration Obstacle System (AIOS) resulted in substantial drop in infiltration. Number of terrorists operating in the valley has gradually reduced and as per the latest estimate, approx 400 are only left, but the face and modus operendi too have undergone a transformation. Technology is being exploited to the hilt and there are no more gun-tottering Jihadis in the streets. The terrorists nowadays rely on surgical, swift and silent attack on unsuspecting security personnel. These are timed to coincide with an important event and mainly aimed at disrupting any peace initiative. Post 2008, agitation dynamics and its exploitation by the terrorist organisations have enhanced the challenges for the security forces manifolds. In the assessment of most of the security experts, 2019 is going to be a very crucial year for the future of J&K. Effect of the trump doctrine, Parliament elections and the internal dynamics of Pakistan will have an overbearing effect on the emerging situation.

Police and PMF. Most of the focus interviews have highlighted the inadequacy of the police and PMF in combatting insurgency in the state. However, operational commanders do give credit to the police SOG and CID as being able to effectively handle complex situations and take part in some major operations with army. Thus, there is no dearth of talent but a trust deficit does exist in arming the police completely based on the past experience of police being susceptible of being subverted. Not withstanding the concern, the police feels that army too could become irrelevant in hinterland if the police is active. Both the stakeholders thus have a reason for not building the capacity of police to handle law and order sites. Law and order being a state subject, the primary responsibility of building police training system, infrastructure and resources, lies with State governments. However, the Central Government has been rendering support to some States in the formulation of training policy, research, improving law enforcement, standardisation and modernisation through exchange of knowledge, coordination and budgetary allocation. The Centre as part of the Seventh Plan has recently taken the initiative and decided to set up 20 Counter insurgency and Anti-Terrorism Training Centres in Bihar, Jharkhand, Assam, Orissa and Chhattisgarh. Also adequate funds have been allocated to Bureau of Police Research and Development (BPR&D) in the 7th plan for development of the police training system throughout the country. *However the state which is most affected does not figure in the list or worse still left out deliberately. Any future counter-terrorist strategy in the valley would have to be Police-led support by army rather than army-led support by police.* There is thus a need to look at capacity building of the police and PMF for the future. Training is the first and most important step towards that goal. While the

Central Paramilitary Forces (CPMF) have recently well-developed integral infrastructure and resources for training, the police forces are generally lagging behind. An adequate and efficient police training system, infrastructure and resources are required to be built up in the States to meet current training requirements. Holistic development of the training system is thus the need of the hour and the Army needs to take a lead. The results of a survey conducted in 2014 clearly show through the views of junior (93%), mid level(97%) and senior officers(92%) of the Army that there is a dire need for capacity building.

Narcotics Trade. J&K is strategically located between the Golden Crescent and the Golden Triangle. The narcotics trade has increased over a period of time and the recent recoveries of drugs in LoC trade are an indication of the growing nexus between terrorism and drug trafficking. The Delhi Police recently has claimed to have exposed a narco-terrorism network with its ring leader being a member of Pakistan-based terror outfit Hizbul Mujahideen. The police had also said that the group seems to be raising its funds for its activities from the narcotics business. The recent drugs haul in Kashmir and other instances of arms, explosives and narcotics being smuggled under the cover of overland trade should serve as a wake-up call to those who advocate throwing open the borders for trade. The narcotics trade has had an effect on the youth of the state also. A large number of youth are said to be addicted to drugs[72] especially in Baramullah. Unemployed youth and drug addicts are a dangerous combination for a state which is fighting a counter-terrorist campaign. Thus, cross-border trade is a security hazard and it should only be allowed to increase after adequate infrastructure is in place which can detect illegal trafficking of drugs and weapons.

Operation (Op) Sadhbhavana

Op Sadhbhavana, the Indian Army's military-civic action (MCA), was launched in 1998. The doctrine of sub-conventional warfare released in December 2006 also gives a central place to Winning the Hearts and Minds (WHAM) through civic action. The initiative was conceptualised as part of the overall counterinsurgency strategy, with the added expected benefit of the collection of discrete intelligence. It was aimed at achieving two goals:

- To wrest the initiative from the terrorists
- To reintegrate the population to the national mainstream.

This was envisaged to be accomplished by restoring the infrastructure that was destroyed during the insurgency and by human resource development in

Jammu and Kashmir, thus presenting a humane face of the Army to the local population. At the core of these actions is the belief that "human security is the key element of national security, which can only be ensured through human and infrastructure development." The general principles guiding *Op Sadhbhavana* are as follows:

- Projects must have a high impact, so they must be based on popular demand
- Planning must be centralised, but its execution must be decentralised
- Projects must be initiated mainly at the village level
- Projects must be aimed at self-empowerment of people
- Projects must be sustainable
- There must be an integration of civic activities with state administration and community development plans
- Such initiatives must respect local religion, culture and traditions.

The focus of *Op Sadhbhavana* was on Quality education, Women's empowerment, Health care, Community development and Infrastructure improvement. From the tasks initially set out, a large number of them have been achieved. Most of the infrastructure which was damaged during insurgency is also in place. The civil administration is also functional and has also been carrying out developed work. Off late most of the work carried out by the army has only complemented the state initiatives. During the interactions with various sections some common perceptions which came about are as follows:

- The word op linked to Sadhbhavana is being looked with suspicion. People feel that all activities done by the army is not from the heart but is for an ulterior motive.
- Some Army officers and troops on ground feel that Op Sadbhavana has lost its relevance and is seen as more of a forum for projection and ribbon cutting rather than looking at it from an op perspective.

Surrenders from Nepal. Surrenders from Nepal is a critical issue and needs to be analysed in depth as to the motive of these surrenders. The Government of J&K in an affidavit filed in the Supreme Court on August 2013 has bluntly admitted that 282 ex-militants have entered into J&K via Nepal since the Rehabilitation & Surrender Policy was revised in J&K in November, 2010. The State Government has also admitted that 134 wives of the militants with 432 children born in Pakistan were also welcomed to J&K. This admission was made by the Government of J&K in reply to a writ petition filed by J&K

National Panthers Party. The figure could be much more now. The Return & Rehabilitation Policy was authored by the coalition government in J&K headed by Mufti Mohd Sayeed in 2004. According to the cabinet order dated November 22, 2010, the surrender application could be filed before the Indian High Commission in Pakistan so that an appropriate entry permit could be issued to the person who desired to surrender in J&K. The government selected four entry points for the purpose of entry for the terrorists who intended to surrender. Four points expressly mentioned were Poonch, Rawalakote (Poonch), Uri-Muzaffrabad (Uri), Wagah (Punjab) and Indira Gandhi International Airport, New Delhi. However, presently the state administration facilitates entry of terrorists and individuals of PoK into J&K whom the J&K Government finds fit. These terrorists safely fly to Kathmandu from where they are picked up by the J&K Police and provided I-cards to enable them to cross over from Nepal to India. These groups of terrorists accompanied by their wives and children, all Pakistani nationals, are escorted by J&K Police to J&K. **The mute question remains as to when the first policy failed, how could a second secretive policy succeed.** The methodology of movement of these persons along with families through an official passport via Nepal cannot be carried out without the full cooperation and support of Pak intelligence agencies. Further, any route open for normal human trafficking would also be prone to movement of terrorists and anti-national elements. When a heavily defended LC cannot prevent terrorists from entering the valley, a porous boundary of Indo-Nepal could easily be prone to infiltration. Some of the critical aspects which need a thorough analysis are:

- How easy is it to get passport and sanction for persons of PoK origin?
- The funds for travel, as a single person has to take return tickets while going to Nepal. For a whole family the amount is considerable.
- The infrastructure and the support mechanism for their transfer from Airport
to the border. Who are the persons manning it?
- The methodology of receiving the families and the criteria for selection?
- The efficacy of the spotters used on Indo-Nepal border?
- Why is that the immigration in Pak was not alarmed at the increased number of people not returning back and surrendering in the valley?
- Why are the so-called surrenderees not targeted by the terrorists?

EXTERNAL SCAN

Background

Strategic Location. Jammu & Kashmir is strategically located in relation to both continental Asia as well as the Indian peninsula. Jammu & Kashmir's location and its diverse borders pose unique challenges and afford immense opportunities to shape our national security strategy. Its location provides Jammu & Kashmir has a land border of about 7600 km. The total area is 222,236 sq km (85,806 sq miles) with a population of 10.1 million. PoK is an area of 13,297 sq km (5,134 sq miles). Physically, the state is contiguous to CAR in North, Pakistan to its West and TAR to its East.

This is an area which has attracted bitter rivalries between India and Pakistan since the last six decades. J&K continues to be a region of heightened activity on account of global security concerns. Jammu & Kashmir's size, strategic location and concern for security environment extends from the Middle East to the Central Asian Republics in the north to Nepal and Bangladesh in the East. Jammu & Kashmir's security concerns are defined by a dynamic global security environment. The regional environment will be briefly scanned to derive the Opportunities and Threats arising from the region.

Relevant Regional and Global Environment. The countries which directly or indirectly influence the militancy in J&K include Pakistan, Afghanistan, Nepal, China and Bangladesh. Taliban in Afghanistan and Pakistan with Saudi Arabia's petro-money is a major stakeholder in this environment of destabilisation in J&K though no conclusive proof of the same is available in the open domain. In the Global environment, the countries that influence security environment in J&K are USA, EU and Supra-national actors like UN, ASEAN and SAARC.

Pakistan for its part is the key factor and involved both covertly and overtly as it obsessively believes that Kashmir should have acceded to it post-1947 partition rather than with India. These countries either directly provide shelter, facilities for training, arms and ammunition or simply act as a transit route for the men and material to and from this region. Ineffective administration in Nepal has been an easy route of transit for the militants due its internal political turmoil and state-sponsorship from the intelligence agencies of Pakistan. Bangladesh has in the last few years cooperated with India in weeding propagators of terror from its soil against India. India in return is expected to return favours by revisiting water sharing arrangements and borders

70 — *Jammu and Kashmir: A Battle of Perceptions*

J&K GEO-STRATEGIC ENVIRONMENT

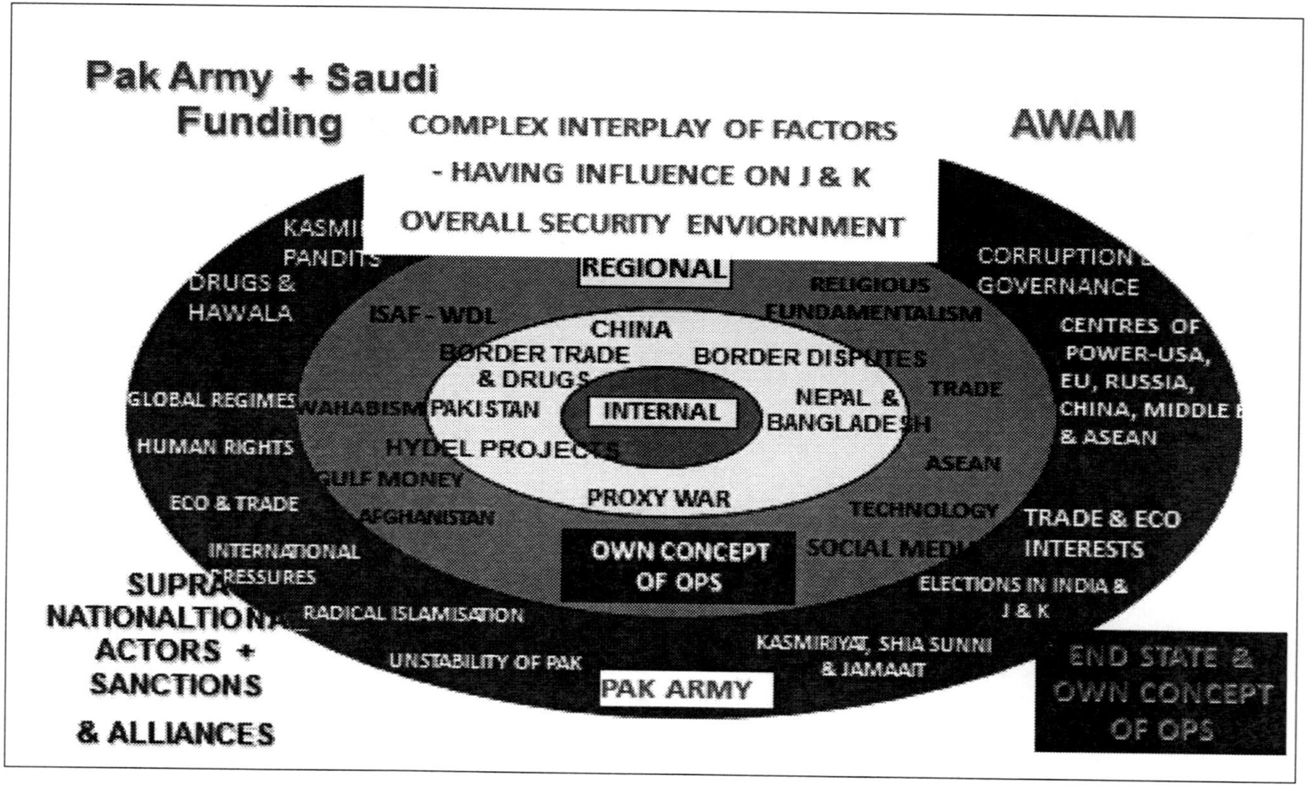

demarcation issue. These issues are critical to Bangladesh's politics. The security environment in the landlocked state of J&K has close linkages with the issue of accession, religion and is influenced by the geographical and strategic disposition. Happenings in the balance of region coupled with historical linkages affect and influences security situation in J&K. For the purposes of scanning the relevant regional environment, Pakistan, Afghanistan, China and Nepal have been identified so as to define the regional environment.

Pakistan

Points of Dissension

- **Natural Resources of Energy and Energy Requirements.** All major rivers of Pakistan flow through J&K (Indus, Chenab, Jhelum and Ravi) and its Hydroelectricity capacity and generation in J&K is an important factor between India and Pakistan. These rivers are critical to Pakistan's need for hydroelectricity, agriculture and drinking needs. These rivers are also source of major floods and relief during drought. The plains of Punjab are key to its agriculture and which in turn is dependent on these rivers flowing through J&K.

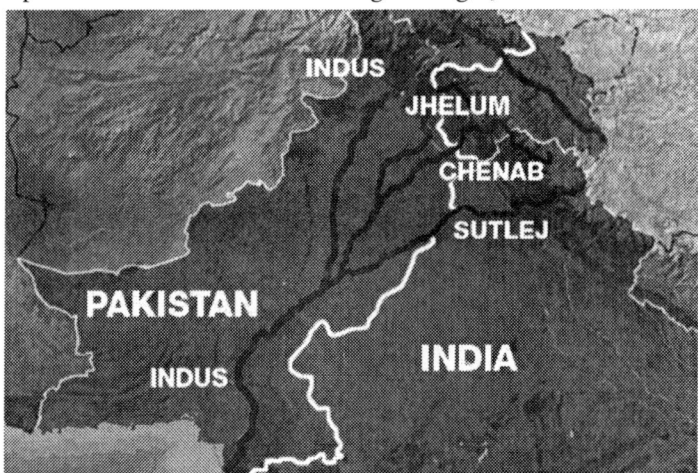

- **Nuclear Capability.** Pakistan is believed to have stockpiled approximately 580-800 kg of highly enriched uranium (HEU) sufficient amount to build about 90-100 nuclear weapons. In 1998, Pakistan commissioned the Khushab research reactor and recently commissioned the facility's fourth reactor, which is capable of yielding 10-15 kg of weapons-grade plutonium annually. Pakistan has adequate delivery means available for nuclear weapon delivery including aircrafts and SSMs. It has been reported in September 2012 that Pakistan has developed tactical nuclear weapon capability. The new weapon is a 60-km ballistic missile launched from a mobile twin canister launcher. Named Hatf IX (Nasr), it was test fired on May 29, 2012. Pakistan's strategic objective[73] has been expanded to the acquisition of a "full-spectrum capability" comprising a land, air and sea-based triad of nuclear forces, to put it on a par with India.

- o **Progress has been made in the miniaturisation[74] of weapons,** or Hatf II with a range of 180 km and Nasr or Hatf-IX with a range enabling their use with cruise missiles, both air and surface-based (Ra'ad or Hatf VIII and Babur or Hatf-VII respectively) as also with a new generation of short-range and tactical missiles (Abdali of 60 km).
- o **Pakistan has steadily improved the range and accuracy of its delivery vehicles,** building upon the earlier Chinese models (the Hatf series) and the later North Korean models (the No-dong series). The newer missiles, including the Nasr, are solid-fuelled, which are quicker to launch than the older liquid-fuelled versions.

- **Aspirations of Ethnic Groups.** *Pakistani politics has to contend with the strongly held regional aspirations of ethnic groups, which are yet to reconcile to their exposure to perceived Punjabi dominance since partition. The country thus has a questionably large populace who are first loyal to their tribe, then to their religion and grudgingly to Pakistan.* However, amongst the few issues that unites the Pakistan nation as one is the issue of Kashmir and Islam. Fissures and difference in opinion is surfacing by moderates trying to voice it but so is the radical religious intolerance.

- **Role of Islam and Fundamentalism.** Islam is the central rallying point and the core of fabric that binds Pakistan into a one nation. It gives Pakistan its identity. Fundamentalism has firmly established itself in the Pakistani state. The issue of Kashmir is played as a catalyst and an adhesive in uniting Pakistan Islamic fervour against India.

- **Civilian Governance with Military "Pre-eminence".** The Army has primacy in Pakistan; it has ruled Pakistan for over half its existence. It acts as the primary guarantor of Pakistan's stability and remains the country's most powerful institution.

- **Rise of Religious Extremists.** Sectarian, ethnic and regional groups are another major source of Pakistan's problems. The religious groups have played a role in politics since the inception of the state and have often benefited from periods of strong state support.

The emergence of Pak Taliban, sustenance of pro-Kashmir militant groups and free run to likes of Hafiz Sayeed in PoK and other parts of Pakistan have led to creation of an ideal infrastructure and environment that propagates violence and hatred. Supported by Pakistan, the major militant groups are Jammu Kashmir Liberation Front, Harkat-ul-Jihad-al-Islami, Lashkar-e-Toiba, Jaish-e-Mohammed, Hizbul Mujahideen, Harkat-ul-Mujahideen and Al-Badr.

- ISI. The ISI is a professional arm of the state and has a credible network in the region. While it is actively involved in various covert ops in the entire region, but it primarily focussed on India, Afghanistan, Nepal and Bangladesh. ISI coordinates and executes proxy war of terror in J&K along with Pak Army and militant groups. It focusses on causing instability in India. The Army's dual role in combating terrorism and at the same time promoting the MMA and so indirectly supporting the Taliban (through the ISI) is coming under closer and closer international scrutiny.[75] Pakistan's state sponsorship of militancy against India by abetting militant groups and Taliban has led to its own turmoil. Pakistan is currently unstable and on the edge of chaos. The West had turned a blind eye towards existing instability and the indirect protection of Al Qaeda and promotion of terrorism till the occurrence of 9/11. Post the twin tower bombings and its leads indicating Pakistani involvement along with Taliban and Al Qaeda, the USA forced Pak to choose sides in the international war on terror. This major event has shown the Paki complicity in almost all major terror incidents all over the world and the power in global security scenario waking up to harsh Pak reality. Indirectly Pakistan (through the ISI) has been supporting terrorism and extremism – whether in London on 7/7 or in Afghanistan or Iraq.[76] The US/UK cannot begin to turn the tide until they identify the real enemies from attacking ideas tactically – and seek to put in place a more just vision. This will require Pakistan to move away from Army rule and for the ISI to be dismantled and more significantly something to be put in its place.[77] Without US funding, Pak position will become increasingly tenuous. China has endeavoured to pitch in place of USA in Pak by expanding its ties to "all weather friendship" as quoted by Pakistan leadership.

- **Indo-Pak Trade.** The bilateral trade between India and Pakistan stood at USD 2.6 billion during the year 2012-13 and certainly it can be raised to much higher levels if sustained and serious efforts are made. There is vast scope which needs to be properly explored and exploited. This is noteworthy that while India has accorded Pakistan the Most Favoured Nation (MFN status) for trade and commerce but Pakistan so far has refrained from taking this essential reciprocal step. For permanent peace and mutual friendship, the two countries have to improve situation on the borders, promote trade ties and step up frequent people-to-people contacts, scale up cultural exchanges and promote sport activities for overall mutual trust and confidence. Will Pakistan respond sincerely and positively to look ahead for a bright future in the regions including the area under study, i.e., Kashmir?

Threats for Jammu & Kashmir. Pakistan's strengths, which translate into threats for Jammu & Kashmir, are:

- **Ability to interdict the lines of communication.** Jammu & Kashmir is connected with rest of India by a single arterial road for all its requirements. Pakistan has in the past threatened/attempted to cut off/severe the state from India in all the previous wars, and also restrict/deny access to the riches of the CAR.

- **Nuclear Weapons offset India's Conventional Military Edge.** Its nuclear status and threat of irrational rationality has effectively offset own conventional military edge in J&K. Pak nuclear weapons falling into the hands of terrorists is a a global concern.

- **Large and Professional Military.** Pakistan has the twelfth largest military in the world, which is well trained and equipped in the regional context. Military leadership is strong and effective. Its military strength is half of that of India with a relatively much less area to guard.
- **Strong Intelligence Network.** The intelligence structure under the ISI is strong and controls large parts of the states functioning. This allows Pakistan to play a proactive and inimical role in fermenting and supporting militancy in Jammu & Kashmir.
- **Islam as a Binding Factor.** Tenets of Islam bind its population into a cohesive national asset which leads to a national mobilisation as soon as an Indian threat is perceived by Pakistan. Issue of Kashmir is an emotive issue across the many sections of Pakistan Muslims.
- **Double Talking and Ineffective Leadership. Pakistani leadership has shown traits of double talking and speaking lies.** The Kargil War in the Indian context or taking advantage of the US year after year in the Global War on Terror should serve as ideal reminders to the Indian security establishment.
- **Ambiguous Nuclear Threshold.** As against Jammu & Kashmir's clearly defined nuclear doctrine of "No First Use" and "Massive Retaliation", Pakistan's articulation of use of nuclear weapons and lack of retaliation capability puts constrains on Jammu & Kashmir's conventional superiority.

Opportunities for India. Pakistan's internal weaknesses seem to overshadow its internal strengths owing to inadequate attention having been paid to certain key developmental areas. Some of these weaknesses are opportunities which India can exploit:

- **Weak Pak Economy.** Jammu & Kashmir should leverage its economy potential to economically marginalise Pakistan in the increasingly liberalised global economic order.
- **Inadequate Heavy Industrial Base.** Pakistan is heavily dependent on imports for critical industrial goods. India should identify these dependencies and develop own potential to meet Pakistani requirements in a way which makes it economically beneficial to both.
- **Lack of Water, Minerals and Food Resources.** Pakistan is heavily dependant on India for import of critical items for its sustenance. India must develop capability to control SLOCs leading into Pakistan to

choke its imports. Develop potential to regulate flow of water from Jammu & Kashmir.

- **Socio-economic Divide.** Inadequate investments in education, health and social upliftment programmes have led to serious strains on the social fabric with a growing gap between "haves" and "have-nots". This can be exploited by India in highlighting the same by effective perception management of population of Jammu & Kashmir and at the same time developing it in J&K to a desired standard.
- **Trans-LC Indo-Pak Trade.** The dormant trade potential between the two countries and the sincere exchanges possible across the LC is a major opportunity for the people of both the regions.
- **Deepening Ethnic Fault Lines.** While the Shia-Sunni divide, Baluchi separatism and trans-national loyalties of Pashtuns had frequently challenged Pakistan's central authority in the past, these have come to the fore again especially post-US military intervention in Afghanistan and Pakistan's cooperation in war against terrorism. These ethnic divides can be exploited by India to highlight to the people of Jammu & Kashmir. The Shia community in and around Budgam district has voiced concern of acts of violence against its community getting replicated in J&K also. The threat of it may likely manifest more with influx of terrorists from Afghanistan post–International Security Assistance Force (ISAF) withdrawal.

People's Republic of China

As a part of the study on J&K, an external geopolitical scan suggests that China is also becoming an important aspect in the Geopolitical game being played in the region. The "**New Great Game**"[78] is alive after all, only the alignments have undergone metamorphosis and will continue to evolve in the near future. Through this Focus Article, an attempt is being made to explain this evolution, as well as suggest opportunities and threats for India.

China[79] and India launched a security and foreign policy dialogue in 2005 and consolidated discussions related to the dispute over most of their rugged, militarized boundary, regional nuclear proliferation. Indian claims that China transferred missiles to Pakistan, and other matters continue; Kashmir remains the site of the world's largest and most militarized territorial dispute with portions under the de facto administration of China (Aksai Chin), India (Jammu and Kashmir), and Pakistan (Azad Kashmir and Northern Areas).

India and Pakistan resumed bilateral dialogue in February 2011 after a two-year hiatus, and have maintained the 2003 ceasefire in Kashmir, and continue to have disputes over water sharing of the Indus River and its tributaries. UN Military Observer Group in India and Pakistan has maintained a small group of peacekeepers since 1949; meanwhile, India does not recognize Pakistan's ceding historic Kashmir lands to China in 1964.

China has deliberately kept the border dispute with India pending with little intent or resolve to find a settlement as it has with most of its neighbours. Over the last few years, People's Liberation Army (PLA) has been testing Indian reaction by continuing its transgressions in areas across Leh-Ladakh in Jammu and Kashmir. The Jhelum River is the only major Himalayan river which flows through the Kashmir valley. The Indus, Tawi, Ravi and Chenab are the major rivers flowing through the state. Jammu and Kashmir is home to several Himalayan glaciers. With an average altitude of 5,753 metres (18,875 ft) above sea-level, the Siachen Glacier is 70 km (43 mi) long making it the longest Himalayan glacier. China has influence or proximity to all these water source and Siachen by having Aksai Chin under its control.

China's Position on Kashmir. China's position has been shifting since 1950s but for the last decade it has been more or less the same as that of the Western countries which is to see Kashmir as disputed between India and Pakistan. The stapled visa for Kashmiris was an experiment by China that should be understood in the context of India's approach toward the Dalai Lama and Tibetan exiles. The period when this issue was alive is the period when there were new developments within Tibetan diasporas seem to want to give a message to India that its neutrality on Kashmir while Sino-Pakistan relation being very important can shift unless India restricts further the political activities of Tibetan exiles in India. China has been clear that it will not accept an independent new state in the region. Actually, it is in China's interest for the dispute to continue and for India and Pakistan to be on loggerheads with each other. This fulfils the primary agenda of preventing any new independent state in the region that may have a domino effect on Uighur Muslims and Tibetans and the secondary agenda of keeping India, the only possible competitor to China in Asia, tied down in South Asia through a permanent rivalry with Pakistan. China will not allow Pakistan to weaken further and one of the reasons is to prevent more Uighur separatists getting radicalized and trained in Pakistani territories. One cannot deny the inexorable advantage that geography has given PoK. Being the only link between the People's Republic

Map – China's Disputed Borders

of China (PRC) and Pakistan, PoK is truly the "umbilical cord" – a bond that is symbolical of the very deep relationship between the two countries. The PRC has at various forums asserted that it only has an economic interest in PoK and has openly denied the presence of PLA personnel in PoK. China would never allow the Kashmir dispute to be settled on terms that were favourable to India, because that would leave China with no border with Pakistan. In other words, should the Kashmir dispute be settled so that PoK (which includes the so-called Azad Kashmir and Gilgit-Baltistan) is awarded to India, the "umbilical cord" will be snapped, leaving China's "all-weather friend" orphaned. Such an explanation merits a deeper analysis of China's long-term perspective on PoK and its growing interests in PoK. Are these interests an indication of the permanent presence of China in PoK? Is China creating Gilgit-Baltistan as a "buffer state" to stem the spread of Islamic fundamentalism into Xinjiang? China had been blocking all UN resolutions to declare Azhar Mahmood a terrorist. It is surprising to see a shift in China's position in the recently concluded BRICS summit statement. At the time of printing of this book global pressure has resulted in China changing its stance and lifting the technical hold that it had placed on the issue.

Foreign Policy and Diplomacy. China has leveraged its multi-lateral and bilateral ties backed by strong economic clout to further its national vision. China is an established regional power and an aspiring global superpower. It has to demonstrate to the world its leadership capability by engaging countries in all aspects for promoting peace and stability in the world and in its neighbourhood in particular. India and China must engage on its aspiration to promote peace for mutual gains as an opportunity.

Industry and Technology. China has a developing industrial base. Ambitious Chinese expatriates have started returning to become entrepreneurs. China's industrial output has increased by almost 50% since 2000 and hence its demand for commodities has skyrocketed, driving up prices. China's industrial and technological needs require phenomenal energy. To secure its energy requirements, it has been working and spending huge amount of money to develop land routes for inflow/outflow of resources and products from land routes other than SLOCs. China SLOCs are vulnerable to blockage and interdiction in IOR, East Sea and South China Sea. China is extremely sensitive to any development that affects its flow of energy requirements. Hence the land routes development in the area of TAR and through Aksai Chin to CAR and Pakistan neighbouring J&K is critical to China.

Map: China-Central Asia Infrastructure Development

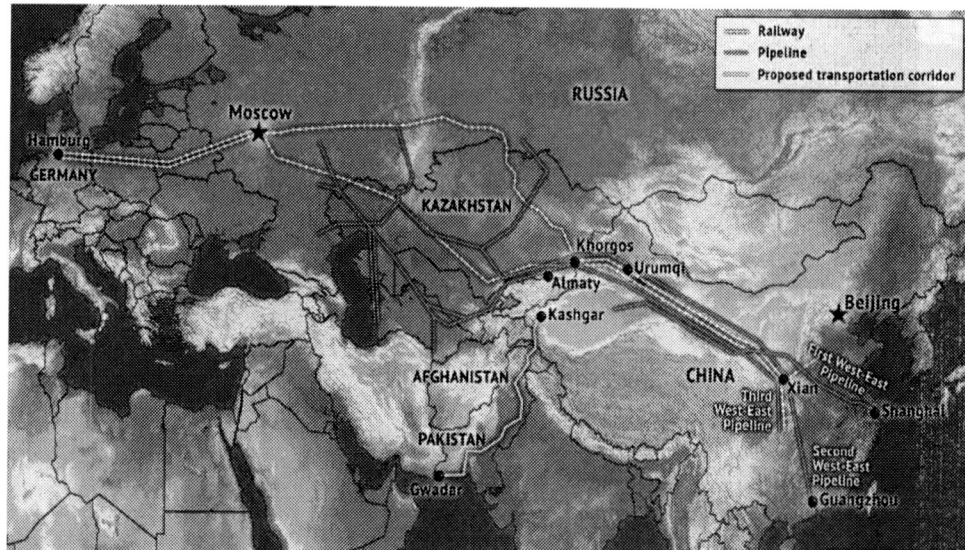

Opportunities and Threats

Opportunities

- **Global Aspirations.** China aims to be a responsible power and all revelations of its involvement with separatist groups stand counter to its claims. India can exploit this sensitivity of China to its own advantage.
- **Regional Leverage.** China's economic and military rise is seen as a threat by other regional and global powers like USA, Japan, Australia and ASEAN nations. In this context, all these countries view India as a suitable ally. India can exploit these new equations to deal with China from a relative position of power.
- **Demographic Divisions and Ethnic Unrest.** Large population with number of ethnic minorities has led to faults among the people. Outbreak of ethnic disturbances and terrorist attacks by separatist groups occur periodically in outlying minority areas of Xinjiang, Qinghai and Tibet. This can be exploited by India vis-à-vis the issue of Jammu & Kashmir. It's in mutual interest of both India and China that internal disturbances do not receive external support in each other territory.
- **Import Energy Requirements.** Low indigenous energy resources juxtaposed against the enormously growing energy demands. It necessitates import of crude through pipelines and sea routes, which is a strategic vulnerability.

Map: Overlapping Claim in the South China Sea

- **Authoritarian Regime.** While the strict enforcement of policies had hitherto fore provided the impetus for growth, the changing socio-economic milieu is increasingly being seen as a detriment to national cohesiveness. This can be exploited by India vis-à-vis Jammu & Kashmir and the issue of huge Tibetan diaspora in India.

Threats

Threats. Relatively large geographical expanse, comparable population size, geographical proximity and a simultaneous economic rise make India and China natural competitors. This equation of rivalry coupled with Chinese headway in economy and military development leaves India vulnerable to a number of threats. The possible threats posed to India under the circumstances therefore are:

- Keep India embroiled in local and internal conflicts by developing proxies like Pakistan in its neighbourhood and propping internal armed struggles like insurgency in NE and LWE and thus blunt its larger growth prospects. China's ambiguity on the issue of J&K coupled with stapled visa to J&K residents till few years ago is a threat both diplomatically and militarily.
- Establish strategic military bases all around J&K thus posing a multidirectional military threat to it.
- Increased presence in ASEAN and Asian Development Bank along with being a permanent member of Security Council has ensured limiting India's influence in these major Supra-national actors.
- **Military.** China is rapidly developing its military potential which is much beyond its defensive requirements, which includes a blue water maritime capability and strategic nuclear forces. Rapid infrastructure development in TAR coupled with that in Aksai Chin is a developing threat to India and its capability in Jammu and Kashmir. Increase in the defence budget is a cause of concern for India.
- **Border Disputes.** China's deliberate decision to delay resolving of disputed borders with India and in particular along Jammu & Kashmir indicates a strategic design to keep the pot simmering.

- **Effective Foreign Policy.** China is subtly keeping India guessing on the issue of Jammu & Kashmir. While it has extracted commitment on issues of its own concern of Dalai Lama and Tibet, it has refrained to remove ambiguity on its stand on J&K.
- **Chinese Clout in Multilateral Regional Fora.** In fora like the SCO, SAARC, ASEAN and many others where it even holds observer status, it has scuttled Indian advances by strategic intervention. All these fora can be a source of major international embarrassment for India if issue of J&K autonomy or independence is permitted to be discussed.
- **China–Pak Partnership.** This strategic collusion has seen a deepening of relations with brisk Chinese activities in PoK and along the Karakoram highway. This alliance poses a major threat to India and more so militarily in Jammu & Kashmir.
- **Competition.** This competition for raw material, energy and water can easily conflagrate into a rivalry if it goes out of control.
- **Systematic Approach to Modernisation of Capability.** Military being an important element of CNP, China is engaged in developing a revolutionized, modernized and regularized People's Army with own unique characteristics. It is endeavouring to transform the armed forces from numerical superiority to qualitative superiority, from manpower to technology intensive. Its endeavour is also to train high-quality personnel and improve the modernization of the weapon systems at a breakneck speed that is detrimental to India.
- **Insurgencies.** Chinese support to Pakistan and its "all-weather friendship" by covertly developing its nuclear, military and infrastructure needs in PoK and rest of Pakistan is a great morale booster to continue abetting its proxy war with India. China has not yet even once clearly stated or denounced any of Pakistani acts of violence. Though in last decade or so China has shown some concern about rising Muslim fundamentalism through Af-Pak region. India must highlight the issue of Islamic fundamentalism as threat to the entire worls and more so in China buffer state of Xinjiang. Increase in insurgencies in Jammu & Kashmir through proxy countries is a threat to China's buffer states. India must leverage it.
- **China's Influences in IOR.** The Indian Ocean is becoming increasingly important to China's economic and security interests. To protect its

economic and security interests and to balance a "rising India," China appears to be pursuing a simultaneous approach of cultivating relations with many states in the Indian Ocean littoral, as well as developing a "String of pearls" of bases and access rights to key facilities in the region. China's encirclement of India comes full circle by its increased presence not only at sea but on land borders also with its increased military bases at TAR and Aksai Chin coupled with infrastructure development by its military engineers in PoK.

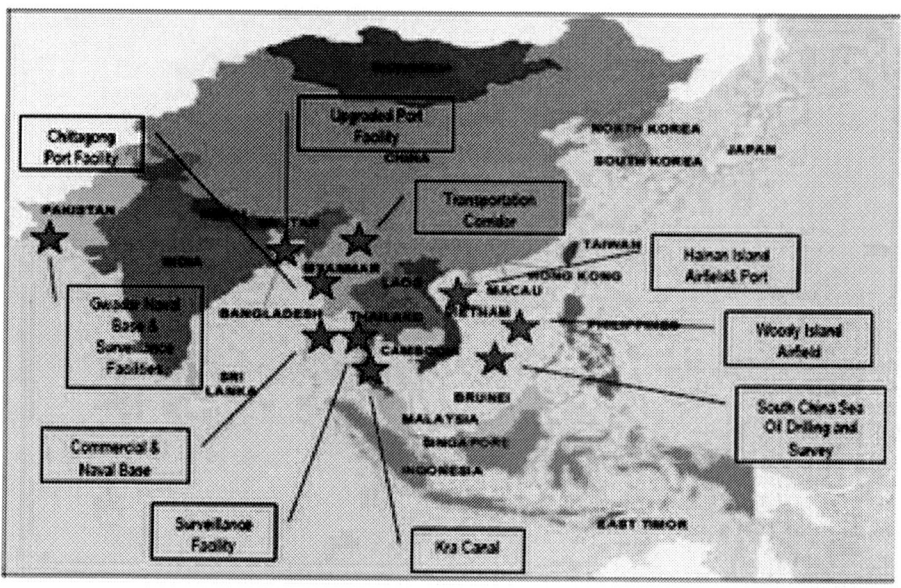

Afghanistan

The strategic location of Afghanistan has been both a source of prosperity and misfortune. Until the discovery of sea routes in the sixteenth and seventeenth centuries, its land routes attracted the attention of merchants, thus turning it into the hub of world commerce. Since the late 1970s, Afghanistan has experienced a continuous state of civil war. In 1979, the USSR occupied Afghanistan. They were defeated and forced to withdraw with the clandestine help of the USA in the late 80s. However, due to the terror strike in the USA in Sep 2001, the Taliban government was overthrown. The country was devastated in all respects due to these events. In December 2001, the UN Security Council authorized the creation of an ISAF to help maintain security and assist the Hamid Karzai administration. The country is being rebuilt slowly with support from the international community and dealing with Taliban insurgency. Afghanistan derives its belief and core values from Sunni Islamic ideology. The tenets of Islam govern the affairs of the country. Further, Afghanistan is an amalgamation of various tribes and ethnic groups; hence, strong tribal affiliations and integral tribal cultures direct affairs in this diverse country. The only national interest of the country is to establish a sovereign, democratic, diverse and unified republic based on Islamic laws and ensure national unity and equality amongst all ethnic groups and tribes residing in the country. Afghanistan has a total area of 647,497 sq km divided into three distinct regions – the Central Highlands, the Northern Plains and the Southwestern Plateau.

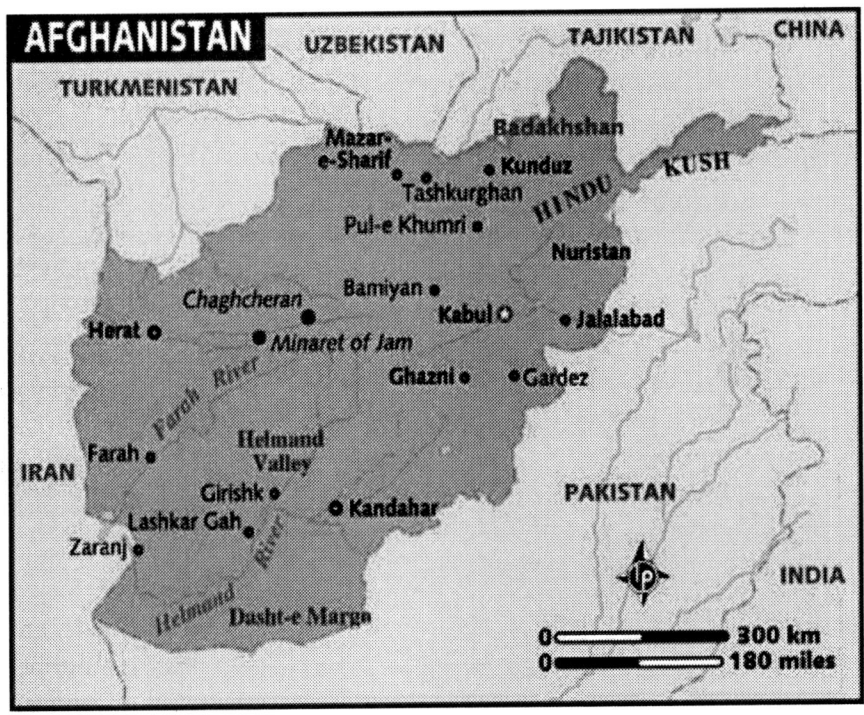

The war-torn country has got a fragmented society on tribal and strong ethnic lines with practically no social binding factor which can be considered to help unite the country in near future. However, Islam being the common religion provides some sort of binding factor. The control of the government does not extend far beyond capital Kabul. The ANA is still in the "building up" stage and currently does not appear to be capable of handling the demands of internal and external security independently. The ANA is racing against the deadline of the planned US withdrawal in 2014 to achieve self-sufficiency.

Opportunities and Threats

Opportunities. India has a lot of opportunities in Afghanistan:

- **Favourable Disposition towards India.** India has acquired a good reputation and credibility amongst the Afghan people following its efforts in rebuilding Afghanistan. India also should reconsider its position on the Durand Line as a legitimate boundary between Afghanistan and Pakistan. Coupled with India's nation-building efforts in Afghanistan, supporting a long-standing Pashtun aspiration may provide India the much needed leverage in the region.

- **Security Forces.** Gives India the opportunity to assist in developing and training of the Afghan security forces, thereby enhancing its influence. Common training process will also facilitate inter-operability, which may be of value in future against common adversaries. Opportunity to gain military presence by establishing training missions.

- **Consortium of Donor Nations.** India's presence as part of the consortium of Nations to help in development of Afghanistan provides it a strategic foothold, thereby also securing its economic interests in the region.

Strategic Depth to Pakistan. Pro-Pakistan government in Afghanistan provides strategic depth to Pakistan. By increasing its presence in all aspects of security and economy in Afghanistan India will negate the Pakistan strategic depth and at the same time leverage it as an opportunity against Pakistan. Therefore, the post-ISAF arrangement in Afghanistan is of acute importance to India to ensure continued Indian presence diplomatically, economically and militarily.

Threats

- **Unstable Afghanistan.** An unstable or a divided Afghanistan will be a source of instability in region, leading to threats from multiple sources, namely terrorist groups, drug trade etc. The likely inflow of mujahids who are battle-hardened and emboldened post-US withdrawal from Afghanistan will be threat to India in Jammu and Kashmir. It will primarily depend on Pakistan Army ability to manage a deal or an understanding with Taliban.

- **Security Cover to India's Infrastructure Investments Post-2014.** The withdrawal of US Forces in 2014 may result in a security void for Indian projects.

- **Chinese Interests.** China will be a competitor to influence and leverage its economic advantage in Afghanistan. A volatile Afghanistan will not be in China's interest either economically or militarily as it will be a constant threat to its Gwadar port activities as well as a factor in Uighur militancy in Xinjiang province.
- **Pakistan's Interests.** Noticing a decline in its influence in Afghanistan, it is likely to put impediments in the Indian initiatives in Afghanistan, by supporting terror attacks against Indians. Major possibility of channeling the battle-hardened and emboldened Taliban as well as ISIS elements post getting a grip of the situation in Afghanistan, to J&K for the "cause of Jihad."

Allowing the ISIS to Flee from Syria and Iraq a Big Mistake?

Given below is the net intake of ISIS cadre from different parts of the world.[80] At a conservative estimate, even if 50% of the Cadre is likely to have fled or given a safe passage through the under-siege areas, approximately 1250 each will be headed towards Europe and Afghanistan (elements belonging to CARs, Pakistan and China as well). It is but natural that an attempt will be made by the ISIS cadre that they exfiltrate to the countries of their origin or near regions so that they can find sympathisers and supporters while they mingle into known surroundings. Afghanistan is already witnessing ISIS in its new Avatar, the Islamic State in Khorasan (ISKP).[81]

As a result, Europe and Afghanistan are likely to be on the boil in the coming years. Due to the operational space available, Afghanistan per se, will also become a catchment area for Jihadi organisations to recruit battle-hardened Mercenaries to further their cause. It is no surprise that China plans to create a buffer by opening up a base in Afghanistan. Beijing has long refrained from engaging militarily beyond its borders. However, as some recent reports suggest, this situation may soon change. Ferghana news reported that China will build a military base in the northern province of Afghanistan, and, according to the news agency, the Ministry of Defence of Afghanistan is already expecting a Chinese expert delegation to discuss the location and further technicalities for the base. If these reports are true, China will fully fund the new military base in Badakhshan, covering all material and technical expenses, including both lethal and nonlethal weaponry and equipment.[82] There is a school of thought that suggests Pakistani jihadi elements like the JEM, HuM and the LET are not likely to involve the ISIS and loose nationalistic space in Kashmir,[83] but history suggests that they have no inhibitions in utilising foreign mercenaries

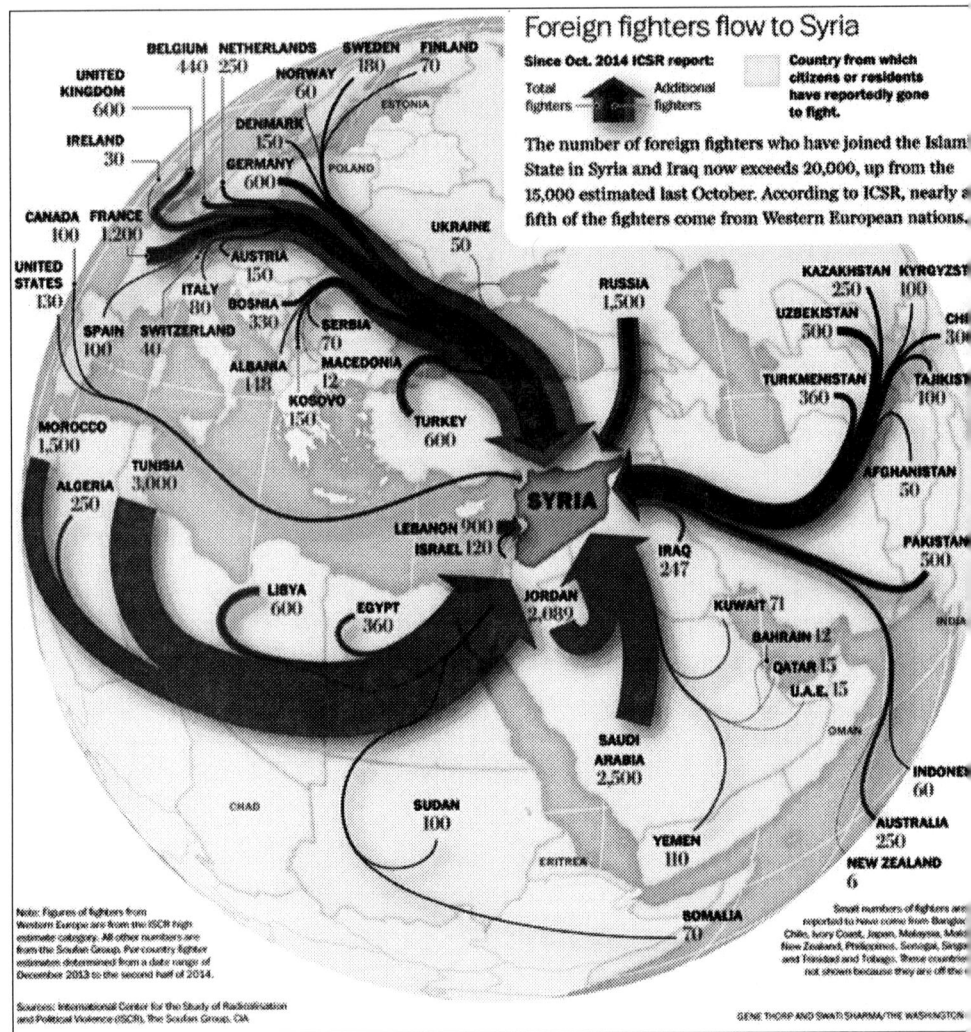

in Kashmir[84] as force multipliers, and therefore, the day is not far when we see some of these mercenary elements of ISIS in Kashmir if steps to the contrary are not taken now. Pakistani Jihadi elements could also recruit the ISIS cadre to carry out 26/11 type of attacks on Indian commercial centres like Mumbai, Bangalore, Kolkata, Gurugram and Pune which also have a sizable expat population. Although India has been keeping a close watch on the situation in Syria and Iraq, mainly due to the presence of Indian Diaspora as contract workers in the region during the early part of the conflict, more needs to be done in order to exorcise the ISIS from the IN-AF-Pak region.

Nepal

Relations between India and Nepal have traditionally been close since ancient times as a result of geographical location and common religious, linguistic and cultural identities that overlap the two countries. Independent India and Nepal initiated their special relationship with the 1950 Indo-Nepal Treaty of Peace and Friendship and accompanying letters that defined security relations between the two countries, and an agreement governing both bilateral trade and trade transiting Indian soil. The 1950 treaty and letters stated that "neither government shall tolerate any threat to the security of the other by a foreign aggressor" and obligated both sides "to inform each other of any serious friction or misunderstanding with any neighbouring state likely to cause any breach in the friendly relations subsisting between the two governments." These accords cemented a "special relationship" between India and Nepal that granted Nepal preferential economic treatment and provided Nepalese in India the same economic and educational opportunities as Indian citizens. The Indo-Nepal border is open; Nepalese and Indian nationals may move freely across the border without passports or visas and may live and work in either country.

The Federal Democratic Republic of Nepal has traditionally maintained a non-aligned policy and enjoys friendly relations with neighbouring countries. As a small, landlocked country wedged between two larger and far stronger powers, Nepal maintains good relations with both the People's Republic of China and India. Nepal's most substantive international relations are perhaps with international economic institutions, such as the Asian Development Bank, the International Monetary Fund, the World Bank, and the South Asian Association for Regional Cooperation, a multilateral economic development association. Nepal also has strong bilateral relations with major providers of economic and military aid, such as France, Germany, Japan, Malaysia, Switzerland, the United States, and particularly the United Kingdom, with whom military ties date to the nineteenth century. Nepal today is struggling to overcome the birth pangs of its nascent democracy since its "Jan Andolan Phase-II" in 2006. It has managed a tottering government which is influenced by India and is trying to balance growing Chinese influence and reach in Nepal. Acute poverty coupled with lack of governance has made it a thriving transit point and route for illegal and nefarious activities and militant groups.

Opportunities
- Major Indian influence in Nepal diplomatically.
- Ethnic, cultural and historical linkages.

- Economic dependence of Nepal on India.
- Intellligence sharing.

Threats
- Influx of J&K militants through Nepal.
- Unmanned porous border.
- Growing Chinese influence in all spheres.
- Increasing ISI activity.
- Arms and FICN influx.
- Growing Muslim conversion in terrai belt of Nepal due to flow of money from ISI and Middle East.

USA and Supra-national Actors (ASEAN, BIMSTEC, SAARC, UN)

USA. United States of America is a federal republic on the continent of North America consisting of 50 States including the non-contiguous States of Alaska and Hawaii. The United States is the world's greatest economic power in terms of gross national product (GNP) and is among the greatest powers in terms of GNP per capita. The nation's wealth is partly a reflection of its rich natural resources. With only 5% of the world's population, the United States produces nearly one-fifth of the world's output of coal, copper, and crude petroleum. The agricultural sector produces nearly one-half of the world's corn (maize); one-fifth of its beef, pork, mutton, and lamb; and more than one-tenth of its wheat. However, the United States owes its economic position more to its highly developed industry, than to its natural resources or agricultural output.

Global Influence. The USA today is the most powerful nation in the world. USA is far more capable of projecting forces beyond its territory, than any other country in the world. In addition, the quality of its armed forces is rivalled by few and equalled by none. It has bases or base rights in 40 countries. In the last 10 years, homeland security has emerged as the primary security concern that drives the US foreign and economic polices the world over. Post-9/11, there has been a shift in the US strategy to counter the threat posed by terrorism. USA today does not hesitate to adopt a proactive approach to counter terrorism in the world and the proliferation of material, technologies and expertise necessary for acquisition of WMD. In this rapidly changing world order, deterrence has been replaced by pre-emption, containment has given way to the policy of engagement and unilateralism has gradually crept into US policy. America's ultimate challenge is to transform its power into moral consensus.

Geo-Strategic Relations

- **Changing Geopolitics.** Today, the global world order is undergoing a major upheaval be it in terms of the rise of China or the recent revolutions shaking the world. In this environment, the US-India relations assume importance. The US President had described India as the "Closest Partner" of the USA during his meeting with Prime Minister Manmohan Singh on the sidelines of the UN General Assembly session in September 2013. The same thought has been expressed by President Trump to PM Modi too. This would also balance US' increasingly Sino-centric approach to Asian affairs.

- **Pakistan.** The Trump administration has shown a change of strategy and warned Pakistan to cut its umbilical chord to Terrorist organization or face aid cuts. The US has four vital national interests in Af-Pak:
    o To prevent Pakistan's nuclear weapons and materials falling into hands of Islamic extremists.
    o To ensure that Afghanistan does not again become a sanctuary for terrorists.
    o To avoid war between India and Pakistan.
    o To prevent the Taliban and its radical collaborators from gaining control of Pakistan.

- **US-China.** Managing the rise of Chinese power and economy is likely to be the most important strategic challenge for US and India in the next two decades. Containment is not an option but attempting together to shape Chinese policies in positive directions is the main viable option. Washington should abandon any thoughts of a G-2 convergence. Taiwan is a major issue between the two countries. The Republic of China remains a focus of difficulties in the relations between the United States and the People's Republic of China. Although the PRC has never governed Taiwan, the PRC claims Taiwan as a 23rd province and has repeatedly threatened to take it by force. **USA stance on J&K will be of criticality in counterbalancing China's support to Pakistan on the issue of J&K.**

- **US-Saudi Arabia.** Within the Arab fold, the diplomatic rise of an assertive Saudi Arabia is evident, all the more remarkable given predictions in some quarters of the immediate demise of the Saudi system following 9/11. The renewal of Saudi engagement is prompted by its diminishing regard for the implications of the U.S.-led freedom and democracy agenda in the region. Saudi Arabia now promotes pan-Arab nationalism as an antidote to political Islam, whereas Saudi funding of Wahabi-Salafi form of Muslim sect in J&K and rest of India is a form of religious radicalism. The political murder of journalist and US national Jamal Khashoggi at the Saudi consulate in Turkey will test the relationship further.

- **US-Af-Pak.** Following the September 11, 2001, attacks in the United States, believed to be orchestrated by Osama bin Laden, who at the time was residing in Afghanistan under asylum, the United States launched Operation Enduring Freedom. This major military operation was aimed at removing the Taliban government from power and to capture or kill Al Qaeda members. Following the overthrow of the Taliban, the U.S. supported the new government of Afghan President Hamid Karzai by maintaining a high level of troops to establish the authority of his government as well as combat Taliban insurgency. Both Afghanistan and the United States resumed diplomatic ties in late 2001. The United States has taken the leading role in the reconstruction of Afghanistan with providing billions of dollars for building national roads, government and education institutions, as well as the entire national military of the country. In 2005, the United States and Afghanistan signed a strategic partnership agreement committing both nations to a long-term relationship. Afghan President Hamid Karzai came under fire in 2009 from the Obama administration for his perceived unwillingness to crack down on government corruption. After winning the 2009 presidential election, Hamid Karzai began to deal with corruption in his country. Since 2002, the United States Armed Forces has been gradually raising its troop level in Afghanistan. As of 2013, there were approximately 62,000 U.S. troops stationed in the country, which have now been downsized to 10,000.

- **US-Pak.** Few relationships in the post–World War II period have experienced such wild fluctuations as that of the US and Pakistan. The sweep of revolutionary developments in Iran, the Soviet intervention in Afghanistan and with it the perceived threat to the security and survival of Pakistan coupled with concerns for regional stability brought USA and Pakistan very close. Pakistan continues to remain a strategic ally for the US because of its cooperation for the US fight against global terrorism, support to facilitate the democratisation of

Afghanistan, and providing US an access to the energy-rich CAR region. **The relationship still has a tinderbox quality, driven by differences over CIA drone strikes in Pakistan's tribal belt, the Afghan war and, most contentiously, the Haqqani network.** The arguments are well worn: American officials say the Pakistani military's ISI is covertly aiding the insurgents; Pakistani officials deny the accusation. But a new boldness from the Haqqanis that aims at mass American casualties, combined with simmering political tension, has reduced the room for ambiguity between the two countries. Inside the administration, it is a commonly held view that the United States is "one major attack" away from unilateral action against Pakistan—diplomatically or perhaps even militarily.

- **Conclusion.** There is optimism with regard to the long-term prospects for the US-India relationship. America will continue to be guided by its National interests and will continue with its policy of engagement and enlargement to extend its sphere of influence. It will opt for cooperation rather than confrontation. The combination of our largely overlapping vital national interests and shared democratic values should produce a bright future for strategic collaboration between New Delhi and Washington in future decades. **It is in India's strategic interest to develop and leverage the relationship with USA in dealing with issue of J&K as a bilateral issue with Pakistan. USA understands Indian viewpoint on this aspects as of now.**

Opportunities and Threats

Opportunities

- **US–India Military Cooperation for South Asian Stability.** We need intensified interaction between the two militaries on military doctrine, force planning, weapons acquisition, interoperability, joint exercises, intelligence exchange, and threat assessments. LEMOA agreement is a prime example.

- **Cooperation in Afghanistan.** India will be a major player in Afghanistan whether the US likes it or not. That should be regarded in Washington as a positive factor.

- **US–India Diplomatic Synergy for Countering Chinese Influence in Asia.** Managing the rise of Chinese power is likely to be the most important strategic challenge for both countries in the next two decades.

US viewpoint to counter Chinese overt support to issue of J&K will be critical importance should it happen.

- **Pressure on Pak for Resolution of Terrorist Support.** There should be intimate, intensive and utterly private US-India talks on how to deal with a turbulent and increasingly chaotic Pakistan in the period ahead, including examining the policy implications of various specific scenarios regarding deteriorating events in Pakistan. USA has always deflected all attempts by Pakistan to involve USA or to internationalise J&K by stating that it's a bilateral issue between India andPakistan although it's a known fact that USA is deeply involved in back-channel talks in intervention and normalisation of relations between India and Pakistan frequently.

Threats.

The major threats to India in the long term arising as a result of changing US strategy in South and SE Asia and/or a dynamic bilateral relationship are enumerated below:

- **Reconciallation with Pak.** The US Administration's efforts to solve the Pakistan problem and to bring to bear as many external resources and capabilities as possible to try to begin to improve the situation in Pakistan are a threat to our security.
- **Economic Dependence/Involvement with China.** Washington's preoccupation with economic cooperation with China seems to be reducing due to trade tarif war but any resolution in present staus will affect Indian Government calculations related to the US-India bilateral relationship and regional and Asian security. But if the US treats China in a privileged fashion and downgrades the quality of its substantive interaction with New Delhi, it is unlikely to produce spontaneous concessions from the Indian side on other matters of importance to Washington.
- **Align with Pakistan Against India in Afghanistan.** Washington does not object to India's economic development activities in Afghanistan, but is apparently sensitive to Islamabad's complaints that India's real objective in Afghanistan is to deprive Pakistan of the strategic depth. So the Administration may not give sufficient weight to India's views regarding Afghanistan as compared to those of Pakistan.

- **Deterioration of Relations over Iran.** Iran is another knotty issue in US-India relations and a potential source of considerable bilateral tension. The Obama Administration is embarking on a diplomatic effort to persuade Tehran to suspend its nuclear weapons activities. It seeks to enlist India in applying a much more stringent sanctions regime concerning Iran, which India may not accede to for various reasons. Waiver for India to import oil as well as all activity in Chahbahar port inspite of sanctions on Iran is a positive step for India.
- **US Naval shift to Asia-Pacific by 2020.** US Defence Secy Leon Panetta's assertion at the Shangrila dialogue in Jun 2012 that 60% of the US Naval Fleet would be shifted to the Asia-Pacific region by 2020 is an indirect cause for concern. Considering the fact that the second and third largest economies in the world are in Asia, it would be reasonable to assume that Asia will become the centre of gravity of the global economy in the near future. Although the US policymakers continue to deny that the shift is to contain Chinese domination of the area, it appears that the US is in fact engaged in a well-calculated strategy to contain and encircle China. If this is true, it would be a grave mistake. Historically speaking, the rise of new great powers has been accompanied by a period of tensions and wars when the existing great powers resisted the required adjustments in the international order. A conflict between China and the US would not be in the interest of either one of them and also India.

International & Regional Forums. Terrorism has no boundaries. India has maintained that J&K is a bilateral issue with Pakistan since 1972 Shimla Agreement. Pakistan has been keen to internationalise the issue through the forums of UN, ASEAN and SAARC. It has used every possible opportunity to internationalise the issues diplomatically.

United Nations. There have been attempts by Pakistan and the insurgent groups to internationalize the issue of insurgency in J&K. The Hurriyat has attempted to raise the issue either through UN or various Human Rights groups internationally. Some groups have been lobbying for a plebiscite under the aegis of United Nations. This needs to be guarded against. **Since the last two decades, India has managed to keep the UN away from any discussion on Kashmir by diplomatic manoeuvres and assistance from USA, Russia and leveraging its growing economic clout with various Supra-national actors.**

NOTES

1. http://kashmirstudygroup.com/awayforward/mapsexplan/historical.html, accessed on November 30, 2017.
2. http://www.rarebooksocietyofindia.org/book_archive/196174216674_10153460989311675.pdf, p. 180, accessed on March 15, 2018.
3. Tavleen Singh, *Kashmir: A Tragedy of Errors*, New Delhi 1995, p. 240.
4. Snedden, Christopher, *Understanding Kashmir and Kashmiris*, Oxford University Press, 2015, p. 170.
5. https://www.dailyo.in/politics/july-13-jammu-and-kashmir-kashmiri-pandits-martyrs-day/story/1/4963.html, accessed on March 18, 2018.
6. Prem Nath Bazaz, *Struggle for Freedom in Kashmir*, New Delhi, 1954, pp. 162-6.
7. http://shodhganga.inflibnet.ac.in/bitstream/10603/63964/11/11_chapter%204.pdf, accessed on December 02, 2017.
8. Balraj Puri, *Kashmir: Towards Insurgency*, New Delhi, 1993, p. 19.
9. Prem Nath Bajaj, *Democracy through Intimidation and Terror*, New Delhi: Heritage Publishers, 1978, p. 15.
10. Balraj Puri, *Kashmir: Towards Insurgency*, New Delhi 1993, pp. 19, 31.
11. Alastair Lamb, *Kashmir A Disputed Legacy 1846-1990*, Roxford, 1991, pp. 255-271; Victoria Schofield, *Kashmir in Conflict*, New York, 2000, pp. 114-116.
12. https://www.deccanherald.com/content/298279/whats-mystery-indira-abdullah-accord.html, accessed on December 05, 2017.
13. Schofield, op. cit., p. 125.
14. http://www.indiatogether.org/peace/kashmir/intro.htm, accessed on December 24, 2017.
15. Lamb, op. cit., pp. 295-326.
16. Puri, op. cit., p. 52.
17. https://www.bbc.com/news/world-asia-18738906, accessed on December 25, 2017.
18. http://www.indiatogether.org/peace/kashmir/intro.htm, accessed on December 25, 2017.
19. Praveen Swami, *The Kargil War*, New Delhi 1999, pp. 71-2, Human Rights Watch, *India's Secret Army in Kashmir*, New Delhi, 1999, pp. 71-2; Amnesty International, *Disappearances in Jammu and Kashmir*, 1999.
20. Schofield, op. cit., pp. 207-8.
21. https://www.thehindu.com/thehindu/2000/11/20/stories/01200001.htm, accessed on December 27, 2017.
22. https://idsa.in/system/files/monograph/monograph61.pdf, accessed on December 27, 2017.
23. https://idsa.in/system/files/Monograph7.pdf, accessed on December 28, 2017.
24. https://www.google.co.in/url?sa=i&rct=j&q=&esrc=s&source=images&cd=&cad=rja&uact=8&ved=2ahUKEwjmhKL2wMHdAhXYWysKHSu0Aq8QjRx6BAgBEAU&url=http%3A%2F%2Fwww.indiandefencereview.com%2Fnews%2Fkashmir-india-china-pakistan-triangular, accessed on March 18, 2018.
25. Raina, A.N., "Geography of Jammu and Kashmir", p. 50; Singh, R.L. (ed.), "India: A Regional Geography", p. 361.
26. https://www.google.co.in/url?sa=i&rct=j&q=&esrc=s&source=images&cd=&cad=rja&uact=8&ved=2ahUKEwiK4u_kw8HdAhXMMI8K HdQrDp4QjRx6BAgBEAU& url=http%3A%2F%2Fgeominjk.nic.in%2Fmaps.htm&psig=AOvVaw1MklZtGZ_8nXGVhc KUZtgE&ust=1537256211392864, Accesed on August 21, 2018.
27. http://www.jkeducation.gov.in/.
28. http://jkhighereducation.nic.in/.

29. Journal of Business Management & Social Sciences Research (JBM&SSR), Vol. 2, No. 4, April 2013.
30. http://pib.nic.in/newsite/erelease.aspx?relid=72572.
31. http://himayat.in/index.php?r=himayatOverview/overview.
32. http://himayat.org/, accessed on November 24, 2018.
33. http://nsdcudaan.com/Uploaded/Newsletter/Udaan_newsletter_5th%20edition(1).pdf.
34. http://indiatext.net/hdi-india/.
35. Parmu, R.K., *A History of Sikh Rule in Kashmir, 1819-1846*, Srinagar: Department of Education, Jammu and *Kashmir* Government, 1977.
36. Hogan, Patrick Colm, *Imagining Kashmir: Emplotment and Colonialism*, University of Nebraska Press.
37. Bhagavan, Manu Belur, *Heterotopias: Nationalism and the Possibility of History in South Asia*, Oxford University Press, Vol. 1, p. 153.
38. Snedden, op. cit., p. 184.
39. https://www.reuters.com/article/idUSDEL291796, accessed on January 14, 2018.
40. www.susmitkumar.net/index.php/history-of-kashmir-conflict, accessed on January 14, 2018.
41. Ibid.
42. www.greaterkashmir.com/news/opinion/the-return-of-migrants/247099.html, accessed on January 14, 2018.
43. India Today's Report in 1993, accessed on January 14, 2018.
44. Sultan Shaheen, Kashmir: Where Sufis are Rishis and Rishis are Sufis! J&K Insights, www.jammu-kashmir.com/insights/insight990901.html, accessed on January 18, 2018.
45. Snedden, op. cit., p. 45.
46. Ibid.
47. www.greaterkashmir.com/news/opinion/profiling-bulbul-shah/165273.htm, accessed on January 20, 2018.
48. kashmirreader.com/2017/08/29/tribute-hazrat-mir-syed-ali-hamdanira, accessed on January 21, 2018.
49. Sultan Shaheen, op. cit.
50. http://www.claws.in/images/publication_pdf/264924915_MP77-SWOT-Choner-18-10-18.pdf, accessed on Novemcer 29, 2018.
51. http://visionofhumanity.org/app/uploads/2017/11/Global-Terrorism-Index-2017.pdf, accessed on April 20, 2018.
52. islamicvoice.com/a-handy-compendium-on-madrassas-in-jk.
53. http://www.satp.org/satporgtp/countries/india/states/jandk/terrorist_outfits/Hurriyat.htm.
54. http://en.wikipedia.org/wiki/All_Parties_Hurriyat_Conference.
55. http://www.dailyexcelsior.com/pak-efforts-to-unite-hurriyat-fail/, accessed on November 24, 2017.
56. http://www.dailyexcelsior.com/another-split-in-hurriyat-conference/.
57. http://www.risingkashmir.com/hurriyat-split-again/.
58. Economic Survey of J&K 2017, p. 3.
59. Economic Survey of J&K 2017, p. 92.
60. Economic Survey of J&K 2017, p. 147.
61. Economic Survey of J&K 2017, p. 109.
62. Economic Survey of J&K 2017, p. 99.
63. Economic Survey of J&K 2017, p. 169.
64. http://www.bharat-rakshak.com/LANCER/idr00013.htm.
65. http://www.thehindu.com/opinion/lead/Understanding-Article-370/article11640894.ece.

66 economictimes.indiatimes.com/articleshow/63599977.cms?utm_source= contentofinterest& utm_medium=text&utm_campaign=cppst, accessed on January 20, 2018.
67 https://www.indiatoday.in/india/story/pdp-bjp-afspa-article-370-jammu-and-kashmir-government-240640-2015-02-17, accessed on January 20, 2018.
68 Kanungo, Sujata, Echoes from Beyond the Banihal-Kashmir: Human Rights and Armed Forces, Vij Books and Publishing, p. 30.
69 https://www.thehindu.com/todays-paper/tp-opinion/Where-the-state-pays-for-teachers-of-hate/article16561058.ece, accessed on November 12, 2018.
70 https://www.amarujala.com/national/jammu-and-kashmir-terror-funding-several-j-k-bank-accounts-under-nia-lens, accessed on November 20, 2018.
71 Chadha, Vivek, "Life Blood of Terrorism: Countering Terrorism Finance", Bloomsbury, 2015, pp. 27, 35, 41.
72 http://drugabuse.imedpub.com/drug-addiction-in-kashmir-issues-and-challenges.php?aid= 20596, accessed on November 21, 2018.
73 http://www.thehindu.com/opinion/lead/dealing-with-pakistans-brinkmanship/article4171664.ece.
74 Ibid.
75 http://news.bbc.co.uk/2/hi/programmes/newsnight/5388426.stm.
76 Ibid.
77 Ibid.
78 https://en.wikipedia.org/wiki/The_New_Great_Game.
79 https://www.cia.gov/library/publications/the-world-factbook/geos/ch.html.
80 https://www.washingtonpost.com/world/foreign-fighters-flow-to-syria/2014/10/11, accessed on January 21, 2018.
81 Taneja, Kabir, ORF Issue Brief No. 220, The Fall of ISIS and Its Implications for South Asia, pp. 5-6.
82 https://thediplomat.com/2018/01/chinas-military-base-in-afghanistan, Accessed on January 21, 2018.
83 Taneja, p. 7.
84 Santhanam, K., Jihadis in Jammu and Kashmir: A Portrait Gallery, Sage Publications, 2003, p. 59.

CHAPTER 3
Systems Analysis

APPLICATION OF SOFT SYSTEM METHODOLOGY IN JAMMU AND KASHMIR PROBLEM SOLUTION

Kashmir as a Soft System

Soft systems methodology (SSM) is an approach to organizational process modelling (business process modelling) and it can be used both for general problem solving and in the management of change. Although soft systems thinking treats all problems as ill-defined or not easily quantified, hard systems approaches, like systems analysis (structured methods), operations research and so on, assume that the problems associated with such systems are well-defined, they have a single, optimum solution, a scientific approach to problem-solving will work well, and that technical factors will tend to predominate.[1] In the context of Jammu & Kashmir problem, the Soft Systems Approaches assume relevance for the following reasons:

- The problem is "messy" as defined by Ackoff and Peter Checkland,[2] i.e., it is poorly defined. This was very evident as almost most of the stakeholders could not come to consensus as to who are the key stakeholders, what is the Centre of Gravity, what are the system boundaries and how does one define "Normalcy" that one is aiming to achieve?
- Stakeholders interpret problems differently (no objective reality).
- Human factors are important.
- There is a need for creative or intuitive approach to problem-solving.
- Outcomes are learning, better understanding, rather than a "solution."

Methodology

The Seven-Step Methodology as subscribed by Checkland in 1981[3] is recommended for dealing with the J&K problem. The steps are represented schematically below.

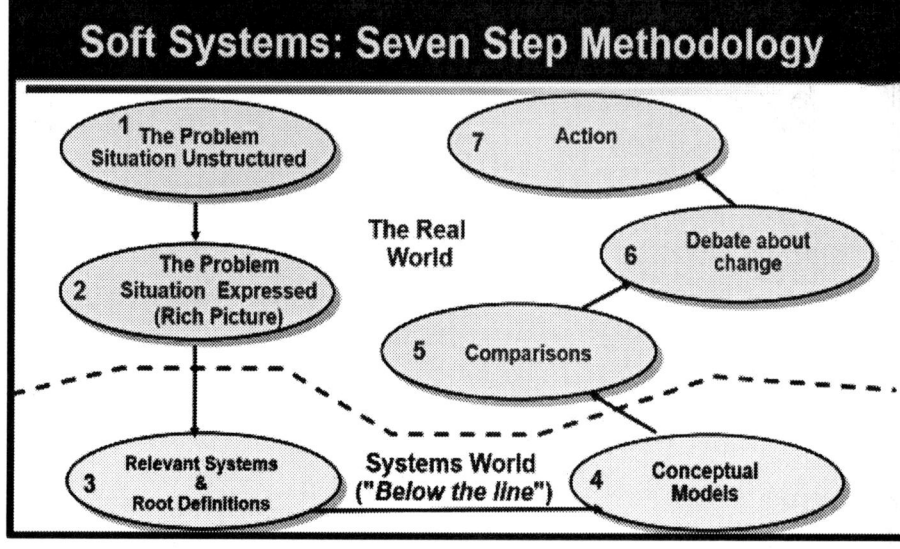

Step 1 – **Problem Situation Unstructured/Data Collection.** Start point is the collection of information about the "Mess." Data collection techniques such as focused interviews, questionnaires and interactions with various sections of the stakeholders as well as additional documentary evidence from related researches, analysis by varied strategic analysts, books, monographs, research papers, articles and internet uploads will allow to consolidate the sufficient information on this particular unstructured problem.

Step 2 – **Analysis/Rich Picture.** The rich picture below captures the essence of the conflict situation as **perceived by the author** and conveys the self-explanatory portrait of situation in J&K. A cursory glance at it will make the uninitiated also realize the complexities involved. In fact it might look like a garbled confused state of mind at first glance, which actually explains the problem very well.

Relevance of the Awaam. Further detailed analysis also revealed that of all the possible actors, Awaam holds a critical position of leverage around which the entire situation pivots at any given point. The following spray diagram elucidated the relevance of Awaam as the Centre of Gravity in J&K. The diagram also indicates all possible actors which need to be considered while undertaking any analysis on the problem related to J&K. The spray diagram gives out the actors and stakeholders at play in a clearer manner. Missing out

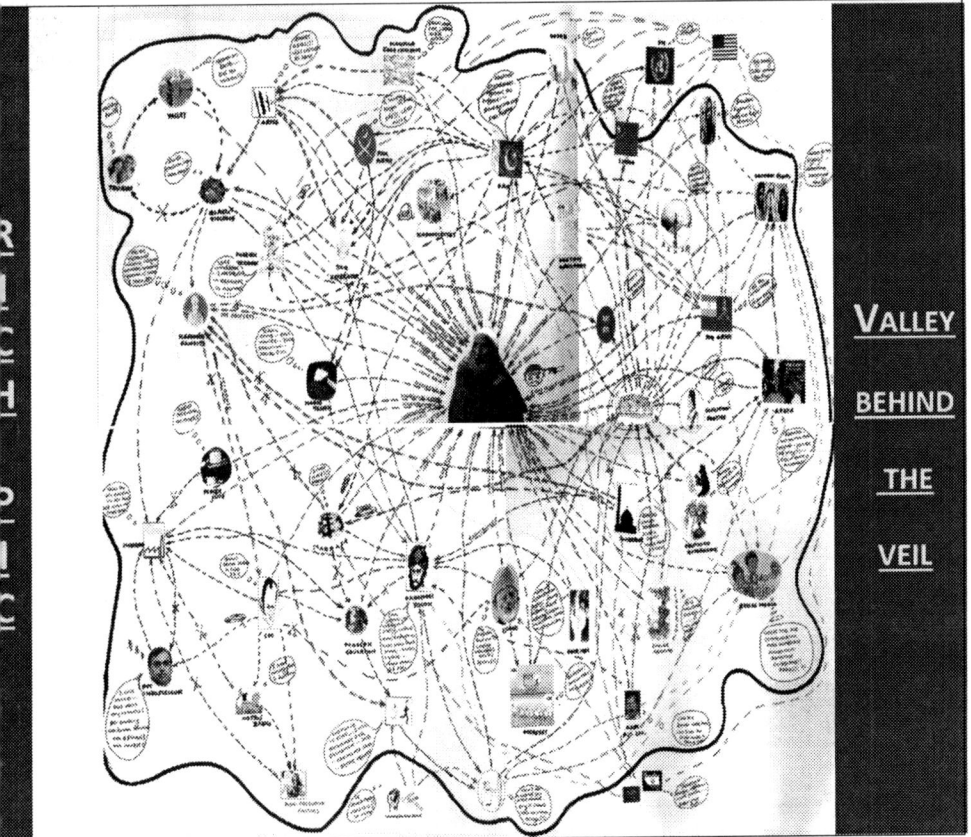

any one of the stakeholders/actors could make the research lopsided and incomplete.

Step 3 - Relevant Systems (RS) and Root Definitions (RD). Some of the related RS and RDs are stated below. As through this focus article, it is intended to highlight the use of SSM methodology as one of the possible alternate methods for the problem solution, the list is only indicative and by no mean exhaustive.

- Relevant Systems
    - **RS 1.** External abetment to the J&K problem.
    - **RS 2.** Poor/Lack of governance.
    - **RS 3.** Religious fundamentalism.

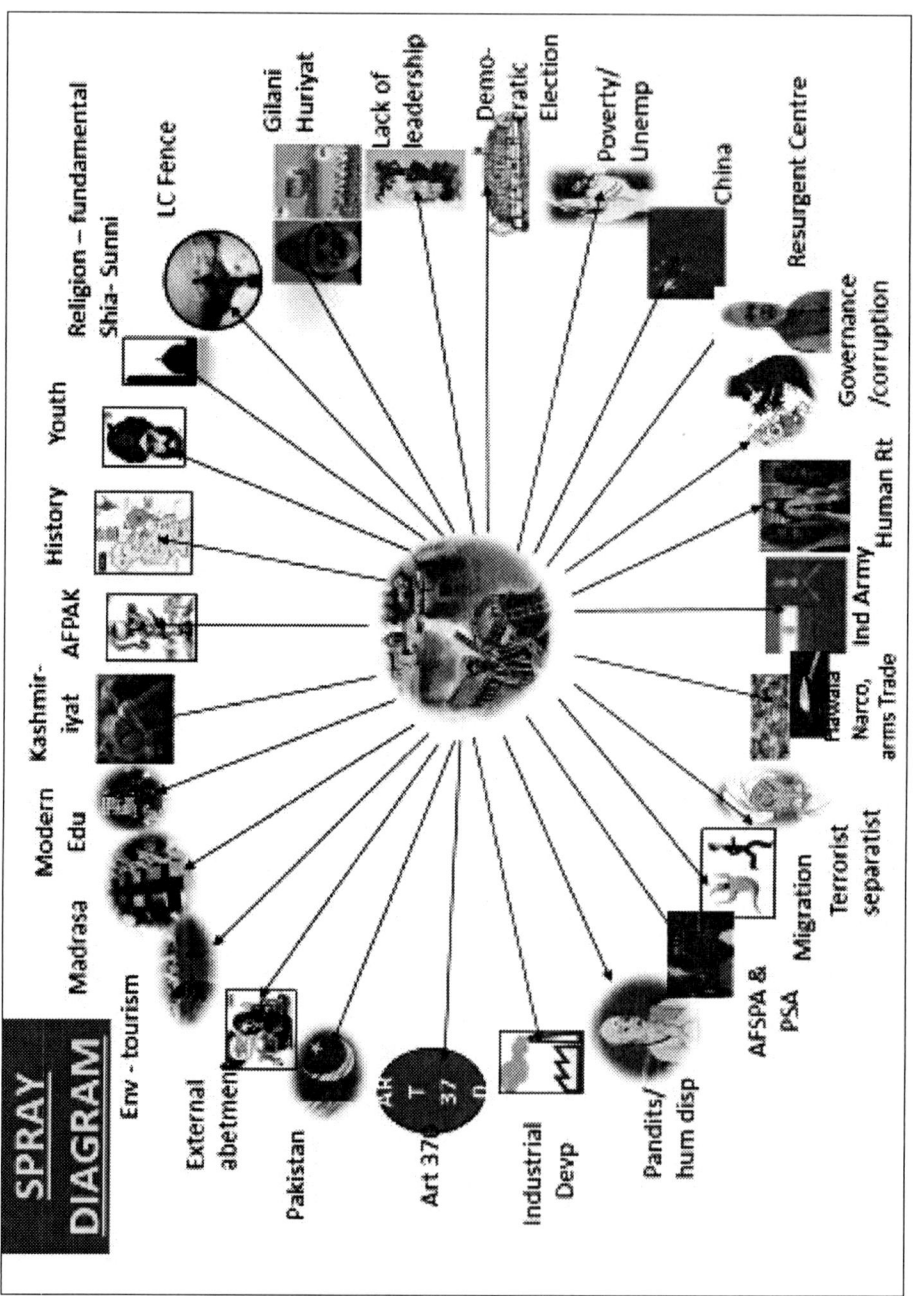

- o RS 4. Lack of resident leadership.
- o RS 5. E-10 – Economy, education, employment, employability, efficiency, e-governance, expansion (development), empowerment, elections, emancipation

- **Root Definition (Covered only for RS1)**
  - o RD 1. A synergised multiagency approach based on institutional mechanism, joint strategies and tactics and standard operating procedures in order to prevent any trans-border abetment to actors/elements inimical to Indian interest in J&K by isolating external influence over the environment and events in the J&K; reducing region's vulnerability to terrorism; and minimize the damage and recover from attacks that do occur despite the preventive mechanisms in force.

CATWOE Analysis

- o Customers. All citizens of India.
- o Actors. Govt and relevant agencies (As shown in the Spray Diagram).
- o Transformation. A synergized multiagency operated security measures by devising institutional mechanism, joint strategies and tactics and standard operating procedures in order to prevent any trans-border abetment to actors/elements inimical to Indian interest in J&K by isolating external influence over the environment and events in the J&K; reducing region's vulnerability to terrorism; and minimize the damage and recover from attacks that do occur despite the preventive mechanisms in force.
- o Weltanschauung (World View). Synergy and interagency cooperation is required for Internal Security.
- o Owner. Government of India.
- o Environment. Elements outside the system which are taken as given, but nevertheless affect its behavior (USA, Afghanistan, China, Iran, Saudi-Arabia, UN etc).

Step 4 – Conceptual Model.

Conceptual Model. This could be also achieved by analyzing various existing model such as such as US Anti-terrorism Model based on organisation structure as depicted above, to arrive at an ideal model.

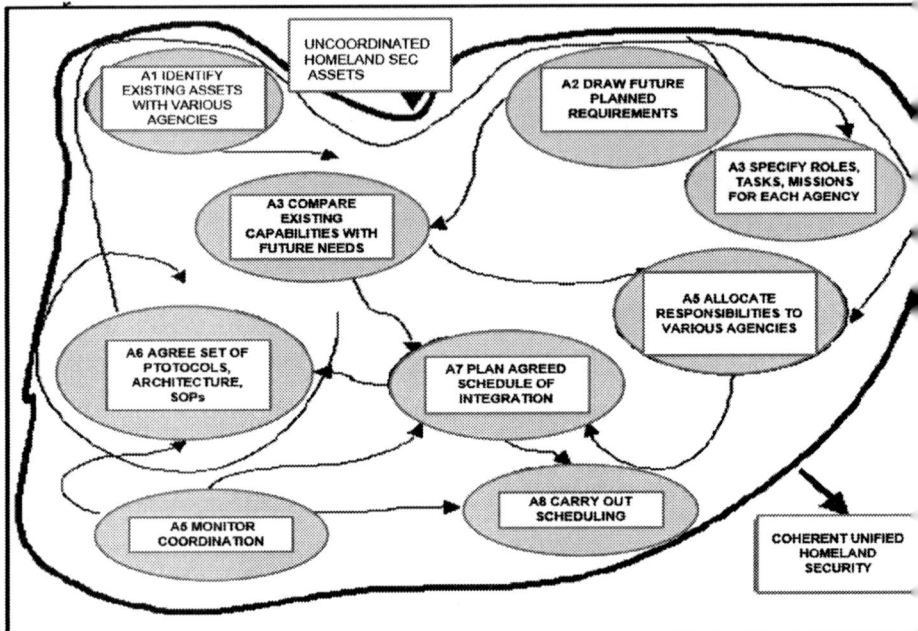

- Measure of Performance. E1 – efficacy (Does the security mechanism work is the transformation effected?); E2 – efficiency (What is the relationship between the output achieved and the resources consumed to achieve it?); E3 – effectiveness (Is the longer term goal stated at Root Definition 15 (a) achieved?).
- Once the complete conceptual model is arrived at the level of resolution, a higher level is undertaken to further refine the root definition.

Comparison with the Real World and EVR Congruence before Action

Comparison of these conceptual models with real world has to be undertaken in order to get the desired results. This could bring out systemically desirable and culturally feasible changes which could be implemented according to a systematic action plan. This needs to pass the EVR congruence in Strategic Management terminology.[4]

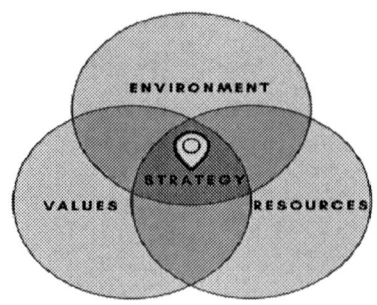

Conclusion

The Kashmir problem does not have a cut-and-dry solution as is the case with many social science-dominated qualitative issues and problems. It is therefore pertinent that a comprehensive analysis be done keeping in mind all stakeholders, breaking the problem into smaller manageable Relevant Systems and further define them through Root Definitions before comparing these again with happenings, systems and strategies in the real world. This will further reduce personnel biases and objectivity which is extremely important for credible research and resultant problem solving.

SYSTEMS THINKING APCH – CAUSAL LOOP DIAGRAMS

Introduction. The IS situation in the Valley can be analysed by employing the Sys Dynamics Apch involving the Causal Loop Diagrams (CLD). The IS situation falls under the "complex" and "unitary" category of Sys Apch. "Unitary" as the participants (Central and State govt, Security Forces and the People of Kashmir) have similar values, beliefs, interests and share a common purpose of achieving "Peace and Prosperity" in the Valley. "Complex" as the situation has a large number of sub-systems that are involved in many more loosely structured interactions, the outcome of which is not pre-determined. In this part, "the IS situation in the Valley" is studied as a whole system. The success of this system lies in the connectedness and inter- relationships of various elements (sub-systems). The dynamics of the systems give cause and effect relationships among the various elements (factors) of the system. This study of cause and effect relationships will give a vital insight into the behaviour, working and the analysis of this dynamic system.

First Questionnaire Analysis. A first detailed questionnaire was prepared and responses analysed in 2014; the details of this are given in Appendix A. Some other world views summarized from interviews are as under:

- **Militancy in J&K.** All sections except Kashmiri Pandits felt in 2014 that the Local young boys are not interested in Jihad but join militancy for lack of employment.

- **External support.** 46.9% Awaam, 68.8% Surrendered Militants, 82.9% Kashmiri Pandits and 92% of JKP soldiers felt that PAK/ISI is responsible for continuation of militancy in and Pak's interference in J&K is aimed at fulfilling its Political agenda and not a genuine concern for the "Awaam" of J&K.

- **Comparison with PoK.** All sections fully understand that Life of a common man is better in Kashmir than PoK.
- **Decline in Infilt.** SF appreciate that the erection of LC fence is the main reason for decline in infiltration across LC.
- **Hurriyat Sp.** Hurriyat generally enjoys the sp of Awaam in valley except elderly people specially people in Govt service who feel that Hurriyat is the political wing of militant organizations.
- **Religious Fundamentalism.** Religious fundamentalism is on the rise; however, Awaam did not feel in 2014 that it has become more important than the concept of 'kashmiriyat."
- **AFSPA.** All sections of the society except Awaam in Kupwara sector and specifically those not employed with state/central govt felt in 2014 that AFSPA is essential for functioning of Security Forces in J&K. All sections of the society understand the importance and necessity of immunity provided by AFSPA; however, Awaam had mixed opinions about its continuation.
- **Deployment of SF and CAPF.** All cross sections of population feel that the deployment of Indian Army and CRPF troops is necessary for continuation of peace and stability in J&K.
- **Surrendered Militants.** All sections of the society in 2014 except offrs/JCOs/OR posted in the valley and Kashmiri Pandits feel that a large number of militants have surrendered because of rehabilitation policy of the govt and surrendered militants have further helped in containing militancy in J&K.
- **Role of Local Media.** Situation in valley had improved to the extent that citizens have full freedom of expression and peaceful assembly in J&K but Local media is still not performing its role towards Awaam in J&K.
- **Governance.** People felt that corruption is rampant in the various state departments and there is lack of employment for the youth. Some expert feel that 99-years lease clause should be exploited to attract investments from businessmen who are not domicile of J&K. More than 60% of Awaam had access to internet in 2014 and e- governance should be exploited to increase transparency as well as efficacy of government schemes.

- **LC Trade.** Majority of the population felt that Free trade across LoC will help improve socio-economic condition of J&K.

- **Infrastructure Development.** Special initiative by the Central government in terms of Infrastructure development in J&K has significantly helped development in J&K.

- **Kashmiri Pandits Rehab.** All groups unanimously agreed that Kashmiri Pandits who have migrated to Jammu, Delhi and other places should be rehabilitated back in Kashmir.

- **Special Status & Alienation.** People in the valley felt that Article 370 of Indian constitution as applicable to J&K should continue while fringe groups like Kashmiri Pandits, JKP and Surrendered Militants felt that J&K should become federal state in the Union of India like all other states.

- **Methodology of Counter-Terrorist Operations.** There is a need for review of the methodologies for conduct of CT ops. Army should gradually move from hinterland to LC and start operating from large bases.

- **Sadhbhavna.** People had mixed opinions about Sadhbhavna. Some sections believe in its continuation while others feel that this aspect should better be left to the state government agencies.

- **Surgical Strikes.** Interestingly majority of the Officers (82.76%) in 2014 agreed that surgical strikes should be undertaken, well before they were actually undertaken in 2016.

- **Perception Management.** Majority of officers were of the opinion that Perception Management is not being done correctly.

- **Capacity Building of J&K Police and Para-Military Police.** An overwhelming majority (93.6 %) were of the opinion this was dire need of the day in 2014.

Second Questionnaire Analysis – July 2018. A lot of water has flowed under the bridge since 2014 and after the Burhan Wani incident, there is a propensity of educated youth of the Valley to join militancy. Therefore, a need was felt to understand the aspirations and attitudes of the College-going students of the valley. The services of Professor Sujata Sriram, Tata Institute of Social Sciences (TISS) were requisitioned by Centre for Land Warfare Study (CLAWS) for this research. The survey was conducted by engaging the trustworthy civil society members having unquestionable acceptability among the youth with no footprints of Army or any other government agencies. The principals and professors were taken into confidence by explaining that TISS is conducting this survey like it does in various parts of the country, especially troubled zones, in a routine manner. It was also told that TISS is undertaking this survey independently to ascertain the feelings of the youth as also what their aspirations are. An effort was made to ensure that group dynamics do not play out. However, some influence of group dynamics or inherent desire to maintain secrecy for certain questions of the survey, e.g. "Do You consider Yourself to be an Indian", "Radicalisation", "Affiliation to Religious Organisation" and so on cannot be ruled out. The details of the Questionnaire and analysis by TISS as well as through in-house resources are attached in Appendix B and the salient issues from it are as under:

- The sample of survey represents the most volatile section of the society (the millennials) and apparently most alienated as well. Hence, extrapolating it to entire population could see the moderation in anti-India sentiments.
- There is a definite sense of alienation if not rage in the millennials.
- There are pockets in both North and South Kashmir, where anti-India feelings are at higher levels. Some impact of incidents in the run-up to the date of survey or at the time of survey also needs to be factored in.
- There is quite a sizeable percentage of population even in areas greatly affected by ongoing turmoil who have opted to be called Indian and hence if harnessed well the situation could further improve.
- Preference for Central Government jobs (61%) corroborates the aspect of hope for a better future within Indian framework. This provides a great opportunity for coaching institutes to flourish in J&K. This will also provide an alternative to the youth from just going to Religious places in their free time. However, most youth want to see a change and a lasting solution for Kashmir.
- Social Media influence in the society is clearly discernible (81%) and its role as a catalyst to lend momentum to radicalisation process in the Valley is undeniable. A very large percentage of youth are inclined towards religion in their spare time (84%), which may reflect the current trend of youth tilting towards radicalisation.
- There lies a great opportunity to utilize technology to our advantage. Social media platform apps specifically made for Kashmir by our tech

wizards at Bangalore could assist in improving perceptions as also become platforms for positive governance and change.
- An interesting finding was that only 50% of youth wanted Kashmiri Pandits to return (as against 84% in 2007 through a CSDS conducted survey), which could be an indicator to the widening divide between Pandit Community and Muslims of the Valley. This does not augur well for future and efforts must be made to facilitate dialogue between Pandits and prominent mainstream Muslim leaders from the Valley.
- The teenagers and millennials who have been interviewed are slowly losing theconnect with the Pandits. Another reason could be the "we against them" syndrome across the Banihal which is also being fed through politics and TV channels.
- Army remains the most trusted agency amongst all the Security Forces operating in the Valley despite years of conflict, but overall trust figures are not flattering. It would therefore prudent to consider what best practices could be co-opted to improve the acceptability.
- One disturbing issue is the low trust on Police and CAPF. Introspection and dramatic change have to be carried out by the home ministry. Sweeping powers and corrupt practices of the police and SOG have led to a sense of rage against these organisations. The Police has not only to be built up but cleaned of malpractices too.
- Religious teachers (65%) and teachers (92%) in schools and colleges seem to be a trusted lot, these being mutually exclusive. There is a reason to engage with them through well thought out approaches and strategy by the home ministry. The key lies in Religious and social rehabilitation of a demographic group who are presently trying to find themselves in religion.
- Family is the most trusted entity. 97% youth opined that they trusted and spent time with their family members.
- The survey quite closely validates the description of the situation in the Valley as "stable, but fragile". Hence, if all the agencies including the civil administration work closely and in unison (synergy has improved, but a lot of it still remains compartmentalized) to wrest the initiative from Separatist-Terrorist-Pakistan troika, there is a great probability of the goal materialising.
- International perception management becomes extremely important as is suggested by the answers to the question on UNHRC report as

well as the choice of viewing international news channels (28%). The MEA will have to get its act together in this field. Think tanks like ours can also play a pivotal role by organizing seminars and sharing strategies through cooperation with international think tanks through visits.
- A road map of well thought out initiatives in the field of education, sports and entertainment could counter growing radicalisation footprints.
- There is a definite need for social, economic, political empowerment of the youth through well thought out strategies otherwise the empty spaces will be taken up by a radical strain of religion.
- It is good to see 50% still feeling proud to be a Kashmiri. Such ethno-sub-nationalistic thinking will bring them closer to their core culture of Kashmiriyat and Sufi Islam which has a unique identity and needs to be reinforced lest the inimical forces of Radical Pan-islamisation should take over.
- The overall findings from the data collected point out that the millennials are dissatisfied but hopeful. But this is a common phenomenon in many parts of the country and the world and is not a reason to be alarmed as being catastrophic.
- Concerted and coherent effort through a whole of the government approach can pull the entire young population back to the mainstream.
- In the proxy war being orchestrated by our adversary, we have a definite advantage of being able to collect and analyse data through reliable tools. But this advantage will only bear fruition in case we utilize the data and the trends to our advantage through concrete action.
- Artificial Intelligence was also utilized in conjunction with Chirag Nagpal, a student of Carnegie Melon University, USA (details are attached as Annexure to Appendix B). Some of the major findings of this exercise are given below:
  - Trust on the Indian Armed Forces, deployed in Kashmir, seems to be most highly positively correlated with the sense of being Indian, across all the three major geographical regions of the Kashmir Valley. This is expected, since the Indian Army has played an active role in fighting armed militancy and also undertaken numerous civic actionprograms aimed at Human Development in the region through the "Sadbhavana" (Goodwill) program. This campaign has included setting up of co-educational Junior and High Schools,

- Vocational training centers and Healthcare and Medical Camps.
- We also found that Trust on Local and Police agencies seems to not be correlated with this sense, suggesting an opportunity for the Local Police totake up similar civic action programs to reach out and play a more active role in creating a nationalistic and democratic sense of belonging to the Union of India.
- Interestingly we found that, a large number of participants who responded that their primary purpose of Social Media was to express opinions a political dialogue also had a positive disposition towards the Indian Union. This suggests that Social Media, although infamous for its deleterious effects in the Valley, does provide a platform for the youth to engage in political discourse, encouraging state instruments to play a more active role on Social Media in positively engaging the population through these media.
- Amongst the population with a general lack of trust on the Indian State and its instruments, such mistrust extends to even other Non-State Instruments, including the Private Electronic Media.
- The effects of both Traditional and Social Media seem to be positively correlated with the responders age too, which is contrary to public opinion about social media being more popular with the younger population.
- While one would expect this to be the case for electronic and print media, the fact **that social media's influence on separatism seems to increase with age is an interesting discovery.**

Interviews

Depth interviews were also carried out with senior retired Army, Police, IAS officers as well as media personalities and politicians. The responses collected from these depth interviews which will assist in system analysis and simulation has been summarized as below:

- **Autonomy.** J&K is presently most powerful state. Autonomy demand is only symbolic, actually Valley was never neglected.
- **Economic development.** Governance and economic prosperity are important factors. Maj issues today are poor implementation, poor accountability and poor delivery.
- **Role of Army.** Army has done its bit in stable areas and now needs to thin out from these areas and focus on anti-infiltration deployment. Infiltration still continues to be a challenge.

- **AFSPA.** AFSPA issue is more of a political gimmick. Army cannot operate without legal protection so AFSPA should continue.
- **ISIS Migration.** Army should not express this concern publicly but be prep internally to handle the situation. Army should be prepared for worst case scenario and irrespective of threat should thin out from hinterland to LC.
- **Sadhbhavana.** No longer relevant in the present format. Army should disengage gradually and hand over to administration.
- **Perception Management.** Enough is not being done presently. Also, the Army should only aim at good behaviour and good work.
- **Media Management.** SF failed to exploit media as a tool. There is a need to have "looking up officers" as Public Relations Officers. Media should be exploited extensively by retired General officers.
- **Social media.** Usage of social media especially by youth is on the increase. This aspect has tremendous potential for counter propaganda and perception management.

Historical Baggage

Though J&K comprises three distinct geographical and ethnic regions, it is the dynamics of Kashmir valley which has played a major role in deciding the fate of the state. There has been a lot of political, security and ethnic turmoil in the valley and the baggage of history has impacted the future development of the state. Consequently, the relevance of past history and its very deep rooted relation to IS situation would have a bearing while analysing military aspects and future courses of action.

Turmoiled History. Power equations have changed over a period of time and it is always the human behaviour of trying to be at the centre of power which has been the main reason for neglecting the aspirations of the state. Almost all the important leaders have played with the emotions of the people to achieve their objectives. Maharaja Hari Singh initially signed the standstill agreement with both countries because he wanted to retain power himself. *The history is not very clear if the whole state seemed to have accepted its transition towards India.* Pandit Nehru in his exuberance and idealism philosophy agreed on a plebiscite. However, the Sher-e-Kashmir, Sheikh Abdullah whose ideas swayed between independence and amalgamation with India or Pakistan had a hidden agenda himself. So much so, Pandit Nehru, his one-time best friend and later foe, seems to have started to distrust Sheikh on realizing that the man himself nurtured feelings of ruling Kashmir if it became independent. This put Nehru in a precarious situation. The person who was given the onus of steering the plebiscite had himself tasted the blood of power. There was no doubt that Sheikh with his enormous clout and an iconic image had coxswained the people of Kashmir into dreaming for Azadi. The seeds of separatism were thus sown during this period. The propping up of parallel leaders to reduce the followings of the Sheikh also added to the confusion. The people were thus confused as what they actually wanted and were generally influenced by the perception of leaders. Most of the political leaders barring a few had myopic views, had visions to suit their political agenda and were amenable to manipulation. The blatant rigging of elections in 1987 was yet another classical example of political parties trying all means to come to power. Finally, to add to the woes, Pakistan jumped into the fray yet again with a well laid out proxy war to manipulate the situation created by our own undoing. Thus, over a period of last seventy years, no single state of the Indian Union has seen such a huge shift in the aspirations of the people from Azadi to becoming part of Pakistan to being part of India, with three totally different scenarios with the Awaam of Kashmir also swaying as the wind blew. **The dust seems to have finally settled with a past which is full of distrust and perplexing aspirations difficult to fathom.** Thus, dealing with a Kashmiri in the valley definitely needs a *Kashmiri outlook* and cannot be compared with any other state. There is a need to mould them gradually to our mainstream rather than force them to accept a particular thought. As Peter Senge brings out that *the harder you push, the harder the system pushes back.*

Kashmiri Psyche. This turmoiled historical baggage has given rise to specific character to the psyche of Kashmiri populace. The character of the Kashmiri[5] has also been highlighted by Walter Lawrence in his book 'The Valley of Kashmir' in 1895. A net assessment study was undertaken as a project by College of Defence Management, Secunderabad, in 2014 in which personalities from all walks of life were interviewed and a Psyche was reconstructed. Few of its derived facets, which have got further substantiated by a survey carried out by the Tata Institute of Social Sciences for CLAWS on Simple Random Samples (SRS) in July 2018 in the colleges of Kashmir (N=503), were presented in the recently conducted seminar on "Mapping of Perceptions in J&K" on 18 August 2018. Few of its extrapolated facets are highlighted as under:

- Kashmiri does not know whom to trust, namely, state/Central government, SF/terrorists/police or even his neighbour.
- He does not know what he wants Azadi or to be with India or Pak or better life.

- He has over a period of time developed a dual personality. He speaks his mind and feelings differently in group/mob and individually. He sings the song based on the audience.
- He feels oppressed because he feels that he has always been ruled by others over the years.
- Turmoil of history and continued oppression has made a Kashmiri adapt himself to his perceived owner. In such circumstances, he is forced to survive by quickly adjusting himself to changing environment. This has led to him being projected as a liar.
- A normal Kashmiri feels that it is the responsibility of the government to take care of them and freebies over a period of time have made him lazy.
- He has a lot of free time and indulges himself in group discussions which results in hardening of stand. An average Kashmiri is politically aware of the environment.
- The youth of Kashmir have been victims of violence and have developed a hatred for the SF due to the perceived violence and humiliation of their parents and relatives. Thus, he has developed traits of a rebel over a period of time which is presently manifesting in the aggressiveness which he portrays to the environment.
- Romanticized notion of a utopian state, escaping the unbearable world, social misfit syndrome, existential anxiety, desire to be a "good muslim" and even as petty a thing as a failed love life is drawing him towards terrorist recruitment when he sees a small trigger as that of a funeral of a slain militant.

Sufism. The most dominant influence on the Kashmiri Muslims, in terms of their Kashmiriyat, is that of the *Rishi* order of Sufis. The detais of this very important aspect have been covered in Chapter 2 of this book. After understanding this aspect, one realizes why the colour of Islam in the valley is still so deeply mystical and deeply respectful of other religions. It is extremely depressing to see people with such mystical traditions living in such violent times. It is difficult to see Kashmir living permanently in the grip of obscurantism and fundamentalism.

Terrorists/Militants

The terrorist groups' activities can be divided into **two categories: activities that sustain the group's existence as a cohesive entity and activities that allow terrorists to sustain series of successful attacks.** Admittedly, these two categories are interrelated. Terrorist groups' ability to sustain a series of successful attacks can turn this success into a recruitment campaign or use the success to reinforce their members' confidence in the group and, hence, bolster group cohesion. In the event of terrorist attacks, social media postings can serve as a force multiplier and accelerator that can amplify the carnage and spread anxiety and fear beyond the immediate victims of a terrorist attack. Despite efforts to counter radicalization and recruitment on social media platforms, a range of challenges persist. Perhaps the greatest challenge to these efforts is the ability by threat actors to upload commentaries and videos in real-time. Terrorists can utilize live streaming functions, such as Twitter Periscope, Facebook Live, and YouTube 360 Degrees. There is currently no reliable machine learning technology, sentiment analysis software or artificial intelligence programs that can monitor and vet all content in real time. The probability of false positives is high when utilizing said technology. As a result, time-consuming human analysis will be necessary to filter out false positives.[6]

Terrorist organizations, over the years, have successfully used social media tools to recruit, propagate and raise funds for their dreadful agendas. Sermons by so-called charismatic extremists have succeeded in influencing youths to join terrorist organizations and carry out sinister attacks across the world. One of the key reasons behind using mass media heavily is because ultimately these anti-social elements are trying to legitimize their unlawful activities, as most of them have a mass following online and have a possibility of gaining greater audience.[7]

If the organisation wants to prevent a particular attack or alleviate an immediate threat, or try to bring in a semblance of peace, then counterterrorism activities should focus, in general, on the second category. **In comparison, if policymakers want to completely dismantle the terrorist organisation over the long term, then counter-terrorism activities should include a significant emphasis on the first category, which is undoubtedly a more holistic approach.** Unfortunately, our strategy over a period of time has focussed primarily on the second aspect that is to try and get a semblance of peace for the government machinery to function.

Organisational and Operational Tools

Having divided terrorist groups' activities into two categories, we next identify certain basic tools that terrorists use – with varying degrees of sophistication— to sustain these activities. The six organizational tools (terrorist capabilities that sustain group cohesion and existence) are:

- Ideology.
- Alienation through Radicalisation.
- Leadership.
- Recruitment pools.
- Publicity.
- Finance.

In addition to these organizational tools, the operational tools used by terrorist groups to sustain a series of successful attacks are:

- Command and control.
- Weapons.
- Operational space.
- Operational security.
- Overground workers (OGWs).
- Cyber space.
- Agitational space.

Organisational Tools of Terrorists

- **Ideology.** With regards to terrorism, the term ideology means the consensus of grievances and objectives that a terrorist group is trying to address through violence. In this context, terrorists' ideologies may take on many forms—e.g., religious or political—but still serve the same purpose—motivating actions, unifying members, and linking the organization to communities for which it purports to fight. In Kashmir, the ideology is different for different groups. While HM is basically fighting for an Azad Kashmir which comes under Pakistan, the LET and JEM seem to have more religious lineages with the ultimate aim of merging with Pak. Thus, the ideology is a mix of *ethno-religious separatism* and Islamic extremism. The huge influx of madrassas in the valley, the rise of the Wahabi/Salafi group, the fiery speeches of Terrorist leaders calling for jihad, the change in the dress code and the massive protests after the Friday congregations are all indicators of growing influence of religion in the day-to-day life of an individual in the valley. **The guidance of Islam could be used as a uniting force to keep all the people true to the cause – that is "to fight to liberate land from infidel occupation".** Factors used to rouse sentiment to join jihad and exacerbate the feeling of fundamentalism keywords such as Al wala' wal bara' which symbolizes a belief that Muslims owe allegiance to

Muslims alone and must reject non-Muslims as allies or friends[8]; *Fatwa*, A religious edict, often issued by a religious authority in response to a question seeking clarification of Islamic doctrine; *Jihad*, literally "to struggle" but often used to refer to armed struggle, etc., are no longer a validation to join a terror campaign.

- **Alienation through Radicalisation.** It is extremely critical to analyse the nuances of *growing fundamentalism* in the Valley. Although the sense of Alienation from the Indian mainland is present in the Awaam due to many other reasons like cultural differences, historical baggage and dysfunctional governance, it is a well-known fact that state-sponsored militancy has dramatically transformed the Sufism and Kashmiriyat-influenced people of Kashmir into a fractured and radically influenced society which, in turn, has given rise to religious fundamentalism.[9] Radicalisation of society in Kashmir feeds to the further alienation of the people,[10] which is the aim of the terror groups and it seems to be the first step for gradually bringing the youth into the main line of militant actions.

- **Leadership.** Leadership represents second organizational tool for any terrorist organisation. In insurgency and terrorism, terrorist groups tend to coalesce around charismatic individuals who attract and inspire supporters. **There are many terrorists who are more than willing to get into the shoes of a slain leader. Power and money will always have takers.** A strategy to take on the leaders will definitely give an operational advantage; however, in the longer run, slain terrorist leaders also provide a grander sense of martyrdom for the cause to the youth and which motivates others to take on the cause, a case in point being the Burhan Wani incident. Hafiz Saeed and Maulana Azhar are state-sponsored rogues but Syed Sallauddin is one leader who has the potential to be won over as he himself had taken part in elections and his group had earlier agreed to a ceasefire.

- **Recruitment.** In the valley, there is an adequate pool of disgruntled, unemployed youth both educated and uneducated for recruitment by anti-national elements. Typically, a strategy of **systematic entrapment** is employed whereby individuals are instructed to undertake operations that are progressively more serious in nature. The objective is twofold: first, to induce inductees to greater acts of disobedience and violence and second, to slowly distance these individuals from mainstream civil society to the point that they have no real option but to remain with the militants. In most cases, the procedure seems to follow a standard pattern that starts out with youth being used to target SF via stone pelting for money, progressing through more serious vandalism and then being OGWs wherein they provide logistical support for strike teams. The more resilient and motivated youth are then assigned jobs of a more serious nature like grenade throwing and snatching of weapon before they join the mainstream groups for more serious actions. **The individuals booked under PSA and who spend time in jails with hardcore terrorists provide an ideal breeding ground for potential recruits.**

- **Publicity.** For the insurgents, the need to win over the population is being reflected in their conduct of operations which have very limited collateral damage. **A comparison of the terrorist strikes in the valley and that of other terrorist organisations in the world show a marked difference in the methodology of operations.** The propaganda strategy of the terrorists here stem around their actions of avoiding any civilian casualty while at the same time capitalizing on the mistakes of the Security Forces. The terrorists have managed to not only identify themselves as freedom fighters but have also been portrayed as fighting for Jihad, both factors providing them the unconditional support of the population. Informal interaction with the civil populace has clearly brought out that an average Kashmiri may not share any info about a terrorist willingly. The mainstream media is also not helping by showing the support for Terrorists on prime time. This is creating a perception that the terrorists are winning ground.

- **Finance.** The aspect of finance is one of the most important organisational tools for a terrorist organisation. The terrorist organisation can only sustain its operations if there are adequate means to generate funds for the cause. It has been learnt from reliable sources that rerouting the hawala funding from Saudi Arabia, Iran and the Kashmiri diaspora seems to be the primary means of funding. Notably, the terrorist organisations both in PoK and valley do not use these resources solely for their terrorist operations but they sponsor a number of charities in the PoK. Thus, it is difficult to separate the funds the organization uses to support health clinics from those used to support terrorist activities. Therefore, although money is key for terrorist organisations to sustain their activities, it also plays an organizational role—group cohesion—by bolstering their relationship to local communities and further legitimizing their activities in J&K. The balance of payment in LoC trade and narcotics, Haj tourism cancellations as well as sale and distribution of ancestral property assets between families on both sides of the LoC seem to be the new source of financing the movement in the valley. A new trend yet not fully discovered and investigated is the Hurriyat- and Pakistan-sponsored "scholarship scandal" wherein students are being sent to SARRC and other countries thereby financing terror in kind.

Operational Tools of Terrorists

- **Command and Control.** For the purpose of this Issue Brief, *command and control* is the mechanism that terrorist groups use to plan, coordinate, and execute their attacks. Notably, terrorist leaders often attempt to build a degree of redundancy into their command and control network in order to coordinate activities. In the initial stages of insurgency, a hierarchy of mid-level leaders met periodically to formulate basic strategic guidance, allowing the leaders discretion in the way that they achieve their overall objectives. This network was facilitated by a system of radio-transmitting stations. The capability of interception and breaking of codes by our forces led to reduced usage of radio communication. This had severely hampered the command and control setup in the valley. However, of late the terrorists seem to have shifted to sophisticated methods of communication including internet to transmit messages. The terrorist groups also seem to have adopted the Al Qaeda model of decentralized command and control system to avoid being intercepted. This apparently allows substantial autonomy to individual local groups to carry out their actions and make it more **difficult to predict any major terrorist incidents**. Moreover, when members of "hardcore" or the central leadership decide to conduct a specific attack, they seem to rely less on the leaders of terrorist groups operating in Valley. The suicide attack on Uri in 2016 could be classified as a classic strike from ***line of march concept***. Planned and conceived by the top terrorist leadership in PoK, the group infiltrated with the sole purpose of carrying out its attack with the help of OGW cells in the valley. The point of concern is the ease with which the entire operation was executed. An analysis of the incident along with the

Mumbai and Pathankot attacks clearly brings out that major suicide attacks in future will also be planned and executed from Pak/PoK with utmost secrecy and limited support from terrorist groups. Hardcore OGWs could be used to provide the necessary logistics support and interface for completing the task. They could also use sophisticated GPS to guide them to the target. Major terrorist strikes would continue to be executed by hardcore cadres from outside.

- **Weapons and Equipment.** Notwithstanding the fact that there is an adequate quantity of weapons hidden in the Valley, more still seem to be coming in. Movement of terrorists without weapons or at the most with just a pistol to pre-designated caches in order to launch attacks has become a trend.

- **Operational Space.** In addition to command and control network and weapons, terrorist groups also need time and space to plan, train for, and execute their attacks. The operational space will range from urban neighbourhoods to sanctuaries within the state and transnational sanctuaries. Each terrorist organisation needs to have an area which provides these groups with a wide range of opportunities to plan, train, and conduct operations, stockpile weapons, and protect their primary leaders. Thus, it is an operational requirement to have bases in the valley where the terrorists make themselves comparatively safe. These areas could be traditional hideouts like the Lolab and Rajwad RF or places like Srinagar downtown, Sopore downtown or Pulwama town, where the density of population and houses makes it extremely difficult to conduct operations. Operational space for each terror cell in terms of a jurisdiction or territorial limitation seems to be clearly demarcated by their handlers.

- **Operational Security.** It is primarily the ability of terrorist groups to keep security forces from discovering the plans and people involved in terrorist activities. We would, therefore, expect that terrorists expend considerable resources to protect the integrity of their operations. The terrorist organisations of late have switched to cell-like structures to maintain operational security, with individual members associated with local cells that operate relatively independently. As a result, those in individual cells are not always aware of others' plans, reducing the potential for informers or infiltrators to discern any given attack. Terrorist groups have also switched on to sophisticated methods like encrypted software and mediums like Facebook, WhatsApp, Facetime and other applications whose servers are not in our country. Thus, the terrorists seemed to have moved one notch ahead as far as technology is concerned while our SF apparatus does not have the requisite infrastructure to intercept and monitor the communications.

- **OGWs.** They have always been the mainstay for an insurgency movement and need to be discussed in detail separately in the same chapter.

- **Cyber Space.** Groups like Al Qaeda, LeT, and Islamic State of Iraq and Syria (ISIS) have successfully created online "madrasas" that has put a significant dent in the young and vulnerable population across the world from the West to the East and irrespective of their religious inclination. They have also succeeded in gathering massive "sympathizers" online where evidently these sympathizers are readily available to provide physical support on the behest of several online videos posted on their terrorist organization's websites and YouTube (online video channel). There cannot be denying that social media has steadily been converted into a lethal mind game by the terrorist organizations to carry out their dreadful radical and terror campaign. It still remains a question that why the US has not actively pursued stringent policy on these social media platforms so as to work on a mandatory policy for all these media organizations to curb terrorist organization's freedom of speech, despite the knowledge about social media platforms like Twitter, Facebook, Google, YouTube, WhatsApp, Skype, Tumblr and Instagram owned by the US corporations having been misused by the terrorists.

- **Agitational Space.** Although the word "Agitational terrorism" was first coined in 2009,[11] the effect of it has been seen mainly since the Burhan Wani incident wherein organised stone-pelting mobs stopping the proceedings by security forces at an encounter spot have become almost a norm. The Organisational tools of Finance and Alienation through radicalisation have a deep connect for successfully employing this operational tool.

What do we do India?

- Insurgents must be isolated from the population, their cause, and support. While it may be required to kill or capture insurgents, it is more effective in the long run to separate an insurgency from the population and its resources, thus letting it die. Confrontational military action, in exclusion, is counterproductive in most cases; it risks generating popular resentment, creating martyrs that motivate new recruits, and producing cycles of revenge. Even carefully targeted military operations against insurgents can create risks for the population. An operation that kills five insurgents is counterproductive if collateral damage and resentment leads to the recruitment of 50 more insurgents. ROE should address lesser means of force and nonlethal means when such use is likely to create the desired effects, and SF can do so without endangering themselves, others, or mission accomplishment.

- If India has to eliminate terrorism threat from social media, the government should create awareness about cyber terrorism and set up highly competitive and efficient cyber-security think tanks which will monitor and report suspected terrorism-related activities. A database should be maintained on the accounts of users who frequently search these words online. Just merely by eliminating provocative video and text contents from YouTube, Twitter or Facebook will not be sufficient to stymie the growth of terrorist web. The symbiotic relationship that has taken root must be prevented. India, as a country, is fast evolving into one of the largest internet users in the world, and therefore is much more susceptible to the challenges posed against its national interest in the backdrop of growing misuse of social media at the hands of terrorist. It is only but need of the hour to congregate an agile foundation for cyber security, where the government agencies must work on a robust monitoring and filtering of anti-national activities conducted online.
- Working on leaders who have the potential to shift sides for money or power needs to be relentlessly pursued as the gains far outweigh the efforts of Counter-Terror operations.
- Checkmate the Radicalisation Campaigns in schools, religious institutions, educational institutes and Prisons through socio-scientific methods and assistance.
- Implement a detailed perception management strategy on prime-time channels; seeing is believing.
- Ruthlessly target Terror funding in real terms as well as in kind. In this regard, carrying out detailed checks on agents supporting terrorists

and discreetly investigating the funding for all persons from the state whose children are studying abroad, including Politicians and Bureaucrats, may pay rich dividends in unearthing the scandal.

- Make our Intelligence networks across the LoC more proficient so that we can track the Line of March type of major terror attacks more efficiently.
- There is a need to identify the potential hideouts and address them with increased frequency so as to deny the terrorists the operational space for planning and conduct of operations. Police and PMF should be the mainstay of sanitisation operations in towns while SF should be completely responsible for the forests.
- Upgrade to modern interception techniques, hardware and software in order to breach the operational security of the Terrorists and always stay one step ahead.
- Procure the best technology to ensure resource control measures without an invasive bent. An effective counter infiltration grid coupled with a technologically enabled checking system for all vehicles entering the Valley both from PoK and Jammu would go a long way in completely denying the most important ingredient providing capability to a terrorist, i.e., weapons and ammunition.

Overground Workers

Introduction. OGWs have always been the mainstay for an insurgency Movement. Previously, OGWs were primarily involved in logistics support and intelligence gathering. Of late, the distinction has blurred considerably with OGWs also capable of carrying out small-scale strikes while retaining the capability to mix rapidly with the population. OGWs also become a significant tool for strategic communication and recruitment by their handlers in J&K. It is a well-known fact that OGWs can constantly work towards development of a negative sentiment in the minds of the so-called grey population or fence sitters in an insurgency.

Resource Control and its Flip Side. Resource control measures including establishing check points, Cordon and Search operations create a sense of alienation in the minds of the populace. On the other hand, the comparative freedom of movement available to terrorists due to limited resource control measures emboldens the terrorists to change their strategy by trying to mix up with population. The attack by Pakistani terrorists at Sunjuwan gives this clear impression that the group had infiltrated months ago and were assisted by OGWs.[12] Movement without weapons or with pistol has thus become the order of the day. **Thus, a present-day terrorist may not be easy to identify and would operate in the grey area between that of an OGW and terrorist.**

Recruitment. In the Kashmir valley, there is an adequate pool of disgruntled unemployed youth both educated and uneducated for recruitment by anti-national elements. Radicalisation seems to be the first step for gradually bringing the youth into the main line of militant actions. Typically, a strategy of **systematic entrapment** is employed whereby individuals are instructed to undertake operations that are progressively more serious in nature. The objective is two-fold: first, to induce inductees to greater acts of disobedience and violence and second, to slowly distance these individuals from mainstream civil society to the point that they have no real option but to remain with the militants. **The individuals booked under Public Safety Act (PSA) of J&K and who spend time in jails with hardcore terrorists provide an ideal breeding ground for potential recruits.** In most cases, the procedure seems to follow a standard pattern that starts out with youth being used to target SF via stone pelting for money, progressing through more serious vandalism and then being OGWs wherein they provide logistical support for strike teams. The more resilient and motivated youth are then assigned jobs of more serious nature like grenade throwing and snatching of weapon before they join the main stream groups for more serious actions. Thus, *are the immediate solutions of today in the form of bookings of youth under PSA the problems of tomorrow?*

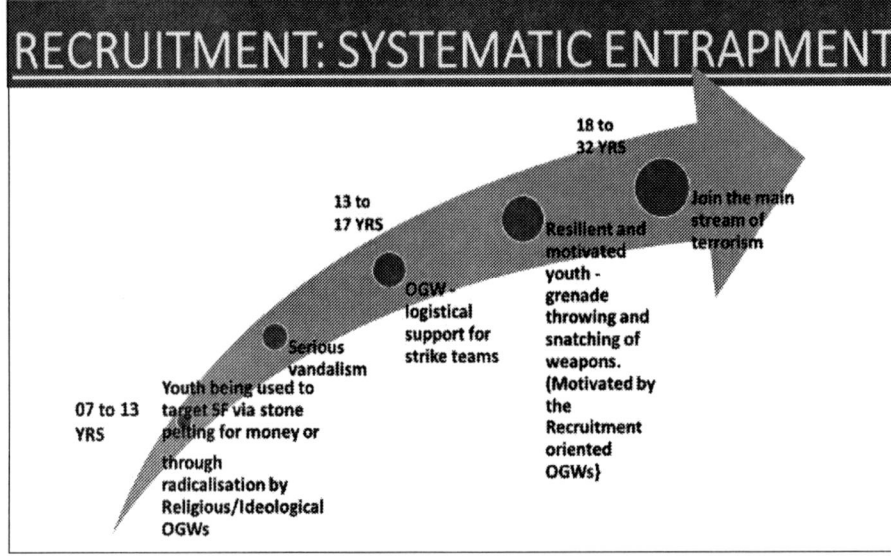

Effect of Sense of Alienation/Isolation. As sense of alienation increases, the support for grey population (separatists and OGWs) increases, who in turn are able to influence the perception of people more adversely. Adverse perception further alienates the people and vice versa. This is a mutually reinforcing loop and a vicious cycle which needs to be broken; otherwise the recruiters of terrorism will never find a dearth for new foot soldiers to further their cause.

The Jammu and Kashmir police are revising the list of suspected OGWs of militants and have called many of them for questioning in all districts as part of their efforts to cut the support network of militants and freeze their movement. All district headquarters have been asked to update the list of suspected OGWs and call them for questioning, if needed, to get an update on the militant network. Names of over 270 locals, suspected to be OGWs, have been circulated to all the district SPs in the Valley to get the latest information on them. Police have already started picking up youth during night raids in Pulwama, Shopian and Kulgam districts of south Kashmir. In the last week of August 2017, 12 youth were detained during raids across Pulwama in a single night.[13] But the moot point is that does such action provide the required impetus to anti-terror and counter-terror operations in the Valley?

Categorisation of OGWs

To fight this most important tool of terrorism and proxy war, it is important to categorise the OGWs so that separate response strategies can be made for each one of the categories. Although operating as larger network, the OGWs in Kashmir can be broadly categorised under the following heads (the categorisation has been done on the basis of experience of the author who has carried out a net assessment and system analysis study on the security situation in Kashmir, in order to give a de-novo look at the issue of OGWs by categorizing them for the sake of strategic communication and perception management/improvement):

- OGWs for Funding & Logistic Support (OGFWLS).
- OGWs providing Ideological and Radicalisation Support (OGWIRS).
- OGWs for Recruitment of Terrorists (OGWR).
- OGWs generating negative Perceptions and Sentiment amongst the Awaam (OGWPS).

Response Strategies

- OGFWLS are easy to identify as these can be caught in the act during a counter-terror operation or by intelligence agencies tracking cyber funding and physical currency as funds for terror. The National Investigative Agency (NIA) in early February 2018 had established links between terrorists, Hurriyat and stone-pelters, tracking the flow of funds, which led to charge sheeting.[14] More recently on 30 August 2018, Syed Saluddin's son, Shakeel was arrested by NIA for funding of terrorist activities through Hawala racquet.[15] Their capture and later indicting is not questioned by the populace to a large extent as they are caught in the act with a trail behind them.

- OGWIRS and OGWR can be grouped together for the purpose of response strategies. These workers are omnipresent in all walks of life. They could be sympathisers, belong to families of killed militants, teachers, religious teachers, separatists, members of larger networks like Al Qaeda or off-shoots of ISIS ideology, Pakistani proxy war agents or even disgruntled elements of society. Though these workers look benign at the face of it, they are the most dangerous to society as well as the security forces. They make their presence felt in all walks of life including the funeral processions of killed militants. Merely picking them up in night raids will only alienate the society further. On the contrary, launching intelligence-based sting operations over a period of time, gathering proof of their damaging activities of recruiting, radicalising or merely pushing the youth into militancy by handing them over guns, will expose them in the eyes of the Awaam. This proof will not only be useful for convicting these elements but also form a tool for strategic communication with the Awaam, showing them how their children are being misled for an unjust cause. Long drawn out stake-outs will garner richer dividends as against perceived arbitrary arrests.

- The last category is that of OGWPS who are the fence sitters and they are just keeping the pot boiling by creating an atmosphere of fear, dejection and helplessness in the youth. These are again omnipresent and cannot be targeted merely on hearsay, due to their democratic and constitutional rights of protest and liberty of expression. An endeavour to change their mindset through psychological and social rehabilitation as well as strategic communication could be an answer to bring them back into the mainstream.

Conclusion. There is definitely a need to jointly map the OGWs, terrorists and anti-national elements through a multi-agency effort so that the intelligence picture generated is in sync with ground realities and not based on perceptions of various agencies. Due care should also be taken to ensure that police gets the credit for any operation launched based on joint intelligence as their empowerment in the long run will be beneficial. The PSA provides an ideal tool to book anti-national elements and OGWs to prevent them from disrupting peace and security. However, care should be taken to ensure that only hardcore OGWs are booked under this act. Random booking of youths under this act completely eliminates their chances to come back to society and thus would be readily available to the terrorists for indoctrination. Further the time spent in jails should also be monitored so as to prevent them from interacting with hardcore terrorists and fundamentalists. Remember that the Perception and Psyche of the Awaam is the key to the solution of the problem and highest standards of propriety and well thought out strategic communication for the different categories of the OGWs will separate the fish from the pond.

Causal Loop Diagrams

Defining the End Game and Major Factors. The desired end state in the Valley is achieving "Integration with India." This can only be achieved when the Centre of Gravity, i.e., the Awaam or the common people desire to be part of India. The state of "Peace and Prosperity" will then fall into place, as it is more a function of good governance. Peace and Prosperity will encompasses a safe and peaceful environment devoid of threats of violence from militancy, communal clashes and external forces; a prosperous and well-governed society in which the social, economic and political aspirations of the Awaam are fulfilled; and a secular society well integrated with India. This desired end state of "Awaam Support (Sp) for National Integration" is driven by two key factors/elements:

- Militant Activities.
- Sense of Alienation & Resentment.

CLD - Overall IS Situation in Valley

Factors Considered
- Awaam Sp for National Integration.
- Militant Activities.
- Sense of Alienation & Resentment.

Cause and Effect Table

S.No.	Cause	Effect	Type of Relationship
(i)	Sense of Alienation & Resentment	Awaam Sp for National Integration	Opposite
		Militant Activities	Similar
(ii)	Militant Activities	Awaam Sp for National Integration	Opposite
(iii)	Awam Sp for National Integration	Sense of Alienation & Resentment	Opposite
		Militant Activities	Opposite

CLD – Overall is Situation in Valley

Feedback Loops. As Alienation and Resentment of the Awaam increases, the sp for National Integration decreases and vice versa. As sp for National Integration increases, the Alienation and Resentment decreases. This is a mutually reinforcing loop. As Militant Activities increase, the sp for National integration decreases and vice versa. As sp for National Integration increases, the sp for Militancy decreases. This is also a reinforcing loop. The Sense of Alienation also has a similar effect on the Militant activities, in that as the Alienation increases there is increased sp for the Militant Activities. This is a "Success to Successful" Archetype; with increase in Alienation and Resentment, Awaam sp for National Integration decreases which in turn gives a boost to Militancy, which further decreases the National integration.

Leverage Pts. Two leverage pts are of Sense of Alienation and Resentment and Militant Activities. The alienation needs to be reduced and at the same time the militant activities need to be controlled. A strategy needs to be divised to ensure a disconnect between the Alienation and the Militant Activities.

CLD 1 - Sense of Alienation and Resentment. It would include:

- **Factors**
    o Religious Values and Beliefs.

o Perception of People.
o Aspirations of People.
o Grey Population.
o Central Forces Ops.

Cause and Effect Table

S.No.	Cause	Effect	Type of Relationship
(i)	Religious Values and Beliefs	Perception of People	Opposite
		Sense of Alienation & Resentment	Similar
(ii)	Perception of People	Sense of Alienation & Resentment	Opposite
(iii)	Grey Population	Perception of People	Opposite
		Sense of Alienation and Resentment	Similar
(iv)	Central Forces Ops	Sense of Alienation & Resentment	Similar
(v)	Sense of Alienation & Resentment	Grey Population	Similar
		Religious Values and Beliefs	Similar
		Central Forces Ops	Opposite
(vi)	Social Media	Perception of People	Similar/Opposite
(vii)	Historical Grievances	Perception of People	Similar

CLD 1 – Sense of Alienation and Resentment

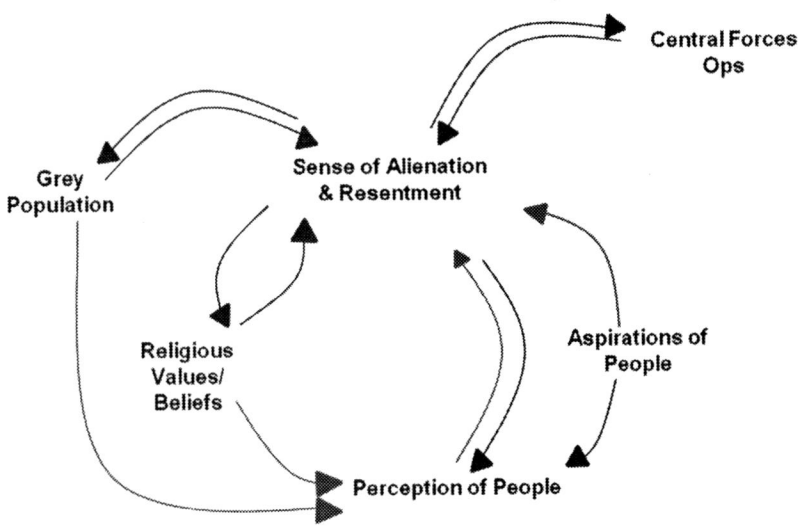

Feedback Loops. There are basically two reinforcing loops as under:

- As sense of alienation increases the sp for grey population (separatists & OGWs) increases, who in turn are able to influence the perception

of people more adversely, adverse perception further alienates the people and vice versa. This is a mutually reinforcing loop.
- More fundamental and non-accommodative religious values/beliefs colour the perception of people thereby increasing the sense of alienation, further affecting the religious beliefs. This also is a mutually reinforcing loop.
- Sense of alienation is also increased by the ops conducted by the Central Security forces, i.e., the Army and CRPF.
- The Perception is also affected by the Social Media and historical grievances.
- The Aspirations of people if met will decrease the sense of alienation and also improve their perception.

Archetypes. "Success to Successfull": The two reinforcing loops work in tandem and further increase/decrease the Sense of Alienation and Resentment.

Leverage Pts. Perception of people, which if managed, will make these loops positive reinforcing loops.

CLD 1(a) – Religious Values/Beliefs. They would include:

Factors

- Kashmiriyat.
- Radicalisation.

Cause and Effect Table

S.No.	Cause	Effect	Type of Relationship
(i)	Kashmiriyat	Religious Beliefs/Values	Opposite
		Communal Harmony	Similar
(ii)	Radicalisation	Kashmiriyat	Opposite
(iii)	Religious Values/Beliefs	Radicalisation	Similar
(iv)	Sufism	Kashmiriyat	Similar
(v)	External Influences	Radicalisation	Similar
(vi)	Pak Sp	External Influences	Similar
(vii)	Pan Islamic movement	External Influences	Similar

CLD 1 (a) – Religious Values/Beliefs

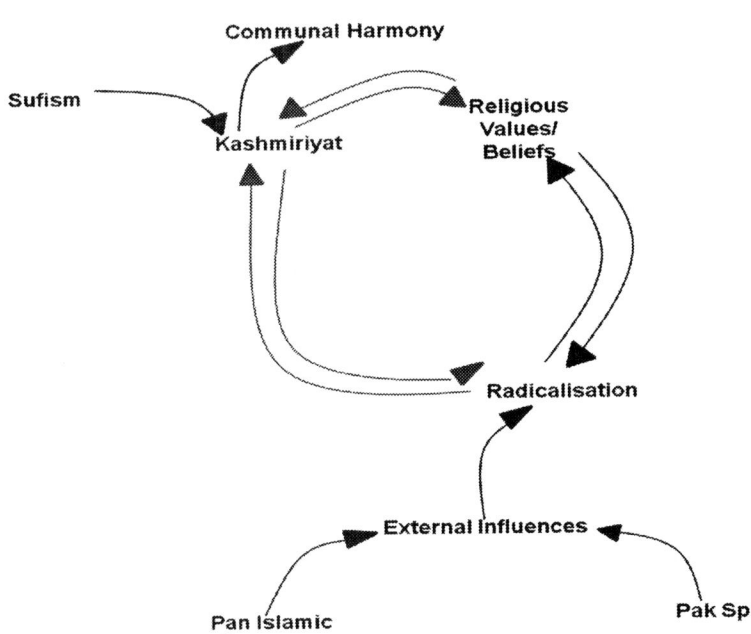

Feedback Loops

- As sense of Kashmiriyat increases, the religious values/beliefs become more accommodative and moderate. As the Religious values/beliefs improve, the Radicalisation of the society reduces, which in turn further improves the Kashmiriyat. This is a reinforcing loop.
- The Kashmiriyat affects Communal Harmony. As Kashmiriyat improves, Communal harmony improves.
- The Radicalisation is fostered by external influences comprising Pak Sp and Pan Islamic Movement sp.

Leverage Pts. Fostering of Kashmiriyat and controlling the external influences on radicalisation.

Archetypes. The two reinforcing loops act in tandem to create a "Success to Successful" Archetype.

CLD 1(b) – Perception of People.

Factors

- Social Media.
- State cap for governance.
- Aspirations of people.

Cause and Effect Table

S.No.	Cause	Effect	Type of Relationship
(i)	Social Media	Perception of People	Similar/Opposite
(ii)	State Capacity for Governance	Aspirations of people	Similar
		Social Media	Similar
(iii)	Aspirations of people	Perception of People	Similar
(iv)	Historical Grievances	Perception of People	Opposite

Feedback Loop. It has two reinforcing loops:
- Good governance ensures that the aspirations of the people are met which in turn realizes in better Perception of people, further giving sp to governance.
- Good governance also ensures positive feedback on the social media, which improves the perceptions.

Archetypes. "Limits to Growth" in case the social media has an opposite effect. The reinforcing loop is offset by the action of the balancing loop. The best strat is good offence. In this case it is better to mitigate or control the effects of the Social Media before it can create substantial impact on results.

Leverage Pts. State capacity for governance and Social Media.

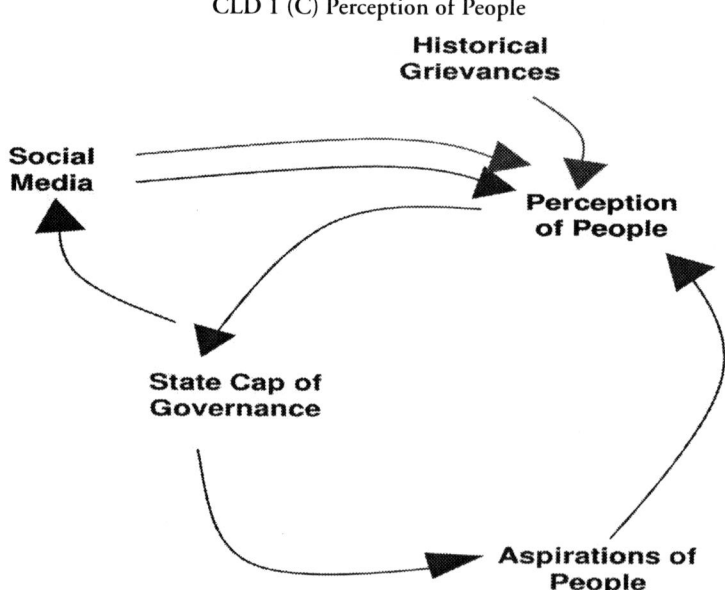

CLD 1 (C) Perception of People

CLD 1(b) (i) – Aspirations of People
Factors

- State Capacity of Governance.
- Prosperity.
- Rehabilitation of Surrendered/Returned Militants.
- Political Environment.
- Aspirations of Youth.
- Aspirations of Kashmiri Pandits.
- Aspirations of Jammu and Ladakh Regions.

Cause and Effect Table

S. No.	Cause	Effect	Type of Relationship
(i)	Aspirations of People	Perception of People	Similar
(ii)	State Capacity of Governance	Aspirations of people	Similar
		Political Environment	Similar
(iii)	Aspirations of Youth	Aspirations of People	Similar
(iv)	Aspirations of Kashmiri Pandits	Aspirations of People	Similar
(v)	Aspirations of Jammu and Ladakh Regions	Aspirations of People	Similar
(vi)	Rehabilitation of Surrendered/Returned Militants	Aspirations of People	Similar
(vii)	Prosperity	Aspirations of People	Similar
(viii)	Political Environment	Aspirations of People	Similar

Feedback Loop. It has two reinforcing loops:

- One of Good governance - Aspirations of the people - Perception of people, as already explained previously.
- The other is of Good governance - Political environment - Aspirations of the people - Perception of people. This is a reinforcing loop.

Leverage Pts. State Capacity for governance.

Archetypes. "Success to Successful".

CLD 1(b) (i) - ASPIRATIONS OF PEOPLE

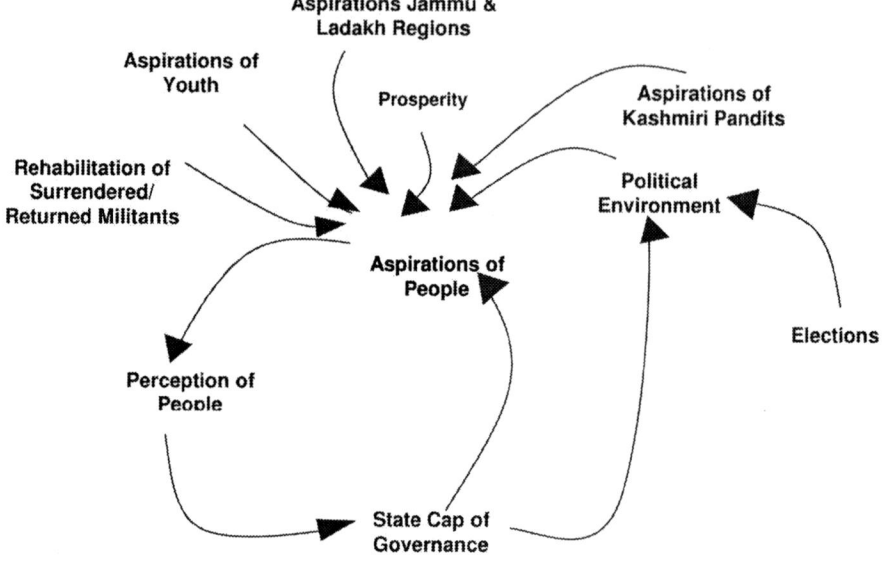

CLD 1(b) (i) (aa) – Prosperity.

Factors

- Aspirations of People.
- Social Inequality.
- Employment (Emp) Generation.
- Economic Activity.

Cause and Effect Table

S.No.	Cause	Effect	Type of Relationship
(i)	Aspirations of People	Economic activity	Similar
		State cap for governance	Similar
(ii)	Social Inequality	Aspirations of people	Opposite
(iii)	Emp Generation	Prosperity	Similar
		Aspirations of Youth	Similar
(iv)	Economic activity	Emp Generation	Similar
		Industrial Activity	Similar
(v)	Prosperity	Aspirations of People	Similar
		Social Inequality	Similar

CLD 1 (b) (i) (aa) Prosperity

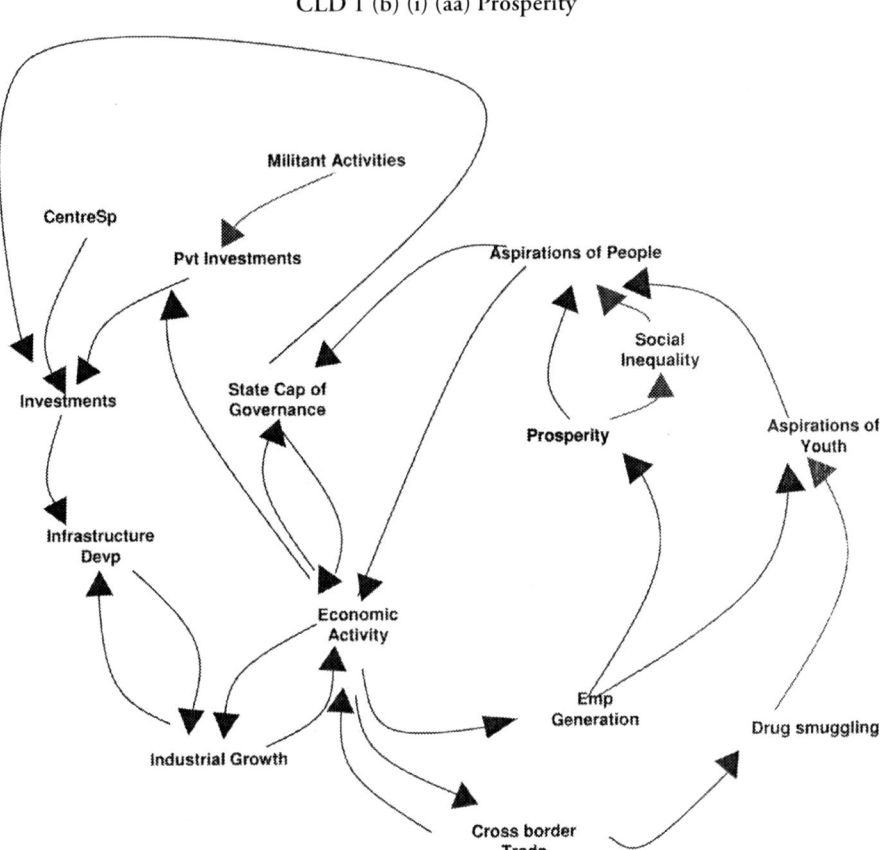

Feedback Loop. It has following loops:

- One loop is of Prosperity fulfilling the Aspirations which in turn motivates people to aspire for more, fuelling demand and economic activity. Economic activity in turn generates emp bringing about prosperity. A reinforcing loop.
- Emp generation also fulfils Aspirations of the youth who add on to the overall fulfilment of the aspirations, further contributing to the reinforcing loop.
- Another loop formed is of Aspirations of people generating confidence in governance further strengthening the economy of the state.
- The loop of Industrial growth - governance - investments - infrastructure development - industrial growth strengthens the CLD of prosperity. This is a reinforcing loop.
- The loop of economic activity generating cross-border trade which

increases the drug smuggling, leading to greater drug addiction in youth and adversely affecting the aspirations of the people and in turn reducing economic activity is a balancing loop.

Archetypes. "Success to Successful", multiple reinforcing loops act in cohesion. There is another archetype "Limits to Growth" when the economic activity loop interacts with drug smuggling balancing loop.

Leverage Pts. State capacity for governance and Economic activity.

CLD 2 – Militant Activities.

Factors

- Org Structure.
- Resources Available.
- Militant Actions.
- Grey Population.
- Central Forces Operations.
- Awaam sp for National Integration.

Cause and Effect Table

S.No.	Cause	Effect	Type of Relationship
(i)	Org Structure	Militant Activities	Similar
(ii)	Resources Available	Militant Activities	Similar
(iii)	Militant Actions	Militant Activities	Similar
		Central Forces Ops	Opposite
(iv)	SF Ops	Militant Activities	Opposite
		Sense of Alienation & Resentment	Similar
(v)	Awaam sp for National Integration	Militant Activities	Opposite
		Central Forces Ops	Similar

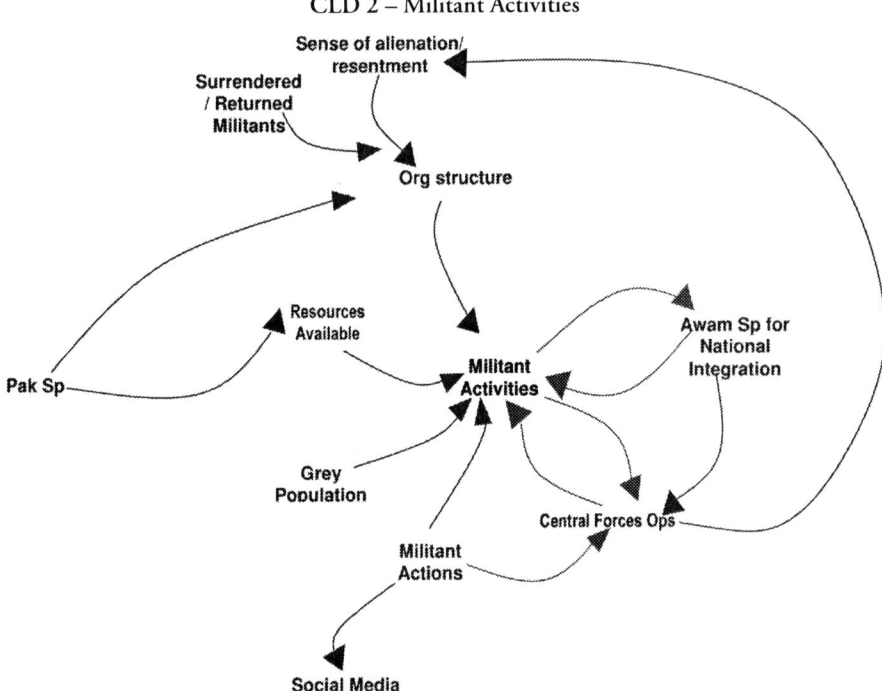

CLD 2 – Militant Activities

Feedback Loops

- First feedback loop is a reinforcing loop wherein Militant Activities reduce Awam's sp for National integration which adversely affects the Central Forces (Army and CRPF) ops thereby increasing effectiveness of Militant Actions.
- Second loop is a balancing loop. Central Forces ops reduce militant activities but at the same time cause harassment to the Awam, increasing their alienation & resentment. This makes them sp the Militancy more.

Archetypes. "Limits to Growth" comprising one reinforcing and a balancing loop.

Leverage Pts. Central Forces ops.

CLD 2(a) - SF OPs

Factors

- CI/CT Ops.
- Int Ops.
- Militant Activities.
- Awam Sp for National Integration.
- Unified HQ.

- Counter Infilt Ops.
- JKP Ops

Cause and Effect Table

Sl.No.	Cause	Effect	Type of Relationship
(i)	CI/CT Ops	SF Ops	Similar
(ii)	Int Ops	SF Ops	Similar
(iii)	Militant Activities	SF Ops	Opposite
(iv)	Unified HQ	SF Ops	Similar
		Int Ops	Similar
(v)	Awaam sp for National Integration	SF Ops	Similar
		Int Ops	Similar
		Sense of alienation	Opposite
(vi)	SF Ops	Awaam sp for National Integration	Similar
		Militant Activities	Opposite

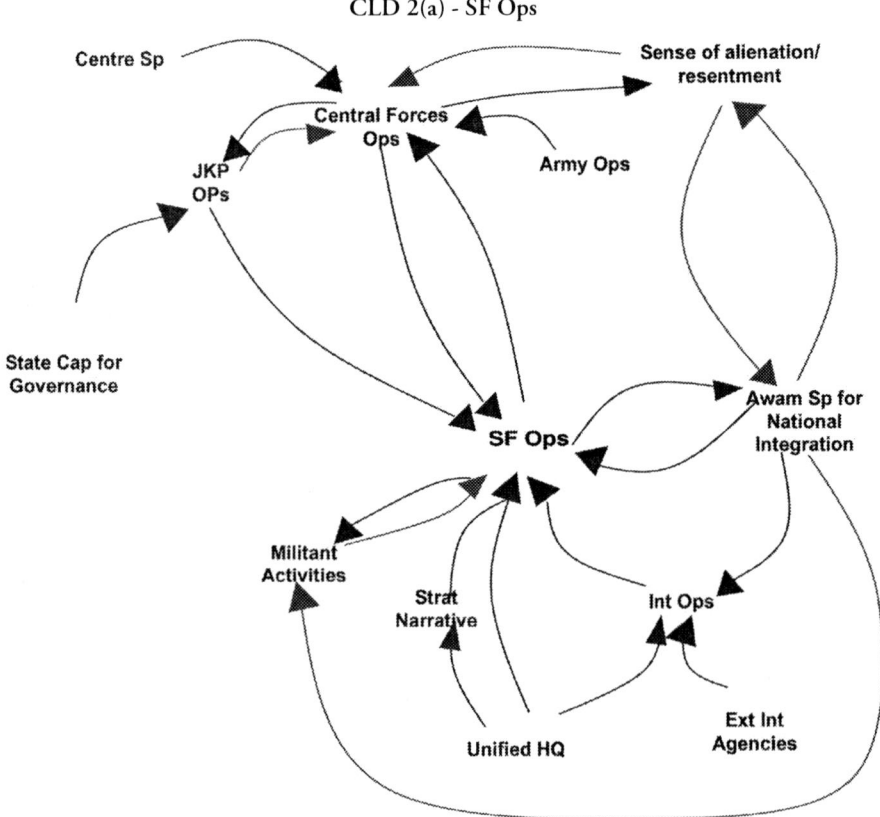

CLD 2(a) - SF Ops

Feedback Loops

- First feedback loop is a reinforcing loop wherein increased effectiveness of SF ops leads to better Awaam sp, which in turn reduces effectiveness of the Militant Activities and improves SF ops. Within is another reinforcing loop of better SF ops leading to better Awam sp, which leads to better intel generation and better SF ops.
- Second loop is a balancing loop. Increase in SF ops leads to increased resentment which decreases the Awaam sp adversely affecting the SF ops. Overall drop in SF ops reduces the Central Forces ops.
- Third is again a balancing loop. Central Forces ops contribute towards increased effectiveness of the JK Police ops, but as the police become more effective, the need of the Central forces reduces.
- Fourth is again a balancing loop of the Militant Activities and the SF ops. As the success of the SF ops improves, the militants change their strategy. The SF also tend to put their guard down. The militants take advantage of this and attack the SF weaknesses thereby reducing its effectiveness.

Archetypes. "Shifting the Burden" comprising two balancing loops and a reinforcing loop. In this archetype, an increase in SF Ops seems to be solving the militancy but it in turn also creates an additional problem of increasing the resentment which leads to increased militancy. We seem to be solving the same problem over and over again. A strat needs to be devised to address the real cause rather than the symptoms.

Leverage Pts. Central Forces ops and Int Ops.

CLD 2(b) (i)- Army OPs

Factors

- CI/CT Ops.
- Int Ops.
- Counter Infilt Ops.
- CRPF Ops.
- Militant Activities.
- Awam Sp for National Integration.
- Jt Ops.
- Sense of Alienation/Resentment.

Cause and Effect Table

S.No.	Cause	Effect	Type of Relationship
(i)	Int Ops	Army Ops	Similar
(ii)	Awam sp for National Integration	Army Ops	Similar
(iii)	Jt Ops	Army Ops	Similar
(iv)	Counter Infilt Ops	Army Ops	Similar
(v)	Army Ops	CI/CT Ops	Similar
		Perception Mgt	Similar
		Sense of Alienation/Resentment	Similar

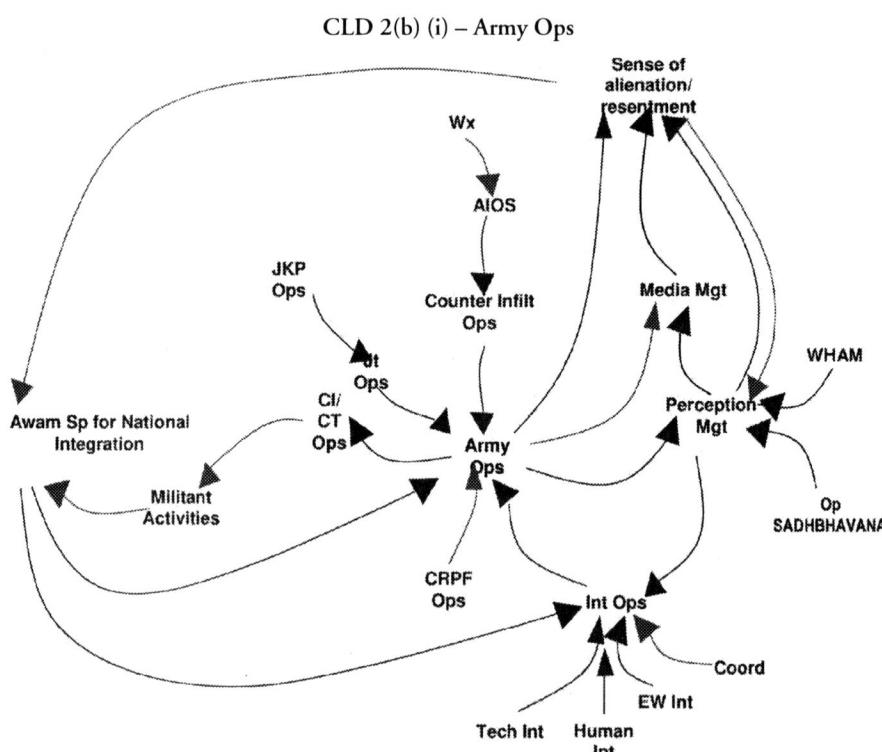

CLD 2(b) (i) – Army Ops

Feedback Loops

- First loop is a balancing loop. Increase in Army ops leads to increased resentment which decreases the Awaam sp adversely affecting the Army ops.
- Second is a balancing loop. Army Forces ops increase the effectiveness of the CI/CT ops which reduces the Militant activities thereby

increasing Awam sp and in turn increasing the effectiveness of Army Ops.
- Third loop involves the Media. With increase in Army ops, the probability of collateral damage increases. This draws Media criticism increasing the alienation and reducing effectiveness of Army subsequently. This again is a balancing loop.

Archetypes. "Escalation" Archetype is created by the two balancing loops of Army ops and the Media, which undermine the effect of Army ops.

Leverage Pts. Perception Mgt, Media.

CLD – Overall CLD

NOTES

1. https://www.burgehugheswalsh.co.uk/Uploaded/1/.../Soft-Systems-Methodology.pdf.
2. www.open.edu/openlearn/ocw/...php/.../Introducing-systems-approaches_ch1.pdf.
3. Ibid.
4. Thompson, John L., Understanding Corporate Strategy, Cengage Learning EMEA, 2001, p. 53.
5. http://www.rarebooksocietyofindia.org/book_archive/196174216674_10153460989311675.pdf, pp. 273-283, accessed on March 15, 2018.
6. https://qrius.com/terrorism-social-media, accessed on Feb 22, 2018.
7. www.dailyexcelsior.com/social-media-and-terrorism, accessed on Feb 22, 2018.
8. Ibid.
9. http://www.claws.in/images/publication_pdf/ Psychological Aspects in Kashmir: Why Kashmiriyat Has Won Against Haivaniyat=ASChonker(Final).pdf, accessed on August 2018.
10. Ibid.
11. http://www.satp.org/satporgtp/sair/Archives/sair8/8_35.htm, accessed on March 2, 2018.
12. https://www.indiatoday.in/india/story/sunjuwan-attack-terrorists-were-operating-in-india-for-10-months-conducted-recce-of-army-camp-1167509-2018-02-12, accessed on March 2, 2018.
13. https://economictimes.indiatimes.com/news/defence/jammu-and-kashmir-police-revising-list-of-suspected-over-ground-workers-of-militants/articleshow/65664094.cms, accessed on September 5, 2018.
14. https://economictimes.indiatimes.com/news/politics-and-nation/jk-terror-funding-nia-chargesheet-reveals-nexus-between-terrorists-hurriyat-and-stone-pelters/videoshow/62758073.cms, accessed on September 6, 2018.
15. https://timesofindia.indiatimes.com/india/nia-arrests-hizbul-chief-syed-salahuddins-son-shakeel-in-jk-terror-funding-case/articleshow/65611181.cms, accessed on September 6, 2018.

CHAPTER 4
Psychological Aspects of Kashmir and their Solutions

Psycholigical Aspects
- Although these aspects have been discussed in Chapter 2, linkages and effects need to be studied in greater depth in order to derive solutions.
- Kashmiriyat per se is the ethno-national and social consciousness and cultural values of the Kashmiri people. Emerging around the 16th century, it is characterised by religious and cultural harmony, patriotism and pride for their mountainous homeland of Kashmir. There is no rocket science required to come to conclusion that this culture of Kashmir needs to be rejuvenated and reinforced.
- To study Kashmiriyat, we must understand the basic tenets of "**Human Behaviour.**" As human beings, we all have our own values, beliefs and attitudes that we have developed throughout the course of our lives. Attitudes are a powerful element life in Kashmir; these are long enduring and hard to change—but not impossible! If we were to draw an iceberg, the deepest part is Cultural and social norms which get developed over Centuries. Kashmiriyat is this "Culture" of Kashmir. Within this Culture too there is a small visible portion and a major unseen portion which is below the surface and is constantly evolving, and sometimes mutating through changes in Attitudes, Values, Beliefs as well as Feelings and Perceptions.[1]
- Pakistan's "inner front strategy" as well as the "misperception strategy" has tried to target the invisible culture of Kashmir by proactively creating narrative after narrative which is also slowly affecting the values, beliefs and attitude of the people of Kashmir. Through proxy war elements, the temperature is set to below boiling point and it takes a small incident to boil. Some of the aspects which need attention are:

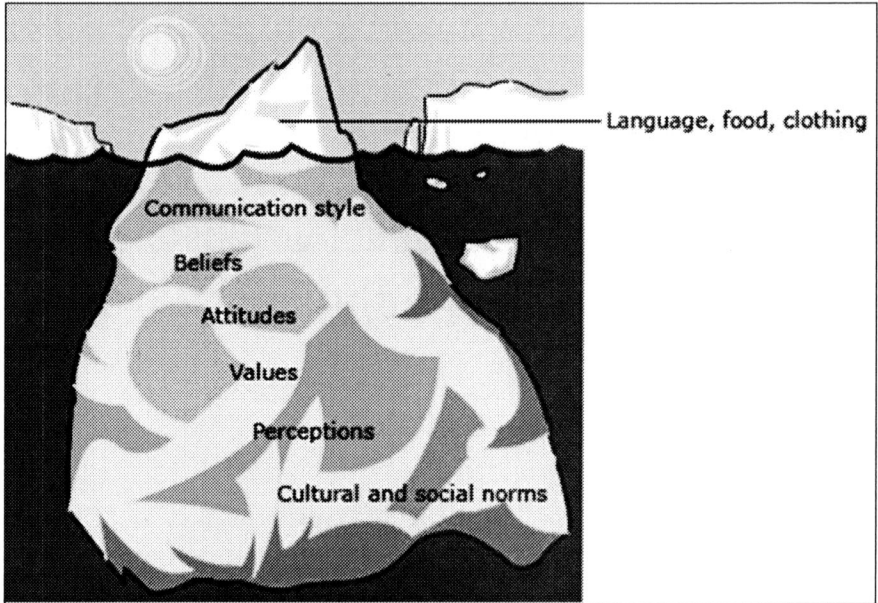

- **Spread of Fundamentalism.** Although this topic has also been dealt in great detail in Chapter 2, some additional points need to be highlighted under the Psychological aspects. Around the year 2007, many Kashmiri Muslims saw the Indian government's moves to increase cooperation with US and Israel as a proof that it is a part of a global anti-Muslim axis. This was overplayed by communication networks. These networks also spread ideas of fundamentalist ideas propagated by Tablighi Jamaat and Ahl-e-Hadith.[2] The Tablighi Jamat acted as the pull for even secular Sufi Muslim youth of Kashmir as it urges the muslims to invite (dawah) the ways of a good muslim (deen) in their own lives so that other non-believers can join their ranks. Religious scholars in Kashmir point out that Ahl-e-Hadith has four sub-schools—Jamait-ul-ahl-e-Hadith (puritan), Difai (ultra-puritan), Guraba (religio-political ultra-puritan) and Sout-ul-Haq, represented by ISIS, where a nonconformist is "wajib-ul-qatl" (eligible for murder)[3].
- **Turmoiled History.** Power equations have changed over a period of time and it is always the human behaviour of trying to be at the centre of power which has been the main reason for neglecting the aspirations of the state. Almost all the important leaders have played with the emotions of the people to achieve their objectives. Most of

the political leaders barring a few had myopic views, had visions to suit their political agenda and were amenable to manipulation. The alleged rigging of elections in 1987 was yet another classical example of political parties trying all means to come to power. Finally, to add to the woes, Pakistan jumped into the fray yet again with a well laid out proxy war to manipulate the situation created by our own undoing. Over a period of last seventy years, no state of the Indian Union has seen such a huge shift in the aspirations of the people from Azadi to becoming part of Pakistan to being part of India, with three totally different scenarios with the Awaam of Kashmir also swaying as the wind blew. Dealing with a Kashmiri in the valley definitely needs a *Kashmiri outlook* and cannot be compared with any other state. There is a need to mould them gradually to our mainstream rather than force them to accept a particular thought.

o **Kashmiri Psyche.** This particular aspect has been explained in great detail in Chapter 3 on System Analysis; hence, it is not being reproduced here but is extremely important in the context of Psychological Aspects.

The Current International Situation

- The Kashmir situation cannot be seen in isolation and there is a need to understand the current international environment. After the Cold War ended, Terrorism has changed significantly from politically motivated to ideological extremism, driven by religion and ethno-nationalism. Extremism, as part of the problem has also spread globally with the common theme "unstructured chaos" with the goal to co-opt or coerce the targeted population to support their extremist ideology by systematically delegitimized the government, create anarchy, and gain control of the targeted population. Violent extremism could, therefore, be stated as of the main driving forces of global terrorism. Globally, violent extremists have leveraged technology and communicated their concept of violence to their followers through various media, primarily social media such as Facebook, Twitter, YouTube, etc., and used languages tailored for their specific global audiences. As the result, foreign fighters from around the world, including Muslims from England, France and Europe joined forces with the terrorist group who efficiently utilized extremist concept to fight for the caliphate.

- In a recently concluded International Seminar on Countering Violent Extremism, the Vice Chairman, China Institute of International Studies, China, Maj. Gen. Nhang Jianguo articulated the current situation on the ISIS front. He said that in recent years, with the joint efforts of the international community, the "ISIS" has been badly hit in Iraq and Syria, and the international war on terror achieved great progress. Presently, although the "ISIS" is gone as a "state", it still exists as an organization and the violent extremist ideology it advocates still lingers, which has made terrorism one of the uppermost security threat to the international community. He also mentioned that after the collapse of the "ISIS", the over-spilling effect of violent terrorism is outstanding, with violent extremists speeding up their evacuation and committing crimes back in their home countries, and violent terrorist activities operating on high levels. Fighting against violent extremism with forces cures only the symptoms but not the disease. Coupled with the impacts of game played by big powers and geopolitical factors, the international community is still confronted with multiple new challenges and new problems to cope with in the field of counter-terrorism.

- In the same Seminar Mr Elyaminne Settoul, Lecturer in political science, Conservatoire national des arts et métiers explained the high number of French jihadists. He explained that France is host to Europe's largest Muslim population. Whilst the share of converts engaged in radical militancy can at times be substantial, it is established that the majority of fighters who joined the Islamic State were raised in Muslim cultural heritage families (practicing or not). Consequently, the potential pool of French candidates to jihad is structurally larger than in most European countries. Although French jihadists display a great diversity of sociological and geographical origins, the bulk of the recruiting ground hails from disadvantaged urban areas. Located at the periphery of most large cities in France, the banlieues are places of social marginalization, where inhabitants are the primary victims of discrimination in access to housing, employment and in their relations to the police. Socially mixed when they were first built in the 1960s, French banlieues have progressively become ethnicized and ghettoized from the 1980s onwards. Undercurrents unfold in a multitude of binary oppositions that oversimplify the reality: whites/visible minorities; policemen/banlieue youth; rich/poor; Israelis/Palestinians. Such otherization of "them" against "us" creates an environment conducive to breakaway and radical attitudes.

International Solutions Addressing the Cognitive Domain

- **The British Experience.** The three-fold response of the UK government to the recent spate of terror-related incidents in the country has yielded rich dividends. Firstly, the social media companies were given an ultimatum to eradicate/filter radicalizing offensive literature and videos from their platforms in UK. This resulted in a 98% decrease in such online literature which could lead to radicalization and recruitment. Secondly, they have upgraded their artificial Intelligence monitoring system to identify probable recruiters, overground Workers and radicalized elements. Thirdly, they have taken the assistance of Non-governmental organizations like the "London tigers" to spread the message of peace and well-being through their community development programs in order to prevent people from undertaking violent extremist acts as also reach out to suspected affected cases.

- **The Indonesian Response.** First Admiral Dr M. Anan Majid, Vice Dean, National Security Faculty, Indonesian Defence University explained the concept of Network-Based Conflict Early Warning and Response System (CEWERS). It is a concept which illustrates various activities to conflict prevention. The assumption in CEWERS concept is usually referred to the analogy that conflict is a cycle, which includes, conflict prevention steps, intervention to stop violence (peacekeeping), negotiation to create peace (peace-making) and also the effort to develop positive peace in order to establish long-term resilience. He also explained the efforts of **"Bela Negara"**, the community empowerment strategy from Indonesia which has been instrumental in not only countering violent extremism but also has successfully built social resilience against radicalization through synergetic cooperation between the government and the communities through smart power. Badan Nasional Penanggulangan Terorisme (BNPT) as the Indonesian agency that works to prevent terrorism could not achieve as much through hard power that interactions with local Ulema and community groups that generated the adequate soft power could do.

- **The Singaporean Concept.** Dr Jolene Jerard, Deputy Head of the International Centre for Political Violence and Terrorism Research, Singapore, explained the effect of radicalization in the society of Singapore and the counter measures being undertaken by their government.

- The **TRIDENT** concept incorporates/addresses the Transforming power of technology, Recruitment and radicalization, Innovativeness, Dense pollination of ideas, evolving trends, new tradecrafts and last but not the least Trusted networks which can be utilized for this fight. The concept envisages the use of transformative power of technology to prevent recruitment and radicalisation and thereby be ahead in the field of innovation by understanding the vectors in a way that could save lives and prevent families from getting destroyed.

- There is a need to be ahead of the terrorists and their masters in Innovation and the learning curve. This could be done through intelligence breakthroughs. A recent case was that of weaponizing the family unit as a tool for jihad.

- Addressing the cognitive domain through a dense pollination of ideas is the universal approach that the handlers and overground workers are exploiting for leading unknowing youth into the trap of fighting for an unrighteous jihad. Radical Islam may not be the only guiding light for the disenchanted.

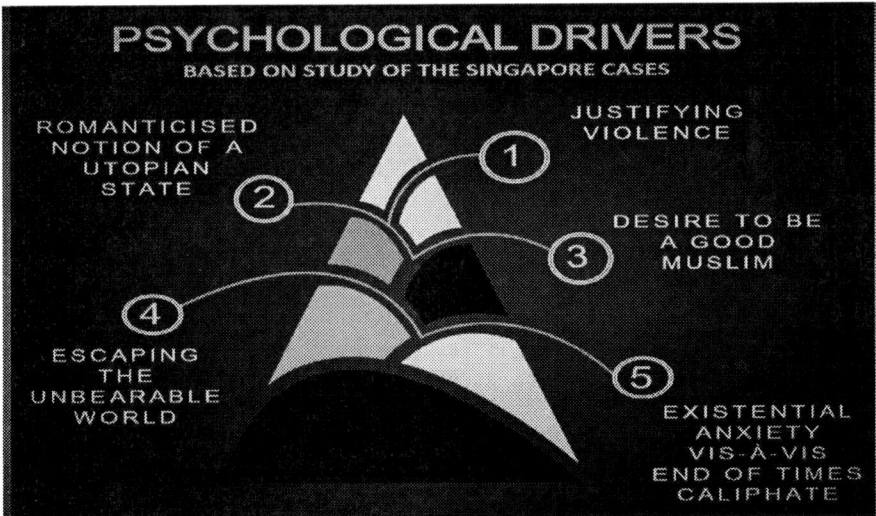

- Evolving trends (a sequence of critical events of consequence) give us an insight of the things to follow. Hence, trend analysis is of utmost importance in the business of countering violent Extremism.

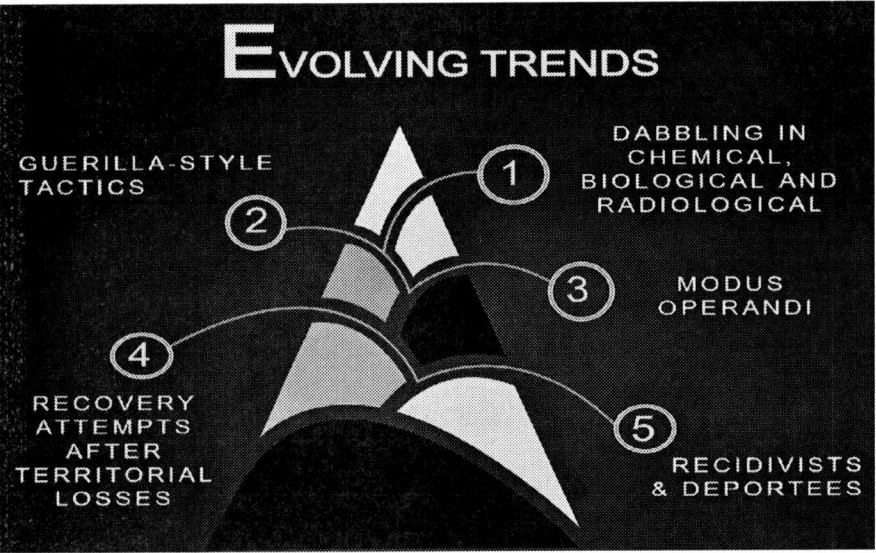

- New tradecraft being employed by the extremists like Inghimasi[4] attacks or lonewolf attacks and its psychoanalysis will help us in getting into the minds of the extremists. An ear to the ground in this regard will pay rich dividends.

- Lastly, trusted networks like security agencies, educational institutions, grassroots organisations and community groups are important to counter the extremist networks.

Strategic Communication Solutions in the Kashmir Context

- If the Psyche of the people is the Centre of Gravity, then Communication strategies like Perception improvement will directly address the Centre of Gravity. Perception management/improvement includes all actions used to influence the attitudes and objective reasoning of foreign and domestic audiences and consists of Public Diplomacy, Psychological Operations, Public Information, Deception and Covert Action. The main goal is to influence friends and enemies, provoking them to engage in the behavior that is suitable to achieve the desired end state. While the exercise of perception management has been carrying on in the Kashmir valley for years, by way of "Sadhbhavna" and other measures, these are being rejected of late, by the radicalized youth as a symbol of state hegemony, as these do not have the foot prints of traditional governance. There needs to be a more focused and concerted approach towards the same which is carried out at all levels over a sustained manner. We need to make a counter-narrative to the Idea of Radicalization through picturization of the success story of development and freethinking futuristic India as a Nation too as compared to many nearly failed states in the vicinity.

- Everyone seems to understand what is wrong in the back drop of proxy war, but one is yet to see a comprehensive concept model which can form a part of a holistic solution to the problem.

The PRIME ANTENNA Concept Model. This is a holistic concept model which requires the participation of many organs of the government so that the Centre of Gravity is addressed at all levels coherently and simultaneously.

An antenna is a non-intrusive tool or device which is omnipresent yet quietly listens and not gets in the face of communities. It is a widely accepted device which gets the ideas of the world to your living room. For obvious reasons, a concept like the TRIDENT would have been outwardly rejected by the Kashmiri Awaam due to the name. The Acronym PRIME ANTENNA is explained below:

- **Promote Kashmiriyat/Sufi Culture.** *Kashmiriyat* is believed to be an expression of solidarity, resilience and patriotism **regardless of religious differences**. Largely funded from abroad, the masses of people remain secular. Nothing could demonstrate this better than the fact that ordinary Kashmiri Muslims are even today eagerly awaiting the return of their Pandit brothers and sisters who had left the valley at the height of militancy. It has surprised many observers that, contrary to the general experience of communal rioting in most parts of the sub-continent, Kashmiri Muslims have been looking after the homes and hearths of their migrated Kashmiri Pandit brothers for years in the fond hope that one day there would be peace and they would be able to return.[5] This culture and Sufi Islam will show the world the benevolent and secular side of Islam. There is a need to leverage this culture. Is it not possible to have a week-long world Sufi festival in Kashmir? Let us as a nation provide the requisite security to cultural Sufi artists from across the world to come and teach and perform in Kashmir and let the excerpts from this festival run on the media channels for a month and the results will be evident.

- Respond Full spectrum. In order to have a holistic approach of going after the organizational and operational tools of terror as discussed in chapter 2, for long-term effects a full-spectrum response as given below will pay rich dividends.

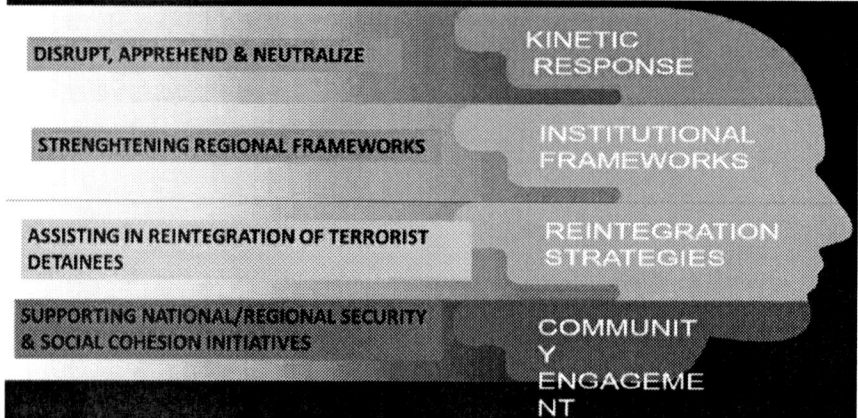

It is of utmost importance that we understand the characteristics of radical Ideology when we plan for the full-spectrum response and the graphic below can serve as a useful guide.

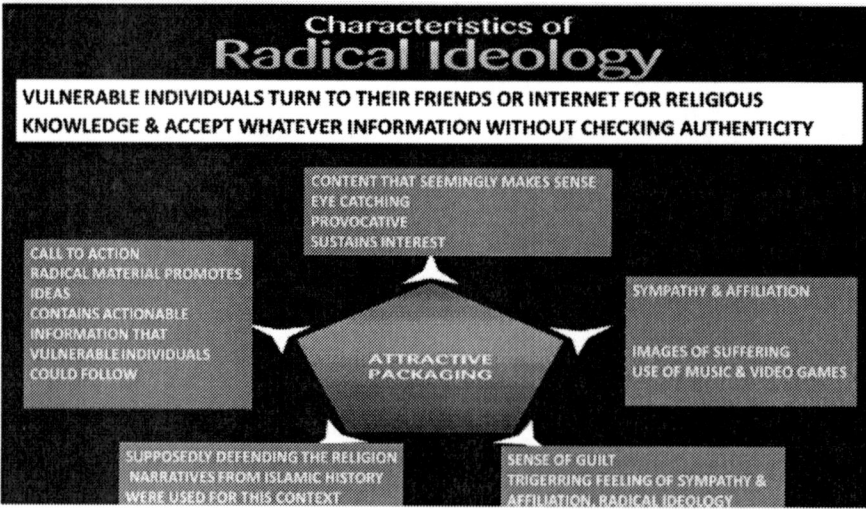

- Integrate the Power of Technology. If the above graphic is seen with a microscopic eye, one would realize that it is the power of technology that is being utilized by the extremists and their handlers in order to derive the desired results in terms of recruitments and to keep the pot boiling. According to the Survey attached at Appendix B, more than **80% youth of Kashmir region use Social Media** (SM). Around **75%** said the contents were **Not Very Truthful** (28%) or **Sometimes Truthful** (34%). Around **32%** affirmed getting influenced by SM and **28% had heard people getting radicalised** through SM. There is a distinct need to integrate the power of technology to deter such activity. Social Media platforms and Vernacular media can only be reined in if one understands the science and technology behind their functioning. Artificial Intelligence to monitor suspicious activities, creating mobile apps to counter radical propaganda and as a support system to vulnerable portions of the society, which will also ensure that data can be accessed without circuitous permissions from foreign-based social media companies, is just a gallon in an ocean of possibilities. Today, not only the Kashmiri society but also the whole country needs social leaders as much as political leaders and it is not a figment of anybody's imagination that these can be created through the proper use of technology. The use of the power of information communication technology and its intensity can be better controlled by the legitimate state than the proxy war identities. The widespread use of networks by the extremist groups has helped the violent extremist activities infiltrate into every aspect of social life. As a result, an all-dimensional situational awareness system of the network threats posed by violent extremism should be built to effectively identify, track, investigate and control such activities as communication and propaganda by violent extremists by collating massive network information through various means. Meanwhile, data and information obtained should be put together and comprehensively studied so as to paint a holistic picture of the activities conducted by the violent extremist groups through networks. Currently, some countries have already built the data model (DM) of network activities by the violent extremist groups, which would provide important information support.

- Manage Perceptions Internationally. One of the biggest feeders to separatism and extremist views in Kashmir is the International Perception that grave injustice is being done to the people. According to the Survey, 28.6% youth believed only International news channels. We have failed as a nation by not creating a positive perception in our favour. The narrative of Partition and the grave atrocities by Pakistani raiders on the Kashmiri people is not known by nine out of ten people internationally who matter. A concerted effort in this regard is due. The threat of ISIS pan-Islamization ideology is far from over and a concerted effort by the world community will be required to fight it. This aspect can be leveraged as a symbol of intolerance to terrorism of any kind in the international arena, to improve the world's perception on Kashmir too. There will be a requirement of enhancing the diplomatic effort for a few years at least.

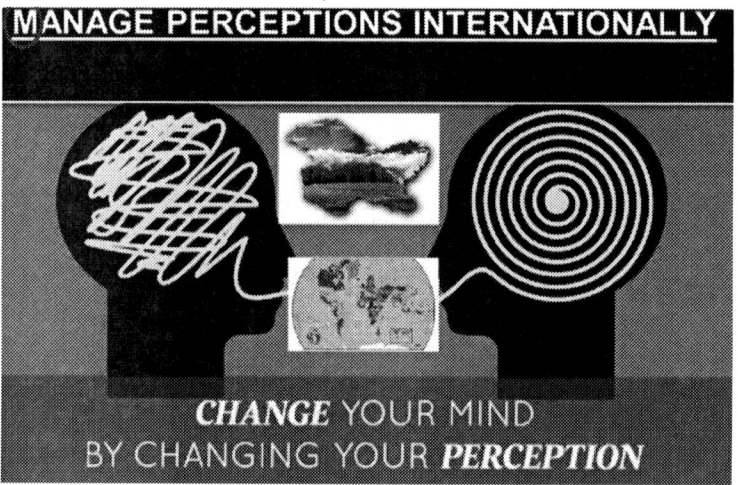

- Engage. Engagement with the people of Kashmir especially the youth is the need of the hour. Generalizations of "us" against "them" as is being picturized by many TV channels will only lead to a negative loop in the system. Mr Dineshwar Sharma's appointment as an Interlocutor was received coldly by Kashmiris,[6] may be because of internal politics of supremacy within the then functional state government. Here is a chance under the Governor's rule for the Centre to make a genuine effort to reach out to the people through dialogue. He must not be seen though only interlocuting with the peaceniks. There is a need to enlarge the envelope to include slain terrorist families and know their mind. Engaging with the network of mothers of slain militants and making them feel a sense of loss will reverse the openness with which the families have started offering their children for the cause of extremism. Engagement amongst the three regions of the state is as important in order to eradicate the Banihal and the Zojila divide. Religious rehabilitation is another area of engagement that can be undertaken as a challenge. **Trust on Religious Institutions and Leaders appeared to be far more** as around **65%** respondents expressed a great deal of trust (**21%**) or some trust (**44%**) in Survey; **84%** said that they visited **Religious Institutions** in spare time with **40% doing so frequently**. Needs no gain saying that for this endeavour to be successful it is important to win the confidence of the expert panel of religious teachers and scholars. Experiments in order to give weightage to their "waaz" as a tool of governance may be incorporated in order to win their confidence to start with. Engaging and training the teachers will also pay rich dividends as after the family, the teachers are the most trusted (91.9% of respondents trusted them as per the above-quoted survey carried out in the colleges of Kashmir).

  Engagement through sports is a great area where pent-up emotions can be redirected. There is a need of constructing 2800 sports fields in the valley itself. Self-worth in the own body through the power of sports could start a movement against the demented thought process of death and destruction as the only alternatives.

- Assuage Feelings through Greater Autonomy. Demand for "Greater Autonomy or Self-Rule" has been the major bone of contention between the centre and state govts over the decades. Political will has to be garnered in order to work out a formula which may not be detrimental to the spirit of our constitution and the idea of India.

- Networks Can Only Beat a Network. Since the violent extremist groups have taken networks as their major vehicle to spread violent terrorist ideas and inflict psychological intimidation, efforts should be made to strengthen online and offline propaganda, innovate methods and means, engage in psychological intervention, refute extreme arguments, and clean up the infiltration of the violent terrorist ideas. For example, YouTube proposed the "reorientation scheme" in July of 2017, prioritizing in sending video clips involving anti-extremist ideas to users likely influenced by the violent extremist groups like the "ISIS" to restrict the network propaganda and recruitment by the violent extremist groups. We should plan to create a network of young Kashmiri entrepreneurs and name them the "Kashmir Leopards" or even better as "Lolab leopards", "Kulgam Kings", "Pulwama Panthers", create a network of positive change which works for peace and prosperity in the state, there is a need to create a network of social leaders in the state. The state has been relying to get panacea from the political leaders for far too long and an alternate system of leadership needs to be created in order to fill the vacuum.

- Trends - Identify through regular Analysis to be ahead in the Proxy war. A central body needs to be created within the NIA which continuously monitors events and trends with the help of trained analysts to remain ahead in the proxy war. A core group could be created from domain specialists available in leading think tanks of the country who could carry out trend analysis and advise the National Security Council on a weekly basis.

- **Empower.** There is a dire need to empower the youth politically. An initiative to train children to understand the power of ballot in schools and colleges will wean them away from inimical forces advocating democratic boycott. Social empowerment will entail the reemergence of the institution of "Mokdam" or the village elder who can influence the young minds through his position which is devoid of political affiliations. Ex-servicemen settled in villages can be utilized for social causes and empowerment. Technical training centres for employment generation will also help in economic upliftment. Psychological conditioning through positive narratives in print and social media will assist in countering terrorist agenda. The circle of spaces has to be filled through empowerment else they fill be filled by a negative agenda. Good governance would also undoubtedly lead to empowerment of the people. Mental health support through premier social science institutes is also a means of empowerment.

    This empowerment will not only lead to rehabilitation of the people who want to come back to the mainstream but also make the community more resilient against the machinations of terror and evolve a strong partnership between the government and the community.

- **Name and Shame Pak Propaganda and OGWs.** At the UN Human Rights Council meeting in Geneva, New Delhi, for the first time,[7] used its "right to reply" to send a strong message to its neighbour. Diplomatic offensives have also been taken up to serve the cause of naming and shaming Pakistan as perpetrator of proxy war and violent extremism in India and these efforts need to be continued. OGWs have always been the mainstay for an insurgency Movement. Previously, OGWs were primarily involved in logistics support and intelligence gathering. Of late the distinction has blurred considerably with OGWs also capable of carrying out small-scale strikes while retaining the capability to mix rapidly with the population. The comparative freedom of movement available to terrorists due to limited resource control measures has emboldened the terrorists to change their strategy of trying to mix up with population. Intelligence sources need to isolate and put them to justice. Caution may be a virtue to avoid a "catch them and bump them off culture by the Police" which may be prevalent in earlier phases of militancy as discussed by David Devadas in his book *The Generation of Rage in Kashmir*. Families of terrorists killed in encounters are also playing a negative role in vitiating the environment and appear as martyrs. These elements also need to be tackled and shown in bad light through credible sting operations.

- New Tradecraft - Negate it. Learn from the world of the new tradecraft being employed like the Inghimasi attacks, lone wolfs and many more in order to negate these. Understand the constantly evolving support ecosystem shouldering this extremist movement through a core group from think tanks which can find solutions against the new tradecraft being employed.

- Address the Cognitive Domain through Narratives of Peace and Prosperity. A significant share of terrorists is looking for a sense of identity and self-worth. Narratives of peace and prosperity and success stories highlighted over FM channels and social media will provide them an alternative. Psychological rehabilitation as a preventive strategy will pay rich dividends. Mental health camps and social scientists will be the drivers in this regard.

A comprehensive CAPS strategy from Correction to Support as given below will address the cognitive domain to a large extent.

NARRATIVES AND THEMES.......

The SPEAR (S - STRENGTHENING SOLIDARITY, P - PRESERVING HARMONY, E - EMBRACING DIVERSITY, A - ADVOCATING ENGAGEMENT, R - RECIPROCATING RESPECT) narrative could be one good example of creating alternate narratives to fear, terror, death and despondency.

Conclusion

The above model could form a basis of tackling the Psychological aspects related to Extremism and wean the population towards peace and prosperity. Psychology in the Valley is deeply intertwined with society and religion and therefore the mantra for success can be from heads to hearts to hands (action) towards peace and prosperity.

NOTES

1. http://www.claws.in/images/publication_pdf/570745787_IB-118-ColASChonker(Final).pdf, Psychological Aspects of Kashmir, accessed on August 20, 2018
2. Devadas, David, The Generation of Rage in Kashmir, Oxford University Press, p. 15.
3. https://timesofindia.indiatimes.com/india/how-mosques-and-mobiles-are-radicalising-kashmir/articleshow/59507200.cms, accessed on August 16 2018.
4. https://www.secureamericanow.org/inghimasi_isis_s_deadly_tactial_approach, accessed on July 28, 2018.
5. www.greaterkashmir.com/news/opinion/the-return-of-migrants/247099.html, accessed on July 29, 2018.
6. https://www.thehindu.com/news/national/why-was-jk-cold-to-interlocutor/article20551716.ece, accessed on June 30, 2018.
7. https://economictimes.indiatimes.com/news/politics-and-nation/for-the-first-time-india-uses-right-to-reply-to-cut-short-paks-kashmir-blame-game/articleshow/47918727.cms, accessed on July 29, 2018.

CHAPTER 5
SWOT Analysis and Short-Term Strategies

Introduction

After having carried out a detailed analysis of the Psychological landscape affecting the Psyche of Kashmiris, let's get back to scientific analysis for generating short-term strategies. Although a detailed internal and external scan has already been carried out in Chapter 2, some of key issues need to be further elaborated. The state of Jammu and Kashmir comprises three regions, namely Kashmir, Jammu and Ladakh. The State is further divided into 22 districts: 2 in Ladakh and 10 each in Jammu and Kashmir. The number of Tehsils and CD Blocks are 82 and 142, respectively. There are as many as 6652 villages and 68 urban areas besides seven urban agglomerations.[1]

Geography. Only a small portion of its total area of J&K, approximately 85,000 square miles (220,000 square km) is well suited to human settlement. Of particular note is the fertile Valley of Kashmir, a valley roughly 80 miles long and up to 35 miles wide (130 × 55 km) astride the upper Jhelum River. It supports an economy based on tourism, handicraft industries and intensive agriculture. Two other favorable areas are of note: the foothills of the Himalayas, together with a narrow strip of the adjoining plain, in southern Jammu, and the northwestern extension of that region, comprising the greater part of PoK. These mainly agricultural areas are all relatively well-irrigated and, where not cleared for cultivation, support rich coniferous forests. Between southern Jammu and PoK on the one hand and the Valley on the other is the Pir Panjal mountain range, which, despite its rugged nature, supports a moderately dense and partially migratory population dependent on largely terraced agriculture, pastoralism, and forestry. Through these mountains must pass the overland traffic connecting the Valley with the plains of India. In the immediate aftermath of the partition of the state in 1947-48, this traffic was funneled through the Banihal Pass, which, at an elevation of 9,290 feet (2,830 meters), was often closed by winter snows. This problem has been mitigated, however, though not entirely eliminated, by the construction of the Jawaharlal Nehru Tunnel at a significantly lower elevation, and by increasing reliance on air transportation. A much easier and formerly much more heavily utilized route to and from the Valley ran through the Baramula gap by which the Jhelum River flows to what are now PoK and Pakistan. Along the North Eastern flank of the Valley runs the main range of the Himalayas. This enormous mountain chain extends from the eastern border region of the North-West Frontier Province of Pakistan southeastward to and well beyond the southern border of Jammu and Kashmir. Forested on their windward southwestern flanks, the Himalayas present a dramatically different, largely barren, aspect to the northeast. There the terrain gives way to the high, arid regions of Pakistan-occupied Baltistan, administered as a part of the Northern Areas, and Ladakh. These two thinly populated regions, comprising well over half the total area of the state, form a western extension of the Plateau of Tibet and are compartmentalized by a series of mountain ranges, generally paralleling the main crest of the Himalayas. They support scattered patches of agriculture, largely dependent on small-scale irrigation works, along with sheep, goat and yak-based pastoralism. An even more barren area, further to the northeast, is known as the Aksai Chin (White Stone Desert), which is held by China since the 1960s.[2]

Demography. Jammu and Kashmir has a Muslim majority population. As per 2011 census, though Islam is practiced by about 67% of the population of the state and by 97% of the population of the Kashmir valley, the state has large communities of Buddhists, Hindus (inclusive of Megh Bhagats) and Sikhs. In Jammu, Hindus constitute 65% of the population, Muslims 31% and Sikhs 4%. In Ladakh, Buddhists constitute about 46% of the population, the remaining being Muslims. The people of Ladakh are of Indo-Tibetan origin, while the southern area of Jammu includes many communities tracing their ancestry to the nearby Indian states. In totality, the Muslims constitute 67% of the population, the Hindus about 30%, the Buddhists 1%, and the Sikhs 2% of the population. Buddhists, Hindus, Sikhs and a few Christian, Jain, and Zoroastrian communities were once natives and made up a vast majority of the whole Kashmir province, but because of economic changes, riots, political tension, military involvement, and foreign extremists resulted in vast majority of the followers of these religions to settle in the growing and

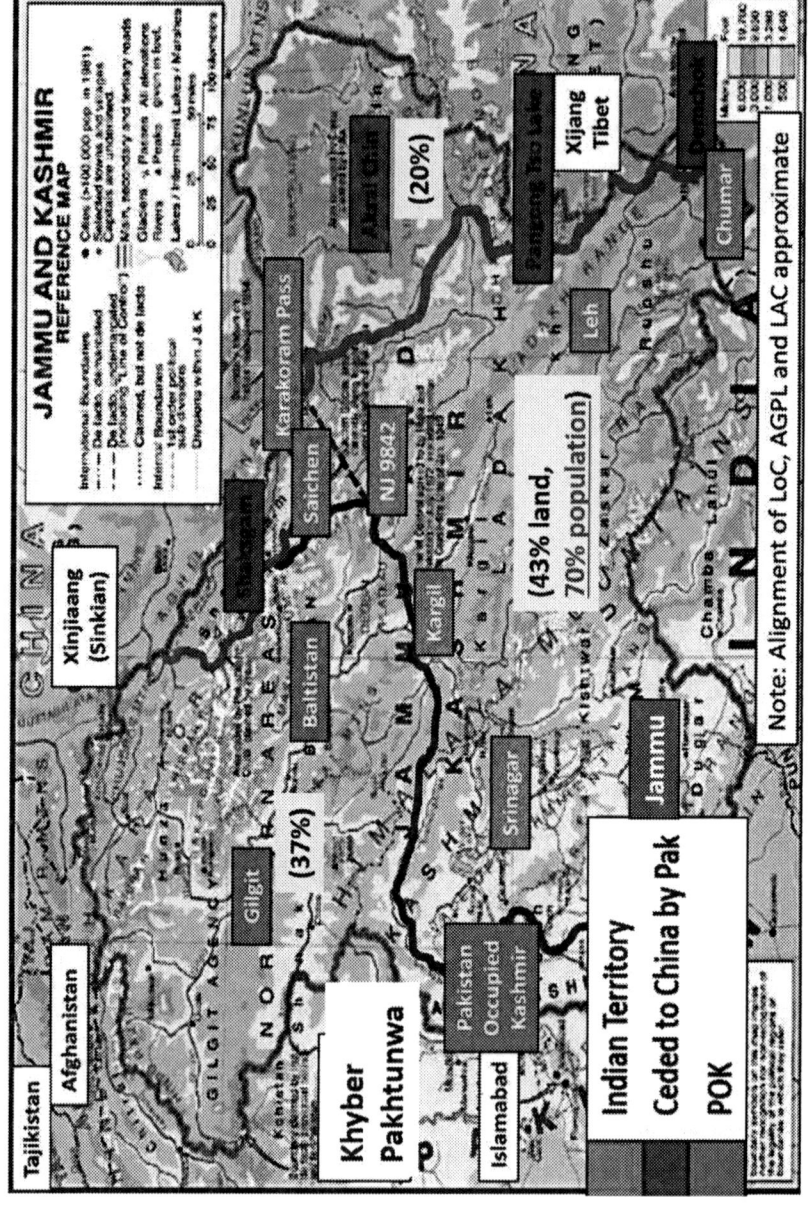

Jammu and Kashmir: Reference Map[3]

advancing neighbouring regions and major cities in India over the years. Hindu pandits were specifically affected in this region due to their status in the local society. Approximately 95% of the total population of 160,000–170,000 of Kashmiri Pandits (i.e., approximately 150,000 to 160,000) left the Kashmir Valley in 1990 as militancy engulfed the state and are settled as internally displaced people in Jammu, Delhi and other parts of the country due to the ongoing violence.

Jammu and Kashmir: A Demographic Profile[4]

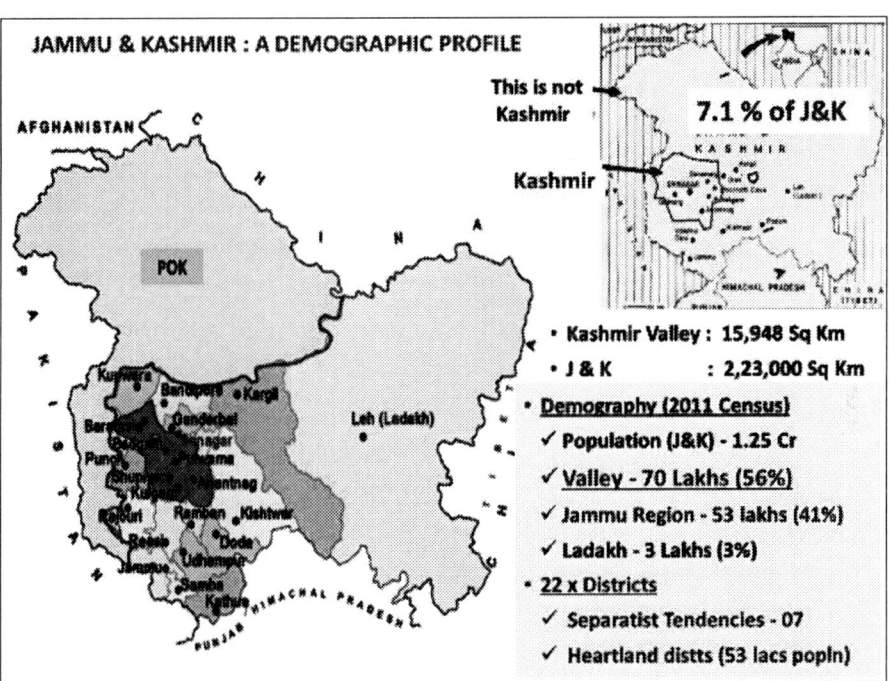

The above map shows the demographical profile as per 2011 Census and was also presented in the system analysis study conducted by the College of Defence Management, Secunderabad, during the National Seminar on Mapping of Perceptions in J&K, the way ahead on 18 August 2018.

While the issue of Kashmir appears to be rather simple on the face of it, the multi-dimensional nature of the problem and sheer number of actors, many of them hidden, with stakes of some form or the other have ensured that this problem takes on the character of the proverbial "Gordian knot." It is increasingly being understood that merely "eliminating" poster boys and dreaded terrorists will not take the situation to a logical and favourable conclusion and therefore much more and in a more coherent form needs to be done. Towards this end, a need was felt that a SWOT analysis be carried out to identify and implement short-term strategies to commence the process of stabilisation.

SWOT analysis (or **SWOT matrix**) is a strategic planning technique used to help an organization identify the *Strengths, Weaknesses, Opportunities,* and *Threats* related to competition or project planning. It is intended to specify the objectives of the business venture or project and identify the internal and external factors that are favourable and unfavourable to achieving those objectives. Users of a SWOT analysis often ask and answer questions to generate meaningful information for each category to make the tool useful and identify their competitive advantage. The following needs to be understood before further reading:

- Strengths and Weakness are frequently internally related, while Opportunities and Threats commonly focus on environmental placement.
- **Strength.** Existence of a competency and ability of the State to successfully apply it or exploit a critical factor to develop competitiveness.
- **Weakness.** Absence of a specific competency or inability of the State to apply the same successfully or non-exploitation of a critical factor that diminishes its competitiveness.
- **Opportunity.** An opportunity is an external condition that could positively impact the State's critical performance parameters and improve competitive advantage provided positive action is taken in time.
- **Threat.** A threat is an external condition that could negatively impact the State's critical performance parameters and diminish competitive advantage provided positive action is not taken in time.
- **Steps Undertaken For this Anaysis.**
    - Step 1 – Identifying Strengths and Weaknesses of J&K.
        - Identifying the environment analysis problem.
        - Identifying drivers that influence the relevant internal environment.
        - Discussing and evaluating the drivers.
        - Determining whether the driver is a strength or a weakness.

- Establishing performances and ranking them to establish priority.
- Establishing the importance/impact of each driver.
- Calculating cumulative values.
- Step 2 – **Identifying external opportunities and threats**
  - Identifying drivers that influence the relevant external environment.
  - Discussing and evaluating the drivers to establish trends over the time horizon of the scan.
  - Determining whether the driver is a threat or an opportunity.
  - Establish the magnitude and impact of these drivers and rank them to establish priority.
  - Establish probability of occurrence of threat/opportunity.
  - Calculate cumulative values.
- Step 3 – **Preparation of SWOT Summary.** Enter the rank-ordered list of Strengths, Weaknesses, Opportunities and Threats and thereafter develop the SWOT matrix.
- Step 4 – **Use SWOT Analysis to identify possible strategies:**
  - Build on Strengths.
  - Resolve Weaknesses.
  - Exploit Opportunities.
  - Avoid Threats.

ANALYSIS OF STRENGTHS

Strengths

- **Geo-Strategic Location.** J&K is located in the northern part of the Indian sub-continent in the vicinity of the Karakoram and western mountain ranges. It falls in the great northwestern complex of the Himalayan Ranges with marked relief variation, snow-capped summits, antecedent drainage, complex geological structure and rich temperate flora and fauna. Its location at the confluence of India, Tibet, Afghanistan, Pakistan and the Central Asian republics makes it geo-strategically one of the most important regions of the world. Major rivers which irrigate the north western parts of the Indian sub-continent, namely the Indus, Jhelum (including Kishenganga) and Chenab pass through the state. The state lies on the old silk route between ancient China and Central Asian republics. It's vicinity to the China Pakistan

Economic Corridor (CPEC), the flagship project for China's Belt Road Initiative (BRI) also enhances its Geo-strategic potential. This is the only Indian state which provides the opportunity to Pakistan and China to employ concentrated forces together as a collusive threat. Due to its deep mystic moderate Islam culture, it has the potential of reversing the cultural Jehadi threat to the Uighur region of China in the North,

- **Growing Economy/GSDP.** Jammu and Kashmir will show a growth of 8.49% in GSDP in the last fiscal, State Economic Survey Report 2017 said.[5] The report which was tabled by Minister for Finance Haseeb Drabu in State Legislative Council said GSDP at constant (2011-12) prices for 2017-18 is estimated at Rs. 1,09,136.52 crore as against the estimate of Rs. 1,00,597.57 crore for 2016-17, indicating growth of 8.49% in the last fiscal.

- **Water Resources with Hydro-power potential.** State of Jammu and Kashmir is bestowed with significant hydel potential which when exploited fully will provide a strong impetus for the growth of the State's economy. The development of this potential would need huge resources, technical expertise, administrative reforms, congenial environment, proper regulation and management, besides competitive marketing, Policy formation and private participation. The optimal exploitation of the available hydel resources in the State would not only meet the State's demand but will also supply power to the Northern grid to boost the overall development of the State. The estimated hydropower potential of the State is 20,000 Megawatts (MW), of which about 16480 MW have been identified. Out of the identified potential, only 2693.45 MW (16% of identified potential) has been exploited so far.[6]

- **Availability of Minerals.** The mountains surrounding the different valleys of the State of Jammu and Kashmir have varied mineral wealth.[7] However, economic viability of mining these resources remains a problem.

- **Natural/Local Resources.** J&K is richly endowed with natural wealth like forests, water bodies, rivers with rich hydroelectric potential, minerals, climate and natural beauty. Extreme cold climate and natural air conditioning all year long is a big plus for many industries. J&K's forest and tree cover has increased marginally by 253 sq kms over the last two years. The increase, based on satellite data and subsequent "ground truthing", has put the total green cover at 23,241 sq km which is 10.46% of total 222,236 sq kms of state's geographical area, India State of Forest Report (ISFR)-2017 by Forest Survey of India has revealed. In 2015, the state's forest cover was reported to be 22,988 sq kms[8].

- **Democratic Govt Setup.** J&K like all other states of India is governed by a democratically elected government. The state of Jammu and Kashmir retains a special status within the union government of India. Unlike the rest of the states, which are bound by the Indian constitution, Jammu and Kashmir follows a modified version of that constitution—as delineated in the Constitution (Application to Jammu and Kashmir) Order, 1954—which affirms the integrity of the state within the Republic of India. The union government has direct legislative powers in matters of defence, foreign policy, and communications within the state and has indirect influence in matters of citizenship, Supreme Court jurisdiction, and emergency powers. Under the constitution of Jammu and Kashmir, the governor, who is head of state, is appointed by the president of India and is aided and advised by an elected chief minister and a council of ministers. Jammu and Kashmir is the only state in India which enjoys special autonomy under Article 370 of the Constitution of India, according to which no law enacted by the Parliament of India, except for those in the field of defence, communication and foreign policy, will be extendable in Jammu and Kashmir unless it is ratified by the state legislature of Jammu and Kashmir. Subsequently, jurisdiction of the Supreme Court of India over Jammu and Kashmir has been extended. Jammu and Kashmir is the only Indian state that has its own official flag and constitution, and Indians from other states cannot purchase land or property in the state.
- **High TeledDensity.** At teledensity of 94.34 per square kilometer,[9] J&K betters a number of states in India. In a survey conducted by CLAWS recently through TISS, it has come to light that nearly 80% youth of the state are using social media on their mobile phones.
- **Handicraft Industry.** Handicraft activities occupy an important position in the economic structure of J&K State. Being environment friendly, these activities are best suited to the state as they are more labour intensive and less capital intensive in nature, therefore having scope for employment generation at a large scale.[10] The Kashmir handicraft

products have earned worldwide fame for their attractive designs, functional utility and high-quality craftsmanship. In absence of other manufacturing industries in the state, handicrafts remained a key economic activity from time immemorial. The artistic imagination and craftsmanship of the Artisans reflected through a wide range of products has delighted the connoisseurs world over for centuries. Crafts like Shawls, Crewel, Namdha, Chain Stitch, Wood Carving, papier-mâché, Costume Jewellery, Kani Shawls and the Carpets hold a significant share in the overall production and export of the State. Silken carpets in particular constitute a specialty having no parallel in quality and design at national level and, therefore, occupy an important position in the international market. The handicraft sector of the state has great contribution towards foreign exchange earnings to the state and country in particular. Total revenue generated from this sector was Rs 2650 Crore with Rs 1151 Crore being earnings from exports.[11] This is just the tip of an iceberg as compared to the huge potential and demand for these products world-wide.

- **Kashmiriyat.** It is the ethno-national and social consciousness and cultural values of the Kashmiri people. Emerging around the 16th century, it is characterised by religious and cultural harmony, patriotism and pride for their mountainous homeland of Kashmir.
    - **Origin.** Kashmir has historically been an important centre for Hinduism and Buddhism. Islam was introduced in the medieval centuries, and Sikhism also spread to the region under the rule of the Sikh Empire in the 18th and 19th centuries. Kashmir has a significant place in the mythology and history of all four religions. The region is home to many legendary Hindu and Buddhist monuments and institutions. The Hazratbal shrine houses a relic that is believed to be the hair of Muhammad, the prophet of Islam. In his journeys seeking religious enlightenment, Guru Nanak travelled to Kashmir. *Kashmiriyat* is believed to have developed under the rule of Muslim governor Zain ul Abedin and the Mughal emperor Akbar, both of whom gave equal protection, importance and patronage to Kashmir's different religious communities.
    - **Philosophy.** Kashmir's existence is characterised by its insular Himalayan geography, harsh winter climate and isolation in economic and political terms. The region has also seen political turmoil and foreign invasions. *Kashmiriyat* is believed to be an

expression of solidarity, resilience and patriotism regardless of religious differences. It is believed to embody an ethos of harmony and a determination of survival of the people and their heritage. This culture embraces Sufi Islam propagated by the likes of Bulle Shah and Shah Hmadani in the 14th Century. To many Kashmiris, *Kashmiriyat* demanded religious and social harmony and brotherhood. It has been strongly influenced by Kashmir Shaivism, Buddhism and Sufism, carrying a long-standing conviction that any and every religion will lead to the same divine goal. However, the impact and importance of *Kashmiriyat* has been concentrated in the Vale of Kashmir only, which is the real historical Kashmir. The farther regions of Gilgit, Baltistan, Jammu and Ladakh have not been influenced by this philosophy, as these regions are not Kashmiri in terms of culture, language or ethnicity. Conscious efforts to revive *Kashmiriyat* have been made by various communities of Muslims and Hindus through united opposition to violence in the state. Efforts to promote *Kashmiriyat* through cultural activities, social programmes and literature have increased throughout Jammu and Kashmir and amongst expatriate Kashmiri communities. In 2007 poll conducted by the Centre for the Study of Developing Societies in New Delhi, 84% of people in Srinagar wanted to see the return of Kashmiri Pandits.[12] However, in a survey conducted by TISS for CLAWS and projected in the National Seminar on Mapping of "Perceptions in J&K - The Way Ahead," only 50% of the college students in the age group of 18 to 27 years wanted the Kashmiri Pandits to come back, thus showing a deterioration in the trend.

- **Low Population Density.** In 2011, population density for Jammu & Kashmir was 124 people per square kilometer of land area.[13] Population density of Jammu & Kashmir increased from 59 people per square kilometer of land area in 1981 to 124 people per square kilometer of land area in 2011 growing at an average annual rate of 28.13%. This is very low as compared to the national average of 382 persons per square kilometer.

- **Well Established Security Forces (SF).** The security forces structure in the state consists of the state police, the CAPFs, Indian Army deployed on the Line of Control and the Line of Actual control as well as the

Rashtriya Rifles the Counter terror force of the Indian Army deployed in the state since 1993. Territorial Army battalions have also been raised within the state which are based on the concept of Home and Hearth Battalions drawing their manpower from the local population. These are normally working in support of the counter-terror network within the state.

All in all, the state has a balanced security structure both at the border and in the hinterland.

- **Reasonably high literacy rate.** Considering the tough terrain and hinterland of the state, a literacy rate of 68.74%[14] is reasonably high and needs to be tapped to full advantage.

- **Youth bulge.** Today, over 70% of Jammu and Kashmir's population is estimated to be under 35. If this huge demographic potential is utilized fruitfully, it could become a great source of strength.[15]

- **Reasonable HDI & Low poverty.** Human Development Index, HDI, makes use of four parameters for measuring and ranking countries/states according to their social and economic development which includes the Life Expectancy at Birth, Expected Years of Schooling, Mean Years of Schooling and Gross National/State Income per Capita. HDI scores ranges from 0 to 1, with 1 being the best possible score to attain. At present, the overall average **HDI** Score of India is 0.6087 and J&K is at tenth position within the Indian states at 0.649.[16]

- Tourism. Tourism is not only a growth engine but also an export growth engine and employment generator. The sector has a capacity to create large-scale employment both direct and indirect, for diverse sections of society from the most specialized to unspecialized work force. J&K has a great promise for development of tourism in view of its inherent potential. Availability of good quality and affordable hotel rooms plays an important role in boosting the growth of tourism. Presently, there are 1508 registered hotels and restaurants in the state apart from 84 tourist bungalows and huts. The Govt is taking all possible steps and making all efforts to develop world-class tourism infrastructure at tourist destinations and circuits. Development of national and internationally important destinations and circuits through three Mega Circuits, i.e., Buddhist Circuit for Leh, Sufi Circuit for Kashmir and Spiritual Circuit for Jammu agreed to by Ministry of Tourism, Govt of India, is a judicious mix of cultural, heritage, spiritual and eco-tourism to give tourists a holistic view about J&K.

- **Cold Climate.** The climate of the state varies from being moderate to extremely cold. Perched in the Himalayas, the state is endowed with winter temperatures ranging from 0°C till -60°C in the Ladakh and the Karokaram ranges. This naturally available air-conditioned environment may become a boon for the industry which is particularly overdependent on Air-Conditioning/Refrigeration. Cold climate also acts as a defence line from traditional and non-traditional threats and is a source of tourism. History and culture of artisan wood, fabric and papier-mâché is also due to cold climate where people in winters have plenty of time to utilize it as a source of livelihood.

ANALYSIS OF WEAKNESSES

Weaknesses

- **Geographical and Ethnically Distinct Regions/Conflicting Interests.** The State of Jammu and Kashmir comprises three geographically and ethnically distinct regions, namely Kashmir, Jammu and Ladakh each one having its own dynamics and interests like culture and religion, which are more often than not conflicting in nature. Each of the regions has a different majority religious belief system. The three regions of the state seem to be polarised on religious lines. The distribution on religious lines is given in the Introduction Chapter.

- **Troubled History/Historical Baggage.** Power equations have changed over a period of time and it is always the human behaviour of trying to be at the centre of power which has been the main reason for neglecting the aspirations of the state. Almost all the important leaders have played with the emotions of the people to achieve their objectives. Maharaja Hari Singh initially signed the standstill agreement with both countries because he wanted to retain power himself. Pandit Nehru in his exuberance and idealism philosophy agreed on a plebiscite.[17] However, the Sher-e-Kashmir, Sheikh Abdullah whose ideas swayed between independence and amalgamation with India or Pakistan, had a hidden agenda himself. So much so that Pandit Nehru, his one-time best friend and later foe, seems to have started to distrust Sheikh on realizing that the man himself nurtured feelings of ruling Kashmir if it became independent. There was no doubt that Sheikh with his enormous clout and an iconic image had coxswained the people of Kashmir into dreaming for Azadi. The seeds of separatism were thus sown during this period.[18] The propping up of parallel leaders to reduce the followings of the Sheikh also added to the confusion.[19] The people were thus confused as what they actually wanted and were generally influenced by the perception of leaders. Most of the political leaders barring a few had myopic views, had visions to suit their political agenda and were amenable to manipulation. The alleged blatant rigging of elections in 1987[20] was yet another classical example of political parties trying all means to come to power. Finally, to add to the woes, Pakistan jumped into the fray yet again with a well laid out proxy war to manipulate the situation created by our own undoing. Thus, over a period of last seventy years, no state of the Indian Union has seen such a huge shift in the aspirations of the people from Azadi to becoming part of Pakistan to being part of India, with three totally different scenarios with the Awaam of Kashmir also swaying as the wind blew. Thus, dealing with a Kashmiri in the valley definitely needs a *Kashmiri outlook* and cannot be compared with any other state.

- **Lack of women empowerment.** The main barriers to women empowerment in J&K[21] are:
  o Violence against women.
  o Lack of decision-making authority.
  o Lack of participation in political affairs.
  o Poor and low status of women.
  o Lack of education.
  o Lack of awareness.
  o Inadequate and unorganized health care delivery system.
  o Under/unemployment leading to poverty.
- **Revenue Deficit.**[22]

Growth and Composition of Expenditure

Chart 1 depicts the trends in total expenditure both in terms of economic classification and expenditure by activities.

The toal expenditure of the State inceased by 9.87 per cent from Rs. 43845 crore in 2015-16 to Rs. 48174 crore in 2016-17. The revenue expenditure components has increased by 9.31 per cent and capital expenditure ecomponent has increased by 12.3 per cent during the same period.

Chart 1: Total Expenditure: Trends and Composition

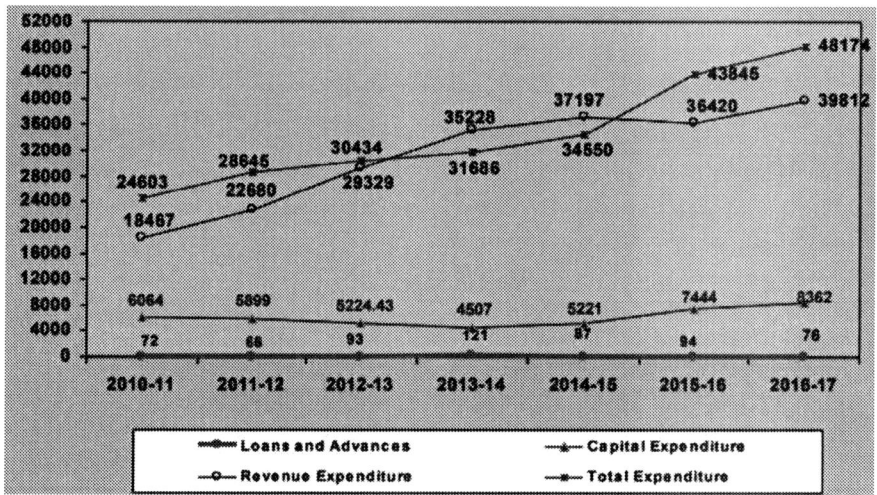

Paucity of resources and other limitation adds to the severity of the issues which need focused attention to make conditions conducive for the economic and social growth. The multipronged strategy for mobilization of additional resources, improvement in tax and nontax collections, cost recovery of user charges, expenditure compression, particularly establishment related and increase in efficiency levels shall be of prime importance. The major areas of concern are put forth as under:

o There is a steep rise in salary and pension bills, administrative costs, burgeoning hidden subsidies including power deficit, rising interest liabilities and loan repayments, deficit on account of Non-tax Revenue, increased interest payment outgo.

o Revenue Expenditure has increased unabated, the major reason being periodical increase of salaries, regularization/appointment of new employees, power revenue deficit, interest liability and subsidies.

o Revenue generation from the both tax and non-tax sources has not recorded impressive jump commensurate to our demands and requirements.

o Dependence on borrowings is more indicative now to maintain at least constant level of Capital spending. Major borrowings are through open market and negotiated loans apart from public account. Financing of Capital spending in the wake of ever expanding Revenue Expenditure and squeezed resources is another challenge to handle.

o The degradation of infrastructure created due to absence of adequate maintenance grants is another area of concern and needs to be addressed by way of providing adequate funds in the capital/ revenue expenditure whichever is applicable on a fixed basis.

- **Inhospitable Terrain.** The territory of the state is divided into seven different challenging physiographic zones closely associated with the structural components of the Western Himalayas. Infrastructure challenges to bridge the zones are immense. Although the terrain provides protection from our adversaries to a large extent, the sense of isolation it also creates within the people of geographically distinct regions far outweighs the advantages. The seven zones include:
  o **The Plains.** The plains of the Jammu region are characterized by interlocking sandy alluvial fans.
  o **The Foothills.** Rising from 2000 to 7000 ft, the foothills form the outer and inner zones.
  o **The Lesser Himalayas.** The Pir Panjal constitutes the first mountain rampart comprising the western-most part of the Lesser Himalayas.

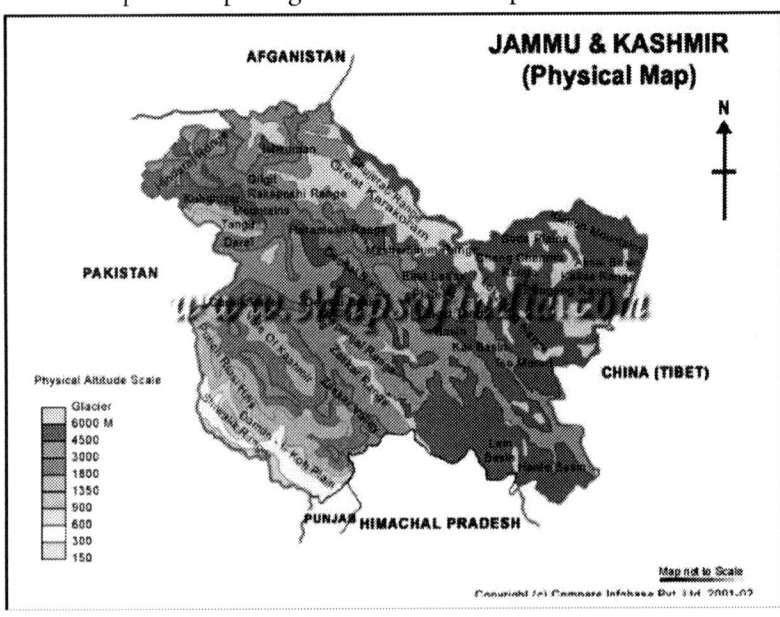

  o **The Greater Himalayas.** This contains ranges reaching more than 20,013 feet (6100 m) in altitude.
  o **Valley of Kashmir.** Between the Pir Panjal and the western end of the Great Himalayan ranges lies a deep asymmetrical basin called the Valley of Kashmir.

o **The Upper Indus Valley.** The valley of the upper Indus river follows the geological strike (structural trend) westwards from the Tibetan border to the point in the Pakistani sector where it rounds the great mountainous mass of Nanga Parbat to run southwards in deep gorges cut across the strike. In its upper reaches, gravel terraces flank the river; each tributary builds an alluvial fan out into the main valley. The town of Leh stands on such a fan, 11,483 ft (3500 m) above sea level.

o **The Karakoram Range.** The Karakoram region contains some of the world's highest peaks. As the altitude rises, majestic peaks appear; K_2 (Godwin Austin) the second highest peak in the world (28,264 ft or 8,615 m) occupies the most important position.

- **Fragile Internal Security (IS) Situation.** Number of terrorists operating in the valley has gradually reduced and as per the latest estimate, approximately 300 are only left, but the face and modus operandi too have undergone a transformation. Technology is being exploited to the hilt and there are no more guns tottering Jihadis in the streets. The terrorists nowadays rely on surgical, swift and silent attack on unsuspecting security personnel. These are timed to coincide with an important event and mainly aimed at disrupting any peace initiative. Post-Burhan Wani, agitation dynamics in 2016 and its exploitation by the terrorist organisations have enhanced the challenges for the security forces manifolds. In the assessment of most of the security experts, 2019 is going to be a very crucial year for the future of J&K. Effect of the Trump doctrine, Parliament/State elections and the internal dynamics of Pakistan will have an overbearing effect on the emerging situation.

- **Political Unpredictability and Varying Ideologies.** J&K is a unique state and has been on politically volatile right from independence. Reason for four Indo-Pak conflicts, the state has been in turmoil for the last 29 years. Compulsions of collation and regional aspirations will always be a hindrance in good governance and solution to the deadlock. A school of thought in the state is of the view that, the prime cause of failure to break the deadlock in the State is that all suggested solutions are based on the misguided notion that the 2,000 square kilometers Kashmir Valley represents the entire State of Jammu and Kashmir; that the political aspirations of all the people in the State are identical or nearly identical and that the contradictions among them, if any, can be easily reconciled. None of these formulations enjoys any

universal support in Jammu, Kashmir and Ladakh. The two prime factors are:
- o The State of Jammu and Kashmir houses a number of religious and ethnic groups.
- o The political aspirations and needs of the people of Jammu and Ladakh – who constitute almost half of the State's population and inhabit about 90% of the State's land area – and Kashmiri Pandits and Muslims are conflicting.[23]

- **Poor Governance.** The constitutional exclusivity guaranteed by Article 370 impinges on the administration and governance in the region,[24] which is essential to maintain peace, prosperity and tranquillity in the state. Several social welfare legislations passed by the parliament are not adopted by the J&K legislature. In some cases, they are adopted in a watered-down form that undermines the effectiveness of social and economic transformation envisaged by the policy. This is further compounded by dysfunctional district administration, which has led to abysmally low levels of education, employment and economic activity in the region. Instability in Kashmir is also due to subversion of institutions of governance including democratic institutions, lack of deliverance of governance and abdication of responsibility of society.

- **Corruption.** The Centre for Media Studies (CMS) in its annual corruption study – CMS India Corruption Study 2017 – has placed Jammu and Kashmir along with Karnataka, Tamil Nadu, Andhra Pradesh as most corrupt among 20 surveyed states. Further the study says that more than 33% respondents stated that state government is not "committed at all" towards reducing corruption in public services.[25]

- **Rising Fundamentalism.** Militancy has dramatically transformed Sufism and Kashmiriyat influenced people of Kashmir into a fractured and radically influenced society which in turn has given rise to religious fundamentalism. This has affected all aspects of the society including Kashmiri institutions such as political parties, government and non-government organisations, militant groups, educational institutions, self-help groups and many other such organisations within and outside Kashmir Valley. Rise of fundamentalism also signifies a transformation in the mindset of Kashmiri people from being accommodative and tolerant society to a more static, traditional and conservative society which is not averse to use of violence and advocates extremist outlook.

- **Lack of Industrial Base and Infrastructure.** The state of Jammu and Kashmir located far away from the market, and the major raw material source base, has historically remained isolated from the major industrial development action happening in the plains. The geographical isolation has restricted state's industrial activity to a selected few sectors in which it either had impressive expertise or had raw material locally available. At one point of time, forests were the main wealth-making resources till the sector was nationalised and new conservation norms took over.

- **Lack of Private Investment.** Under the Make in India programme, new initiatives have been taken in "Ease of Doing Business" to facilitate the investors to boost industrial sector in the state and create employment opportunities for unemployed youth of the state both skilled and unskilled. Employment generation being another focus area of Make in India programme, the Industrial Policy 2016 targets to create 15,000-20,000 employment opportunities per year as compared to an average of 5000 in last decade[26] for the skilled and unskilled youth. However, in spite of various sops, there is strong resistance by the private industry to invest in areas of the state other than the ones which are close to rail heads and good markets.

- **Unemployment.** Currently youth unemployment is one of the major challenges faced by the state of Jammu and Kashmir. With the number of educated unemployed youth running in lakhs,[27] the need for employment creation through youth entrepreneurship is undeniable. While hindered by the overall employment situations in the state, this challenge has its own specific dimensions and therefore requires specific targeted responses.

- **Growing Agitational Dynamics.** Although the word "Agitational terrorism" was first coined in 2009[28], the effect of it has been seen mainly since the Burhan Wani incident where-in organised stone pelting mobs stopping the proceedings by security forces at an encounter spot have become almost a norm. The Organisational tools of Finance and Alienation through radicalisation have a deep connect for successfully employing this operational tool.[29]

- **Fragile Geology.** Composed of varied regions and rock types, the Geology of J&K is fragile and prone to degradation in case utilization of the natural resources is not regulated. Recent cases of destruction caused due to floods, cloudbursts could be a direct result of overutilization of resources.

- **Poor Connectivity with Mainland.** Although we have come a long way from the days of Partition where all surface connectivity to the state was from the newly formed Pakistan, a lot needs to be done still to improve the surface (road and rail), air and data connectivity to the state from the Indian mainland.

- **OGWs and Fence Sitters Activities.** OGWs have always been the mainstay for an insurgency movement. Previously OGWs were primarily involved in logistics support and intelligence gathering. The comparative freedom of mov available to terrorists due to limited resource control measures has emboldened them to change their strategy of trying to mix up with population. Thus, OGWs are merging as a potent force and need to be given equal weightage while dealing with them. As per the Pakistani strategy of targeting the Cognitive domain of the population, the OGWs are playing an increasing role in radicalization and creating a perception of hopelessness amongst the youth thereby acting as recruiters. These OGWs and fence sitters would continue remaining actively involved in assisting the cause of the militants.

ANALYSIS OF OPPORTUNITIES

Opportunities. The opportunities emerged from the *internal scan* as pertaining to J&K. These are listed below.

- **Divided families across LC.** The Centre for Dialogue and Reconciliation's *Living on the Margins – Complex Narrative of People Living on the LoC*[30] aims to add an alternative, humanist angle to the discourse on borders, which are often simply seen as a stage for wartime theatrics or as symbolic communication channels – and which ignore the communities that live along them. The study focuses on the overall problems faced by people on both sides of the 758-km LoC, including divided families, and offers recommendations to underscore these concerns. The core of the study is to help "make a shift from mutual distrust and hostility to mutual trust and friendship with a holistic approach." By bringing the borderlanders to the centrestage and humanising the discourse on the LoC, the study seeks to include their residents in the process of encouraging peaceful negotiations to resolve cross-border issues between the two countries.

- **Divided and dwindling Hurriyat.** Awaam is getting more and more disillusioned and APHC is losing its sway in the valley. As per general perception, lack of ability to lead people led to this factionalism and the difference in these pro-freedom leaders adversely affected the united cause. The meaningless basis of identity crisis parted them from the public too. The recent split in Hurriyat Conference (M) has on one hand disappointed the people of Kashmir and on the other hand has let the cat out of the bag. Kashmiris are demanding accountability from these leaders who claim to be representing the mass aspiration.[31] Geelani's age is also an issue of concern with no formidable leader to step in his shoes.

- **Indo-Pak Trade.** The dormant trade potential between the two countries and the sincere exchanges possible across the LC is a major opportunity for the people of both the regions.

- **Indo-China Relations.** Indo-China relations, though out of the cool box of the 1960s to the 1980s decades, have gone through a roller-coaster ride in the recent past, especially in the Doklam case. The CPEC through PoK remains a bone of contention and China's support to Pakistan, be it on the issue of NSG membership or the issue of nomination of global terrorists, borders on collusivity. In spite of the upheavals, there is a sense of maturity and outreach at the leadership level which should turn out in to a great opportunity.

- **Education and Job Opportunities in other States.** Due to various reasons ranging from lack of raw materials to the security situation in the state, the number of private education institutes as well as Industrialists have not invested in the state, which forces the youth of the state to look outwards to the rest of India. Going out of the state and exploring new avenues widens the horizon and thinking of the people towards national integration.

- **Semblance of Stability in Internal Security Situation.** In spite of the ups and downs over the years, the present state of security in the state can be at best narrated as one of unease and mistrust, that is to say that there is a sense of functionality where the security situation in the state is bordering on the line between militancy and a law and order situation.

This Semblance whenever it is achieved is the biggest opportunity for other coherent efforts to establish peace and prosperity in the state. Unfortunately, this state, whenever it has been achieved in the past has not been fully exploited as it has not been seen in the light of conflict resolution theory.

- **Ease of Doing Business/E-Technology/Governance.** Ease of Doing Business is an index published by the World Bank and it is an aggregate figure that includes different parameters which define the Ease of Doing Business. Out of total 372 recommendations of the Business Reform Action Plan (BRAP), J&K state has successfully implemented 270 recommendations and uploaded 262 replies. As per the dynamic ranking by the Department of Industrial Policy and Promotion (DIPP), J&K stands at 22nd.[32] The advent of E-technology in every sphere of life and Governance world over is a huge opportunity to further improve the ease of doing business and in turn the quality of life of the people of J&K.

- **Central Govt Schemes and Programmes.** The Central Govt has launched a number of schemes for skill development, micro-financing, electricity for all, cooking gas for all, women empowerment, Employment generation schemes, housing for all, etc. There lies a huge opportunity for the people of the state to participate in the schemes to achieve prosperity for all.

- **Deteriorating US-Pak Relations.** For years together, US has propped up Pakistan for serving their own interests in the region, so much so that they have even offered a blind eye to Pak-orchestrated terrorist attacks in India. The Trump doctrine has showered in a hope of change in support and aid to Pakistan. In February this year, US has asked Pakistan to act against the Haqqani network and other militant groups and address international community's concerns about terror financing. Deputy Assistant to the President and the US National Security Council's Senior Director for South and Central Asia, Lisa Curtis made the remarks during her meetings with Foreign Secretary Tehmina Janjua, Interior Minister Ahsan Iqbal and Chief of the General Staff Lt Gen Bilal Akbar.[33] Although it seems that the US is addressing its concerns in Afghanistan, the rhetoric also suggests that Pakistan has been asked to rein in or face the consequences. The developing story could yield dividends for India in terms of new opportunities.

ANALYSIS OF THREATS

Threats. The threats emerged from the *external environmental scan* as pertaining to J&K. These are listed below.

- **Radicalisation of Society.** Militancy has dramatically transformed Sufism and Kashmiriyat. It has influenced people of Kashmir into a fractured and radically influenced society which in turn has given rise to religious fundamentalism. This has affected all aspects of the society including Kashmiri institutions such as political parties, government and non-government organisations, militant groups, educational institutions, self-help groups and many other such organisations within and outside Kashmir Valley.[34] Radicalisation is different than disaffection and is due to ideological manipulation of an individual or society, while dissent or disaffection is due to hopelessness, frustration and anger. Rise of fundamentalism also signifies a transformation in the mindset of Kashmiri people from being accommodative and tolerant society to a more static, traditional and conservative society which is not averse to use of violence and advocates extremist outlook. Slowly but steadily, Islamic schools and madrasas have gained importance amongst the valley population. As madrasas focus on the Islamic identity, they weaken the concept of Kashmiriat. Many of the madrasas, which are affiliated to Salafia Trust, Jamait-e-Islami and Deobandi School of thought, are focusing on establishing orthodox Islam thought and practices which in turn erode the core values of Sufism. Shariah traditions as advocated by orthodox Islam, advocate shunning of local traditions such as shrine worship and advocate strict "Purdah" by women. Reducing the influence of Shia maulvis is another motivating factor for the fundamentalists. Around the year 2007, many Kashmiri Muslims saw the Indian government's moves to increase cooperation with US and Israel as a proof that it is a part of a global anti-Muslim axis. This was overplayed by communication networks. These networks also spread ideas of fundamentalist ideas propagated by Tablighi Jamaat and Ahl-e-Hadith.[35] The Tablighi Jamat acted as the pull for even secular Sufi Muslim youth of Kashmir as it urges the muslims to invite (dawah) the ways of a good muslim (deen) in their own lives so that other non-believers can join their ranks. Religious scholars in Kashmir point out that Ahl-e-Hadithhas four sub-schools—Jamait-ul-ahl-e-Hadith (puritan), Difai (ultra-puritan), Guraba (religio-political ultra-puritan) and Sout-ul-Haq, represented by ISIS, where a nonconformist is "wajib-ul-qatl" (eligible for murder).³⁶ Radicalisation is the biggest threat to Kashmiri society today.

- **Pak Proxy War and Obsession with Kashmir.** Kashmir is an integral part of India as defined in the constitution, but the state is in turmoil due to Pakistan's cross-border terrorism and proxy war. Pakistan, on the other hand, insists that Kashmir is a disputed territory and that it is merely providing moral and diplomatic support for an indigenous freedom struggle in Kashmir. Pakistan's obsession with Kashmir has led to four conflicts and has the potential of a nuclear stand-off.

- **Pak-Taliban Relations.** The fall of the Najibullah government in 1992, and the subsequent four years of chaos, set the stage for the rise of the Taliban in 1996 and created an opportunity for Pakistan's ISI to emerge as both the Taliban's financer, organizer and principal patron. The Taliban, in turn, gave Pakistan's ISI an unprecedented opportunity to exert its control over Afghanistan and its government. An opportunity that Pakistan's government has pursued for the last 20 years. Spill-over of these battle-hardened radicalized fighters from Afghanistan to J&K is a threat in being especially if the Taliban rules the roost in a given scenario in Afghanistan.

- **Pan-Islamic Wave.** Although the rise of the Islamic caliphate of the ISIS has been nipped in the bud but the idea is still at large and remnants of its militant organs have migrated to many provinces of Afghanistan. There is a school of thought that suggests Pakistani jihadi elements like the Jaish-e-Mohammad (JeM), Harkat-ul-Mujahedeen (HuM) and the LET are not likely to involve the ISIS and loose nationalistic space in Kashmir, but history suggests that they have no inhibitions in utilising foreign mercenaries in Kashmir as force multipliers and therefore, the day is not far when we see some of these mercenary elements of ISIS in Kashmir if steps to the contrary are not taken now.³⁷

- **Unsettled borders with Pak & China.** Unsettled borders with both Pakistan and China in a time when the CPEC is being constructed through disputed territory has made the two brothers in arms come even closer to each other. It is in China's interest for the J&K dispute to continue and for India and Pakistan to be on loggerheads with each other. This fulfills the primary agenda of preventing any new independent state in the region that may have a domino effect on Uighur Muslims and Tibetans and the secondary agenda of keeping India, the only possible competitor to China in Asia, tied down in South Asia through a permanent rivalry with Pakistan. China will not allow Pakistan to weaken further; one of the reasons is to prevent more Uighur separatists getting radicalized and trained in Pakistani territories and the other of course is the CPEC. It has put all its eggs in one basket, i.e., the CPEC as far as the BRI is concerned and therefore it needs to create space around it, in order to allow it to succeed.

- **Misuse of Media.** The Vernacular Press in the Valley is the focus of attention of the militant groups. Facing the gun, it has little choice except to publish distorted and exaggerated stories. The people in the Valley who would rather believe what is printed in the local Press rather than the news put out by All India Radio and Doordarshan, get worked up by the provocative militant-inspired writings and often come out in the streets to stage protest demonstrations. The foreign media which often have a problem understanding the nuances and background, then project the demonstrations as a reflection of the spontaneous support of the people for the militants and secession. This is the chain reaction sought to be achieved. The diabolical hand of Pakistan is behind this orchestrated campaign against India. Disinformation, false reports and rumors are floated by militants and these are forced on the local media.

- **Drugs & Hawala Money.** Due to squeeze in international funding very little is available with Pakistan to fund the proxy war in J&K. As per reports, Pakistan is extensively using funds generated through illegal drug trade to support this agenda. Pak narcotic smugglers, who are controlled by ISI, are reportedly getting 2.5 billion dollars from illegal narcotic trade. Hawala route is also being used by ISI as well as Islamic Fundamentalist groups based in Middle East. Legitimate businesses are being used as fronts to deliver money to J&K terrorist organisations.

- **Dependence on Central Aid.** Grant-in-aid represents the significant component from the union government in the budgetary resource base of the State Government. The grant-in-aid from union government in absolute terms has remained 49% in 2016-17 vis-à-vis total revenue receipts and 42.75% vis-à-vis total expenditure.[38] This huge dependence on Central aid does not inspire confidence amongst the investors in the state machinery.

- **Terrorist Activities Spilling to other Regions.** Separatists are making all-out efforts to spill over the instability to South of the Pir Panjal

Ranges as well as east of Zojila, the vulnerable areas that can be targeted by the ISI and separatists in the Chenab Valley, Poonch-Rajouri and Kargil. The Government should ensure that these areas are not alienated and should be paid due dividends for ensuring peace. Any effort of communal disharmony needs to be curtailed with iron hands and politicization of issues, such as juvenile rape case of Kathua, should not be allowed to communalize the entire region. Such opportunities should not be handed over to the separatists and the ISI to reignite instability in the areas that are comparatively peaceful.[39]

- **China's Increased Involvement in PoK and Gilgit-Baltistan.** China is increasingly becoming a major stakeholder in the conflict due to its high-value investments on the CPEC. It is in China's interest for the dispute to continue and for India and Pakistan to be on loggerheads with each other. This fulfills the primary agenda of preventing any new independent state in the region that may have a domino effect on Uighur Muslims and Tibetans and the secondary agenda of keeping India, the only possible competitor to China in Asia, tied down in South Asia through a permanent rivalry with Pakistan. China will not allow Pakistan to weaken further, one of the reasons is to prevent more Uighur separatists getting radicalized and trained in Pakistani territories and the other of course is the CPEC. It has put all its eggs in one basket, i.e., the CPEC as far as the BRI is concerned and therefore it needs to create space around it, in order to allow it to succeed. This can only be done in case the focus continues to be in Afghanistan on one flank and Kashmir on the other.

RANK ORDERING OF SWOTs

The *strengths and weaknesses* were duly analysed as per their *importance* and *likely impact* they would have on state of J&K. For this purpose, the interviews taken to establish the fields in the Analytical Hierarchy Process during the Net Assessment study of the state of J&K carried out by College of Defence Management in 2014 were taken as the base which was further reinforced by the views taken by the youth social leaders from J&K who had participated in the National Seminar on Mapping of Perceptions in J&K - the Way Ahead, recently conducted by CLAWS. These were given a value of importance as well as value of impact on a scale of 1 to 9 and a comprehensive figure arrived at by multiplying both these values for rank ordering them. The tables indicating the above methodology are as given below.

Analysis of Strengths vis-à-vis Importance

S.No.	Factors	Strengths									Importance/Impact									Cum Value
		Maj			Med			Minor			High			Med			Low			
		9	8	7	6	5	4	3	2	1	9	8	7	6	5	4	3	2	1	
1	Geo-Strategic Location				x									x						36
2	Growing Economy/GSDP					x							x							35
3	Water Resources with Hydropower Potential		x									x								64
4	Availability of Minerals				x									x						36
5	Natural/Local Resources		x										x							56
6	Democratic Govt Setup	x										x								72
7	High Teledensity					x								x						30
8	Handicraft Industry		x											x						48
9	Kashmiriyat			x									x							49
10	Low Population Density				x									x						36
11	Well-Established SF		x									x								64
12	Reasonably high literacy rate				x									x						36
13	Youth Bulge		x									x								64
14	High HDI & Low Poverty			x										x						42
15	Cold Climate			x							x									63
16	Tourism		x										x							56

185

Analysis of Weaknesses vis-à-vis Importance/Impact

S.No.	Factors	Weaknesses									Importance/Impact									Cum Value
		Maj			Med			Minor			High			Med			Low			
		9	8	7	6	5	4	3	2	1	9	8	7	6	5	4	3	2	1	
1	Geographical Distinct Regions			x								x								56
2	Troubled History		x									x								64
3	Lack of women & youth empowerment				x								x							42
4	Revenue Deficit				x									x						36
5	Inhospitable Terrain				x								x							42
6	Fragile IS Situation	x										x								72
7	Political unpredictability & varying ideologies	x									x									81
8	Poor Governance	x										x								72
9	Corruption		x									x								64
10	Rising Fundamentalism			x									x							49
11	Lack of Industrial Base & Infrastructure		x											x						48
12	Lack of Private Investment		x											x						48
13	Unemployment			x								x								56
14	Growing Agitational Dynamics			x								x								56
15	Fragile geology				x									x						36
16	OGW & Fence Sitter Activities		x									x								72
17	Poor Connectivity with Mainland			x										x						42

SWOT Analysis and Short-Term Strategies

The above *opportunities and threats* were duly analysed as per their *importance* they would have for the state of J&K and the *probability of occurrence*. For this purpose, the interviews taken to establish the fields in the Analytical Hierarchy Process during the Net Assessment study of the state of J&K carried out by College of Defence Management in 2014 were taken as the base which was further reinforced by the views taken by the youth social leaders from J&K who had participated in the National Seminar on Mapping of Perceptions in J&K - the Way Ahead. These were given a value of importance on a scale of 1 to 9 and a value for probability of occurrence from 0 to 1 and a comprehensive figure arrived at by multiplying both these values for rank ordering them. The tables indicating the above methodology are as given below.

After doing the above exercise, the strengths/weaknesses and opportunities/threats were *rank ordered* for all values *above 48 and .45* respectively. The rank-ordered SWOT is given in the following table:

Rank-Ordered SWOT

#	STRENGTHS	#	WEAKNESSES
1	Democratic govt Setup	1	Political unpredictability & varying ideologies
2	Well Established SF	2	Fragile IS Situation
3	Youth Bulge	3	Poor Governance
4	Water Resources	4	OGW & Fence Sitter Activities
5	Cold Climate	5	Troubled History
6	Tourism	6	Unemployment
7	Natural/Local Resources	7	Growing Agitational Dynamics
8	Kashmiriyat	8	Political unpredictability & varying ideologies
9	Handicraft Industry	9	Geographical Distinct Regions
		10	Rising Fundamentalism
		11	Lack of Industrial Base & Infrastructure
		12	Lack of Private Investment
	OPPORTUNITIES		**THREATS**
1	Semblance of Stablity - IS situation	1	Radicalisation of Society
2	Deteriorating US-Pak relations	2	Pak Proxy War
3	Divide & dwindling Hurriyat	3	Drugs & Hawala money ingress
4	Indo-Pak/Afghanistan trade	4	Misuse of Media
5	e-Governance/e-Technology	5	Increased Involvement of China
6	Central Govt Schemes & Programmes	6	Pak-Taliban Relations
7	Education & job opportunities in other states	7	Pan-Islamic Wave

Comparison of Oppurtunities vis-à-vis Probability of Occurrence

S.No.	Factors	Oppurtunities									Probability of Occurrence									Cum Value
		Maj			Med			Minor			High			Med			Low			
		9	8	7	6	5	4	3	2	1	0.9	0.8	0.7	0.6	0.5	0.4	0.3	0.2	0.1	
1	Divided families across LC	x														x				0.36
2	Divide & dwindling Hurriyat	x											x							0.63
3	Indo-Pak trade		x										x							0.56
4	Indo-China relation		x													x				0.32
5	Education & job opportunities in other states		x											x						0.48
6	Semblance of Security in IS situation	x										x								0.72
7	Ease of Doing Business/e-Governance/e-Technology			x									x							0.49
8	Deteriorating US-Pak Relations		x									x								0.64
9	Central Govt Schemes & Programmes		x											x						0.48

Comparision of Threats vis-à-vis Probability of Occurence

S.No.	Factors	Threats									Probability of Occurrence									Cum Value
		Maj			Med			Minor			High			Med			Low			
		9	8	7	6	5	4	3	2	1	0.9	0.8	0.7	0.6	0.5	0.4	0.3	0.2	0.1	
1	Radicalisation of Society	x										x								0.72
2	Pak Proxy War	x										x								0.72
3	Pak-Taliban Relations			x									x							0.49
4	Pan-Islamic Wave	x													x					0.45
5	Unsettled borders with Pak & China			x										x						0.42
6	Misuse of Media		x									x								0.64
7	Drugs & Hawala money ingress		x								x									0.72
8	Dependence on Central Aid				x										x					0.3
9	China's Increased Involvement		x										x							0.56
10	Spilling of terrorist acts		x											x						0.48

STRATEGIES AND RECOMMENDATIONS FROM SWOT ANALYSIS

The various strategies (namely, the Strength-Opportunity, Weakness-Opportunity, Strength-Threat, Weakness-Threat and Mandatory Strategies) that have been worked out based on SWOT analysis are given in subsequent paragraphs.

Strength-Opportunity (SO) Strategies

- To leverage the well-established Security Forces through Governor's office till an elected government is formed, for improving governance and create environment for improving the Centre-State relationship and reaping benefits of central govt schemes.
- Utilize the democratic setup of the country to conduct the Panchayati elections, empower the Panchayats to reduce the impact of fundamentalist organizations.
- Educated youth bulge must be given assistance and help by public and private players to exploit education/job opportunities in other states by establishing special setup and close monitoring.
- Exploit the situation after relative normalcy to harness the tourism potential of the state by conducting tourism fests at various locations with major involvement from the local educated youth thereby generating revenues and employment opportunities.
- State/Centre govts to harness hydro-electric potential by bringing in private players through lucrative schemes for generation of employment opportunities for the locals.
- Exploit potential of handicraft/horticulture industries of J&K through Indo-Pak trade improving revenue deficit and generating employment.
- Exploit the Cold climate regions of the state to establish Servers, data storage and mining for the e-technology industry which requires huge air-conditioning plants in case done in hot climate areas.

Weakness Opportunity (WO) Strategies

- When stabilized, exploit the Internal Security situation in the state, initiate process of meaningful devolution of powers at the various lower levels, namely regional, district and panchayat levels to reduce effect of fundamentalists, thus bringing in political stability.
- Leverage technology and high internet penetration in the state to exploit

potential of e-governance to overcome rampant corruption and bring in transparency in administration.
- To contain the fragile IS situation to present levels by maintaining balanced presence and non-intrusive posturing of Indian Army ensuring control over IS situation.
- Boost Indo-Pak/Afghanistan trade through tax concessions/loans such as to reduce unemployment.
- The state govt machinery to bring in more transparency and accountability of its governance by exploiting e-governance to check corruption and poor governance.
- SF to maintain balance between restrain and firm handling of situation such as to avoid giving trigger to local population for any anti-govt agitations turning to IS instabilities
- Well-established SF and state government to work in synergized manner to ensure stable/controlled IS situation remains so and its fragile character is not exploited by fundamentalists and terrorists.
- Leverage deteriorating US-Pak relations to force Pakistan to stop providing material and psychological support to Agitational dynamics and OGWs in the state.
- Leverage the idea of Kashmiriyat and family values to negate the Pan-Islamic wave of radical Islam.

Strength-Threat (ST) Strategies

- The state govt to preserve and give boost to the idea of Kashmiriyat by effective use of all sorts of media wherein the Kashmiris retain their identity and cultural cohesion to counter spread of radicalization in the state.
- Democratic govt once re-elected, along with established SF to be proactive and transparent in media handling to avoid misuse by the fundamentalists/terrorists.
- The well-established Indian Army's Anti Intrusion Obstacle System (AIOS) to be further strengthened with use of technology to further reduce infiltration and foil Pak proxy war designs in the valley.
- Well-established SF to strengthen police forces and NIA to put effective mechanisms in place to check the spread of drugs and hawala money in the state.
- Leverage the idea of Kashmiriyat to re-settle willing Kashmiri Pandits back in the valley by providing them concentric security arrangements,

along with opportunities of employment through private industry in outer perimeter. This can then become the, meeting point with other communities of young job seekers in the valley, thereby reducing the threat of a radicalized society.

Weakness-Threat (WT) Strategies
- To exploit the IS situation in the state on stabilization to strengthen the administrative mechanism, improve governance, and enhance transparency in public funds spending in order to create positive public perception about the elected govt body.
- To harness the availability of local and natural resources to set up small-scale industries by providing suitable concessions to private industries and generate employment.
- Exploit democratic setup to ensure balanced allocation of resources for growth of regions in consonance to peculiarities and requirement of same. This will take care of the negative sentiment generated by geographically separated regions.
- Ensure transparency and fairness in electoral process (to start with in the Panchayat elections) and functioning of same to avoid any political crisis/uncertainties.
- Strengthen Govt education mechanism by placing trusted personalities at the helm of affairs and bring in free education to counter radicalization.
- To work out modalities for time-bound transfer of control of IS situation in the hinterland from Indian Army to state and central police forces.
- Promote investment in horticulture industry by private and govt agencies through tax holidays/waivers to generate employment and engage educated youth.
- Improve private investments and Infrastructure in the state to counter the threat of Increased Chinese influence through the construction of CPEC.
- Create infrastructure to develop additional tourist hubs/centres other than traditional locations to generate employment and more revenue.

Mandatory Strategies
- Maintain IS situation stable/controlled by synergized actions of army, police and civil administration at all hierarchal levels.
- Make a sustained effort to capture and indict OGWs with appropriate

proof of their nefarious activities which are stealing the future of the youth of the state.
- Army to insure effectiveness of Anti Intrusion Obstacle system (AIOS) and LC management to keep infiltration under check such as to foil Pak's proxy war plans.
- Bring in more transparency and accountability of governance through use of technology and strictness such as to build its credibility amongst local populace.
- Fairness and transparency to be ensured in electoral process and media reporting by administration and army.
- Strengthen state police forces through well-established security forces to check drugs and Hawala money and also to maintain present stable/controlled IS situation as law and order situation.
- Reduce presence of army from hinterland (South of Banihal to start with) through timebound well-planned coordinated effort such as IS situation is managed and controlled by police forces in hinterland.
- Strengthen education and health mechanism in the state to check radicalization and weaning away of youth from mainstream.
- Generate employment for educated youth by building up industrial base through PSUs and bringing in private investors.
- Engage Pak through Multi-track diplomacy, Indo-Pak trade and boost handicraft/agriculture/horticulture industry of the state.
- Infrastructure development be paced up for generating employment and also allowing flow of commodities thus boosting states economy as well.
- RRG is an acronym for the Religious Rehabilitation Group.[40] Formed and officially launched in 23 April 2003, RRG is a voluntary group consisting of individual ulama and a community of asatizah (Islamic scholars and teachers) in Singapore. Initially, RRG's primary objective was to rehabilitate detained Jemaah Islamiah members and their families through counselling. However, it has since broadened its scope to include misinterpretations promoted by self-radicalised individuals and those in support of ISIS. A similar arrangement could be worked out with the participation of the local religious Ulema so that the effect of Radicalisation is reduced/removed through religious counselling.
- Carry out social empowerment through interaction with community leaders and programmes in order to wean people away from Radicalisation.

- Utilise trained specialists to carry out Psychological and Social rehabilitation of radicalised elements of society.

Recommendations

It is strongly recommended that the short-term strategies derived from SWOT analysis be studied in consonance with the coherent mid-term and long-term "whole of the government" strategies of the government so that there is a holistic and continuous approach to the problem at hand. We cannot afford that today's solutions become fixes that fail in the overall context of the Issue at hand.

Conclusion

Decades of Militancy and support from across the border have resulted in the state of J&K becoming one of the poorest in terms of Governance. The vacuum created by this lack of governance is being filled up either by efforts by the Army, which again is being perceived negatively of late, or by the Terrorists/OGWs who are implementing a well laid out Pakistani subversion plan. A relook at Governance in a more comprehensive manner needs to be carried out which will assist in creating positive perceptions amongst the Awaam.

The turmoil since 2016 resulted in unending clashes between people and security forces, caused killing and injuring of civilians, burning of Government property, and tremendous loss of Industrial production and services coupled with the halt in Economic activities in the backdrop of long spells of curfews and hartals. The Tourism sub-sector and industrial/business activity which is the backbone of Kashmir economy came to a grinding halt during the period. With regular cycles of unrest since 2008 disrupting the social life and hitting the economy hard, the biggest challenge for the government is two-fold:

- To prevent re-occurrence of such events
- To calibrate the economic and social policy to what in the short run is the "new normal."

Political turmoil, misplaced priorities, one-upmanship, rampant corruption and a total sense of insecurity may have led the Central government to break the alliance in J&K and consider Governor's rule. At this juncture announcement of Governor's rule, when the Awaam was probably fed up of ineffective governance and a general sense of despondency this could be a blessing in disguise for the troubled state.

Although it is accepted that many of the the above-mentioned strategies derived through scientific analysis, may already being pursued, but this SWOT Analysis could form a basis for the present disposition in the state as well as for the elected representatives of the state as and when the present situation is resolved, to form a holistic response.

NOTES

1. http://shodhganga.inflibnet.ac.in/jspui/bitstream/10603/161434/14/9.%20chapter%203.pdf, accessed on August 25, 2018.
2. http://kashmirstudygroup.com/awayforward/mapsexplan/jammu_kashmir.html, accessed on August 25, 2018.
3. https://www.google.co.in/url?sa=i&rct=j&q=&esrc=s&source=images&cd=&cad=rja&uact=8&ved=2ah UKEwjmhKL2wMHdAhXYWysKHSu0Aq8QjRx6BAgBEAU&url=http%3A%2F%2F www.indian defen cereview.com%2Fnews%2Fkashmir-india-china-pakistan-triangular conflict%2F&psig=AOvVaw3z9shxD3IBiwJlZ_p0aHWf&ust=15372 5434867493, accessed on August 24, 2018.
4. The map was projected as a part of System Analysis Study conducted and projected by College of Defence Management for National Seminar on Mapping of Perceptions in J&K - the Way Ahead, Held at Manekshaw Centre on August 18, 2018.
5. http://www.business-standard.com/article/pti-stories/j-k-gsdp-to-grow-at-8-49-pc-in-2017-18-survey-118011000858_1.html, accessed on May 27, 2018.
   6https://www.business-standard.com/article/pti-stories/j-k-exploits-just-16-of-hydro-power-potential-despite-growing-demand-survey-118022500370_1.html, accessed on August 22, 2018.
7. Official site of Department of Geology and Mining J&K, accessed on August 22, 2018.
8. https://www.greaterkashmir.com/news/op-ed/increasing-forest-cover-of-j-k-an-inside-perspective/276625.html, accessed on August 25, 2018.
9. https://www.trai.gov.in/sites/default/.../Telecom%, accessed on July 18, 2018.
10. http://jkslbc.com/Handicrafts.php, accessed on July 18, 2018.
11. Economic Survey of J&K 2017, p. 113.
12. http://en.wikipedia.org/wiki/Kashmiriyat.
13. https://knoema.com/atlas/India/Jammu-and-Kashmir/Population-Density, accessed on May 28, 2018.
14. censusindia.gov.in/2011-prov-results/data.../india/Final_PPT_2011_chapter6.pdf.
15. https://www.livemint.com/Opinion/qtleLNGIy8RKgh3o5i5LjN/Managing-Kashmirs-youth-bulge.html, accessed on August 22, 2018.
16. https://en.wikipedia.org/wiki/List_of_Indian_states_and_territories_by_Human_Development_ Index, accessed on August 22, 2018.
17. Pandit Premnath Bazaz, The History of the Struggle for Freedom in Kashmir, Kashmir Publishing Company, New Delhi, 1954, p. 657.
18. Ibid.
19. http://ikashmir.net/distortionsreality/chapter3.html, accessed on August 22, 2018.
20. www.jammu-kashmir.com/archives/archives2015/kashmir20150805d.html.
21. https://www.researchgate.net/publication/321085190_Women_empowermentIssues_ and_challenges_in_Jammu_and_Kashmir, accessed on August 22, 2018.
22. Economic Survey of J&K 2017, pp. 289-290.
23. http://www.bharat-rakshak.com/LANCER/idr00013.htm , accessed on July 23, 2018.

24 https://www.orfonline.org/research/governance-jk-alienation/, accessed on July 8, 2018.
25 http://www.greaterkashmir.com/news/kashmir/j-k-among-most-corrupt-states-survey/271724.html, accessed July 8, 2018.
26 Economic Survey of J&K 2017, p. 107.
27 https://www.greaterkashmir.com/news/news/jk-has-6-lakh-jobless-youth/114847.html, accessed on July 23, 2018
28 http://www.satp.org/satporgtp/sair/Archives/sair8/8_35.htm, accessed on March 2, 2018.
29 http://www.claws.in/images/publication_pdf/1027785870_Cissuebrief.pdf, Tools of terror in J&K, p. 5.
30 https://thewire.in/uncategorised/understanding-the-lives-of-those-living-along-the-loc, accessed July 9, 2018.
31 http://www.risingkashmir.com/hurriyat-split-again/.
32 https://kashmirlife.net/jk-economic-survey-2017-ease-of-doing-business-161605/, accessed on August 22, 2018.
33 https://www.financialexpress.com/world-news/us-asks-pakistan-to-act-against-haqqani-network-other-terror-groups/1081719/, accessed on August 25, 2018.
34 Dabla, B.A., Social Impact of Militancy in Kashmir, Gyan Publishing House.
35 Devadas, op. cit.
36 https://timesofindia.indiatimes.com/india/how-mosques-and-mobiles-are-radicalising-kashmir/articleshow/59507200.cms, accessed on August 16, 2018.
37 http://www.claws.in/images/publication_pdf/709160172_IB126-min.pdf. Exorcising the ISIS, AS Chonker. Accessed on August 21, 2108.
38 Economic Survey of J&K 2017, p. 287.
39 https://www.vifindia.org/article/2018/july/10/strategy-of-military-and-non-military-measures, accessed on July 12, 2018.
40 https://www.rrg.sg/about-rrg/, accessed on July 21, 2018, The organization was highlighted by speakers in the recently comcluded strategic dialogue on "Countering Violent Extremism" at Strategic Studies Centre, Thailand, which was attended by the author.

CHAPTER 6
A Peek into the Future: Scenario-Building Exercise

FOR MID-TERM AND LONG-TERM STRATEGIES

General. Having formulated the various short-term strategies consequent to an in-depth SWOT analysis, the next step in formulation of the Kashmir Valley Strategy is to carry out the exercise of scenario analysis to arrive at plausible medium and long-term strategies which should be integrated with the SWOT strategies. Having gone through the chapters on system analysis and psychological aspects of Kashmir and its solutions, the readers would realise that the system in the state is so complex and dynamic that it is practically impossible to do justice to scenario-building exercise without going into the intricate details of the socio-economic-religious, security, external as well as the administrative environment. The time horizon chosen for building and analyzing scenarios is Year 2035 with a time step of three years, six years and eight years in the first, second and third steps, respectively. Factors already analyzed earlier in the book will not be discussed again, although these will be utilized in order to prepare the requisite construct for the Scenarios.

Decision Focus
- **Purpose.** Kashmir Scenarios 2035.
- **Time Dimension.** Time period for development of scenario is up to 2035 and the time steps for development of scenario dynamics are:
    o **2019-2022 (3 years).** Post-Parliamentary elections of 2019.
    o **2022-2028 (6 years).** Mid-term time check.
    o **2028-2035 (8 years).** Long-term time check to arrive at long-term strategies.

SCENARIO BUILDING

- o **Departure Point.** The common start-point chosen for the building of these trajectories and scenarios is after the dissolution of the J&K Assembly by the Governor and the results of the local body elections and panchayat elections scheduled for end of 2018. The results of the same will be declared in mid-December 2018. The aftermath of the elections in early 2019 are characterised by violence against elected members. The elections throw up a dilemma for policymakers. In order to assess the situation at departure point, world view of all stake holders was obtained and expert interviews were taken; the world views are summarized as below:
- **Militancy in J&K.** All sections except Kashmiri Pandits feel that the local young boys are not interested in Jihad but join militancy for a number of factors which include a sense of alienation and lack of employment which is being catalyzed by radicalizing forces working for a separatist agenda. It is also getting fashionable amongst the youth to get radicalized and join militancy.
- **Pak Support.** There is a universal agreement that primarily, Pak is responsible for terrorism in J&K over the last 30 years and Pak's interference in J&K is aimed at fulfilling its Political agenda and not a genuine concern for the "Awaam" of J&K. However, lately there is a rise in the number of local militants due to socio-economic and politico-religious reasons.
- **Comparison with PoK.** All sections fully understand that Life of a common man is better in Kashmir than PoK.
- **Decline in Infiltration.** SF appreciate that the erection of LC fence is the main reason for decline in infiltration across LC. Only 10% of the total 200 odd militants are of foreign origin.

- **Hurriyat Sp.** Hurriyat does not enjoy the support of Awaam in valley as it did in earlier times.
- **Religious Fundamentalism.** Religious fundamentalism is on the rise and Awaam feels that it is challenging the concept of "Kashmiriyat." The youth of the region are being systematically driven away from their core values.
- **AFSPA.** All sections of the society except Awam in Kupwara sect and specifically those not employed with state/central govt feel that AFSPA is essential for functioning of Security Forces in J&K.
- **Deployment of SF and CAPF.** All cross sections of population feel that the deployment of Indian Army and CRPF troops is necessary for continuation of peace and stability in J&K.
- **Role of Local Media.** Situation in valley has improved to the extent that citizens have full freedom of expression and peaceful assembly in J&K but Local media is still not performing its role towards Awaam in J&K.
- **LC Trade.** Majority of the population feel that free trade across LoC will help improve socio-economic condition of J&K.
- **Infrastructure Development.** Special initiative by the Central government in terms of Infrastructure development in J&K has significantly helped development in J&K.
- **Kashmiri Pandits Rehab.** All groups unanimously agree that Kashmiri Pandits who have migrated to Jammu, Delhi and other places should be rehabilitated back in Kashmir. However, there is a feeling amongst the muslim community in the valley that they should come back only to their homes and no special ghettoes should be made for them by acquiring land.
- **Spl Status & Alienation.** People in the valley feel that Articles 370 and 35 A of Indian constitution as applicable to J&K should continue while fringe groups like Kashmiri Pandits, JKP and Surrendered Militants feel that J&K should become federal state in the Union of India like all other states.

Domains. Due to reasons mentioned above and carrying out a comprehensive scenario analysis without compromising any particular aspect, the following domains have been identified with respect to Kashmir valley:

- Security and External Domain (SE).
- Social, Economic and Religion Domain (SER).
- Administrative (Admin) Domain.

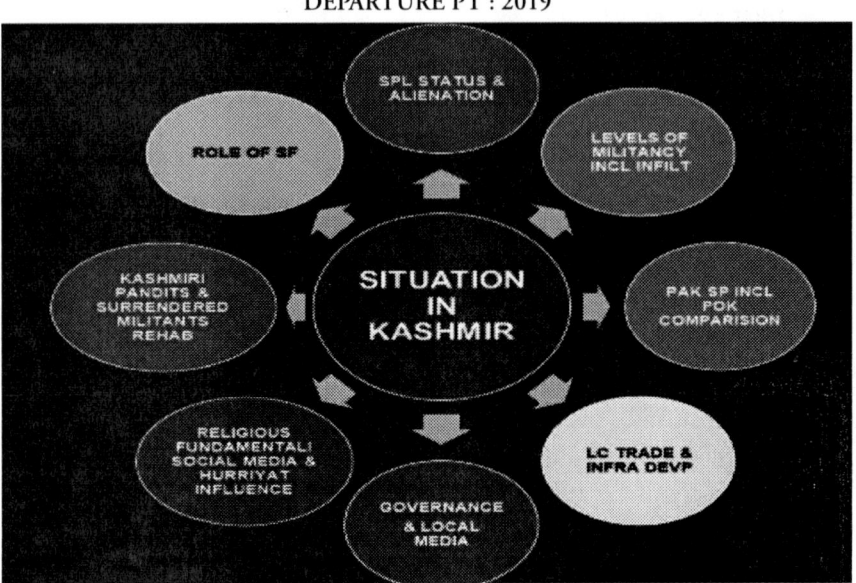

SECURITY AND EXTERNAL (SE) ENVIRONMENT

Key Decision Factors. The Key Decision Factors pertaining to the strategic decision are Political will, Socio-economic security and Human resource development, Governance, Pak's influence: cross border terrorism, Presence of SF, Separatist dynamics and youth, Communal disturbances and the Electoral process.

These issues have already been discussed in detail in the book and hence are not being revisited.

Environmental Forces (not being discussed in detail as already covered in the Book)

- **Internal.** These include Internal security problems in J&K, rising internal law and order unrests including stone-throwing incidents, strikes and obstruction of operations of SF, Religious fanaticism and communal issues, Economic development, strong, modern and apolitical military, strong democracy and political system, separatism and quest for independence in the valley, Jammu and Ladakh dynamics.
- **External.** As far as Pakistan is concerned, these factors certainly include unresolved border disputes with India, Kashmir as a core issue, Religious extremism, proclivity to support terrorism in India and Afghanistan,

fragile economy and unstable democratic govt, strong and dominant role of military in national policy, deteriorating relations with US, poor nuclear proliferation record, propensity to increase strategic depth by forging alliances with Taliban and controlling events through the Haqqani network. For Afghanistan, it is the likely instability in it due to migration of ISIS elements and the consequent security implications. China's increasing interest in the AF-Pak region due to its flagship BRI project of CPEC corridor could also lead to changing dynamics in the region.

DRIVERS & PARAMETERS S-E ENVIRONMENT

•ASPIRATIONS OF PEOPLE •PAK MORAL, POL ,DIPLOMATIC, FINANCIAL, MTRL SP •HURRIYAT CONF AGENDA •OGWS & FENCE SITTERS •DOMINATION OF J&K POLITICS BY VALLEY •INFILT •JAMMU & LADAKH REGION DYNAMICS	•ECONOMY •UN-EMP •AFSPA •PERCEPTION MGT BY SF •SOCIAL MEDIA •ELECTORAL PROCESS •AFGHAN SECURITY SIT •GOVERNANCE •COMMUNAL DISTURBANCES /DIVIDE **PARAMETERS** •TER GP RIVALRY	•ROLE OF SF •PAK'S CALIBRATION OF PROXY WAR •MILITANTS DYNAMICS **DRIVERS**
•HISTORICAL BAGGAGE •ILLEGAL FUNDING-DRUGS, HAWALA •APPEASEMENT OF KASHMIRIS	•INFRA-COMN, INDUSTRIAL •ROLE OF HR ORGS •CAPACITY & CAPB OF CAPF & INT AGENCIES •LOCAL MEDIA •CORRUPTION •SURRENDER & REHAB POLICY	•POLITICO-MILITANT NEXUS •LAW & ORDER SIT •ISIS SIT IN AF-PAK-IN
•POK POLITICAL DYNAMICS	•TAPPING OF NATURAL RESOURCES •TOURISM FACILITIES •GROWING LITERACY RATE	•CROSS BORDER TRADE

IMPACT ↑ UNCERTAINTY →

Scenario Logics. The **high impact–high uncertainty** factors are identified as the "**Drivers**" and the **high impact–low uncertainty** factors as the "**Parameters.**" Other factors shall be ignored. The essence of scenarios is not to examine every possibility but to consider the **possibility of drastically different futures**. Hence, based on each scenario logic, separate scenarios need to be developed leading to separate future "end states." Developing a matrix of all drivers and their possible behaviour will lead to possible and plausible grouping to form scenario logics. With this as the basis of analysis, the following plausible scenarios have been formulated while ensuring the direct impact of drivers on the scenario and cross impact of drivers on each other.

DESCRIPTION OF DRIVERS

MILITANTS DYNAMICS
- INCREASE OF RADICALISATION OF YOUTH
- INFLUENCE OF IDEOLOGICAL LEANINGS OF SEPARATISTS
- NON FULFILMENT OF GROWING ASPIRATIONS
- CHANNELIZING THE YOUTH BULGE IN VALLEY TOWARDS JIHAD
- MONITOR VICTIMS OF STATE ACTION
- ACCESSIBILITY TO SOCIAL MEDIA & TECHNOLOGY BY THE URBAN YOUTH
- REHAB & SURRENDER POLICY
- PERCEPTION OF AFSPA
- JIHAD A LUCRATIVE PREPOSITION

ROLE OF SF
- TGT THE LDRSHIP OF MILITANCY & SP STRUCTURE
- CAPACITY & CAPB OF CAPF, STATE POLICE & INT AGENCIES
- AFSPA
- ONE UP-MANSHIP
- PERCEPTION MGT
- EFF CT GRID & COUNTER INFILT
- ABILITY TO DEAL WITH TRIGGERS
- OPs WITH REDUCED FT PRINT

PAK'S CALIBRATION OF JIHAD (PROXY WAR)
- MORAL, POL, DIPLOMATIC, FINANCIAL, MTRL SP
- ENTANGLEMENT WITH INTERNAL TURMOIL (TTP)
- INTERNATIONAL PRESSURE TO CURB CROSS BORDER TERRORISM
- OBSESSION WITH KASHMIR
- RELENTLESS EFFORTS TO DERAIL THE PEACE THROUGH ITS VARIOUS PROXIES – BOTH TERRORIST AND SEPARATIST

Scenarios and Driver Trends

Driver / Scenario	Role of SF	Pak's Calibration of Proxy War	Militants Dynamics
"Chalta-Hai" Kashmir (Status Quo)	IS Deftly Controlled (med)	Spasmodic (med)	Uncomfortable tranquil (med)
Healing Kashmir (More Positive Case)	Firm and Complete Control (high)	Irregular (low)	Restful (high)
Smouldering Kashmir (Worst case)	IS situation blazing and spiralling out of control (high)	Belligerent (high)	Aggressive (high)

A Peek into the Future: Scenario-Building Exercise

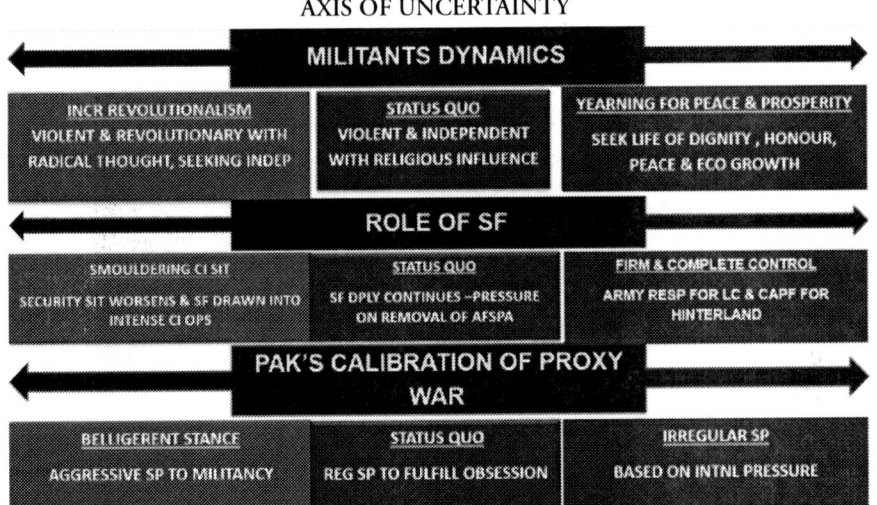

Trajectory 1: "Chalta Hai" Kashmir: Status Quo

- **Trajectory Dynamics/Description.** Security forces continue to maintain pressure on separatists preventing them from regrouping into a viable force. Pak continues with its agenda/policy of abetting terrorism in Kashmir unwilling to let go of its obsession. Separatists continue to pursue their agenda of Azadi with display of violence and unrest under influence of Jihad. Only interplay of **Drivers** is highlighted.
    o **Role of Security Forces.** There is slow improvement in law and order; however, sporadic incidents of unrest continue to affect internal security of the state, with limited marginalisation of armed segments of insurgent outfits and successful integration of moderate factions into electoral process. Uneasy calm continues in J&K; however, occasional incidents of violence occur. SF continue to keep up pressure on militants resulting in effective control of the situation, but sporadic incidents of violence continue to shake the calm. Major separatist groups continue to operate. Intermittent escalation of street protests over a range of "issues" and "codes of conduct" continue. Widespread dissent and protests against AFSPA continue to create turbulence with frequent statements from political hierarchy asking for its withdrawal and admonishing by courts, creating a sense of misperception amongst SF. There is limited coordination amongst police and SF due to varied perceptions. State police remains politicised, coercive and collusive corruption

continues. Certain sections of State Police (SOG) continue to perform and achieve results although under the fear of targeted killings of SPOs and their family members by militants. The complicity of some Policemen in abandoning the force and joining militancy-related activities emerges as a major concern, as terrorist modules operating with the help or participation of Policemen become particularly difficult to identify and neutralize.

- **Pakistan's Calibration of Proxy War.** Pak continues to covertly support terror outfits while endeavouring to engage India in talks on Kashmir. Kashmir issue brought up selectively in international forums. However, increasing economic and cultural engagement marginally balances the rhetoric, leading to uneasy peace at borders, with gradual strengthening of religious hardliners in Pakistan's internal politics, leading to increasing support for cross-border terrorism, appeasement politics, and stifling of moderates seeking peace.
- **Afghanistan.** Pak interference and growing influence of Taliban keeps things on edge with a distinct possibility of influx of terrorists and ISIS ideology to foment trouble into India. Afghanistan's request of support from India is guarded as also the response from India.
- **Militants Dynamics.** Separatists continue to remain vociferous; however, an uneasy calm prevails. There is resentfulness amongst youth due to unemployment, poor governance and SF actions. Alienation of youth remains despite Govt policies to integrate them into mainstream resulting in widespread joining of youth into Jihad. Repeated and often acerbic exchange of views on the issue of withdrawal of the Armed Forces Special Powers Act (AFSPA) from certain areas in the state continues to be voiced. Surrender and rehabilitation policy is marginally successful but fails to incite mass homecoming. Youth detained in jails for stone-throwing incidents are radicalised there and join the cause of militancy on their release.

Trajectory 2: Healing Kashmir: Positive

- **Trajectory Dynamics/Description.** SF continue to maintain firm and effective control on the IS situation resulting in promoting the prospect of enduring peace in the state. Pak continues to covertly support terror outfits while endeavouring to engage India in talks on Kashmir under intense international pressure. Kashmir issue brought up selectively in international forums but without any support from major players. There is a change in sentiments of separatists, with sharply diminishing enthusiasm for the secessionist cause and in favour of Pakistan. Only interplay of **Drivers** is highlighted.

- o **Role of Security Forces.** There is a swift improvement in law and order; however, infrequent incidents of unrest continue to affect internal security of the state. There is complete marginalisation of armed segments of insurgent outfits and successful integration of moderate factions into electoral process. Relative calm continues in J&K; however, occasional incidents of violence occur but with reduced severity and impact without any backing or popular support from Awaam. SF continue to maintain firm and effective control on the IS situation resulting in promoting the prospect of enduring peace in the state. Due to prolonged unfruitful militancy, continuous and cumulative failures of the separatists within J&K and firm control of IS situation by SF, major separatist groups are completely marginalised. Peaceful street protests only over a range of "political" and "governance" issues continue. Due to handing over of control to CRPF and community policing by J&K Police, and complete withdrawal of Army from the IS duties and deployment on the LC, no more dissent and protests against AFSPA and therefore no turbulence and resultant sense of alienation is seen. Political hierarchy exploits conducive environment for effective governance thereby bringing in positive peace. Complete synergy amongst police and SF due to clear perceptions on political strategy has to be followed. State police and CRPF take on the role of effective management of law and order in major towns and cities in the state. Militancy is completely wiped out of the state. Intensive measures to strengthen civil administration and reenergise the Police Force result in infusing greater confidence in the people. The separatists fail in repeated efforts to orchestrate a resurgence of street violence on the 2016 pattern.
- o **Pakistan's Calibration of Proxy War.** Pak continues to covertly support terror outfits while endeavouring to engage India in talks on Kashmir under intense international pressure. However, increasing economic and cultural engagement considerably balances the rhetoric, leading to complete peace at borders. Despite repeated calls by the Pakistan-backed terrorist separatist formations to the

people of J&K to boycott polls – General Elections, Assembly Elections and Local Body Elections – people vote in large numbers, demonstrating faith in the democratic process, as against the politics of the gun. Youth self-help groups act as catalysts for this movement of change. Pakistan is awash with Islamist extremist militancy and organised crime groups, creating a regime of heightened lawlessness and anarchy. In spite of "democracy" in Pakistan, it results in further decline of political and administrative institutions, and a further destabilisation of the economy, threatening the very integrity and existence of the state. Futility of pursuing terrorism as an instrument of state policy is realised by the people, traders and intelligentsia, resulting in greater voices for forging peace with India. Pak endeavours to dismantle terror infrastructure in PoK.

o **Afghanistan.** Pak interference and growing influence of Taliban keeps things on edge with a distinct possibility of influx of terrorists to foment trouble into India. The ISIS develops deep inroads into an already fractured society in Afghanistan, which results in a turf war between Afghanistan National security Forces, Taliban, ISIS and Pak.

o **Militants Dynamics.** There is growing disenchantment of the separatists and Kashmiri youth with violence as a form of grievance redressal. Separatists continue to remain vociferous; however, calm prevails. The reconstruction plan for Jammu and Kashmir is a success, aimed at creating infrastructure development, basic amenities, employment and other income-generating activities and rehabilitation and resettlement of militancy-affected victims. For skill development and making the State's youth employable, schemes like "Himayat" and "Udaan" give encouraging results resulting in dwindling support to separatists. The Indian private sector pitches in by diverting corporate social responsibility funds in to the state youth forums running de-radicalisation programmes in the hinterland. There is yearning for peace amongst youth and separatists due to prolonged militancy and quest for reaping the dividends of positive peace. There is change in sentiments of separatists, with sharply diminishing enthusiasm for the secessionist cause and in favour of Pakistan. Nevertheless, some lingering irritants still persist. The issue of withdrawal of the AFSPA is no more voiced as the Army withdraws from peaceful zones in the hinterland.

Disillusionment with Pak and extremely successful surrender and rehabilitation policy encourages mass homecoming for all groups.

Trajectory 3: Smouldering Kashmir: Worst Case

- **Trajectory Dynamics/Description.** J&K situation is volatile due to aggressive support of Pak, Taliban and global influences of ISIS ideology in the state, threatening to deteriorate to the extent that Pak Army emboldened to launch misadventure. Pak continues to overtly support terror outfits with rhetoric that the only solution lies in implementation of UN resolutions or tripartite talks. There is significant resurrection of terrorism in the state with sleeper cells getting activated resulting in youth participating in escalation of violence. Only interplay of **Drivers** is highlighted.

    o **Role of Security Forces.** Gradual deterioration in law and order situation compounded with regular incidents of unrest/stone throwing continue to adversely affect internal security of the state. J&K situation is volatile due to aggressive support of Pak, Taliban as well as ISIS-inspired local groups in the state, threatening to deteriorate to the extent that Pak Army emboldened to launch misadventure. Armed militancy, kidnappings and selected killing of security forces and their families are rampant in the Kashmir Valley. Terrorist strikes and violence spread and continue to affect the entire country. Long-term policies of national security are adversely affected due to own political, diplomatic and bureaucratic apathy. As a result, security concerns are neglected in Government policies, giving impetus to armed segments of insurgent outfits and alienation of moderate factions from electoral process. Militants give open calls and threats for non-participation in electoral process. Grave situation in Kashmir continues with population alienated, passions against India rejuvenated by the local media. Thousands of people are under the influence of separatists as well as negative propaganda by mainland Indian media, out on the streets to demonstrate against India. SF continue to keep up pressure on militants despite widespread sporadic incidents of violence shaking the calm. Major separatist groups continue to secure direct assistance from their Pakistani patrons. Regular escalation of street protests over a range of "issues" continues, severely crippling the life in the state. Widespread dissent and protests against AFSPA continue to create turbulence with frequent statements from political hierarchy and Judiciary asking for its withdrawal creating a sense of misperception and lowering of morale amongst SF. There is lack of coordination amongst police and SF due to varied perceptions. State police remains politicised, coercive and collusive corruption continues. Defection and rampant complicity of Policemen in militancy-related activities emerges as a major concern threatening the core of CI strategy.

- **Pakistan's Calibration of Jihad Proxy War.** Pak continues to overtly support terror outfits with rhetoric that the only solution lies in implementation of UN resolutions or tripartite talks. Kashmir issue is brought up vigorously in international forums. Due to intense domestic pressure, there is considerable decrease in economic and cultural engagement. There is resurgence in militancy adopting various tactics, including military-style ambushes, suicide attacks, bomb blasts and Improvised Explosive Device (IED) attacks; the militants mainly target SFs as well as moderate elements who try to initiate a dialogue with the Government. As and when peace in J&K consolidates, the establishment in Pakistan displays increasing signs of impatience, with increasing violations of the Ceasefire Agreement in the form of artillery and small arms firing across the Line of Control and International Border (IB), as well as urgent attempts to reach out to the separatist constituency in the State. There is gradual strengthening of religious hardliners in Pakistan's internal politics, leading to increasing support for cross-border terrorism, appeasement politics, and stifling of moderates seeking peace.
- **Afghanistan.** Pak interference and growing influence of Taliban results in heavy influx of terrorists to foment trouble into India. Pak also informally carries out a deal with ISIS and Al Qaeda elements to infiltrate J&K and India without affecting Pak.
- **Militants Dynamics.** Separatists continue to remain vociferous and toe the Pakistani line, and reject any dialogue with Delhi without a role for Pakistan and third-country intermediaries. There is extreme resentfulness amongst separatist youth due to unemployment, poor governance and SF actions. There is a complete alienation of separatists, and Govt policies to integrate them into mainstream are a failure. Repeated and often acerbic exchange of views on the

issue of withdrawal of the AFSPA from entire state continues to be voiced violently. Surrender and rehabilitation policy is completely unsuccessful resulting in recycling of surrendered militants. Youth are booked for stone-throwing under PSA; their parents are harassed by policemen for bribes. These youth are tortured in jails and get radicalised to join militant groups. On coming out of jails they are seen at funerals of slain militants motivating their friends to join militancy. There is significant resurrection of terrorism in the state with sleeper cells getting activated, resulting in youth participating in escalation of violence.

SOCIAL, ECONOMIC AND RELIGIOUS DOMAIN (SER)

Key Decision Factors. Following Key Decision Factors (KDFs) have been identified with respect to Kashmir Valley:-

- **Economic Growth.** Already discussed in SWOT analysis.
- **Regional Disparity.** One of the most astonishing facts about J&K's economy is the disparity in distribution of economy among the three regions.

	Jammu	Kashmir	Ladakh
Population	62 Lakh	58 Lakh	2 Lakh
Area	25.96%	15.67%	58.37%
Villages	3,614	2,029	242
Lok Sabha Seats	2	3	1
Vidhan Sabha Seats	36	47	4
Jobs in Secretariat	10% (approx)	90% (approx)	–
Revenue Generation	70% (approx)	30% (approx)	–
Funds given by Govt.	30% (approx)	70% (approx)	–
Education Fund	30% (approx)	70% (approx)	–
Electricity Supply	23 Mega Watt	350 Mega Watt	–

- **Social Divide.** The Kashmir Valley is dominated by ethnic Kashmiris, who have largely driven the Azadi campaign. Non-Kashmiri Muslim ethnic groups (Paharis, Sheenas, Gujjars and Bakarwals), who dominate areas along the Line of Control, have remained indifferent to the separatist campaign. Jammu province region though has a 70:30 Hindu-Muslim ratio, parts of the region were hit by militants, but violence has ebbed there, along with the Valley. Dogras (67%) are the single largest group in the multi-ethnic region of Jammu living with Punjabis, Paharis, Bakerwals and Gujjars. Ladakh is the largest region in the state with over 200,000 people. Its two districts are Leh (77% Buddhist) and Kargil (80% Muslim population). Union territory status has been the key demand of Leh Buddhists for many years. The state is clearly divided in three distinct regions of Jammu (dominated by Dogras and Hindus), Kashmir (dominated by Muslims) and Ladakh (dominated by Buddhists). The Shia-Sunni divide also exists in valley.

- **Religious Fundamentalism.** Already discussed in SWOT analysis.
- **Empowerment of Youth and Women.** The number of officially registered unemployed youth rose from 4,47,653 to 5,97,332 between Nov 2009 to Dec 2010. Today, over 70% of Jammu and Kashmir's population is estimated to be under 35. Reliable figures are hard to come by but there is evidence of chronic unemployment and underemployment. The available data suggest that the best part of three-quarters of a million people have joined the ranks of working-age people seeking jobs between 2001 and 2011. Official data reveals that the incidence of unemployment amongst youth in Kashmir has continued to rise since 1993. With more and more educated youth entering an already over-saturated job market each year, Kashmir faces a mounting challenge. According to the Mercy Corps findings from an extensive research effort conducted across 10 districts of Kashmir Valley to analyze and understand key factors that are critical to boosting youth entrepreneurship, which was also presented to the state government for right investment and support, Kashmir's youth bulge could eventually yield a demographic dividend in terms of increased productivity and economic growth. Kashmir's burgeoning youth population is an untapped asset and represents a potential opportunity for the positive economic and social change. Large percentages of Kashmir's youth are potential entrepreneurs. Kashmiri youth are highly resilient, educated and motivated but currently lack skills needed to compete in the 21st century and face acute scarcity of employment opportunities in both the public and private sector.
    o **Empowerment of Youth.** Empowerment of youth, besides panchayati raj institutions, in Jammu and Kashmir is the top priority of the Center and the State Govt. Skill Empowerment and Employment in J&K is required to provide options and

opportunities to all youth in J&K, ranging from school dropouts to college educated, to select training program for salaried or self-employment as per their interest.

- o **Women Empowerment.** In a state like Jammu and Kashmir where a huge population of women is unemployed and another significant section consists of widows and half widows, the importance of women's economic independence for their overall dignity and even survival is brought out by the fact that there is a linkage between the physical survival of women and their entry into the workforce. Mothers have a huge influence in Kashmiri families and by empowering and patronizing this segment of society, could have a positive impact on the Psyche of the people.

- **Kashmiriyat.** Already discussed in SWOT analysis.
- **Education System.** J&K Govt provides compulsory and free education upto Elementary Level under SSA. It includes opening/upgradation of schools for Elementary Education, 100% enrollment of children in Educational Institutions and providing of Infrastructural facilities; 79 KGBVs (Kasturba Gandhi Balika Vidayalayas) are functional in the state. The Education Department provides free of cost Text books and mid-day meal upto 8th class. Strengthening of Secondary and Higher Secondary Education Institutes under RMSA has also been a priority of the state govt. The literacy rates are 78% for male and 58% for women; also the urban rate is 69% and rural rate is 54%. The enrolment in Government Schools increased from 14.50 lacs in 2004 to 19.50 lacs in 2009-10. Number of Out of School Children (OOSC) was reduced from 3.76 lacs in 2002-03 to 0.39 lacs in 2009-10. J&K Higher Education Department is the controlling authority for all the Higher Education Institutions of the State. It has seven universities and numerous Government and Non-Government Colleges to look after. There has been a gradual increase in number of govt colleges and enrollment over the years. A total of 45 colleges exist in the Kashmir valley. There are increasing pointers to the claim by some Self-Help Groups that Religious and Militant Radicalization as well as Separatism is being fanned by the Faculty at schools and colleges to a great extent.

Environmental Factors. Critical uncertainties of the future are the environmental factors, changes in which in the future, will impact the "End State". Although discussed in different chapters of the book earlier, based on brainstorming and expert opinion, some of the factors have been further expanded as given below:

- **Economic Growth.** Issues that merit attention are exploitation of hydroelectric power and tourism, investment by corporate houses, opening of trade routes to increase LC trade, industrial development, increase of domestic consumption, creating an Ideal Investment climate, economic reforms including privatization, remuneration of outside money in valley, development of infrastructure, entrepreneurship abilities of Kashmiris, removing disparities between urban-rural communities, investment in software, data storage/mining, food processing and handicraft industries and reduced dependence on central funding.

- **Social Divide.** Checking Social disparities, inclusive of socio-economic development, human resource development, overcoming religious divide, appeasement politics, change of mindset from govt jobs, Jammu-Valley-Ladakh divide and rehabilitation of surrendered militants need to be addressed under this factor.

- **Religious Fundamentalism.** Although Religious fundamentalism has been discussed in great detail in the chapter Psychological Aspects of Kashmir, there is a need to again flag a few issues like radicalization of youth, increasing influence of Jamaitis and its affiliated Falah-e-aam Educational trust, especially in South Kashmir, influence of Salafi (Wahabi) sect of Islam, increase in radical Islam Madrassas, inaccessibility of Sufi literature, monitoring spread of fundamental intolerant Islam at national level, regularization of education in madrassas.

- **Hiring of govt teachers from Salafi and Falah-e-Aam education trusts and funding of these trusts.** Back in 1945, Islamist ideologue Abul Ali Mawdudi called on his followers to "change the old tyrannical system and establish a just new order by the power of the sword." He demanded that members of the party founded in his name "seize the authority of state for, an evil system takes root and flourishes under the patronage of an evil government, and a pious cultural order can never be established until the authority of government is wrested from the wicked." According to a Cabinet decision taken on July 14, 2010, hundreds of jobs were to be handed out to schoolteachers linked to the Jammu Kashmir Jamaat-e-Islami, the party set up in Mawdudi's name. More than 440 Falah-i-Aam Trust teachers were inducted into the State school system in 2010.[1] Seventy-four unskilled workers who lost their jobs when Falah-i-Aam schools were closed down in 1990 also got State government jobs. By hiring the Falah-i-Aam teachers, the NC evidently hoped to build bridges with its decades-old Islamist adversaries. But the costs of the decision are being borne now. No great imagination is needed to see what the Jamaat hoped to get from the party affiliates whose salaries is now being paid by the Jammu and Kashmir government—and the tragedy that could lie ahead in case corrective action is not taken to change the perception of these teachers. The details of the Jamaat-e-Islami movement have already been covered in Chapter 2 of the book. Political patronage to ideologicaly inclined organisations and teachers, to increase vote banks in the Valley can lead to dire consequences due to the heady concoction that these organisations are creating in the minds of the youth.

- **Empowerment of Youth and Women.** Already discussed in great length earlier in the book, however, some issues that merit interest are limited representation of women in jobs, influence of separatists in maintaining status quo, meeting rising aspirations of the young and positively channelizing the youth bulge, requirement of genuine NGOs for uplifting the women, channelizing resources for the victims of state action as well as for health and education of women, accessibility to social media and technolgy to the youth, consistency in implementation of policies/schemes, capacity building of the youth, enhanced amenities in border areas, acquiring skills for self-employment anf private sector jobs and last but not the least, changing the perception of youth from seeking govt jobs to private sector jobs.

- **Kashmiriyat.** This factor has been dealt with adequately in the chapter on psychological aspects in Kashmir.

- **Education System.** Improvement in basic and rural education standards as well as infrastructure for higher education is important. Monitoring the education system including the syllabi through local bodies without creating ripples, integration with national education system, exposure to modern higher education and blossoming of a number of schools on the lines of Goodwill schools are also the need of the hour. While we are at it, there is a definite need to keep a discreet watch on the activities of Jamaat-affiliated teachers appointed in 1994 and 2010. If a need is felt, there may be a case for improving their perceptions so that they can impart secular values.

Analysis of Environmental Factors. The above-listed environmental factors have been analyzed based on their "range of variation – degree of uncertainty" and "strength of impact on environmental outcomes – end states". As a result of this analysis, they are classified as shown in the table.

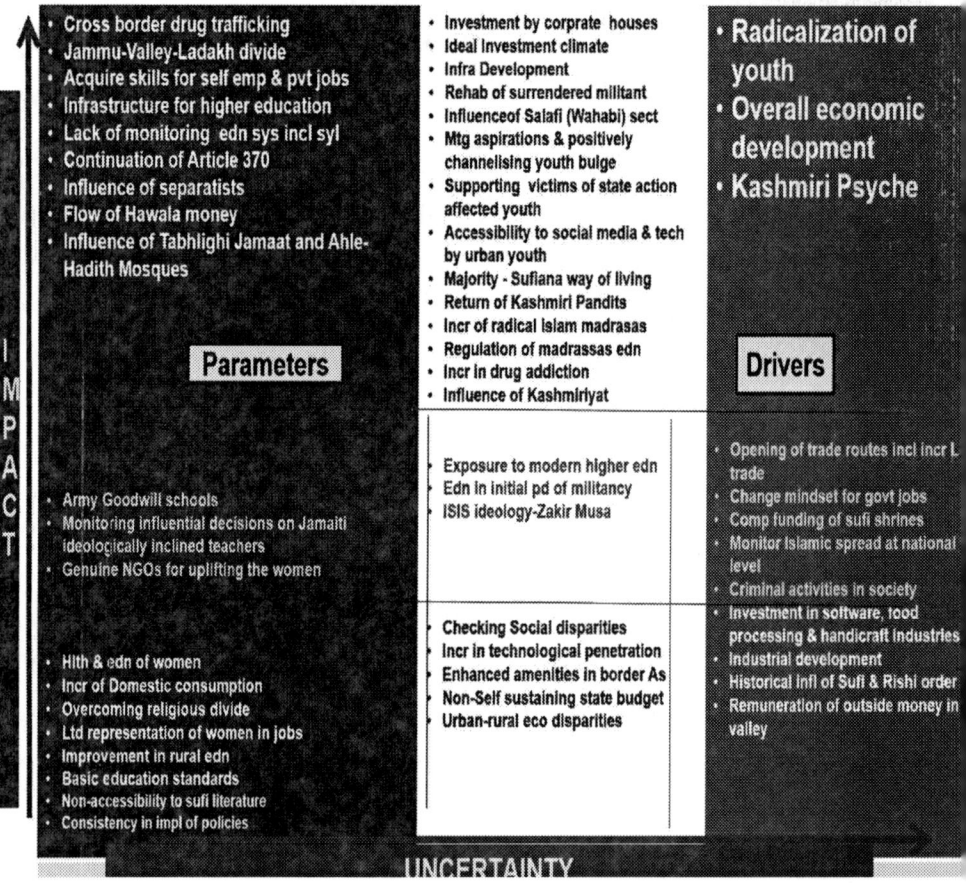

Drivers. Having plotted the environmental factors on the impact – uncertainty matrix, there are three drivers considered on the Economic, Social and Religion Domains; these also include the factors in the Medium Uncertainty – High impact and High Uncertainity – Medium Impact. The drivers will include these also and the description of the three drivers are given as under:

DESCRIPTION OF DRIVERS

RADICALISATION OF YOUTH
- Infl of Salafi (Wahabi) sect of islam in valley
- Supporting victims of state action, spl the stone pelters in getting emp
- Accessibility to social media & technology by the urban youth
- Incr influence of Jamaitis/Tablighi Jamaat
- Incr of Ahle-Hadith mosques- connected ISIS ideology
- Regularization of edn in madrassas
- Meeting the aspirations of the youth
- Salafi & Falah-e-Aam edn trust funds
- Criminal activites in society
- Positively channelising the youth bulge
- Monitoring Islamic spread at national level
- Rehabitation of surrendered militants
- Incr consumption of drugs
- Deradicalizing pgmes by youth SHGs

OVERALL ECONOMIC DEVELOPMENT
- Ideal Investment climate
- Infra Development
- Devp of employable skills
- Rehab of surrendered militant
- Change of mindset for pvt jobs
- Incr trade incl across LC
- Investment by corporate houses

Kashmiri Psyche
- Return of Kashmiri Pandits
- Majority - Sufiana way of living
- Competitive funding of sufi shrines
- Dominated by outsiders
- Systemised feedback
- Perception of being victimised
- Art of untruth, misinformation & lies
- Habit of Appeasement & subsidies

- **Radicalization of Youth.** The radicalization of youth with increase in radical Islam madrasas and influence of Salafi (Wahabi) sect of Islam and Ah-le-Hadith Mosquesin the valley—This driver includes positive channelizing of the youth, specially the victims of the state action and the surrendered militants, accessibility to technology and social media by the urban youth and influence of Jamaatis in the society, the regulation of the education in Madrassas and monitoring of the funding of Salafi and Falah-e-Aam education trusts, monitoring activities of the Tablighi Jammat as also the Teachers and Professors of the Salafi and Falah-e-Aam ideology. It also includes competitive funding of Sufi shrines and monitoring Islamist trends at national level. The aspects of criminal activities in the society and the increase in consumption of drugs in the valley including dependency on drugs as well as proposed deradicalization programmes by Youth Self-help groups. All these aspects will have a bearing on the three spectrums of the driver from the best, status quo and worst-case trajectories.
- **Overall Economic Development.** The overall economic development will include aspects relating to meeting the aspirations of the Awaam specially the youth, infrastructure development, investment by corporate

houses, investment climate and development of employable skills in the Awaam. Rehabilitation of the surrendered militants and changing the mindset of the Awam in aspiring for private sector jobs instead of the govt jobs only.

- **Kashmiri Psyche.** The same has been discussed in detail in the chapter Solutions for Psychological Aspects of Kashmir and hence will not be explained again here.

Parameters. Having plotted the environmental factors on the impact – uncertainty matrix, the Economic, Social and Religion Domain provides the High Impact but low uncertainty factors, which will remain constant. The medium uncertainty – Medium impact and Medium Impact – Low uncertainty factors are also included in the parameters. The parameters will include these also and the description are given as under:

PARAMETERS

- The Jammu-Ladakh-Kashmir divide
- Cross border drug trafficking
- Comprehensive Edn Sys
  - Infra for higher edn
  - Lack of monitoring edn sys incl the syllabus
  - Nationalistic educational activities
  - Army Goodwill schools
  - Exposure to modern higher edn
  - Edn in schools and Colleges affected by ideology
- Flow of Hawala money
- Preventing outside settlements by continuation of Article 370
- Influence of separatists
- Continuation of Article 370
- Acquire skills for self emp & pvt jobs

Axes of Uncertainty. The above stated three drivers are analyzed for the range of possible behaviours in order to form possible groupings to form scenario logics. The axes of uncertainty of each of the three drivers are as shown as under:

AXIS OF UNCERTAINITY

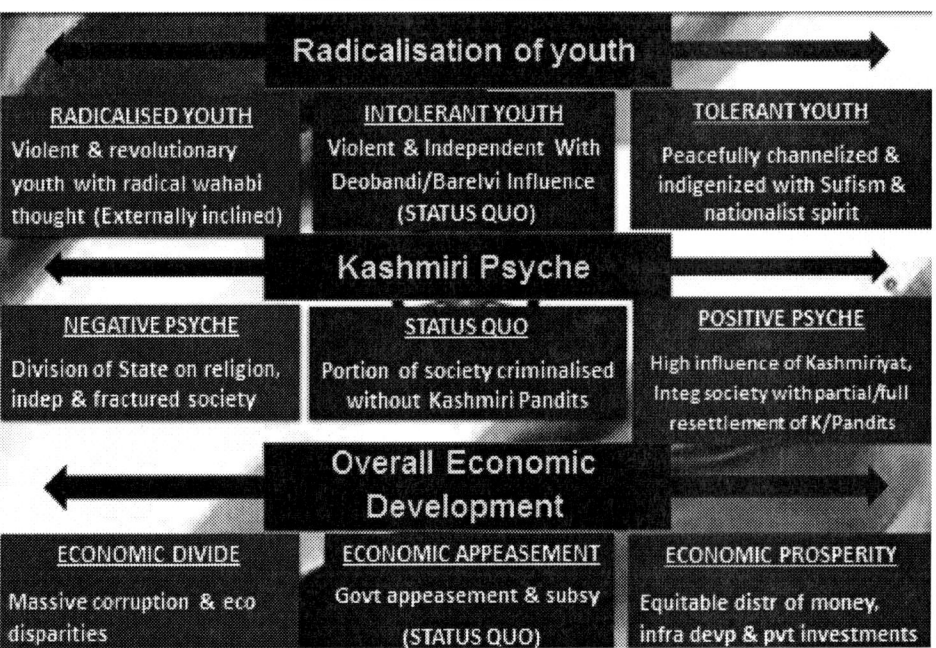

Trajectories. Above-mentioned scenario logics were grouped into three scenarios and are given in subsequent paragraphs as under.

- **Trajectory 1: Taareekh-e-Zamaanah (Status Quo).** The meaning of **Tareekh-e-Zamaanah** is "Reliving of an age". Kashmir has status quo or medium influence of Kashmiriyat in the Kashmiri Psyche and the society remains intolerant with influence of the Deobandi/Barelvi Sect of Islam as well as the Ahl-e-Hadith Mosques in the valley. The teachers in schools and colleges continue to profess negativity thereby creating a toxic mix of radicalization and intolerance in the minds of the youth. Also, the overall economic development remains slow and the system of appeasement continues, with the youth becoming criminalized. Characteristics of this trajectory would be as under:
    o **Radicalisation of Youth.** The Kashmiri youth are intolerant and have adopted the Deobandi/Barelvi sect of Islam and are partly anti-national. They are pulled towards the idea of Tablighi Jamaat and the Ahl-e-Hadith religious teachings. They are easily manipulated and support the call for independence. The support base of radicalized Islamic sect is at the present levels and the Kashmiri Sufiana way of living is fast losing interest. Education in

the Deobandi and Barelvi sect Islamic madrassas and educational institutes continues with limited regulation at the national level and their effects are visible in the society. The funding for the Salafi and Falah-e-aam education trusts continues without much scrutiny and control, giving a militant mindset to the youth. The Sufi education institutes are limited and targeted by the militants. The accessibility to technology and social media is negatively utilized and the youth is channelized into anti-national activities and agitation by utilizing tech for networking of frustrated youth. The youth empowerment schemes like the HIMAYAT and UDAAN are partially successful but the aspirations of the youth are not met as the jobs are available outside the state; therefore, there is large unemployment and the youth bulge is not channelized well. About 2,000 surrendered militants are still unemployed, thus still having a large number of trained persons available for recruitment in valley. There is no clear-cut policy for rehab of the Kashmiri returning from Nepal after staying in PoK for years. Criminal activities in the society are rampant and the majority of the youth is interested in govt jobs. Youth addicted to drugs is on the increase and the years of militancy and its effect on the society are increasingly adverse with none of the NGOs genuinely assisting in rehab and the cross-border drugs smuggling is high due to lack of tech screening facilities at the trade hubs.

o **Overall Economic Development.** Economic conditions are just starting to pick-up, but the larger investments suffer due to lack of safety and security concerns. The areas of concern where the private sector can contribute positively are education, healthcare, employment, rehab of surrendered militants, social growth etc. Corruption continues and the govt continues appeasing the Kashmiri people with subsidies and freebies, both through centre and state govt policies, which is resented by the people of Jammu and Ladakh region. The security scenario and the investment climate in the valley are just starting to pick up with the tourism industry looking good. The Awaam has a mindset of only doing govt jobs and people are not opting for the private sector jobs. This results in larger demand being generated, thus increasing corruption and unemployment in the valley. There is some infrastructure development and the few industries, roads, Railway tracks, buildings etc. have started emerging in the valley. The cross LC trade with Pakistan is under a cloud of suspicion with large number of security-related incidents causing the trade being stopped sometimes, therefore having minimum investments/stakes. The skills required for self-employment and private/govt jobs are nonexistent and need to be developed in the Awaam; the institutes in the valley are inadequate to cater for the skilled manpower for work.

o **Kashmiri Psyche.** The Psyche of the Kashmiri society remains at present levels with the influence of Kashmiriyat reducing from the initial years of militancy. The resettlement of the Kashmiri Pandits back in the valley has not succeeded and there are only few families surviving in the valley despite militancy. The Kashmiri Muslims, Pandits and Sikhs remain divided and the earlier day influence of Kashmiriyat remains a distant dream. The Kashmiri Pandits are not interested in rehabilitation back to the valley and blame the security situation for this. The Sufiana way of living of the Kashmiris is on the back burner as militants target the people following Sufism in the valley. The Sufi shrines and their fund state are in poor state thus making their madrassas and education institutes suffer in popularity amongst the youth as compared to the other sects. The communities in the valley are divided with Muslims and Sikhs based in the valley. The state is further split amongst the Ladakhi Buddhist, the Jammu Hindus and Kashmiri Muslims. The Kashmiri Pysche remains unchanged and issues like lying, corruption, projecting state of victimhood, art of systemized feedback and spreading of misinformation and feeling of being manipulated by others remain. The cross-border drug trafficking continues with the levels reducing due to lesser acceptance in the valley. Stable internal environment improves climate with clear-cut policies and better economic environment ensures enhanced investments, thus, boosting the economy along with lowering of unemployment rate. Despite this, the rural-urban divide continues as the terrain remains inhospitable. The J&K state budget continues to remain dependent on the funding and support of the central govt irrespective of the economic development. The state remains divided into three clearly different regions of Jammu, Kashmir and Ladakh. The influence of the separatists specially the Hurriyat will remain and will continue acting as a nuisance in the Kashmiri society and the valley, preventing

Non-Kashmiris from settling in the valley by continuation of Article 370, thereby ensuring there is no change of demography and the dominant community of Muslims remains in the valley. Comprehensive education system has to include aspects like development of higher education infrastructure, Army goodwill schools, exposure to modern higher education. Influence of education in the initial period of militancy and the inability to monitor the education system including syllabi are focused on. Influence of the Hurriyat and other separatist groups in the valley prevents integration of the society. Easy flow of hawala money inside valley results in the increased criminalization of the Kashmiri society.

- **Trajectory 2: Husn-e-Ghazal (Best Case).** The meaning of **Husn-e-Gazal** is the "best sher in a ghazal". Kashmir has high or medium influence of Kashmiriyat and the society remains tolerant and totally integrated, due to improved economic development resulting in prosperity and employment. Only interplay of **Drivers** highlighted is as under:
  o **Radicalisation of Youth.** The Kashmiri youth is positively channelized and indigenized with Sufism and national spirit and support the Indian Nationhood. The support base of radicalized Islamic sect is reduced and the Kashmiri Sufiana way of living comes to the forefront with limited Wahabi and Deobandi Islamic schools/madrassas. The education in the Deobandi and Barelvi sect Islamic madrassas and educational institutes is controlled at the national level and their effects are visible in the society. Funding for the Salafi, Falah-e-aam and Deobandi educational trusts is scrutinized and controlled and perceptions amongst the youth corrected, thereby reducing their attractiveness. The activities of teachers with these affiliations are monitored in schools and colleges. Special camps are undertaken to address their perceptions and mindsets. The Sufi education institutes flourish in the valley and are regularized by the education department and the state govt. The accessibility to technology and social media is positively utilized and the youth is channelized in positively utilizing technology instead of using it for networking of frustrated youth. The youth empowerment schemes like the HIMAYAT and UDAAN are successful and the aspirations of the youth are met and the youth bulge is positively

channelized. Private sector companies establish recruitment centres to hire skilled youth of the valley. Surrendered militants are rehabilitated and are employed, thus reducing readily available frustrated youth in valley. The militants returning from PoK through the Nepal route have increased and after scrutiny and checks are gainfully utilized in valley itself through a separate rehab policy. The criminal activities in the society reduce as the youth is optimally employed in govt and private jobs. The number of youths addicted to drugs reduces and the years of militancy and its effect on the society reduce with more and more NGOs genuinely assisting in rehab and the cross-border drugs smuggling is brought to minimum levels.

o **Overall Economic Development.** Economic conditions improve with large number of corporate houses taking initiative and investing. The safety and security concerns are put to rest as the levels of militancy are reducing every year. The private sector contributes positively in education, healthcare, employment, rehab of surrendered militants, social growth etc. Corruption is at its lowest ebb and the implementation of centre and state govt policies is good. The security scenario and the investment climate in the valley reach ideal levels. The number of calls for Hartaals and economic shut-downs reduces drastically. The Awaam changes its mindset for private sector jobs and there is an increase in people opting for these. This results in larger demand being generated, thus increasing corporate investment in the valley. There is rapid infrastructure development including industries, roads, Railway tracks, buildings etc. The cross-LC trade with Pakistan increases with more investments/stakes. Skills required for self-employment and private sector/govt jobs increase in the Awam, therefore increasing the employability of youth in the valley. There is a perceptible change in the thinking of the youths to take on private sector jobs instead of yearning only for govt jobs.

o **Kashmiri Psyche.** The Psyche of the Kashmiri society in the J&K state remains positive with the influence of integrated partial/full resettlement of the Kashmiri Pandits back in the valley. The Kashmiri Muslims, Pandits and Sikhs co-habitat peacefully and the earlier days influence of Kashmiriyat prevails in the valley. The return of Kashmiri Pandits in valley takes place after better implementation of rehabilitation schemes and improvement in the security situation. Majority of the people adopt the Sufiana way of living and increase in the tolerance levels of the Awaam. There is better management of the Sufi shrines and competitive funding of the Sufi shrines by regulating funding of all the madrassas and education institutes. There is harmony in the existence of all the communities, specially the Muslims, Pandits and Sikhs. The peaceful co-existence of the Ladakhi Buddhist, the Jammu Hindus and Kashmiri Muslims also continues. Kashmiri Pysche shows signs of changing positively and issues like lying, corruption, projecting state of victimhood, art of systemized negative feedback and spreading of misinformation and feeling of being manipulated by others are getting reduced as the Indian state grows economically and cohesively, and Pakistan's internal condition worsens.

- **Trajectory 3: Shab-e-Gham (Worst Case).** The meaning of **Shab-e-Gham** is "Night of despair". Kashmir has no/limited influence of Kashmiriyat and the state gets deeply divided into three different regions based on communities of Jammu, Kashmir and Ladakh with the Kashmiri Psyche becoming worse and radicalized. The society becomes radicalized and totally disintegrated with influence of Wahabi sect of Islam. There is increased effect of Ahl-e-Hadith mosques and their religious teachers. The youth gravitate towards the ideology of ISIS. The overall economic development remains at appeasement and subsidiary levels with slow progress. Only interplay of **Drivers** is highlighted as under:
  o **Radicalisation of Youth.** The Salafi/Wahabi sect madrassas and education institutes flourish in the valley and the youth is easily attracted to them. The Tablighi Jamaat pulls the youth into its fold and the Ahl-e-Hadith Mosques, through their fiery speeches instigating the youth towards fundamental intolerant Islamic values. Two policemen are lynched outside the jama masjid at Srinagar after Friday prayers. Religious leaders in The Valley as well as in Pak exhort the Kashmiri students studying various parts of India to join Jihad against India. The education in the Deobandi and Barelvi sect Islamic madrassas and educational institutes are also influenced by fundamentalist and Pakistan support. There is no/limited regulation at the national level and their effects are visible in the

society. The indicators start emerging all over India specially in the valley due to bad influence of the Deobandi, Salafi and Jamaiti educational activities. The funding for the Salafi, Falah-e-aam and Deobandi education trusts enhances their attractiveness to the youth and gain substantially as compared to the Sufi institutes. Sufi education institutes are targeted in the valley and there is an ideological shift in the following of Islam in valley wherein, the more radical Salafi sect following dominates Sufism. The overradicalized elements seek the answers in the path chosen by ISIS elements like Zakir Musa. The accessibility to technology and social media is negatively utilized by the youth utilizing technology for propagating a psychological war against India and the Security Forces. Backlash by the mainland Indian media add fuel to the fire. Youth empowerment schemes fail miserably and the aspirations of the youth are not met, resulting in the youth bulge being negatively channelized. The surrendered militants remain unemployed due to poor governance and implementation of policies, thus becoming recycled in large numbers due to frustration. The criminal activities in the society increase and the entire society is criminalized due to unemployment, and murders, robberies, loot etc are normal. The number of youth addicted to drugs increases and the years of militancy shows its effect on the society. The rehab centres and jails are mismanaged and become areas for drug abuse and business; the cross-border drugs smuggling flourishes along the LC.

o **Overall Economic Development.** The security scenario and the investment climate suffer in the valley due to frequent shut-downs/terror strikes and the corporate world is unwilling to invest due to the prevailing security threat. The Awaam continues with a mindset of doing only govt jobs, resulting in larger scale unemployment and increased frustration. The militants start targeting the infradevelopment and corruption ensures that the work quality is not good and most projects fail. The existing cross-LC trade is closed due to large-scale smuggling of arms, ammunition and FICN, and resultant ongoing poor relations with Pakistan. The skills required for self-employment and private/govt jobs are not acquired by the Awaam, thereby decreasing employability of youth in the valley.

o **Kashmiri Psyche.** The Psyche of the Kashmiri society in the J&K state becomes negative. There are large-scale protests by the separatists when the govt tries to develop separate colonies for the Pandits; a few targeted killings and Kashmiri Pandits decide to remain away and refuse all efforts for resettlement back to their respective areas. The majority of the people have an ideological shift from Sufiana way of living to radicalization and terrorism. Police personnel and their families are targeted by local militants in order to create fear in their minds. Poor management of the Sufi shrines and lack of funds including targeting by terrorists cause the Sufis to go underground. Killings of Sikhs and left over Pandits in valley result in communal divide. The muslims are targeted in the other parts of the state in Ladakh and Jammu region (Kishtwar and Poonch). The Shias in Budgam also have problems. The Kashmiri Pysche comes to the forefront in a negative manner and the nation is divided over presence of youth from Kashmir in their state. The issues like lying, corruption, projecting state of victimhood, art of systemized feedback and spreading of misinformation and feeling of being manipulated by others start growing.

ADMINISTRATIVE ENVIRONMENT

Description of Drivers. The drivers that will determine these trajectories are as follows:

- **Centre-State Relations.** This has been and always will be a crucial driver for the political trajectory of the state of J&K. The major factors that constitute this driver are Article 370 and 35A of the Indian Constitution and its different interpretation by the Kashmiris and the Indian government, the stand taken by the concerned stakeholders about the use of the AFSPA for the protection of the armed forces engaged in counter-insurgency operations in the state and Central funding for economic activities in J&K.
- **Governance.** The requirement that all public institutions and processes should serve all stakeholders in a reasonable timeframe and in a transparent manner form, the next driver for the political trajectory. The factors that constitute this driver are effective civil administration providing the desired civic amenities, effective utilisation of central and state funds, desired low levels of corruption and empowerment of local bodies and individual citizens.

Corruption becomes an important issue as the money accumulated by

A Peek into the Future: Scenario-Building Exercise

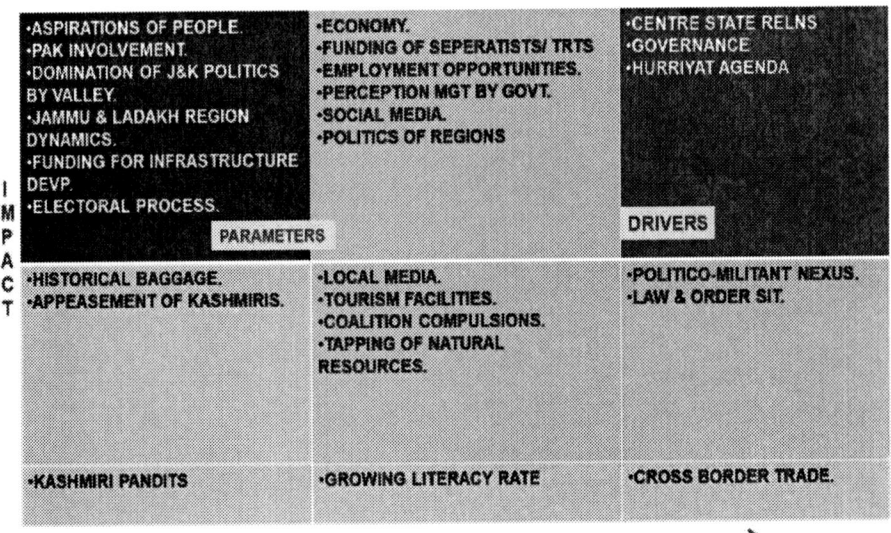

corrupt politicians and policemen goes back into the system in the state, thereby fuelling the militancy indirectly.

- **Hurriyat Agenda.** The APHC claims to represent the Awam of J&K and despite recent setbacks will continue to wield influence over the political trajectory of J&K. The major factors that constitute this driver are factionalism within the Hurriyat Conference, external funding to the Hurriyat and influence of the Hurriyat on the Awaam.

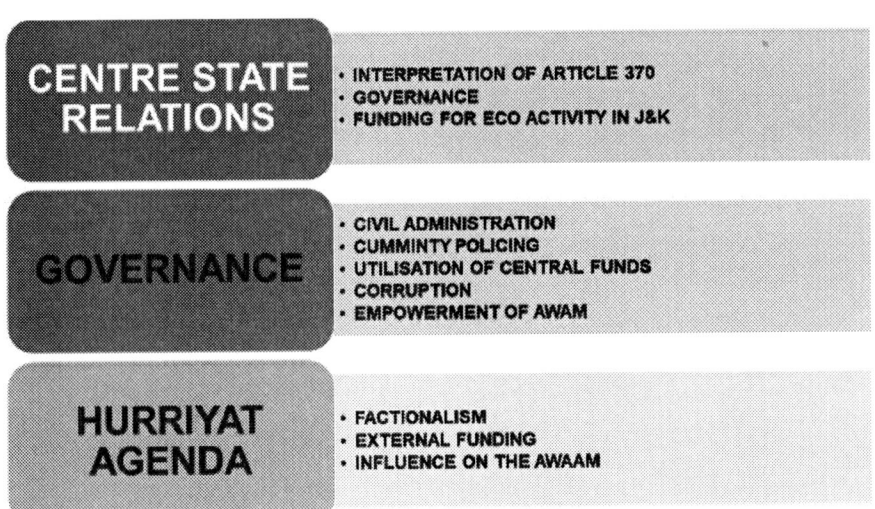

Axes of Uncertainty. The behaviour of the drivers remains highly uncertain and their movement along their respective axis of uncertainty is as shown below:

AXES OF UNCERTAINTY

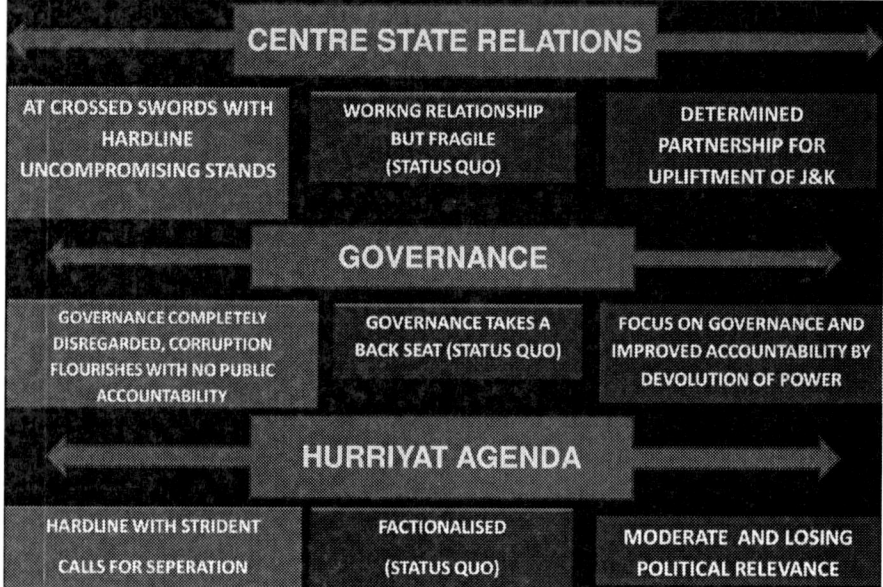

- **Trajectory I: Crawling Kashmir (Status Quo).** After the euphoria associated with the success at the Elections has subsided, political realities come to the fore. Both, the central and state governments are bound by coalition compulsions and find themselves unable to deliver the promises made to the electorate before the elections. They lose no time in playing to the gallery, with the centre blaming the rigid attitude of the state government on Article 370 for lack of progress in the Valley. On the other hand, the state government blames the centre for trying to cut down its powers and hence prevent it from carrying out developmental activity in the Valley. It also raises the issue of withdrawing AFSPA from certain parts of the state. Heated debates on Article 370, 35 A and AFSPA are a common feature in the Lok Sabha and the mass media. To counter the same and to pander to its voter base, the state government demands a return to pre-1953 status for Jammu and Kashmir. This is widely supported by the Awam in the valley, but received with scepticism by the people of Jammu and Ladakh. In the political rhetoric played out almost daily, core issues such as governance and infrastructure development take a back seat. Corruption, always a factor in all government dealings, shows a steady rise in the Valley. The state government goes slow on devolution of greater power and responsibility to local bodies as MLAs feel that their position and primacy will be threatened. As a result, civil administration is ineffective and the lack of improvement in basic amenities and quality of life leads to simmering discontent in the Awam. The law and order situation remains under control mainly due to the presence of security forces. Pakistan uses the situation to its advantage by covertly supporting terror outfits while ostensibly endeavouring to engage India in talks on Kashmir. It also raises the Kashmir issue selectively in international forums. However, its increasing economic and cultural engagement with India marginally balances the situation. Despite the ill health of its stalwart, Syed Ali Shah Geelani, and the factionalism plaguing it, the APHC remains active, receiving funding from external players and creating problems for the government. By 2025, another round of elections has taken place giving rise to new coalitions, both at the centre and state levels. Again, the lack of a clear mandate leads to instability and no clear-cut policy direction to resolve the Kashmir issue. Due to the steady growth of the Indian economy, central funding to infrastructure projects remains but progress remains slow due to sporadic incidents of violence and public agitation. Completion of the railway line to Srinagar gives a fillip to domestic tourism and trade related activities in the Valley, but adversely affects the trader community in Jammu. This causes the opposition parties at the centre and state to raise the ante about abrogation of Article 370 leading to protests in the Valley. With the government busy in politicking, civil administration suffers and corruption levels keep rising in the Valley. The government fails to take necessary steps like implementing e-governance empowering local panchayats etc. in order to curb large-scale corruption. Angry protestors resort to morchas and dharnas to express their displeasure and shake the government out of its inaction. Once again, it is the security forces that handle the tense situation and maintain law and order in the Valley. Pakistan continues to calibrate militancy in J&K leading to strained relations with India. A suspicious India puts in place strict security measures that slows down the cross-LoC trade to almost a trickle. The death of Geelani in 2022 provides a fresh lease of life to the hardliners in the APHC who use the sympathy wave to consolidate their position and renew their demands for independence. As the trajectory plays out in 2035, a third round of elections has taken place with the anti-incumbency factor resulting in the erstwhile opposition parties coming to power at both centre and state levels. Due to the lack of a comprehensive mandate and the resulting coalition compulsions, policy paralysis on J&K continues. The perceived erosion in the status of Article 370 leads to even greater strain in the centre-state relations. This is manifested by constant bickering between the two which is widely reported in the media. As a result, the focus on infrastructure development weakens further and overall development of the Valley lags far behind the planned targets. Governance is placed on the backburner leading to rampant corruption in public life. The law and order situation remains tense and security forces have to carry out frequent flag marches to retain control of the situation. The situation is exploited to the hilt by Pakistan by increasing support to militancy and repeatedly raising the issue in international forums. The immediate result is that a fuming India puts further restrictions on cross-LoC trade bringing it almost to a halt. The situation plays right into the hands of AHPC which uses it to remain relevant in the Valley with a no compromise policy on its demand for independence.

- **Trajectory II: Prospering Kashmir (Best Case).** After celebrating their success in the elections, both governments prepare to bring about a definitive change in the situation in J&K. Realisation of the compulsions of coalitions sets in quickly and both centre and state governments tone down the pre-election rhetoric and agree to make a sincere attempt at a partnership aimed at genuine upliftment of the conditions in the Valley. The centre puts the issue of abrogation of Article 370 on the backburner and the state government puts aside its call for greater autonomy and withdrawal of AFSPA. By 2020, the centre and state governments have overcome the initial tentativeness in their interactions with each other. This is manifested in the smooth and effective functioning of the Unified HQ leading to good law and order situation in the state with minimal human rights issues. The centre shows its appreciation by increasing the funds for employment and infrastructure generation schemes in the state with focus on the Valley. Talks are also on to reduce the footprint of the security forces in the state. This is well received by the Awaam in the valley, as well as the people of Jammu and Ladakh. There is a concerted effort to improve governance by cracking down on corruption and laying the foundations of e-governance in the state. The state government initiates measure for devolution of greater power and responsibility to local bodies adding to the positive climate. Civil administration starts to improve and a visible change for the better is seen in the civic amenities in rural areas. Pakistan tries to play spoilsport by increasing covert support to terror outfits while ostensibly endeavouring to engage India in talks on Kashmir. It also raises the Kashmir issue selectively in international forums. However, due to improved cooperation between the Awam and the security forces the success of these efforts is minimal. Realising that the situation is not moving in the right direction, Pakistan looks to increase economic and cultural engagement with India leading to greater cross-LoC trade which improves the situation in the Valley even further. With the ill health of its stalwart, Syed Ali Shah Geelani, the factionalism in the APHC increases. The hardliners in the Hurriyat have trouble in retaining their primacy due to the improved atmosphere in the Valley. To help them retain their position, external players like Pakistan, Saudi Arabia etc increase the funding to the pro-independence factions of the Hurriyat. By 2024, another round of elections has taken place and the coalition governments both at the centre and state levels have reinforced their positions by getting elected with a greater majority. Encouraged by the faith reposed in them by the electorate and aiming to consolidate their gains even further, the centre-state partnership is now far stronger than before, with the two governments showing more trust and respect for each other. The time is ideal for bold policy measures to be introduced and the governments grab the opportunity with both hands. The centre proposes greater devolution of power and responsibility to the state government in return for greater cooperation from the latter on vital issues related to security and land usage in the state. Encouraged by the good results in the past, the state government also moves towards greater decentralisation of power to the local panchayats. The e-governance system has been highly successful in the urban areas bringing greater accountability to public life and plans are formulated to extend the same to rural areas as well. Central funding to infrastructure projects continues and due to the peaceful situation prevailing in the Valley, infrastructure projects like hydroelectric plants, Zojila tunnel, Jammu-Srinagar rail link, alternate route to Ladakh via Padam and a fully operational Mughal route have been completed within stipulated timeframes. This leads to unprecedented growth in tourism and economic activity. There is still reluctance among the Awam about setting up of industrial parks and SEZs to facilitate the entry of industrial houses in the Valley, but more and more voices in favour of the same can be heard in local and social media, especially among the youth. With Pakistan in a precarious financial state, support to militancy in the Valley is considerably reduced, and the Pakistan government is heard making conciliatory statements to focus on economic and cultural engagements with India while it gets its own house in order. This further improves the situation in the Valley leading to the Army handing over to properly trained paramilitary forces and police in the hinterland and focussing its efforts towards securing the LoC. The death of Geelani in 2022 proves to be the proverbial final straw for the hardliners in the Hurriyat. Moderate factions led by Mirwaiz Umar Farooq gain ascendency in the APHC and commence negotiations with the government for a solution to the Kashmir issue. As the trajectory plays out in 2035, a third round of elections has taken place with much the same results. The APHC participates in elections for the first time but is rejected by the electorate. Stable governments at the centre and state reflect the confidence of the people in their performance. The process of change nurtured from 2019 onwards continues on its path granting significant autonomy to the state while maintaining allegiance to the Indian Constitution. At the same time, on the basis of its strong performance, the state government is able to sell some points of the centre's agenda on security, land holding laws and other common articles of law to the Awam. An ideal compromise is reached with the Awam's aspirations for dignified self-rule being met and the increasing inclusion of Kashmir in the national mainstream. The aspirations of the people of Jammu and Ladakh are also catered for by increased representation in government and adequate funding to promote economic growth. Infrastructure development continues at a rapid pace resulting in excellent all-round growth in tourism, hydroelectric, timber and food-processing industries. 2025 marks a historic occasion as the first ever SEZs are set up in the Valley with corporate groups showing keen interest in the project. With e-governance infrastructure available even in remote rural areas, corruption is at its lowest. Civic activities are planned and executed by local authorities thus giving the Awaam a sense of empowerment. There is a growing realisation in Pakistan that funds spent in support of insurgency in the Valley are unable to give commensurate returns. Faced by growing protests against the poor quality of life in PoK, the Pakistan government decides to follow a similar action plan for development of PoK. A magnanimous India agrees to provide expertise and aid for the same and lifts restrictions on cross-LoC trade. By now, the Hurriyat has been rendered almost irrelevant in Valley politics though Mirwaiz Umar Farooq still retains the respect of the Awaam as a religious leader.

- **Trajectory III: Self-Destructing Kashmir (Worst Case).** Elated with their performance in the elections, both the centre and state governments lose no time in trying to consolidate their gains. As mentioned in their election manifesto, the state government repeatedly raises the issue of AFSPA withdrawal and Article 370 with the centre. Not to be outdone, the centre steadfastly refuses to engage with the state on these issues, instead choosing to emphasise the need to treat the state of J&K as "any other state" of the Indian Union, and blaming the corruption and poor governance of successive state governments for the poor development in the state. By 2020, heated debates on Article 370 and AFSPA are a common feature in the Lok Sabha and the state assembly. The ruling party at the Centre take the matter to the Supreme Court. Separatist local politicians add fuel to the fire by making provocative speeches demanding freedom from the Indian occupation in the Valley with tacit support of the state government. The Centre retaliates by announcing its intentions of putting an end to the appeasement policies followed by its predecessors. It announces special economic packages for Jammu and Ladakh citing their loyalty to India. This causes widespread resentment in the Valley leading to anti-government demonstrations and clashes between the protesting groups and the security forces. Several members of the public and security personnel are injured in these incidents. With attention focussed on these issues, matters such as decentralisation of power to local bodies, governance and infrastructure development are quickly forgotten. Corrupt politicians and bureaucrats make full use of the confusion to divert crores of rupees for their personal gains. The resulting decline in civic activity and quality of life only adds to the anger of the Awaam. The law and order situation becomes precarious with various incidents of stone pelting, gherao of security personnel and government officials and frequent bandhs. Sporadic incidents of IED explosions lead to further clashes between the Awam and the security forces, heightening the tensions in the Valley. Pakistan exploits the situation to the hilt by increasing support to terror outfits by way of funding as well as insertion of armed foreign terrorists from Afghanistan. It also raises the issue of Human Rights violations by Indian security forces at every available opportunity in international bodies. In retaliation, the Indian government cuts off the cross-LoC trade and accuses Pakistan of interfering in its internal matters. The perceived injustice in the Valley leads to all factions of the APHC uniting under the leadership of its stalwart, Syed Ali Shah Geelani, and further inflaming anti-India sentiments in the Valley. By 2028, another round of elections has taken place with the central government re-elected with a similar majority, while there is a change in the state government. The death of Geelani in 2022 provided a fresh lease of life to the hardliners in the APHC who used the sympathy wave to consolidate their position and renew their demands for independence. The political rhetoric in the Valley continued to foment distrust between the central and state governments. With the steady growth of the Indian economy, central funding to infrastructure projects is available, but due to the law and order situation in the valley, no work takes place. Instead, corrupt local politicians in cahoots with the contractors' mafia divert these funds to fill up their own coffers. Corruption in the Valley is at an all-time high. There is also a sharp decline in the number of tourists visiting the state leading to further economic hardships to the Awaam. Angered by the lack of development, violent demonstrations mar the atmosphere in the Valley requiring the increased use of force by security forces. A couple of incidents of high-handed behaviour by armed forces personnel to break up violent protests against the AFSPA are covered widely by the media, causing an inundation of sympathy for the Awaam and anger against the armed forces in the social media. The volatile situation leads to reactivation of sleeper cells of insurgents with active support of the local populace. In 2026, one such group blows up the railway line to Srinagar, greatly affecting life in the Valley. This is greeted with huge support from the Awaam. A heavy crackdown follows, with security forces sparing no effort in trying to find those responsible for the blasts. Cordon and search operations and indefinite detentions for interrogation by the security forces lead to a sense of humiliation in the Awaam, reminding them of the situation in the Valley in the 1990s.

The central government threatens to dissolve the state assembly and impose President's rule in the state. This leads to fresh surges of violence all across the Valley, with attacks on central government institutions. Many people are injured in the police action that follows. In a few areas there are a number of civilian casualties. In retaliation, insurgent elements carry out Fidayeen attacks on security forces camps and kill fifteen jawans and two officers of RR battalions in two separate incidents. With the situation going out of control, the centre imposes President's rule in J&K further alienating the people of the Valley. Presented with an opportunity to denounce India and reassert its claim on J&K, Pakistan steps up support to the "freedom fighters" and starts a diplomatic offensive aimed at reducing the credibility of India's position in the Kashmir issue. It actively abets the infiltration of terrorists from camps across the LoC, leading to further deterioration of the situation. Needless to say, cross-LoC trade is reduced to zero further increasing the economic misery of the people. As the trajectory plays out in 2030, President's rule continues in J&K. The law and order situation deteriorates further with widespread violence against the security forces and government establishments. The steps taken by the armed forces to retain control of the state only strengthen the Awaam's perception of them as an occupying force. Terrorist groups like the LeT and the Harkat-ul-Mujahideen are seen as the saviours of the Awaam and have their tacit as well as active support. The situation resembles a war zone, comparable to the days of the 1990s and the worst period of the insurgency in the state. As a result, there is almost no progress on infrastructure development and economic state of the Valley lags far behind the rest of the country. Special concessions for the Awaam like reservations in colleges, professional courses and employment are withdrawn thus distancing them even more from the rest of the country. Terrorist camps across the LoC actively train and aid infiltration into J&K leading to frequent skirmishes at the LoC. The Kashmir issue catches the imagination of the international community and calls for involvement of the UN/third-party mediators gain ground. Within the state, the Hurriyat in its most hardline avatar spews venom against the Union of India and has the full support of the people of the Valley.

SCENARIO BUILDING

Scenario Logics. The axes of uncertainty of the drivers were plotted on a matrix to identify "scenario logics", as shown below. The logic (1,2,1) would mean the effect of the nine trajectories amongst each other with Best SE Trajectories, Status Quo SER Trajectory and Best ADMIN Trajectory as under:

		SER TRAJECTORY			PL TRAJECTORY		
		Best	Status Quo	Worst	Best	Status Quo	Worst
SE TRAJECTORY	Best				(1,1,1)	(1,1,2)	(1,1,3)
					(1,2,1)	(1,2,2)	(1,2,3)
					(1,3,1)	(1,3,2)	(1,3,3)
	Status Quo				(2,1,1)	(2,1,2)	(2,1,3)
					(2,2,1)	(2,2,2)	(2,2,3)
					(2,3,1)	(2,3,2)	(2,3,3)

Plausible Scenario Logics. The plausible scenario logics are as shown below.

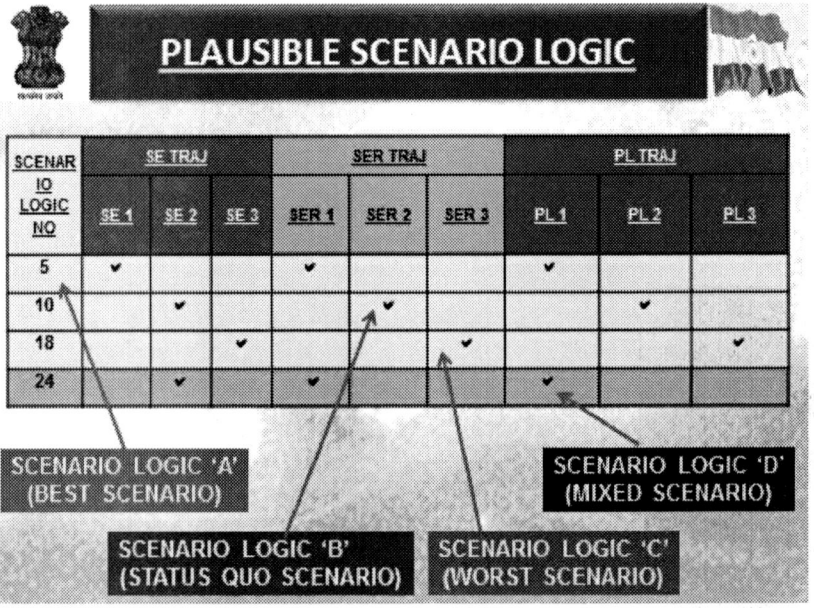

Trajectories to Scenarios. The trajectories are then converted into scenarios by having an interplay of the plausible trajectories of each of the three domains as under:

A Peek into the Future: Scenario-Building Exercise

TRAJECTORIES TO SCENARIOS

SCENARIOS \ TRAJ	SE TRAJ			SER TRAJ			ADMIN TRAJ		
	Best	Status Quo	Worst	Best	Status Quo	Worst	Best	Status Quo	Worst
Scenario 1 (Best)	✓			✓			✓		
Scenario 2 (Status Quo)		✓			✓			✓	
Scenario 3 (Worst)			✓			✓			✓

SCENARIO LOGIC 'A' (STATUS QUO)
SCENARIO LOGIC 'B' (BEST SCENARIO)
SCENARIO LOGIC 'C' (WORST SCENARIO)

Scenario Building

Four Scenarios anticipated for Kashmir Valley for year 2035 are as under:

- **Kashmir in a Status Quo Scenario.** "**Chasm-Baraah**" meaning waiting to welcome or impatiently waiting. Interplay of "Chalta Hai Kashmir" from SE Domain, "Shab-e-Gham" from SER Domain and "CrawlingKashmir" from the Pol Domain.
- **Kashmir in a Best Case Scenario.** "**Ejaaz-e-Maseehaaee**" meaning miracle of Jesus or miraculous cure. Interplay of "Soaring Kashmir" from SE Domain, "Husn-e-Ghazal" from SER Domain and "Shining Kashmir" from the Admin Domain.
- **Kashmir in a Worst Case Scenario.** "**Daagh-Daar**" meaning anything having strains or spots. Interplay of "Smouldering Kashmir" from SE Domain, "Aab-e-Deedar" from SER Domain and "Self-destructive Kashmir" from the Admin Domain.

TRAJECTORIES TO SCENARIOS

DOMAIN & TRAJ \ SCENARIO	SE DOMAIN	SER DOMAIN	ADMIN DOMAIN
	• Role of SF • Militants dynamics • Pak's caliberation	• Radicalised youth • Kashmiri Psyche • Overall eco devp	• Centre-state relations • Hurriyat agenda • Governance
Scenario 1 (Best)	**Healing Kashmir** • SF in control • Low levels of militancy • Irregular sp by Pak	**Husn-e-Ghazl** • Tolerant youth • +ve psyche & Kashmiriyat • Economic prosperity	**Prospering** • Centre-state relns good • Hurriyat irrelevant • Good governance
Scenario 2 (Status Quo)	**Chalta Hai Kashmir** • SF under pressure • Med levels of militancy • Regular sp by Pak	**Yaadgar-e-Zamannah** • Intolerant youth • Criminalised Society • Economic Appeasement	**Crawling** • Diff in Centre-state relns • Hurriyat active • Poor Governance
Scenario 3 (Worst)	**Smouldering Kashmir** • Smouldering of sit • High levels of militancy • Aggressive sp by Pak	**Shab-e-Gham** • Radicalised youth • -ve Psyche & division • Economic Divide	**Self Destructing Kashmir** • Breakdown betn centre-state • Hurriyat leads divide • Governor's rule

Scenario Description
- **Scenario 1: Ejaaz-e-Maseehaaee (Best Trajectories combined together).**
  - Scenario Dynamics/Description. SF continue to maintain firm and effective control on the IS situation resulting in promoting the prospect of enduring peace in the state. Pak continues to covertly support terror outfits while endeavouring to engage India in talks on Kashmir under intense international pressure. Kashmir issue is brought up selectively in international forums but without any support from major players. There is change in sentiments of separatists, with sharply diminishing enthusiasm for the secessionist cause. Kashmir has high or medium influence of Kashmiriyat and the society remains tolerant and totally integrated, due to improved economic development resulting in prosperity and employment. A determined centre-state partnership implements several bold policy decisions to improve the economic and political conditions in the Valley. Focussing on governance and decentralisation of power, the government is able to win the confidence of the Awam, as well as people in Jammu and Ladakh.
  - The interplay of all the trajectories is highlighted as under:
  There is swift improvement in law and order; however, infrequent incidents of unrest continue to affect internal security of the state but with reduced severity and impact without any backing or popular support from Awaam. There is complete marginalisation of armed segments of insurgent outfits and successful integration of moderate factions into electoral process. The separatists fail in repeated efforts to orchestrate a resurgence of street violence on the 2010 and 2016 pattern as the Awaam rises up in rebellion against the militant cause. The centre proposes greater devolution of power and responsibility to the state government and local bodies in return for greater cooperation from the latter on vital issues related to security and land usage in the state. Due to prolonged unfruitful militancy, there are continuous and cumulative failures of the separatists within J&K and firm control of IS situation by SF, with major separatist groups completely marginalised. One sees peaceful street protests only over a range of "political" and "governance" issues continue. Prospect of enduring positive peace, monitored directly by the National Security Council in the state, gets a major boost. Due to handing over of control to CRPF and Police and

complete withdrawal of Army from the IS duties and deployment on the LC, there are no more dissent and protests against AFSPA to create turbulence. Police acts as a people's community force and drops its high-handed behaviour. Political hierarchy exploits conducive environment for effective governance. Complete synergy amongst police and SF due to clear perceptions on political strategy needs to be followed. State police and CRPF are empowered to take on the role of efficient manager of law and order in major towns and cities in the state. Militancy is completely wiped out of the state. Economic prosperity results in sustained economic growth which ensures a boost to areas such as education, healthcare, employment, rehab of surrendered militants, and inclusive social growth. The corruption reduces in the society due to young leaders and the government eases appeasing the Kashmiri people with subsidies and freebies. Central funding to infrastructure projects continues and due to the peaceful situation prevailing in the Valley, infrastructure projects like hydroelectric plants, Jammu-Srinagar rail link, alternate route to Ladakh through Padam and a fully operational Mughal route are completed within stipulated timeframes. This leads to unprecedented growth in tourism and economic activity. Pak military continues to covertly support terror outfits while endeavouring to engage India in talks on Kashmir under intense international pressure. Kashmir issue is brought up selectively in international forums but without any support from major players. People of Pak reeling under severe financial burden and a dwindling economy reject the idea of Jihad for Kashmir and are openly in favour of better ties with India. Increasing economic and cultural engagement considerably balances the rhetoric, leading to complete peace at borders. Despite repeated calls by the Pakistan-backed terrorist separatist formations to the people of J&K to boycott polls – General Elections, Assembly Elections and Local Body Elections – people vote in large numbers, demonstrating faith in the democratic process, as against the politics of the gun. Alternative political parties at the local bodies and the state level have a happy mix of forward-looking Youth leaders coming to the fore to lead the State on the path of progress. Pakistan is awash with Islamist extremist militancy and organised crime groups, creating a regime of heightened lawlessness and anarchy. In spite of "democracy" in Pakistan, it results in further decline of political and administrative institutions, and a further destabilisation of the economy, threatening the very integrity and existence of the state. Futility of pursuing terrorism as an instrument of state policy is realised, resulting in greater voices for forging peace with India. Pak's polity remains deeply divided between military and democratic forces making it difficult to arrive at consensus on Kashmir. Pak endeavours to partially dismantle terror infrastructure in PoK. The Kashmiri youth is positively channelized and endowed with Sufism and national spirit and supports the Indian Nationhood. The support base of radicalized Islamic sect is reduced and the Kashmiri Sufiana way of living comes to the forefront with limited Wahabi, Deobandi, Jamaati Islamic schools/madrassas. The teachers at schools and colleges, and religious Ulema in various mosques are won over by deradicalizing Self-help youth groups supported by corporate sector. There is growing disenchantment of the separatists and Kashmiri youth with violence as a form of grievance redressal. Separatists continue to remain vociferous; however, calm prevails. The reform plan for Jammu and Kashmir is a success, aimed at creating infrastructure development, basic amenities, employment and other income-generating activities, rehabilitation and resettlement of militancy-affected victims. J&K becomes the national hub for data storage servers, bringing in large-scale outsourced jobs for the youth. For skill development and making the State's youth employable, schemes like "Himayat" and "Udaan" give encouraging results due to participation by the private sector resulting in dwindling support to separatists. There is yearning for peace amongst youth and separatists due to prolonged militancy and quest for reaping the peace dividends. Disillusionment with Pak and extremely successful surrender and rehabilitation policy encourages mass homecoming for all groups. There is change in sentiments of separatists, with sharply diminishing enthusiasm for the secessionist cause and in favour of Pakistan. Nevertheless, some lingering irritants still persist. The Kashmiri Pysche undergoes a positive transformation due to deradicalization of society and a connect with the rest of India. A strong bilateral relationship between India and the United States, based on a congruence of strategic interests, acts not only as a hedge against China but also to build indigenous defence capabilities and an industrial base. As part of U.S. rebalancing strategy towards Asia, it draws India into a much stronger strategic partnership and provides technologies and equipment that would enhance India's overall defence capacities and preparedness, apart from enhanced intelligence-sharing and cooperation in the space and cyber domains.

Due to relative internal stability, progress and development, military modernization and incremental upgrading of its military posture, backed by logistics capability and communications infrastructure, India's influence grows beyond the region. With a robust defence funding and collusive support from USA, India is able to narrow the capability gap with China and widens the disparity in conventional capability with Pak. Afghanistan rejects Pak interference and influence through Taliban. The Taliban joins mainstream politics after diligent efforts from the world community. The sphere of influence of the ISIS ideology in Afghanistan is considerably reduced and it is firmly on the path of progress.

o **Snapshots/Milestones.**

2022	2028	2035
(i) Elections in J&K completely peaceful. Hurriyat's anti-India campaign fails. The centre puts the issue of abrogation of Article 370 on the backburner and the state government puts aside its call for greater autonomy and withdrawal of AFSPA. (ii) Anti-talk outfits completely side-lined and fully deactivated. LC ceasefire continues but with occasional violations. Talks continue on reduction of footprint of the security forces in the state. People-to-people contact between India and Pak increases; this is well received by the Awam in the valley, as well as the people of Jammu and Ladakh. (iii) There is a concerted effort to improve governance by	(i) Elections in J&K comparatively calm despite minimal Pak-sponsored terrorism. Hurriyat continues to raise rhetoric for complete independence however with diminishing support from Awaam. The death of S A Gilani proves to be the proverbial final straw for the hardliners in the Hurriyat. Moderate factions led by Mirwaiz Umar Farooq gain ascendency in the APHC and commence negotiations with the government for a solution to the Kashmir issue. In another round of elections, the coalition governments both at the centre and state levels reinforce their positions by getting elected with a greater majority. (ii) Encouraged by the good	(i) A third round of elections has taken place with much the same results. The APHC participates in elections for the first time but is rejected by the electorate. Stable governments at the centre and state reflect the confidence of the people in their performance. (ii) There is yearning for breaking military and political deadlock between Govt of India, Pak and separatists. (iii) Seeing India progressing in leaps and bounds, Kashmiris realise futility of secession, and aspire for their political aspirations to be addressed. The process of change nurtured from 2020 onwards continues on its path granting significant autonomy to the state while maintaining

2022	2028	2035
cracking down on corruption and laying the foundations of e-governance in the state. The state government initiates measure for devolution of greater power and responsibility to local bodies adding to the positive climate. Civil administration starts to improve and a visible change for the better is seen in the civic amenities in rural areas. (iv) Due to religious fundamentalism Pakistan political process weak, preventing major policy initiatives against foreign policy reforms. Growth of religious fundamentalism on upswing. (v) Indian political process results in clear majority verdict, stable Govt at the centre, leading to forging of consensus on steps required to resolve the J&K problem. Border infrastructure projects provided renewed impetus and higher funding. Smooth and effective functioning of the Unified HQ leads to good law and order situation in the state with minimal human rights issues. (vi) Taliban continues to foment violence in South abd SE Afghanistan with active support from radical outfits in Pakistan (Haqqani network). (vii) Militant organisations under Taliban unite against NATO forces in Afghanistan, as well as to wage a defensive jihad against Pakistani forces. (viii) USA scraps the aid to Pakistan completely.	results in the past, the state government also moves towards greater decentralisation of power to the local panchayats. The e-governance system is highly successful in the urban areas bringing greater accountability to public life and plans are formulated to extend the same to rural areas as well. (iii) Pak policy making continues to suffer, with increasing smoothness in bilateral issues with India. However, increasing economic and cultural engagement balances the rhetoric, leading to peace at borders. (iv) Indian policy making passes on to next generation of leaders, with renewed energy and focus on nation-building. Renewed impetus to economic agenda. Security aspects dealt with pragmatically, sustained focus on modernisation and resolution of J&K imbroglio. (v) USA gradual shift of stance away from Pak resulting in greater reliance on India to balance its requirements. (vi) SF continue to completely control the IS situation in Kashmir despite occasional spurt in militant activities/orchestrated disorders created by Pak. Firm control further improves the situation in the Valley leading to the Army handing over to properly trained paramilitary forces and police in the hinterland and focussing its efforts towards securing the LoC. (vii) Pakistan's gradual loss of trust with the international community, including its major ally the US. This gives	allegiance to the Indian Constitution. At the same time, on the basis of its strong performance, the state government is able to sell some points of the centre's agenda on security, land holding laws and other common articles of law to the Awaam. An ideal compromise is reached with the Awaam's aspirations for dignified self-rule being met and the increasing inclusion of Kashmir in the national mainstream. (iv) Militancy completely wiped out. Threat of secession warded off, Pak reconciles to the futility of pursuing a policy of confrontation; however, it continues with rhetoric on Kashmir to satisfy domestic compulsions. The people at large in Pak are in favour of good relations with India due to changed perceptions. (v) Line of Control becomes formalized and is accepted as international border. (vi) Pakistan and Kashmiri activists also reconcile to this idea. Both the U.S. and the EU favour converting the Line of Control to international border. (vii) Focused attention on the developmental aspects with a view to strengthening the infrastructure, creating employment and income generation opportunities, and generally improving the quality of life of the people results in youth, especially victims of state action changing their mindset towards reconciliation. (viii) With a deepening of positive peace, the Government's attention turns increasingly to investments, employment

A Peek into the Future: Scenario-Building Exercise 241

2022	2028	2035
(ix) International players lending their support to sustained dialogue on Kashmir however insist its resolution bilaterally. (x) Symbiotic existence of terrorist camps and Pak army continues. (xi) SF deployment and operations continue as hitherto fore, with more focus on anti-infiltration grid astride LC. (xii) SF actions complemented by effective governance and a whole of govt approach monitored by the NSCS. (xiii) Youth connect model supported by Corporate social responsibility funds kicks of resulting in de-radicalization of the society. (xiii) Youth continue to remain vociferous however 2010 and 2016 like protests do not occur. With the ill health of its stalwart, Syed Ali Shah Gilani, the factionalism in the APHC increases. The hardliners in the Hurriyat have trouble in retaining their primacy due to the improved atmosphere in the Valley. To help them retain their position, external players like Pakistan, Saudi Arabia etc increase the funding to the pro-independence factions of the Hurriyat. (xiv) In PoK, the governance structures created by Pak continue with classical colonialism, political subjugation, systematic exploitation and cultural negation ordained by significant degrees of coercion.	India leverage to put its case more forcefully, thereby managing perceptions positively internationally. (viii) Islamist extremist militancy in Pak creates a situation of extreme instability, compelling it to look towards mending its differences with India in its larger national security interests. With Pakistan in a precarious financial state due to failure of CPEC, support to militancy in the Valley is considerably reduced, and the Pakistan government makes conciliatory statements to focus on economic and cultural engagements with India while it gets its own house in order. (ix) Gradual and sustained growth in Indian economy positively affects the growth in Kashmir resulting in inclusive growth and employment opportunities for the youth. Central funding to infrastructure projects continues and due to the peaceful situation prevailing in the Valley. (x) There is still reluctance amongst the Awam about setting up of industrial parks and SEZs to facilitate the entry of industrial houses in the Valley, but more and more voices in favour of the same can be heard in local and social media, especially among the youth. (xi) A large number of misguided youths, religious teachers and Teachers in academic institutes are deradicalized and brought to the mainstream.	and a restoration of the dynamism of the economy. The aspirations of the people of Jammu and Ladakh are also catered for by increased representation in government and adequate funding to promote economic growth. (ix) The first ever SEZs are set up in the Valley with corporate groups showing keen interest in the project. There is a change in the mindset of the youth to take on private sector jobs. The countries largest data servers are built in J&K, getting a large number of jobs to the state. With e-governance infrastructure available even in remote rural areas, corruption is at its lowest. Civic activities are planned and executed by local authorities thus giving the Awam a sense of empowerment. (x) The Hurriyat is rendered almost irrelevant in Valley politics though Mirwaiz Umar Farooq still retains the respect of the Awam as a religious leader. (xi) India's conventional mil capb gap vis-à-vis Pak widens. Owing to reduction in US aid and non-development for long years, Pak's economy spirals downwards. USA gradually distances itself from Pak due to better alliances with India and Iran. Afghanistan kept comparatively stable by Pak as leverage for employment of effort against India.

o **End State.** J&K would continue to be calm with eagerness to reap positive peace dividends. Internal Security situation improves considerably to a desirable level thereby relieving the Armed forces to focus on capability building. Economy of the state improves with employment and other income generating activities and rehabilitation and resettlement of militancy-affected victims. The predominant role played by SF in controlling the IS situation results in bringing violence down to levels, wherein, the elected representatives of the state and the administrative machinery function effectively. At this stage, political negotiations attempt to find a respectable and long-term solution to the problem at hand. Using a set of win-win strategies, Centre-State partnership succeeds in meeting the aspirations of the Awaam in valley for dignified self-rule, while at the same time cultivating amongst them a sense of belongingness and loyalty to the Indian flag. Peace and prosperity return to the Valley rendering external players and APHC nearly irrelevant. USA's engagement with India increases manifold; Pak suffers partial international isolation due to its inimical policy towards India and support for terrorism. The People of Pak rise in revolt against an anti-India policy and want to mend fences with the Indian people. India develops a strong bilateral relationship with the USA, based on a congruence of strategic interests, as a hedge against China. Instability in Pakistan continues with a possible security threat to India. Despite international pressures and peace overtures by India, Pak continues its unsuccessful fight of proxy war through radicalised youth and foreign militants though to a reduced scale. Pak continues to internationalise the issue by seeking involvement of UN, USA and other international organisations. It reluctantly accepts the status quo while proclaiming importance of resolution of dispute. Due to robust defence funding, military modernization, relative internal stability, progress and development, India is able to enlarge the capability gap with Pak and widens the disparity in conventional capability.
o **Likelihood of Scenario Emerging.** Less likely/plausible.
o **Desirability of the Scenario.** Most Desirable.

- **Scenario 2: Chasm-Baraah (Status Quo trajectories combined together)**
  o **Scenario Dynamics.** Isolation from the mainstream politics and

economic development with unrealistic obsession fueled by state and non-state actors inimical to the Indian National Interests remain the main hindrance to any worth-while development in the situation in J&K. While the Govt agencies continue to maintain the uneasy "balance" in the internal situation, their inability to address the Centre of Gravity – Psyche of Awaam – and other vested interests prevent bringing in normalcy in Valley. The definition of "Normalcy" in such a scenario is "prevention of situation going out of hands of Govt agencies" and not positive peace. Security forces continue to maintain pressure on separatists preventing them from regrouping into a viable force. Pak continues with its agenda/policy of abetting terrorism in Kashmir unwilling to let go its obsession. Separatists continue to pursue their agenda of Azadi with display of violence and unrest under influence of Jihad. On the socio-eco-religious front, under a status-quo scenario, the erosion of the fiber of Kashmiriyat continues and teachers at academic institutions contribute towards that end. While the development sponsored by Centre starts to make a headway, the progress is too sluggish to counter-balance the spread of radical idealism in form of spread of Deobandi-Wahabi/Ahl-e-Hadith influence especially on the unemployed youth. Women in the valley remain marginalized section of the society. After the euphoria associated with the success at the elections has subsided, political realities come to the fore. Both, the central and state governments are bound by coalition compulsions and find themselves unable to deliver the promises made to the electorate before the elections. They lose no time in playing to the gallery, with the centre blaming the rigid attitude of the state government on Article 370 for lack of progress in the Valley. On the other hand, the state government blames the centre for trying to cut down its powers and hence prevent it from carrying out developmental activity in the Valley. It also raises the issue of withdrawing AFSPA from certain parts of the state. The scenario could be further elaborated in succeeding paragraphs. While there is a slow improvement in law and order, sporadic incidents of unrest continue to affect internal security of the state. Limited marginalisation of armed segments of insurgent outfits and successful integration of moderate factions into electoral process reduces the militancy to some effect. At the backdrop of this uneasy calm, occasional incidents of violence continue to occur. SF maintains pressure on militants; however, at the slightest opportunity of complacency and laxity, it suffers episodic casualty. Funded by external and internal (reduced) actors, major separatist groups continue to operate. Intermittent escalation of street protests over a range of "issues" and "codes of conduct" continue. Wide spread dissent and protests against AFSPA continue to create turbulence with frequent statements from political hierarchy asking for its withdrawal creating a sense of misperception amongst SF. Inter-agency coordination remain the key weak area. State police remains politicised, coercive and collusive corruption continues. Certain sections of State Police (SOG) continue to perform and achieve results. The complicity of some Policemen in militancy-related activities emerges as a major concern, as terrorist modules operating with the help or participation of Policemen becomes particularly difficult to identify and neutralize. Pak continues to covertly support terror outfits while endeavouring to engage India in talks on Kashmir. Kashmir issue is brought up selectively in international forums. However, increasing economic and cultural engagement marginally balances the rhetoric, leading to uneasy peace at borders. There is gradual strengthening of religious hardliners in Pakistan's internal politics, leading to increasing support for cross-border terrorism, appeasement politics, and stifling of moderates seeking peace. Pak interference and growing influence of Taliban keeps things on edge with a distinct possibility of influx of terrorists to foment trouble into India. Afghanistan's request of support from India is guarded as also the response from India. There is resentfulness amongst youth due to unemployment, poor governance and SF actions. Alienation of youth remains despite Govt policies to integrate them into mainstream resulting in widespread joining of Jihad. Repeated and often acerbic exchange of views on the issue of withdrawal of the AFSPA from certain areas in the state continues to be voiced. Surrender and rehabilitation policy is marginally successful but fails to incite mass homecoming. The evils of poor governance, unemployment and lack of participation because of apprehensions in democratic process do not allow the economic prosperity in the country resulting in disturbed economic growth. The critical areas such as modern education, healthcare, employment, rehab of surrendered militants and inclusive social development remain neglected. The corruption and opportunism remain the bane in the society and appeasement lobbying continues preventing generating pride in locals of being a Kashmiri. The social divide between "Haves" and "Have Nots" widens. Awaam continues to remain dependent on subsidies and freebies. The lack of modern education, growth of Wahabi and Deobandi Islamic schools/madrassas and steady funding from Islamic states further dampens decaying Sufism. ISIS ideology gains deep roots in an already fractured society. The support base of radicalized Islamic sect starts increasing. The added complexity is provided by Shia and Sunni and Intra-Shia factionalism. The society in the J&K state remains trifurcated on Kashmir Valley, Jammu and Leh and Ladakh demographic divide. While on the surface, the Valley Muslims claim resettlement of the Kashmiri Pandits back in the valley, the terms and conditions of returns and time plan are never discussed. The law and order situation remains the sore point with Awaam playing victimization card at any breach of existing uneasy status quo. There is easy flow of hawala money inside valley, thus resulting in the increased criminalization of the Kashmiri society. The cross-border drug and arms trafficking continues with the levels increasing/reducing at periodic regularity. Lack of private industry and Govt sector being sole employment avenue keeps the unemployment index growing. This results in increased criminalization. Awaam's reluctance to work hard results in the labour intensive tasks in development projects continue to be filled by non-domicile population. The rural-urban divide continues. The social-media and satellite television/internet allow a Kashmiri to develop a world-view and expose him to the developments around the globe. This gives rise to elevation of his aspirations. It also reduces the effects of anti-India propaganda by Pakistan using Pak TV Channels and social media. However, separatists and interested elements start using internet- facebook/instagram etc as a very effective tool of mass mobilization and perception management. The J&K state budget continues to remain dependent on the funding and support of the central govt irrespective of the economic development. The Kashmiri Pysche remains unchanged and issues like lying, corruption, projecting state of victimhood, art of systemized feedback and spreading of misinformation and feeling of being manipulated by others remain. Article 370 continues to prevent Non-Kashmiris from settling in the valley thereby preventing demographic alterations and the Sunnis remain a dominant community in the valley and it gets more and more polarized.

o **Snapshots / Milestones**

2022	2028	2035
(i) Elections in J&K comparatively violent. Hurriyat active, continues with its anti-India campaigning.	(i) The death of Gilani in 2022 provides a fresh lease of life to the hardliners in the APHC who use the sympathy wave to consolidate their position and renew their demands for independence.	(i) By 2029, another round of elections has taken place giving rise to new coalitions, both at the centre and state levels. Again, the lack of a clear mandate leads to instability and no clear-cut policy direction to resolve the Kashmir issue. There is military and political deadlock.
(ii) Central and state governments are bound by coalition compulsions and find themselves unable to deliver the promises made to the electorate before the elections.		
(iii) Anti-talk outfits though sidelined but not fully deactivated. Though LC ceasefire continues but with occasional violations.	(ii) Elections in J&K comparatively calm despite Pak-sponsored terrorism. Hurriyat continues to raise rhetoric for complete independence.	(ii) Kashmiris realise they cannot secede forcibly, yet they have the power to deny political legitimacy to Govt of India unless their political aspirations are addressed.
(iv) Due to religious fundamentalism Pakistan political process weak, preventing major policy initiatives against foreign policy reforms. Cosmetic actions against Hafiz Sayeed. Growth of religious fundamentalism on upswing.	(iii) Pak policy making continues to suffer, with increasing roughness in bilateral issues with India. However, increasing economic and cultural engagement balances the rhetoric, leading to uneasy peace at borders.	(iii) Insurgency reaches a state of stalemate. Indian leaders realise that they have warded off the threat of secession, but peace will remain elusive without Pak's consent and Kashmiris' approval.
(v) Indian political process results in a fractured verdict, unstable Govt at the centre, leading to no forging of consensus on steps required to resolve the J&K problem. Border infrastructure projects lack renewed impetus and higher funding.	(iv) Indian policy-making passes on to next generation of leaders, with renewed energy and focus on nation-building. Renewed impetus to economic agenda. Security aspects dealt with pragmatically, sustained focus on modernisation and resolution of J&K imbroglio.	(iv) India would like the Line of Control to become formalized and be the accepted international border. Even though India maintains that it owns the entire span of Kashmir, it is willing to accept the ceasefire line as the boundary between the two nations.
(vi) Taliban continues to foment violence in South and SE Afghanistan with active support from radical outfits in Pakistan (TTP).		(v) However, Pakistan and Kashmiri activists remain against this idea because they want greater control. Both the U.S. and the U.K. favour creating the Line of Control to be accepted as international border.
(vii) USA reduces aid to Pakistan.	(v) USA aid to Pakistan conditional. USA gradual shift of stance away from Pak resulting	
(viii) International players lend		

2022	2028	2035
their support to sustained dialogue on Kashmir. (ix) Symbiotic existence of terrorist camps and Pak army continues. (x) SF deployment and operations continue as hitherto fore. (xi) SF actions not complimented by effective governance. (xii) Youth continue to remain vociferous and 2010/2016-like protests occur intermittently. (xiii) Kidnappings and killings by militants are on the rise to establish their writ.	in greater reliance on India to balance its requirements. (vi) Civil administration is ineffective and the lack of improvement in basic amenities and quality of life leads to simmering discontent in the Awam. (vii) SF continue to control the IS situation in Kashmir despite occasional spurt in militant activities/ orchestrated disorders created by Pak. (viii) Pakistan's gradual loss of trust with the international community, including its major ally the US. This gives India leverage to put its case more forcefully. (ix) Gradual and sustained growth in Indian economy positively affects the growth in Kashmir resulting in inclusive growth and employment opportunities for the youth. (x) The movement for removal of AFSPA gathers a very strong momentum. (xi) Pakistan uses the situation to its advantage by covertly supporting terror outfits while ostensibly endeavouring to engage India in talks on Kashmir. (xii) The government fails to take necessary steps like implementing e-governance empowering local panchayats etc. in order to curb large scale corruption.	(vi) Focused attention on the developmental aspects with a view to strengthening the infrastructure, creating employment and income generation opportunities, and generally improving the quality of life of the people results in youth especially victims of state action changing their mindset towards reconciliation. (vii) The law and order situation remains tense and security forces have to carry out frequent flag marches to retain control of the situation. The situation is exploited to the hilt by Pakistan by increasing support to militancy and repeatedly raising the issue in international forums. The immediate result is that a fuming India puts further restrictions on cross-LoC trade bringing it almost to a halt. The situation plays right into the hands of AHPC which uses it to remain relevant in the Valley with a no compromise policy on its demand for independence.

o **End State.** Under this scenario, a series of fractured mandates by the electorate gives rise to relatively unstable coalition governments at both central and state levels. Coalition compulsions ensure that no bold political initiatives are taken by central and state government to bring about decisive changes to the situation in the Valley. As a result, centre-state relations remain fragile at best, governance takes a back seat and the aspirations of the Awam remain unfulfilled leading to simmering discontent in the Valley. The APHC exploits the situation to remain relevant and continues to make strident calls for independence. J&K would continue to be calm only on the surface without the semblance of positive peace. Internal Security situation though "managed", violence does not reduce to a desirable level thereby continuing to adversely strain the Armed forces and economy of the state. Although USA's engagement with India increases manifold, it realises due to geopolitical constraints it can't be at the cost of Pak whom it will continue to engage favourably. Instability in Pakistan continues with a possible security threat to India. Pak continues to fight the proxy war through radicalised youth and its homegrown militants supporting them by providing them safe havens while blaming India for repression in the valley. Pak continues to internationalise the issue by seeking involvement of UN, USA and other international organisations. It remains unwilling to accept the status – quo while proclaiming nuclear threat due to dispute.

o **Likelihood of Scenario Emerging.** Most likely/plausible.

o **Desirability of the Scenario.** Less desirable.

- **Scenario 3 : Daagh-Daar (Worst trajectories combined together)**
  o **Scenario Dynamics.** 2019 general elections and those for the state legislature are marred with violence and a low voter turnout. The results are still declared as a face-saver, with anti-incumbency being the order of the day. A right-wing conservative coalition government comes to power at the centre and the state government is a stable coalition composed of the erstwhile opposition parties. However, the party leading the coalition at the centre is not a part of the coalition government in J&K. The new governments come to power with a hope to move towards the resolution of the Kashmir issue. Unfortunately, things start going wrong almost immediately. An India-Pakistan cricket match in Dubai in October 2019 proves to

be the trigger for a series of events that sour the centre-state relations even before they could stabilise. The tightly contested match is won by Pakistan in a close finish triggering celebrations in parts of the Valley and by a group of Kashmiri students watching the same in their college hostel in a Northern Indian state. The local police, at the behest of local right-wing politicians arrest the students and slap a charge of sedition against them. The issue gets quickly blown up by the media, and the J&K government asks the Centre to intervene and drop charges against the students. However, playing to the vote bank that got it elected, the central government refuses to intervene. This causes widespread outrage in the Valley and in turn harsh comments by the J&K government to appease its own vote bank. Although the case against the students is dismissed by the local magistrate and the charges dropped, the students receive threatening calls prompting them to leave the hostel and return to their homes in Srinagar. A few days later, a video clip showing Kashmiri youth being beaten up at an unknown location surfaces in the social media, triggering a panic, with hundreds of Kashmiri youth leaving their jobs and studies and scrambling back to the Valley. Later, the video is proved to be a fake, but with the centre and state governments not on the best of terms, only half-hearted efforts are made to reassure the Kashmiri populace of their safety in other parts of India. This results in large-scale protests in the Valley, with hundreds of people marching to demand the safety of Kashmiris outside the Valley. The demonstrations turn violent at a few places and security forces have to resort to firing to retain control of the situation. The incident gives a shot in the arm to the separatists in the Valley, who renew their calls for freedom from this "repression" by the Indian Union. Pakistan grabs this opportunity to table a resolution in the UN condemning India for violence against the minority community, especially in Kashmir. It also steps up financial and moral support to the separatists. By 2022, with neither the state nor the centre willing to strike a conciliatory note, the Valley simmers with resentment and undercurrents of tension. Several foreign governments issue travel advisories warning their citizens not to travel to Kashmir due to the existing situation. Tourism drops drastically, leading to economic problems which further stoke discontent in the Awaam. The simmering discontent in the Valley continues for much of 2022 with frequent incidents of stone pelting against the security forces. The security forces try their best to engage with the Awam by exercising restraint and continuing to try and win hearts and minds, but the mood in the Valley does not encourage reconciliation. To make matters worse, there are frequent heated exchanges between the centre and the state governments about the status of Articles 370, 35A and AFSPA. Local politicians knowing that separatist views would curry favour with the Awam change positions with impunity, demanding freedom from the Indian occupation of the Valley with tacit support of the state government. The feeling of disenchantment within the Valley provides a chance for the fundamentalists to further their agenda of radicalisation of the populace. This period sees a threefold increase in the number of madrassas in the Valley. These new Islamic schools and ideologically inclined teachers in schools and colleges, flush with funds from Pakistan and Saudi Arabia, attract hordes of discontented youth and set about the task of turning them into soldiers of Islam. While all this is on the teachers appointed in 2010 with Jamaati leanings quietly continue to derail the lives of many a student in schools and colleges by radicalizing them beyond repair. The students take to the path of militancy on attending funerals of slain militants, as the last straw that breaks the camel's back. In the meanwhile, the stalwart of the AHPC, Syed Ali Shah Geelani, who has been ailing for a while, passes away in late 2022. Thousands of mourners pour out into the streets to pay their final respects and security forces have a hard time regulating the crowds. A panicked security jawan inadvertently fires a round in the air resulting in a stampede killing 85 people including women and children, and injuring hundreds more including security persons. The security forces are immediately pushed on the back foot. Separatist groups, terror outfits and religious leaders join hands and exploit the social media to inflame the Awam by portraying the security forces as insensitive killers. Incensed by this perceived insensitivity, there are widespread violent demonstrations against the security forces. Pakistan also keeps the issue inflamed in the international arena and activates terrorist sleeper cells leading to an increase in terrorist activity with ambushes, suicide attacks and IED blasts targeting the security forces. It also tries to divert militants from Afghanistan into the Valley thus increasing the number of infiltrations attempts and increasing the pressure on the already beleaguered security forces. The Ahl-e-Hadith mosques of the Valley fuel the ISIS ideology through its teachings and many youths join in the path of Zakir Musa. With the support of the Pakistani establishment, large-scale smuggling of drugs starts across the LoC as a means to finance the activities of the jihadis. There is a spurt in the use of drugs amongst the disillusioned, unemployed youth in the Valley. The tourism industry is almost at a standstill and in the absence of any infrastructure development and economic activity the economic misery of the Awaam is compounded leading to further anti India sentiments. The next round of elections throws up a different coalition government at the state level while the same combine retains power at the centre. Elected on the basis of its strong anti-India propaganda, the state government shows no inclination to soften its stand and work with the centre for reconciliation and resolution of the issue. Situation in the Valley remains volatile. With all the stakeholders, the central and state governments, Pakistan and the Awaam, unwilling to budge from their stated positions, the political and security deadlock continues. Violent anti India demonstrations continue and security forces are forced to implement curfews to ensure that the law and order situation remains under control. The Awaam is increasingly alienated and the seemingly endless struggle for political self-determination and economic stability has a damaging effect on the Kashmiri psyche. The influence of Wahabi Islam is on the rise with madrassas mushrooming all over the Valley, flush with funds from the hawala route from Pakistan and the Middle East. By 2030, due to increased radicalisation of the youth, the concept of Kashmiriyat suffers leading to increased violence against non-Muslim inhabitants of the Valley. The Shia minority is also targeted in areas like Badgam. This leads to widespread protests in Jammu where attempts are made to carry out an economic blockade of the Valley. In retaliation, terrorists carry out multiple attacks on the Amarnath Yatra in the summer of 2031, killing 200 yatris and injuring many more. In the crackdown by the security forces that follows, cordon and search operations and indefinite detentions for interrogation lead to a further sense of humiliation in the Awam. In the precarious security climate, work on infrastructure projects proceeds at snail's pace with industrial houses evincing no interest in setting up projects in the Valley. Cross-LoC trade is also at a standstill due to strained relations between India and Pakistan. Government funding therefore remains the sole means of livelihood for the Awaam. However, poor governance and ever-increasing corruption means that only a fraction of these funds reach the common man, while most are salted away by the corrupt state officials and contractors. Increasingly frustrated, with no employment prospects and facing economic penury, more and more youth opt for joining the jihadi movement. Separatist and fundamentalist elements continue to operate with increased support of Pakistan. In the midst of this turmoil, the centre increases funding to Jammu and Ladakh regions and announces its plans to form separate councils for governing these areas which have proved their "loyalty to India". It also withdraws special concessions for the Awaam like reservations in colleges, professional courses and employment thus distancing them even more from the rest of the country. This provokes the Awaam further, leading to more protests and demonstrations. The Hurriyat uses this opportunity to further consolidate itself as the voice of the Awaam by making strident calls for mass demonstrations against India and support "Azadi". In 2029, a terrorist group with allegiance to the LeT blows up the Jammu-Srinagar railway line, derailing a train, which results in more severe action by the security forces. Protests against the high handedness of the security forces continue with thousands of people from all walks of life taking to the streets. The terrorist families are continuously harassed and tortured by high handed SPOs under the safety of PSA. The terrorists strike back by attacking the Police memorial school at Srinagar with suicide bombers, killing 56 children. The central government dissolves the state assembly and imposes President's rule in J&K. Pakistan loses no time in taking advantage of the situation and openly protests against genocide in the Valley to suppress what it calls "the Kashmiri Spring". Terrorist camps across the LoC actively train and aid infiltration into J&K leading to frequent skirmishes at the LoC. The Kashmir issue catches the imagination of the international community and calls for involvement of the UN/third-party mediators gain ground.

o **End State.** As the scenario plays out in 2035, political rhetoric in the Kashmir Valley continues unabated with none of the stakeholders willing for a compromise. This results in increasing levels of violence and President's rule in the state continues; Kashmiri resentment with India escalates with vociferous street demonstrations calling for "Azadi". Infrastructure development is at an all-time low (practically zero) and the drop in tourism leads to poor economic development. A disenchanted Awam views the security forces as oppressors and occupiers and provides support to terrorist groups who are viewed as freedom fighters. Support for these violent groups from across the LoC is at a very high level. The Kashmir issue is back on the international centre-stage and calls for UN mediation are on the rise. The hardline Hurriyat Conference becomes the political voice of the Valley.

o **Snapshots.**

2022	2028	2035
• Kashmiri students' support to Pakistan cricket team in end 2019 leads to continuous threats from locals	• Continued problems in centre state relations on AFSPA & Art 370	• Political and security deadlock continues
• Panic scramble of Kashmiris from other states back to Valley due to provocative video on social media	• Threefold increase in number of Wahabi madrassas, radicalisation of youth increases in schools and colleges. Teachers become ideological gurus for stugents to join militancy	• Increasing influence of Wahabism, radicalised youth, communal violence and multiple attacks on Amarnath Yatra
• Centre-state stand off to appease vote banks	• Stampede during Geelani's funeral, violent protests against security forces	• Special package for Jammu and Ladakh leads to violent retaliation, railway line to Srinagar blown up and train derailed
• Violent protests in the Valley leading to lathi charge by security personnel	• Pakistan ramps up support to separatists, activates sleeper cells and aids influx of Afghani militants including ISIS, internationalizes issue	• Security forces crackdown leading to increasing alienation of Awam
• Separatists and Pakistan condemn repression, UN resolution by Pakistan	• Spurt in ambushes, kidnappings, suicide attacks, and IED blasts targeting security forces, families of SF and govt establishments including children at a Police memorial school	• President's rule imposed in J&K
• Increased support to separatists and militants by Pakistan		• Pakistan actively pursues the issue internationally and increases support to separatists, militants
• Travel advisories lead to drop in tourist inflow	• Large scale drug smuggling across LoC to finance the Jihad affecting youth and social fabric	• Amidst political penury, Hurriyat becomes the political voice of the valley
• Governance sidelined leading to discontent in the Valley	• No development, governance at a standstill, economic misery of Awam worsens, corruption at its peak	• UN calls for a debate on a resolution on Kashmir
• Ahl-e-Hadith mosques gain centre stage. Subversion of the minds of the students in schools, colleges and Madrassas is prevalent		

- o Likelihood of Scenario Emerging. Least Likely but plausible.
- o Desirability of the Scenario. Undesirable.

- **Scenario 4 : Naadir-e-Rozgaar (Wild Card)**
  - o **Scenario Dynamics.** "Nadir-e-Rozgaar" means "**unique in the world or rare**" and the scenario unfolds sometime in 2029. The TTP, ISIS and other Islamist outfits have secured control over much of the Pakistani Armed Forces, and thus, the entire state of Pakistan falls into the hands of fundamentalists. Terrorist attacks within Pakistan reach an unprecedented high. Pakistan is taken over by the military and the military uses chemical weapons against the TTP in Waziristan. The international community lays down economic embargo on Pakistan. UN peace-keeping forces are deployed in Pakistan in fear of misuse of nuclear weapons by non-state actors. This forces Pak to reduce its cross-LC activites. Afghanistan is continuing with a civil war and UN-led forces are conducting peace-keeping ops with India being the lead participant.The internal security situation across the country in India improves steadily through implementation of robust and responsive policies. The external terrorist groups are gradually marginalized due to the presence of UN forces in Pakistan and Afghanistan. Prime Minister is visiting Srinagar after successful talks with separatist leaders and all stake holders based on the long-term comprehensive strategies devised in 2014 after victory in general elections. He is making a public statement in Srinagar for having found a lasting solution to the Kashmir problem. Pakistan is not in the loop. While addressing the people at the Harbaksh stadium in Srinagar, a group of Fidayeen manage to sneak in and carryout indiscriminate firing under the clandestine support of the ISI and fundamentalist elements in Pak military. A human bomb explodes near the main dais, killing the Prime Minister, Chief Minister and a large number of top leaders of the State. Another bomb explodes among the people attending the rally leading to large scale loss of human life. A simultaneous attack on all the road and rail tunnels across the Pir Panjal range is laso launched using dirty bombs prepared by smuggling stolen fissile material and chemicals from Pak. Communal tensions flare up. A muslim village in Kishtwar, Udhampur and Rai Bareili is burnt down. Massive riots break out

in Budgam between Shias and Sunnis, Hindu-muslim at Kishtwar and blockade of J&K from Pathankot to Udhampur by the Jammu Hindu community. The rest of the country also has communal violence and a large number of towns are affected. Mass destruction of national property takes place and thousands of human lives are lost. The country comes to a standstill stretching the social fabric of the nation and governments resolve to the limit. The nation-state of India is on the verge of splitting into small clusters based on religion. Under intense pressure from the masses, TF Zulu comprising a package of 10 aircraft strikes Muzzafarabad and a number of training camps, followed by surgical strikes on 20 terror launch pads, causing large-scale destruction. Both countries mobilize for war and the UN peacekeepers start moving out from Pakistan.

Scenario to Strategy Options

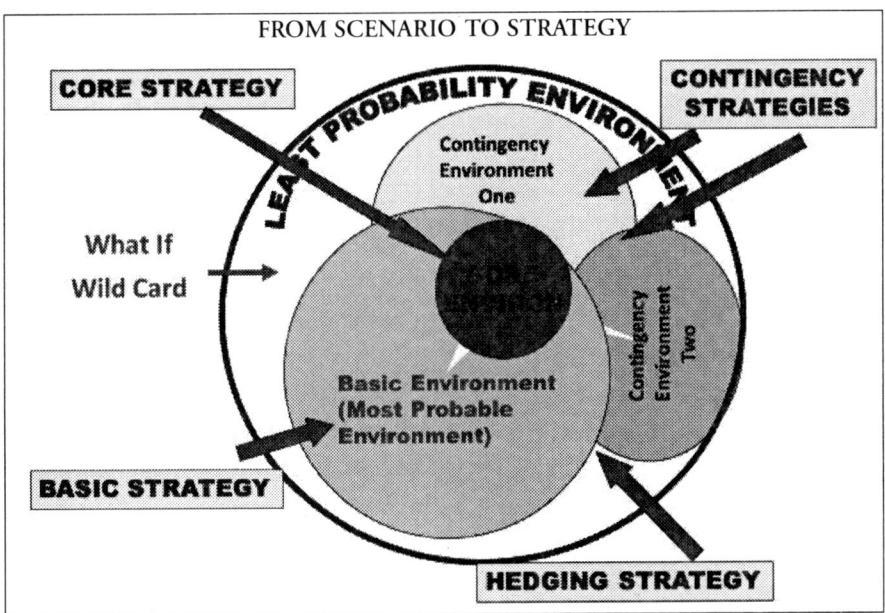

Core Future Security Environment. Key events and trends that will characterize the future over next 10–15 years, irrespective of whichever scenario emerges are as under:

- **Historical Perspective being Manipulated and Aggrieved.** Power equations have changed over a period of time and it is always the human behaviour of trying to be at the centre of power which has been the main reason for neglecting the aspirations of the state. The historical perspective of the awam of being aggrieved and manipulated by its own national and state leaders for short term political gains. This feeling has been constant and is unlikely to be changed.

- **Aspirations of the Awam of Valley.** Over a period of last sixty years, no single state of the Indian Union has seen such a huge shift in the aspirations of the people from Azadi to becoming part of Pakistan to being part of India, three totally different scenarios with the Awaam of Kashmir also swaying as the wind blew. These aspirations are only likely to increase with more technological penetration and awareness.

- **The Jammu-Kashmir-Ladakh divide.** The Jammu province region though has a 70:30 Hindu-Muslim ratio, parts of the region were hit by militants, but violence has ebbed there, along with the Valley. Dogras (67%) are the single largest group in the multi-ethnic region of Jammu living with Punjabis, Paharis, Bakerwals and Gujjars. Ladakh is the largest region in the state with over 200,000 people. Its two districts are Leh (77% Buddhist) and Kargil (80% Muslim population). Union territory status has been the key demand of Leh Buddhists for many years. The state is clearly divided in three distinct regions of Jammu (dominated by Dogras and Hindus), Kashmir (dominated by Muslims) and Ladakh (dominated by Buddhists).

- **OGWs and Fence Sitters Activities.** Over ground workers have always been the mainstay for an insurgency movement. Previously OGW were primarily involved in logistics support and intel gathering. The comparative freedom of mov available to terrorists due to limited resource control measures has emboldened the trts to change their strategy of trying to mix up with population. Thus, OGWs are merging as a potent force and needs to given equal weightage while dealing with them. These OGWs and fence sitters would continue remaining actively involved in assisting the cause of the militants.

- **Strategically Important Location of Kashmir.** Jammu and Kashmir is connected with rest of India by a single arterial road for all its requirements and has access to China and Pakistan; this importance is likely to remain due to major water resources and access to the riches of CAR nations, China and Pakistan.

- **Partially Porous Borders with Pakistan.** The borders with Pakistan are porous as they are recognized as disputed and so far four wars have already been fought with Pak. The PoK also adds a new dimension to the entire problem. This aspect is likely to continue as Pakistan will continue to exploit the LC for infiltrating the terrorists in Kashmir.

- **High Levels of Infiltration.** The levels of infiltration have continued to remain high for the last 28 years except that they have reduced since 2004 after the construction of the LC fence. This trend is going to remain constant and relates directly to the levels of militants in the valley.
- **Advent of the Local Militants.** In the last four years or so the OGWs are targeting the youth in schools and colleges. A heady concoction is being given to them by some compromised teachers, religious preachers and recruiters in funeral processions to motivate them in joining militancy.
- **Flow of Large-Scale Hawala Money and Counterfeited Currency.** This aspect is one of the most important operational tools for a terrorist org. The hawala funding from Saudi Arabia, Iran, Pakistan ISI and the Kashmiri diaspora seems to the primary means of funding. Notably, the terrorist organizations both in PoK and valley does not use these resources solely for its terrorist operations; example, it sponsors a number of charities in the PoK and Pak. Thus, it is difficult to separate the funds the organization uses to support health clinics from those used to support terrorist activities. Therefore, although money is key for terrorist organizations to sustain its activities, it also plays an organizational role—group cohesion—by bolstering its relationship to local communities and further legitimizing its activities in J&K. However, the balance of payment in LoC trade and narcotics[2] seems to be the new source of financing the movement in the valley.
- **Cross Border Drug Trafficking.** J&K is strategically located between the Golden Crescent and the Golden Triangle. The narcotics trade has increased over a period of time and the recent recoveries of drugs in LoC trade are an indication of the growing nexus between terrorism and drug trafficking. The recent drug hauls in Kashmir/Delhi and other instances of arms, explosives and narcotics being smuggled under the cover of overland trade should serve as a wake-up call to those who advocate throwing open the borders for trade without checks and balances in place. The narcotics trade has had an effect on the youth of

the state also. A large number of youth is said to be addicted to drugs. Unemployed youth and drug addicts are a dangerous combination for a state which is fighting a counter-terrorist campaign.

- **Continuation of Article 370.** Jammu and Kashmir is the only state in India which enjoys special autonomy under Article 370 of the Constitution of India, according to which no law enacted by the Parliament of India, except for those in the field of defence, communication and foreign policy, will be extendable in Jammu and Kashmir unless it is ratified by the state legislature of Jammu and Kashmir. Subsequently, jurisdiction of the Supreme Court of India over Jammu and Kashmir has been extended. Jammu and Kashmir is the only Indian state that has its own official flag and constitution, and Indians from other states cannot purchase land or property in the state. The Instrument of Accession of Jammu and Kashmir to India was signed by the Maharaja Hari Singh in October, 1947 and a special status was given to the State through the Article 370. The wordings of Article 370 and its title "Temporary provisions with respect to the State of Jammu and Kashmir" are both significant as they imply that it was designed as a temporary or provisional arrangement. The Article essentially governs centre-state relations pertaining to J&K. Centre-State relations and issues of regional balance within States are similarly dealt with in the case of Gujarat, Maharashtra, Andhra Pradesh, Assam, Sikkim, Manipur, Nagaland, Tripura, Meghalaya, Arunachal etc in Articles 371-A to I and Schedules 5 and 6. Kashmir, in this sense, is not uniquely treated. When objections were raised in the Constituent Assembly regarding the inclusion of Article, an assurance was given by the framers of the Constitution that it would get eroded gradually. This happened to some extent during the premiership of Bakshi Ghulam Mohmmad, but it was not taken to its logical conclusion. So stating the Article as the root cause of all the trouble over J&K and in the fear of demand for a plebiscite, some political parties have been demanding abrogation of the Article. They also believe that this Article has encouraged the secessionist elements in other part of the country. In December 1964, Articles 356 and 357 were extended to the state. Can we amend Article 370 when the Constituent Assembly of the state no longer exists? Or whether it can be amended at all? Some jurists say it can be amended by an amendment act under Article 368 of the Constitution and the amendment extended under Article 370(1). But it is still a mooted question. Equally valid arguments are forwarded by those in favour of and those against its abrogation. Those in favour argue that it has created certain psychological barriers and the root cause of all the problems in J&K. Article 370 encourages secessionist activities within J&K and other parts of the country. They say, at the time of enactment, it was a temporary arrangement which was supposed to erode gradually. They also argue that it acts as a constant reminder to the Muslims of J&K that they have still to merge with the country. Those against its abrogation argue that Abrogation will have serious consequences. It will encourage secessionists to demand plebiscite which will lead to internationalization of the issue of J&K. They further argue that the contention of Article giving rise to secessionist activities is baseless as states like Assam and Punjab, which don't have any special status, have experienced such problems. It would not only constitute a violation of the solemn undertaking given by India through the instrument of accession, but would also give unnecessary misgivings in the minds of the people of J&K, making the issue more sensitive. This article would remain constant with no/minor changes in due course.

- **Kashmir as Part of India and the Constitutional Evidence.** The state of Jammu and Kashmir retains a special status within the union government of India. Unlike the rest of the states, which are bound by the Indian constitution, Jammu and Kashmir follows a modified version of that constitution—as delineated in the Constitution (Application to Jammu and Kashmir) Order, 1954—which affirms the integrity of the state within the Republic of India. The union government has direct legislative powers in matters of defence, foreign policy, and communications within the state and has indirect influence in matters of citizenship, Supreme Court jurisdiction, and emergency powers. Under the constitution of Jammu and Kashmir, the governor, who is head of state, is appointed by the President of India and is aided and advised by an elected chief minister and a council of ministers.

- **Continuation of AFSPA in J&K.** AFSPA has been the biggest thorn in the centre-state relations in the recent past. The longstanding demand of separatists, their supporters and some political parties has been to repeal the AFPSA altogether. However, the politicians of J&K have propounded the idea of a partial revocation from certain areas of the state. Echoing public sentiment, its votaries repeatedly blast the Act as "draconian" in nature and the Army's misuse of the Act to perpetrate human rights violations and excesses. Public sentiment and those swaying with it often term the AFSPA as illegal and unconstitutional. A perusal of the various powers available to the police in J&K under the provisions of the Criminal Penal Code vis-à-vis those available to the Armed Forces under the AFSPA would reveal that the police authorities still enjoy more encompassing and wider powers relating to arrest, search, seizure, summoning of witnesses and preventive detention than the powers enjoyed by the Armed Forces. AFSPA is an enabling provision and Act passed by the Parliament and it assists the Armed Forces in dealing with special situations. The Central Government vide Article 355 of the Constitution of India is duty bound to protect every state not only against external aggression but also internal disturbances and to ensure that every state is governed in accordance with the provisions of the Indian Constitution. It is also an established fact that the judiciary is the custodian of the Constitution. An independent judicial system performs better than any other agency to maintain equilibrium between the liberty of the individual and the powers of the State. It is in this context that the Honourable Supreme Court of India had upheld the constitutional validity of the AFSPA. The Court further observed that the instructions issued by military authorities in the form of "Dos and Donts" while acting under the AFSPA are to be treated as binding and are required to be followed by the Armed Forces. By analysing the issue of safeguard further, it would transpire that the protection envisaged is for only those persons who act in good faith in discharge of their official duties and not otherwise. Acting in good faith would mean to act without any malice. The protection under Section 7 would not be available to a member of the security forces who commits acts which constitute criminal offences not in the discharge of his official duties even in the areas which have been declared as "disturbed". In January 2018, in Shopian District of Jammu and Kashmir, a "disturbed area" under Armed Forces Special Powers Act (Jammu and Kashmir), 1990, an Indian Army convoy was on bona fide military duty. It was isolated by an unruly and violent mob and came under unprovoked and intense stone-pelting by a group of 100-120 stone-pelters who also attacked with petrol bombs.[3] As a preventive measure, warning shots were fired in the air in accordance to the rules of engagement. When the violent mob refused to spare the life of the JCO, the army personnel opened fire with an objective to disperse the violent mob and protect the government servants and property.[4] There were mixed responses on the incident by the state govt and the Judiciary which crates doubts in the mind of soldiers on the ground. The interlocutors' report on Jammu and Kashmir had also recommended review of the AFSPA in the state and said the Defence Ministry needs to consider how to respond "positively" to the issue. The report sought amendments in the Public Safety Act (PSA) which gives sweeping powers to security forces to detain people on grounds of propagating or attempting to create feelings of enmity or hatred or disharmony in the state. The act is extremely important for ops in the valley, particularly so in the wake of people having greater access and knowledge of their legal rights through propaganda and social media. The lack of such an act would have dangerous legal implications particularly due to the propensity of the people to leverage the lack of legal protection to arm twist the armed forces.

- **Domination of J&K Politics by Kashmir Valley.** J&K is a unique state and has been on politically volatile right from independence. Reason for four Indo-Pak conflicts, the state has been in turmoil for the last 25 years. The ethnic divide as enumerated earlier substantiates the feeling of alienation in other two regions. With NCs domination fading away, emergence of PDP in the Kashmir's politics and BJP in the Jammu region, the 2002 elections ushered in the era of collation politics in the state. The prime cause of failure to break the deadlock in the State is that all suggested solutions are based on the misguided notion that the 2,000 square kilometers Kashmir Valley represents the entire State of Jammu and Kashmir; that the political aspirations of all the people in the State are identical or nearly identical and that the contradictions among them, if any, can be easily reconciled. None of these formulations enjoys any universal support in Jammu, Kashmir and Ladakh. There are two prime factors, i.e., the State of Jammu and Kashmir houses a number of religious and ethnic groups, and the political aspirations and needs of the people of Jammu and Ladakh – who constitute almost half of the State's population and inhabit about 90% of the State's land area – and Kashmiri Pandits and Muslims are conflicting.

- **Comprehensive Education System.** The aspects of modern higher education, infrastructure development, and presence of Army Goodwill schools are essential. J&K Govt provides compulsory and free education upto Elementary Level. The Education Department provides free of cost Text books and mid-day meal upto 8th class. There has been a gradual increase in the number of Govt colleges and enrollment over the years. A total of 45 colleges exist in the Kashmir valley. The madrassas need to be regulated and the education system is likely to continue in the present form. Teachers affiliated to religious groups propagating radicalization need to be weeded out at the earliest as they are slowly but steadily providing the miltant poison to the children of Kashmir.

- **Financial aid by Centre**. The state's economy is heavily dependent upon the grants from the centre, the central funded schemes and the security forces deployed in the state. Details have been covered adequately in the chapter on SWOT analysis.
- **Local Media**. The Press in the valley was at the mercy of the militants in the nineties. Correspondents of national dailies who tried to be objective were beaten up and driven out of Kashmir. Any journalist, who does not report the utterances of the various militant outfits, almost all of it propaganda, had to face their wrath. There had been an improvement in the situation in the new millennium but things are deteriorating again. The national press more or less has been objective and truthful in its reports but the same can't be said about the vernacular press. The vernacular press in the Valley is the focus of attention of the militant groups. Facing the gun, it has little choice except to publish distorted and exaggerated stories. Stringers controlled by the militants put out colorful and doctored reports which are a travesty of the truth. The people in the Valley who would rather believe what is printed in the local press rather than the news put out by All India Radio and Doordarshan get worked up by the provocative militant-inspired writings and often come out in the streets to stage protest demonstrations. The foreign media which often have a problem understanding the nuances and background, then project the demonstrations as a reflection of the spontaneous support of the people for the militants and secession. This is the chain reaction sought to be achieved. The diabolical hand of Pakistan is behind this orchestrated campaign against India. Disinformation, false reports and rumors are floated by militants and these are forced on the local media. Proliferation of electronic media has brought in a new dimension. The breaking

news culture and need for sensational reporting to remain relevant has added new challenges for both the govt and the security forces. Freedom of press without much thought to responsibility has many a time resulted in avoidable crisis situation for the authorities. Any attempt to place a curb or restriction on this media has always evoked huge criticism but the fact remains that acerbic reporting by many national news channels is further polarizing the people of Kashmir.

- **Technological Enhancement.** The Social Media is growing rapidly and the present youth has no inhibitions to use technology. Violent clashes in Kashmir between young Kashmiris and security forces of 2010 and 2016 though have petered out, but these conflicts remain highly visible on the Internet, where youth are using social media to continue to air their grievances and advance their cause. "Social media is a paradigm shifter in terms of the tools available to protestors in Kashmir. They no longer need to take illegal measures to protest straight away. Rather, Facebook, Twitter, and the like, have allowed them space to share information, plan protests, and raise awareness in completely legal ways." Violent protests against Security Forces are hardly a new occurrence in the valley. Jammu and Kashmir has experienced similar types of domestic uprisings since 1989. However, the protests in the aftermath of Machil incident in 2010 and the Burhan Wani incident of 2016 saw the emergence of social media as the most powerful tool. The deaths in SF actions during the protests have prompted young protestors, mostly teenage boys, to go viral with online videos that capture the security forces' role in these deaths and blogs publicize their "rock throwing" campaigns. Youth also see the Internet as a way to make visible what is happening in Kashmir to the international community. But many observers believe that these videos will ignite more violence rather than remedy the problem, because the videos and photos keep alive and resonant a memory that feeds continued unrest. The problem is being accentuated by targeted efforts of inimical forces having servers abroad. The advent of social networking technology is a major challenge one has to deal with in today's environment not only in J&K but everywhere.

Core Strategy Options. Strategic efforts, in key national and state endeavours, that can and should be plausibly made to address above-mentioned environment are as under:

- Ensure army completely withdraw and not operate in areas which do not require the cover of the AFSPA, thereby giving a taste of positive peace to the people of these areas, the dividends of which will be contagious. The army may be requisitioned to aid civil authorities as and when required.
- Promote integrated society, encourage and empower all communities to come to mainstream in all fields by equitable arrangements for power and resource sharing.
- Define an integrated national strategic roadmap for J&K involving all instruments of national powers for synergised and coordinated efforts to create a secure environment so that social, economic and political aspirations can be addressed effectively and integrate local populace with national political, social, economic, security, technological and legal mainstream.
- Institute effective measures to check and curb illegal financial assistance from outside India for various radical and fundamentalist purposes by international cooperation, integrating the investigating mechanisms to identify illegal fund flows by combining the efforts of various crime monitoring agencies including narcotics, customs, and other security agencies such as CBI and various state investigating agencies to stem financing of terror.
- Remain alert on the LoC and strengthen the counter infiltration grid to prevent any influx of terrorists by using an array of surveillance eqpt ranging from satl to grnd sensors combined with digital connectivity in comn backed with eff Decision sp sys to enable quick decision making.
- Utilizing electronic, print and social media as a "Force Multiplier" to shape public opinion and to counter false propaganda by launching realistic, coordinated, timely and proactive psychological and information warfare so that the will of the anti-national elements is suffocated and the hearts of the populace are won.
- Upgrade communication systems by adequate investment programmes so that FM channels, television and telecommunication spreads to our remote and border areas to spread the awareness and hasten the process of national integration thereby countering Pakistani propaganda.
- Expose Pakistan-sponsored "proxy" war and apply international pressure more aggressively, highlight the justness of our cause and the support to terrorism by Pakistan, both through state and non-state players, as

- well as strive to isolate Pakistan in the international community utilizing diplomacy, trade, sports and military.
- Ensure assured infrastructure growth by adequate allocation of funds in communication, power, medical and health, public works and education so as to accelerate the achievement of national aim of integrating the Kashmiris with India politically, socially, economically and most importantly, psychologically.
- Develop cities/towns as major tourist destinations as also promote rural tourism so that there is more interaction and integration with rest of the country thereby reducing alienation.
- Meet aspirations of Awam by creating equal opportunities in governance, modern education, employment and development of rural areas through devolution of power through alternate arrangement such as Panchayat Raj.
- Create an integrated Perception management cell as part of the UHQ for countering the social media activities and use the social media as a major medium to effectively manage the perception of the local population.
- Exploit every opportunity of a situation of low violence in the valley for perception management by effective employment of psychological and IW resources.
- Exploit the threat of use of the provisions of PSA to book anti-national elements and OGWs with separate cells to prevent them from disrupting peace and security.
- Educate the traders associations and those involved with tourism on the financial losses likely to happen due to long protests or terrorist actions in the valley. They are a very respected community in the Valley and winning over their support can pay rich dividends.
- Maximise availability of additional troops by redeployment from hinterland to the LoC so as to eliminate the possibility of any influx of terrorists into the valley.
- Exploit insurgent financial weaknesses by controls and regulations that limit the movement and exchange of material and funds may compound insurgent financial vulnerabilities.
- Take advantage of tech and the availability of enforcement agencies and their expertise to deny LoC trade being used for activities which are not in our national interest.
- Prevent opposition to AFSPA through credible perception management

strategy and ensure that the SF do not provide an opportunity to the people to project a case of gross violation of Human Rights.
- Prevent anti-SF propaganda by HR organizations and local media through maximum transparency in modus operandi and regular interaction with these bodies until the perception of the people towards SF alters from an "anti" stance to a "neutral/pro" stance.
- Facilitate emergence of a homogenous society by bridging ethnic divide between Shia-Sunni-Kashmiri Pandits-Buddhist-Sikhs and tribal class through interactive mechanisms, power sharing, empowerment of tribals and removing parochialism.
- Create SEZ for SMEs at major population centres and provide special tax holiday for industries for a limited period to hasten inclusive economic growth.
- Leverage technology and high internet penetration in the state to exploit potential of e-governance to overcome rampant corruption and bring in transparency in administration.
- Provide facilities for the Awaam in having a better understanding of the history of Kashmir with a view of being manipulated by Pak and having interactive e-governance at the state level.
- Iintegrate Kashmir and J&K with India by addressing the issue of alienation amongst Kashmiris through exchange program in universities, with education curriculum of rest of India and vice versa, development of the state and region and promoting trade and commerce through Jammu and LoC fence.
- Create accountability by establishment of an apex committee at state level to monitor agendas. This committee shall also think, plan and execute innovative projects for specific problems in Kashmir, identify and prioritize key issues of planning and development to include communication network, agriculture, tourism, MSMEs etc.
- Chalk out an administrative action plan for infrastructure growth and economic development through nodal centers in form of industrial areas, incorporate NGOs and village authorities/councils in development of roads, tracks, electrification, education, healthcare, small scale industries, etc thereby ensuring inclusive growth as well as empowering the people at the grassroots level rather than only a few wells dug in political parties and their patrons.

Basic Strategy Options

- **Basic Security Environment.** It is the environment of the "most likely scenario", i.e., Scenario 2: Chasm Barrah-Status Quo-is Kashmir (Current state of affairs continues with weak governance, lack of leadership under a fragile but contained internal environment). Some of the desirable and undesirable trends/events would be as under:
    o Desirable Trends/Events. Governance improves, economic development, infrastructure growth and employment better than current state.Kashmiriyat and Sufism re-emerge as religious fundamentalism remains restricted in minor pockets. Jammu-Kashmir-Ladakh and Ethnic divide (Shia-Sunni) reduces, equitable power sharing being talked about. Separatists groups remain divided thereby unable to bring a strong local leadership. Fractured groups managed by GoI to own advantage. Democratisation starts making inroads in the society especially schools and colleges. Student unions are allowed to be formed again with a promise of peaceful representation.
    o Undesirable Trends/Events. Poor governance and lack of basic amenities and infrastructure. Increase in levels of violence.Deep divide resulting in quest for power. Destabilized/radicalized situation accentuated by religious groups and teachers.

- **Strategic Effort Required to Address.** These are the strategic efforts in all endeavours, in congruence with core strategy options, pursuing both simultaneously:
    o Discharge of basic duties linked with governance by developing infrastructure, creation of employability/employment, provision of basic amenities through industrialisation, increase in accountability, check corruption, increase transparency and invigorate economic activity.
    o Meet aspirations of Awaam by creating equal opportunities in governance, modern education, employment and development of rural areas through alternate arrangement such as Panchayat Raj.
    o Reduce violence levels by undertaking SF operations through border management, surrender policies, engaging in talks with people of Pakistan through people to people, intelligentsia and Business entities under the principle of Multi-track diplomacy, as well as effective utilisation of surrendered terrorists for info-based precision CI/CT operations.

- Increase capabilities of Kashmir Police, CRPF and SOG by capability-building measures and increased inter-operability to make it the principle instrument of IS Management.
- Work out modalities for time-bound transfer of control of IS situation in the hinterland from Indian Army to state and central police forces.I ngrain in the state police a culture of community policing.
- Promote Kashmiriyat and Sufism to maintain its relevance through mass media/communication and internet-based information warfare, thereby preventing/checking rapid growth of radical Wahabi-Deobandi cult.
- Facilitate emergence of a homogenous society by bridging ethnic divide between Shia-Sunni-Kashmiri Pandits-Buddhist-Sikhs and tribal class through interactive mechanisms, power sharing, empowerment of tribals and removing parochialism.
- To exploit small windows of stable/contained IS situation in the state, by strengthening the democratic setup further and initiating process of meaningful devolution of powers at the various lower levels, namely regional, districts and panchayat levels.
- To leverage the IS situation in times of peace to improve governance and create environment for improving the Centre-State relationship. Promote good governance by effective execution of economic, social and political reforms through well intentioned development programs, thereby providing positive peace to the Awaam.
- Create conducive situation to speed up restoration of normalcy by relentless joint operations with CAPF in Kashmir to neutralise and wipe out writ of separatists through all out CT operations in valley combined with effective LC management to prevent infiltration.
- Promote integrated society, encourage and empower all communities to come to mainstream in all fields by equitable arrangements for power and resource sharing.
- Ensure unhindered operating space for SF by avoiding media and HR reprimand through building hard intelligence for "clean ops", discourage "number game", increase transparency and promote strong perception management.
- Ensure governance reaches entire state by developing government machinery at grassroots level with panchayats emerging as vibrant and effective institutions.

- Check Pakistan-backed extremism, terrorism and separatism, with Governments, both in New Delhi and Srinagar, taking intensive measures to strengthen civil administration, create international pressure, sensitization of local populace and reenergizing and integrating the Security Force, thereby infusing a greater confidence in the people.
- Define an integrated national strategic roadmap for J&K involving all instruments of national powers for synergised and coordinated efforts to create a secure environment so that social, economic and political aspirations can be addressed effectively and integrate local populace with national political, social, economic, security, technological and legal mainstream.
- Resumption of sustained and meaningful dialogue with the people of Pakistan through multi-track diplomacy channels to create a conducive atmosphere for resumption of talks besides restoration of internal dialogue with diverse political opinions in an inclusive manner.
- Further strengthen the Unified Command so as to give a co-ordinated and planned response to the threat of terrorism in Kashmir. Strengthen apex-level intelligence agencies by incorporating advance techs to gain intelligence and create intelligence network to carry out counter terrorist ops at strategic and operational level thereby minimizing collateral damage.
- Leverage technology and high internet penetration in the state to exploit potential of e-governance to overcome rampant corruption and bring in transparency in administration.
- To contain the fragile IS situation to present levels by maintaining balanced presence and non-intrusive posturing of Indian Army.
- Create SEZ for SMEs at major population centres and provide special tax holiday for industries for a limited period to hasten inclusive economic growth.
- Rationalise SF ops by introducing changes at strategic level through joint planning with central and state governments, media management, target ideology, creation of political will, moulding public opinion, providing favourable political environment and motivating/engaging top leadership.
- Expose Pakistan-sponsored "proxy" war and apply international pressure more aggressively, highlight the justness of our cause and

the support to terrorism by Pakistan, both through state and non-state players, as well as strive to isolate Pakistan in the international community utilizing diplomacy, trade, sports and military.
- o Exploit electronic, print and social media as a "Force Multiplier" to shape public opinion and to counter false propaganda by launching realistic, coordinated, timely and proactive psychological and information warfare so that the will of the anti-national elements is suffocated and the hearts of the populace are won.

- **Capacity building of Police and PMF.** In order to enable State Police to be totally effective and operate independently in the Valley, the following basic measures could be undertaken:
  - o Work towards a stated goal of handing over security of Valley to police and PMF in the next five years.
  - o Maximise joint operations especially in the hinterland.
  - o Give credit to police to improve credibility.
  - o Sharing intelligence, aiding in training to create ability to absorb hi-tech weapons and equipment and minor tactics drills. There is a need to train more police personnel in certain key areas like commando training; intelligence training; basic induction training and specialist training
  - o Establish a Counter-Insurgency Training College to train police personnel each year.
  - o Address the budgetary constraints for increase in manpower.
  - o Address manpower and leadership problems.
  - o Assist in development of instructional staff and training infrastructure. Check out the feasibility of employing retired army personnel and army officers in police training.
  - o Train Police for community policing through NGOs and SHGs.

- **Social Media.** Social media is a major medium which can be used effectively for perception management of the youth. It has a reach which grows exponentially with the type of message it carries. Social media should be used for transmitting messages on the following aspects:
  - o Need for peace.
  - o Incidents of violence in Pak where civs are killed unnecessarily.
  - o Quotes of Sufi saints.
  - o Quotes on Family values.
  - o Achievers of valley.

- **Trans-LoC Trade.** LoC trade has become a security hazard than any meaningful meeting point between people of both sides. Some strategies for the LoC trade route are:
  - Customs officials need to be posted at all the trade route exit points. The responsibility of the security and checking of the trade route should be with CISF with J&K police providing protection.
  - Need to have X-ray machines to scan vehicles for weapons and counterfeit goods. The lack of urgency shown by Government in procuring the X-ray machines shows the total lack of strategic intent.
  - Need to have sniffer dogs which can detect narcotics goods.
  - Need to have a more elaborate arrangement for checking and transhipment of goods. There is also a need to equip these places with mechanical loaders so that transhipment of goods is easy.
  - Gold and valuable items to be carried including money should be restricted as per Government regulations.
  - The value of goods imported needs to be valued correctly so as to avoid the recipient selling off at higher price and the difference being used for anti national activities.

Contingency Strategy Options. There are two different contingencies visualised, i.e., less likely and least likely scenarios, as elucidated below:
- **Contingency Environment 1.** It is the environment of the "less likely scenario", i.e., Scenario 1: "Ejaaz-e-Maseeha," Kashmir prospers due to major political initiatives driven by political will, stabilization of the situation by SF actions, unprecedented economic growth and the imbroglio getting resolved in a manner favourable to India. The desirable and undesirable trends/events would be as under:
  - **Desirable Trends/Events.** Resolution of ethnic differences leading to empowering of all communities and equal representation of all in power sharing. Political reforms leading to strong-willed policies towards economic growth, infrastructure development, equitable growth and good governance. People-friendly operations by SF to put relentless pressure on separatist groups resulting in their marginalisation, thus compelling them for talks. Ideal Centre–State relations and electoral process. Promotion of Kashmiriyat and diminishing fundamentalism. Aspirations of the youth met to a large extent. Good governance and an effective and a secular education system prevalent. Ideologically inclined teachers are

weeded out from schools, colleges and madrassas. The Awaam rejects the idea of Militancy and Separatism. Realisation by Pak of its futility of pursuing a policy of state-sponsored terrorism.

- o **Undesirable Trends/Events.** Under-mentioned trends are expected to be on decline from the present levels. However, their existence itself is undesirable. Governance is driven by ethnic affinity and corruption. Limited economic growth and development in the state. SF operations hindered due to political-militant nexus, HR, media glare and lack of actionable intelligence. Radicalization of youth and increase in fundamentalism in Kashmir. Pak's overt support to terrorism and separatists in Kashmir in the backdrop of extreme instability within with a possible negative fallout. Lack of trust between Centre and State Govt. Creation and exploitation of triggers by the separatists for vested interests and to keep the pot boiling.
- o **Strategic Effort Required to Address.** These are the strategic efforts in all endeavours, to promote and accelerate desirable events and trends and prevent or reduce the impact of undesirable events and trends. Promote good governance by effective execution of economic, social and political reforms through well-intentioned development programs. Ensure governance reaches entire state by developing government machinery at grassroots level with panchayats emerging as vibrant and effective institutions. Promote integrated society, encourage and empower all communities to come to mainstream in all fields by equitable arrangements for power and resource sharing. Create conducive situation for governance by relentless joint operations with CAPF in Kashmir to neutralise and wipe out writ of separatists through all out CT operations in valley combined with efficient LoC management to prevent infilt. Ensure unhindered operating space for SF by avoiding media and HR reprimand through building hard intelligence for "clean ops," discourage "number game" and promote strong perception management. Bring to a complete end Pakistan-backed extremism, terrorism and separatism, with Governments, both in New Delhi and Srinagar, taking intensive measures to strengthen civil administration and re-energize the Police Force, thereby infusing a greater confidence in the people. Resumption of sustained and meaningful multi-track diplomacy dialogue with Pakistani people to create a conducive atmosphere for resumption of talks besides

restoration of internal dialogue with diverse political opinions in an inclusive manner. The Unified Command be further strengthened so as to give a co-ordinated and planned response to the threat of terrorism in Kashmir. The education system be monitored and revamped to avoid negative sentiment amongst the youth.

- **Contingency Environment 2.** This is the environment as a result of the scenario analysed to be "least likely" to emerge – Scenario 3: "Daagh Daar." It contains trends and issues that may give rise to one or more Contingency Environments. These are as follows:
  o Complete breakdown of the relationship between the centre and state governments. This is marked by a lack of trust, and hard and uncompromising attitudes on both sides.
  o Lack of comprehensive understanding of the sensitivities involved in the issue by the policymakers at the centre leading to flawed policies and actions to resolve the issue.
  o Poor governance due to blatant corruption and lack of accountability of elected representatives and public officials.
  o Total alienation of the Awaam from the Indian union. The people of the Valley feel humiliated and angry at the treatment meted out to them by the security forces and the apathetic attitude of the central government towards their concerns. APHC and other separatists foment the feelings of hatred and influence the Awaam into thinking that their well-being lies only in independence from India. In the rest of the country, Kashmiris present for education or professional reasons are viewed with suspicion and subjected to discrimination.
  o Increasing unrest in Jammu and Ladakh and their demand for greater representation in government leading to division of the state into three parts.
  o Operations of the security forces hindered due to the Awaam's support to insurgent elements and involvement of common man in protests and demonstrations. Increased infiltration from across the LoC also stretches the deployments of the security forces.
  o Pakistan's overt support to terrorism and separatists in Kashmir in the backdrop of extreme instability and its success in internationalizing the Kashmir issue. This is characterised by

increasing activities of organisations like LeT, Hizbul Mujahideen etc.
- Economic stagnation in the state despite availability of adequate funding for developmental activities.
- Increase in the inflow of drugs and hawala money from across the LoC.
- Radicalisation of Kashmiri youth in schools, colleges and madrassas and dominance of Islamic fundamentalism in the Valley. The concepts of Kashmiriyat and Sufism lose relevance due to the overwhelming dominance of Wahabi Islam.

- **Contingency Strategy Options.** These strategic efforts will essentially address the issues of contingencies evolving from the least likely scenario. These will normally effect when indicators pointing to such a scenario start to emerge. These are enumerated below:

- **Political Strategies**
  - Build consensus on the way to resolve the Kashmir issue by structured political dialogue between the internal stakeholders consisting of the GoI, government of J&K, respected religious leaders from the Valley, representatives of the Kashmiri Pandits, the people of Kashmir, Jammu and Ladakh and the APHC. This has to be a continuous process and not a one-time effort and should be coordinated by a Constitutional Committee which would consist of eminent persons agreed to by all stakeholders.
  - Encourage the government of Pakistan and the elected representatives of PoK to shun any form of violence and support to militancy, and enter into sustained and meaningful dialogue. In addition, Track II interactions on the resolution of the J&K issue and people-to-people meetings to explore the way ahead can also be effectively utilised to build an atmosphere conducive to consensus for a solution of the issue.
  - Ensure the success of the Panchayat Raj process in the state by greater devolution of power and enhanced funding for local schemes to fulfil the aspirations of the Awam for self-determination/ governance.
  - Promote greater accountability by the development of a strong e-governance framework with details of expenditure, recruitment and decision-making process being published in the open domain and

on departmental websites for the scrutiny of the people. This strategy will also include prompt and exemplary punishments to those found guilty of misuse of public resources or indulging in or abetting any form of corruption.
  o Selecting and appointing suitably qualified and dynamic civil servants and "Think tanks" to ensure that development schemes are executed as planned with focus on taking their benefits to the Awaam. Suitable incentives to be given to such bureaucrats on successful implementations of these schemes.

- **Security Strategies**
  o Continuously sensitise the security forces about the importance of winning the confidence and cooperation of the Awaam by displaying the highest possible restraint while dealing with civic disruptions or during CI/CT operations. Security Forces should adopt a citizen-friendly approach; safeguarding the life and property of innocents; offering special protection to residential areas and activating local bodies to have a system of community watch on elements who pose a threat to security. Human rights violations by security forces personnel should not be tolerated and the guilty should face justice without delay in a transparent and fair process.
  o Police should transform to community policing winning back the trust of the people.
  o Procurement and effective use of high-technology communication monitors and surveillance systems to keep track of and reduce the infiltration rates at the LoC and intercept communications in order to break up the terrorist networks in the state.
  o Continue the high levels of strategic synergy at higher echelons of UHQ and put in place mechanisms for continuing the same at all levels including operational and tactical levels for effective joint CI/CT operations and prevention of cross-LoC infiltration.
  o Strengthen the intelligence network on both sides of LoC as well as the hinterland to be aware of key information well in advance so as to prevent events that affect security with clean and effective operations and minimum collateral damage.
  o Reduce the visibility of the Army in the Valley by making them operate in the background and gradually allow the J&K Police greater role in the maintenance of law and order in the Valley. This

- Modify the scope of Sadhbhavana by utilising Armed Forces only to ensure last-mile implementation of welfare and development schemes in remote areas where the civil administration does not reach to recast the image of the Armed Forces as facilitators of development rather than that of an entity which controls all administrative duties in the Valley.
- Formulate and implement comprehensive media and perception management policies to exploit mass and social media as weapons of psychological warfare in a proactive manner to build a positive image of the Armed Forces.
- **ISIS.** Some of the initiatives that need to be taken are given below:
    - Assist in securing a UNSC resolution for initiating Demobilsation, Disarming and Rehabilitation (DDR) activity in Syria and Iraq.
    - Assist in the reconstruction of these areas by sponsoring skilled labour and engineers.
    - Keep a close watch on the developing ISIS situation in Afghanistan through its Allies' intelligence networks.
    - Protect its assets in Afghanistan and Iran so that they don't become easy targets.
    - Keep a close eye on Pakistani Jihadi elements and their recruiters wooing ISIS Mercenaries.
    - Name and shame Pakistan-based terror organisations and ISI who plan to direct ISIS cadre towards us, on the international stage.
    - Seal its maritime and land borders including the eastern ones bordering Myanmar and Bangladesh as well as beef up the Line of Control in order to contain the recruited personnel in Pakistan.
    - Activate internal intelligence agencies to identify probable sympathisers and supporters to ISIS mercenary attacks.
    - By taking out these actions, India can manage to not only stem the flow of ISIS into our borders, but also ensure that an implosion takes place within the territory of the perpetrators

and supporters of radical Jihadi thought and state-sponsored terrorism. It won't be long before these contained elements of ISIS attack their own sympathisers, i.e., the Pakistanis in their own courtyard. With the CPEC progressing at a fast pace through the heartland of terror, China should be ready to now open bases not only in Afghanistan to ward away the ISIS, but also in Pakistan to protect its long lines of communications.

- **Social and Religious/Cultural Strategies**
    o Implement comprehensive plans for reforms in the education sector to ensure development of human resources through education and training in order to enhance the quality of life of the Awaam. The plans should be aimed at addressing the lack of technical and professional knowledge among the youth which affects their prospects of getting jobs in industrial houses and businesses.
    o Ensure secular education by monitoring radicalizing elements in the faculty at schools and colleges.
    o Implement measures to provide scholarships and other means of financial support like easy term education loans to needy students to enable them to acquire a suitable professional/vocational education of their choice. This will help greater number of youths attain gainful employment and dry up the source of manpower of the insurgents and fundamentalists.
    o Promote the spirit of secularism and Kashmiriyat among the youth by special efforts by the state government to promote the culture, values and languages of all ethnic communities in the Valley through festivals and college fests involving the Awam in large numbers.
    o Crack down on the increasing drug trade across the LoC to stop the destruction of local youth due to addiction and to cut off a source of funds for the radical elements and terror networks in the Valley.
    o Regulate the number of Wahabi/Salafi madrassas and Ahl-e-Hadith mosques being set up in the state by cutting off the source of their funding through the hawala route and at the same time encourage the growth of Sufiana madrassas and schools to promote the Sufi traditions of Kashmir. This must be run concurrently with a compulsory education programme for all children in modern state-

run schools with common syllabus that fosters the values of tolerance and emphasises the centuries old traditions of Kashmiriyat.
- Provide reservation of seats for youth of Jammu and Kashmir in technical and professional higher institutions as extended to similarly affected communities in the rest of the country. This will provide them opportunities for interaction and integration with the rest of the country and help overcome the feeling of alienation so persistent in the Awam.
- Set up adequate healthcare infrastructure to provide basic facilities especially to far-flung rural areas to overcome the current problem areas like infant mortality, women's healthcare issues, mental and physical disorders due to prolonged exposure to militancy etc. in order to develop a sense of belongingness in the Awam.
- Setting up a special task force comprising eminent and inspiring women from all parts of J&K to address problems faced by women like sexual and physical violence, loss of life of family members due to the militancy etc and to formulate measures to provide increased employment to the women in the state.
- Change mindset of youth through motivation to take on private sector jobs rather than only craving for govt jobs.

- **Economic Strategies**
  - Improve the physical connectivity within the state by development of transportation infrastructure in the form of multiple axes of all-weather roadways and railways to end the dependence of the Valley and Ladakh on Jammu for road connectivity. This will help improve accessibility of remote areas thus improving prospects of tourism and other industries as well as facilitate access to the markets for products from these areas.
  - Expand the capacity of Srinagar airport for facilitating tourism and quick movement of perishable commodities to their markets thereby improving the economy.
  - Maintain focus on further development of tourism into an all-weather rather than seasonal industry by increasing the facilities for adventure tourism activities like skiing, trekking etc. in order to increase the revenue from the same.
  - Promote growth of industries based on locally available raw materials like timber processing, horticulture and food processing etc to provide economic development and source of employment to the Awaam.

- o Promote growth of local cottage industries by formation of cooperatives and providing incentives to export of handicrafts in order to exploit their economic potential and generate local self-employment.
- o Provide incentives like tax holidays and exemptions from excise duties, import duties etc. to attract outside capital for industrial development in the state in order to increase employment and lead to overall improvement in the economic condition of the Awaam.
- o Implement policies to tap the potential for generation of hydroelectric power in the state by providing impetus to investment in the sector in order to provide adequate power supply for the industrial activities in the state and for revenue generation. Objections raised by Pakistan on the same can be resolved by exploring the feasibility of selling some of the generated power to PoK at subsidised rates.
- o Plan and implement a roadmap to reduce the dependence of the state on funding from the centre by restructuring public finances to cut down on wastages/non-developmental expenditure and gradual increase in the revenue collection from local sources like usage of electricity and water by industrial units, progressive taxation of high net worth individuals etc.

Environment-Shaping Strategy Options.
Most Desirable Security Environment. The most desirable environment for Kashmir is that of Scenario 1, i.e., Ejaaz-e-Maseeha, Kashmir prospers economically with inclusive growth, under a good governance and internally stable environment. Major features include Political agreement and power sharing amongst all communities, Good governance, Reduction of fundamentalism and promotion of Kashmiriyat, Economic development of Kashmir (not at the cost of Jammu and Ladakh region), infrastructure growth and prevention of corruption, Mitigating feeling of alienation amongst Kashmiris and encourage yearning for a life of peace and dignity shunning the path of violence, Positive role of SF and marginalisation of separatists, Ideal Centre state relations build on foundation of trust, Recognition by Pak of its futility of pursuing a policy of state-sponsored terrorism are some of the other features of this environment.

- **Strategic Effort Required.** These are the strategic efforts in all endeavours that can and should be plausibly made to prevent negative events and trends and promote and accelerate positive trends and events of Basic Environment. It also includes endeavours to induce occurrence of positive events and trends that characterize emergence of "most desirable environment". Long-term strategies required to counter terrorism should comprehensively address all fronts to include political, economic, social and military. Strategies should be evolved from our national aims and objectives to protect core values, i.e., consolidate as a secular federal democratic state with freedom of speech, equality and justice, protect sovereignty and territorial integrity and promote socio-economic growth and develop fully in an atmosphere of positive peace. The following environment shaping strategies are recommended:

o Execute political action plan by state government taking on a dual role of managing demands of Kashmiris as well as central government's intentions through audacious steps by centre and state to generate political will to solve Kashmir problem.

o Define clear-cut political strategy to drive military strategy for effective CT in J&K to create a secure environment so that social, economic and political aspirations can be addressed eff as also enable eff governance.

o Focus on optimum utilisation of aid by ensuring efficient vigilance machinery at district level through a coordinating and monitoring agency, along with exemplary punishment to defaulters, suspension of Govt employees involved in corruption, irregularities and separatist/criminal/politician nexus.

o Create accountability by establishment of an apex committee at state level to monitor agendas. This committee shall also think, plan and execute innovative projects for specific problems in Kashmir, identify and prioritise key issues of planning and development to include communication network, agriculture, tourism, MSMEs etc.

o Break deadlocks by maneuvering alternate strategies over contentious issues rather than pending it in a time warp, through involvement of intellectuals of Kashmir in the peace process.

o Chalk out an administrative action plan for infrastructure growth and economic development through nodal centers in form of industrial areas, incorporate NGOs and village authorities/councils in development of roads, tracks, electrification, education, healthcare, small-scale industries, etc thereby ensuring inclusive growth.

- Remove the roots of terrorism through good governance, by striving to achieve economic well-being, social justice and political aspirations of the populace, eradicating political and beureucratic corruption, thereby strangling the free flow of funds into the terror ecosystem.
- Ensure assured infrastructure growth (not at the cost of Jammu and Ladakh region) by adequate allocation of funds in communication, power, medical and health, public works and education so as to accelerate the achievement of national aim of integrating the Kashmiris with India politically, socially, economically and most importantly, psychologically.
- Address fundamentalist forces by both "strong arm tactics" as well as by the promotion of secular polity by containing/neutralising radical religious groups of the state.
- Develop cities/towns as major tourist destinations as also promote rural tourism so that there is more interaction and integration with rest of the country thereby reducing alienation.
- Create SEZ for SMEs at major population centres and provide special tax holiday for industries for a limited period to hasten inclusive economic growth.
- Improve effectiveness of SF by lucrative surrender policy to engage main groups in homecoming. Surrender policy should be an expeditious process for meaningful rehabilitation, including incentives to undertake self-employment.
- Create political space for operations by SF by introducing changes at strategic level through joint planning with central and state governments, media management, target ideology, create political will, mould public opinion, provide favourable political environment and motivate/engage top leadership.
- Make operations more effective by favourable political environment, employment of SF teams in critical areas, allotment of modern tech resources to reduce collateral damage.
- Improve capability of CAPF by providing special training, eqpt and incentives to carry out efficient CT ops independently so as to enable Army to reduce its foot print from the hinterland and focus on strengthening the counter-infiltration grid astride the LoC.
- Address "Structural" inadequacies in the state apparatus, by strengthening the intelligence structure – human as well as technical,

modernization of Police, PMF and Armed Forces, imaginative media management and coverage, active response and swift governmental decision-making, clear strategy and policy on Internal Security.

- Expose Pakistan-sponsored "proxy" war and apply international pressure more aggressively, highlight the justness of our cause and the support to terrorism by Pakistan, both through state and non-state players, as well as strive to isolate Pakistan in the international community utilizing diplomacy, trade, sports and military.
- Make all possible efforts to improve the existing internal situation, step up diplomatic efforts to expose Pakistan's propensity to support terrorism amongst the international community, and try to exert pressure to make it realize the futility of pursuing the policy of fomenting terrorism thereby increasing the cost in involvement in India's affairs.
- Move from a policy of appeasement and accommodation of populace and separatists to firm action against anti-national elements so as to prevent further spread and encouragement of dissent.
- Adopt proactive policies to confront the terrorists militarily, and at the roots of terrorist ideology – fundamentalists, social evils and sources of terrorism, e.g. narcotics/drug trade by enacting effective anti-terrorist laws and legal framework, modernising and enlarging intelligence networks, Modernising state Police and Para Military Forces in training, equipment and ethos.
- Enhance our economic and military capabilities and widen the gap between India and Pakistan sufficiently, and act as an economic and military deterrence for Pakistan, so as to make it realise the futility of trying to catch up.
- Promote moderate and secular polity by media, intelligentsia and religious institutions. The path of developing a composite culture like Kashmiriyat to serve as a role model.
- Address the outdated education system of Madrassas and schools by quality modernization and laying down guidelines for uniform syllabi which prevents inculcating an ideology of intolerance, violence and extremist indoctrination. Foster public private partnership by incl 'Adopt a School' programme in which businesses are encouraged to become involved in op of Govt schools.

- Upgrade communication systems by adequate investment programmes so that television and telecommunication spreads to our remote and border areas to spread the awareness and hasten the process of national integration thereby countering Pakistani propaganda.
- Utilizing electronic, print and social media as a "Force Multiplier" to shape public opinion and to counter false propaganda by launching realistic, coordinating, timely and proactive counter-narrative through psychological and information warfare so that the will of the anti-national elements is suffocated and the hearts of the populace are won.
- SF to carry out effective perception management by changing its narrative, managing the force ethos, cultural training of its rank and file, keeping in mind the cultural sensitivities of the people to show every Kashmiri that the army is not the enemy of the people by executing Operation Sadbhavana to build a more people-oriented approach where dignity and self-esteem of the average Kashmiri is accentuated.
- Institute efficient measures to check and curb illegal financial assistance from outside India for various radical and fundamentalist purposes by international cooperation, integrating the investigating mechanisms to identify illegal fund flows by combining the efforts of various crime monitoring agencies including narcotics, customs, and other security agencies such as CBI and various state investigating agencies to stem financing of terror.
- Remain alert on the LC and strengthen the counter infiltration grid to prevent any influx of terrorists by using an array of surveillance equipment ranging from satellite to ground sensors combined with digital connectivity in communication, backed with efficient Decision support system to enable quick decision making.
- Strengthen apex-level intel agencies by incorporating advanced technologies to gain intel and create an intel network to carry out counter-terrorist ops at strategic and operational level thereby minimizing collateral damage.
- Have a long-term absolute clear SF strategy and intelligence focus on surviving militant networks and OGWs to prevent sustenance and resurrection of terrorism thereby defeating assistance and safe heavens being provided by Pakistan.

o **AFSPA.** In order to ensure Freedom of Action in CI Operations and legal protection to security forces, maintain AFSPA in present form. Dilution in the law should not be accepted at any cost. **The change of name to some other with equal or same provisions may be tried out as the acronym AFSPA is perceived as draconian by the population.** Further care should be taken during election year to not provide an opportunity to the separatists and politicians to highlight the nuances of AFSPA. The following strategies could be implemented so as to ensure that AFSPA stays:
  ➢ AFSPA jingoism reduces considerably through credible perception management policy of the SF.
  ➢ Highlight severe and timely punishment to SF personnel involved in HR violations.
  ➢ Project humane face of armed forces while conducting operations.
  ➢ Incidents like Pathribal where the preliminary inquiry reveals no involvement of troops or lack of evidence should be handed over to appropriate authority to show more transparency. However, this should only be done after a thorough investigation.
  ➢ It is the responsibility of the SF to provide all assistance to the army personnel involved in any court case. Officers involved in cases where there is continuous hearing could be posted to the formation HQ so that necessary assistance can be provided to him.
  ➢ It may be also be worthwhile to consider whether certain areas could be excluded from the cover of the AFSPA. However, the army should completely withdraw and not operate in in such areas. Clearly, the maintenance of law and order by police forces, which are subject to state laws, does not require the cover of the AFSPA. If the security situation so warrants, the armed forces may be requisitioned to aid civil authorities, as was done for a brief period during the current unrest.
o **PSA.** The PSA also provides an ideal tool to book anti-national elements and OGW to prevent them from disrupting peace and security. However, care should be taken to ensure that only hard core OGW are booked under this act. **Random booking of youths under this act completely eliminates his chances to come back to**

society and thus would be readily available to the terrorists for indoctrination. Further, the time spent in jails should also be monitored so as to prevent them from interacting with hardcore terrorists and fundamentalists.

- **Victims of state action.** Youth, especially unemployed youth who take part in stone-throwing incidents should be placed under PSA only after due deliberation. Some strategies for the youth are as follows:
    - Youth placed under PSA should be kept under a separate rehabilitation centre.
    - Care should be taken to not mix hardcore terrorists and fundamentalists with the youth.
    - Terrorists who are already convicted and not involved in court cases should be moved to jails in other states so that they do not influence other people. **Jails continue to be the hub centre of radicalisation and criminalisation.**
- In order to reduce biased reporting by vernacular and local media, ensure a proactive media campaign by conducting operations with complete transparency and involving media during conduct of operations. The forces should now have the capability to operate with imbedded media. Recording of some of the operations could also be contemplated.
- Need to be proactive on social media. Social media has to be countered back immediately. Battle in the cyber space has to be fought in a systematic manner with all agencies scanning the social media site to assess all the activities and posting necessary responses through pseudo names.
- Need to carry out cyber audit of all cyber traffic emanating from the valley so as to block any unauthorised traffic.
- Need to block unauthorised softwares which can be used by terrorists for transmitting messages.
- In times of emergency there is a need to have the capability to slow down the internet speed when required to make transmission of messages extremely difficult.
- **Surrendered Terrorists.** The surrendered terrorists have the potential of moving back into the fold of terrorism as they are not accepted by the society and are under pressure from state and militants. Some measures which could be undertaken are:

- Rehabilitation policy needs to be streamlined and adequate measures need to be instituted to ensure that the terrorists get their due. **The SF should identify all the terrorists who have not got their due and work towards their speedy rehabilitation.**
- Need to use the platform of UHQ meetings to put forward the details of the surrendered terrorists who have not been given their due.
- The package for surrender policy should be made more attractive so that the remaining terrorists also lay down the arms.
- Need to have a surrender policy for foreign terrorists also. Some of the terrorists who op in valley are more of mercenaries with duty ranging from a year to two years. There are terrorists operating in valley who are convicts on life imprisonment or death sentence in Pak and who have been given freedom to fight for Jehad. A surrender policy with the caveat of temporary citizenship could result in some terrorists surrendering themselves. Even a single surrender could have a severe psychological damage to terrorists' ideology.

o **Artificial Intelligence (AI).** Utilise AI to neutralize the tools of terror as under:
- We could take a leaf out of the UK Home Office which has successfully encouraged the large online content platforms to invest in automated detection technology that can spot and remove radicalizing videos. Collaborating with the UK Home Office Counterterrorism Unit, ASI Data Science built a tool that removes extremist propaganda from the web.[5] The new technology is capable of detecting 94% of ISIS's online propaganda with 99.995% accuracy. Any content that the software is still unsure about would then be passed on for a human to review.[6] The goal is to stop the majority of video propaganda before it ever reaches the internet.
- While on one hand AI can effectively eradicate video propaganda on the internet, it can also be utilised effectively to win over potential turncoats by automatically replacing terrorist propaganda with appealing stories and videos by boosting other sites.

- AI could be utilised effectively to monitor and carry out statistical analysis of the whereabouts of OGWs at various levels to draw patterns which could lead to the recruiters.
- AI tools can be utilized to carry out continuous statistical analyses to highlight the collateral damage that the terrorists and their handlers are effecting by their involvement of innocent youth of the state in their unjust cause.
- On their own, incremental financial transactional activities might not trigger suspicion, but taken together, they create a pattern that an AI machine might identify as fishy. Of course, as with any computer system that can learn on its own, the results are only as good as the data fed into it and the human oversight and controls put on it.
- Use of AI-enabled 3D vehicle CT scanners at entry points as well as Robots to monitor and report ingress without involvement of the human angle are some AI keys to ramp up security.
- Launching of indigenised AI-enabled apps or AI-enabled data mining of on-shore servers could help in breaking the codes used by terrorists to communicate.
- Funerals of slain militants have become the new hot-spots of recruitment by OGWs. AI-enabled drone-borne cameras at checkpoints as well as at public places could help in monitoring and stinging these OGWs who are fuelling the fire in young minds.

Hedging Strategy (For the Wild Card Scenario)
- Development of an integrated and coordinated intelligence network involving all relevant agencies.
- Engagement with all regional players to ensure regional stability and improvement in the internal security situation.
- Strategic and conventional military capability to afford deterrence against state sponsored terrorist activities.
- Use of media to continuously engage our adversary in its futility to carry out state sponsored terrorism
- Continuous improvement in Disaster Management procedures and capability enhancement.

- Need to push for a global forum for war on terror and monitoring of NBC material to prevent its theft.
- **Preparedness**. It is difficult to be "prepared" for something as horrifying as a dirty bomb attack on the lines of communication with a bomb attack on the PM and state leadership in Srinagar. It is of the utmost importance that India's nuclear doctrine is modified to include political signaling of retaliation if the sovereignty and independence of the nation is threatened.
- Ensure that the intelligence network, especially in Afghanistan and Pakistan, needs periodic review and upscaling. There is an urgent need to invest in and expedite our intel and surveillance resources/programmes.
- Coord with USA to ensure close observation of Pak nuclear programme and material, and covert assistance from China and North Korea.
- Enhance own footprints in Afghanistan and extend wholehearted assistance to the Afghan government and strengthen Afghanistan, especially post-withdrawal of the USA. A stable and thriving Afghanistan is a prerequisite for a stable and thriving Asia/India.
- The government to keep Channels of Communication open with all Moderate Factions inside Afghanistan and Pakistan. As a state policy, India doesn't believe in the concept of initiating internal disturbances in other nations. However, in the circumstance of a complete breakdown of the system in Afghanistan and Pakistan, India must remain in touch with moderate factions inside these countries, especially erstwhile Northern Alliance as leverage against the possible Taliban/Pakistan influence.
- **Proactive Strategy**. The main difference between switching from a soft option to a hard option is the capability to identify and analyse a trend/incident in time. There is thus a need for our intelligence agencies to remain one step ahead to read the indicators and predict the security implications.

NOTES

1. https://www.thehindu.com/todays-paper/tp-opinion/Where-the-state-pays-for-teachers-of-hate/article16561058.ece, accessed on November 12, 2018.
2. https://indianexpress.com/article/india/jk-herion-worth-rs-250-crore-bound-for-delhi-seized-5437989/, accessed on November 20, 2018.
3. "All norms followed: Army," *The Tribune*, January 31, 2018, available at http://www.tribuneindia.com/news/jammu-kashmir/ all-norms-followed-army/536710.html. Accessed on July 11, 2018.

4   http://www.claws.in/images/publication_pdf/647959617_StonePeltinginKashmirValley ViolationofHumanRightsofArmedForcesPersonnel_CLAWS.pdf, accessed on November 15, 2018.
5   https://conferences.oreilly.com/artificial-intelligence/ai-eu/public/schedule/detail/70263, accessed on December 06, 2018.
6   https://i-hls.com/archives/81392, accessed on December 06, 2018.

CHAPTER 7
Perception Management/ Improvement Strategies

Introduction

Having taken a peek into the future through the scenario-building exercise carried out in Chapter 6, we are in a much better position to understand what is and will be affecting the situation in the state in the future. Over the coming decades, India's global influence would look set to rise substantially, as the country becomes an increasingly important economy with an enhanced role to play as a major global power in a multi-polar world. However, internal security issues like the J&K problem, Left-Wing Extremism (LWE) and Insurgency in the North East impedes the desired rate of development of our great nation utilising substantial amounts of time and resources in terms of men, material and finances. The state of Jammu and Kashmir has been an integral part of India since 1947. However, segments of the people of this state, namely, the *Awaam* of Kashmir valley have not been able to identify with the Indian nation. For this aim, one should be looking at the parameters of reduction in violence and increase in peace which appear suspiciously out of sync with the emerging environment.[1] These are issues such as governance, radicalism, financial conduits to the Separatists, trust between the people and the security forces/other organs of the Central Government, self-esteem and dignity of the Kashmiri people, the degree of connect between the Centre and the State, tourism and other revenue- and profit-earning activities. Hence, if the desired end state to the J&K problem is to seamlessly integrate the state of Jammu and Kashmir with India, the perception of the target population needs to be managed/improved towards the desired end state.

The Perceptual Process

Having carried out an in-depth net assessment of all the elements in play in J&K with special reference to Kashmir, the readers of this book will now realise that these inputs were extremely necessary for embarking on the process of Perception management/improvement. More often than not, the people responsible for this activity do not understand the nuances and the fact that it is a complicated process which would involve intricate details and appropriate timely action.

PERCEPTUAL PROCESS[2]

```
                    PERCEIVER'S CHARACTERISTICS
                    * NEEDS        * PERSONALITY
                    * LEARNING     * SELF-CONCEPT

PERCEPTUAL          PERCEPTUAL              PERCEPTUAL      B
INPUTS              MECHANISM               OUTPUTS         E
• OBJECTS           •SELECTION              • ATTITUDE      H
• EVENTS            •ORGANISATION           • OPINION       A
• PEOPLE            •INTERPRETATION         • FEELING       V
                                                            I
                                                            O
                                                            U
                    PERCEIVED'S CHARACTERISTICS             R
                    * SIZE         * MOTION
                    * INTENSITY    * NOVELTY
                    * CONTRAST     * STATUS
                    * REPETITION   * APPEARANCE
```

Perception can be defined as the process of receiving, selecting, organising, interpreting, checking and responding to sensory stimuli or data.

RECEIVING

- Sight   74%
- Hearing   14%
- Touch   06%
- Taste   03%
- Smell   03%

Five instruments of knowledge – eye, ear, skin, tongue and nose

Perception management is a term originated by the US military. The US Department of Defense (DOD) gives this definition:

> *Actions to convey and/or deny selected information and indicators to foreign audiences to influence their emotions, motives, and objective reasoning as well as to intelligence systems and leaders at all to influence official estimates, ultimately resulting in foreign behaviors and official actions favorable to the originator's objectives. In various ways, perception management combines truth*

projection, operations security, cover and deception, and psychological operations.[3]

The phrase "perception management" has often functioned as a euphemism for "an aspect of information warfare."

Perception management includes all actions used to influence the attitudes and objective reasoning of all audiences and consists of Public Diplomacy, Psychological Operations (PSYOPS), Public Information, Deception and Covert Action. The main goal is to influence friends and enemies, provoking them to engage in the behavior that you want. DOD sums it up: "Perception management combines truth projection, operations security, cover and deception, and psychological operations."

For the above to take place scientifically, it is most important to firstly identify the audiences/elements. It is for these reasons that the author amended his research topic to "Perception Management **for** J&K" from "Perception Management **in** J&K". While the latter suggests that it is for only internal elements, the former signifies that it is for the complete environment which includes all the audiences (internal, external, affiliated, associated, social, psychological) which are directly or indirectly affecting the emerging situation and the psyche of the people of the state.

The Elements/Audiences

People of the State. The people and their Psyche have already been identified as the Centre of Gravity and therefore they need to be given due importance for the purpose of this exercise. Although the Awaam can be treated as one throughout the state, a word of caution however is to deal with the Awaam of the Kashmir Valley, Jammu region and Ladakh region separately also as is suggested throught the system analysis. If the perception of the people of Jammu and Ladakh region who consider them culturally different than the people of Kashmir is not taken into consideration while planning any activity or project in the Valley, there will be a negative feedback from these two areas and the Banihal and Zojila divide will widen.

Mothers, Fathers and Extended family. The mutually exclusive survey carried amongst the youth of the Valley suggests that 97.6% of the youth impose trust in their families and 80.6% spend their free time with family; hence, this becomes an important audience to address. Currently the family is playing a benign role in mentoring the youth to follow a path towards prosperity as they themselves are getting influenced by the radicalizing elements in society.

Mothers of Slain Militants. During the course of studying the Psychological aspects in Chapter 4, it came to light that the mothers of slain militants do not grieve in public, but in the privacy and mental comfort of interactions with mental health workers or doctors, they tend to break down and grieve. Theory would suggest that they try to show their resolute and hard-shelled side to the public which creates a false sense of bravado for others to emulate by joining militant organisations. It is extremely important to manage their perceptions and make them accept reality, a sense of loss and unnecessary waste of precious life for a senseless cause. This will go a long way in curbing militancy, and for this there may be a requirement of hiring professional mental health workers and social scientists.

Teachers. Survey suggests that 91.6% of the youths impose trust in teachers. It has also been exposed in the internal scan as well as played out in the scenario-building exercise that the ideologically inclined teachers who are now entrenched in many schools and have even climbed the stairs of promotions to reach degree colleges of the state, have their own agenda and are creating a negative impact to the psyche of the educated youth of the state, so much so that even when they go to other parts of the country for higher education, they maintain their connect with their ideological Gurus. With a constant and repeated ideological battering, it is just a matter of time that small triggers make them join militancy. Teachers become a major environment shaping force for the battle of perceptions in Kashmir and need to be perceptually transformed into an extremely positive role for the society.

Religious Teachers/Ulema. In Singapore, RRGs'[4] primary objective was to rehabilitate detained Jemaah Islamiah members and their families through counselling. However, it has since broadened its scope to include misinterpretations promoted by self-radicalised individuals and those in support of ISIS. A similar arrangement could be worked out with the participation of the local religious Ulema in J&K, so that the effect of Radicalisation is reduced/removed through religious counselling. With the advent of the Tablighi Jamaat way of thinking and the mushrooming of Deobandi/Barelvi and Ahl-e-Hadith mosques in the Valley, it becomes imperitive to reach out to the religious Teachers and manage their perceptions positively so that they in turn can counsel the youth against joining the path of militancy, as Survey suggests that 66% youth impose trust in religious teachers.

OGWs. To fight this most important tool of terrorism and proxy war in the Valley, it is important to categorise them so that separate response strategies can be made for each one of the categories. Although operating as larger network, the OGWs in Kashmir can be broadly categorised under the following heads (in order to take a de novo look at the issue of OGWs by categorizing them for the sake of strategic communication and perception management/ improvement as discussed in Chapter 4 of the book):

- OGWs for Funding & Logistic Support (OGFWLS).
- OGWs providing Ideological & Radicalization Support (OGWIRS).
- OGWs for Recruitment of Terrorists (OGWR).
- OGWs generating negative Perceptions and Sentiment amongst the Awaam (OGWPS).

Trader Community. The trader community in J&K is a highly respected community as due to lack of formal sector facilities, this community has been providing jobs and livelihood to the people of the state. Due to their involvement in trade and businesses, they are generally inclined towards peace and prosperity. Managing their perceptions positively could lead to a sequence of motivating actions which could bring the youth to the path of peace and prosperity and positive contribution to society.

J&K Police. Although a part of the SF, this institution needs to be dealt with as a separate entity. It has been discussed in detail that positive peace can only prevail if the law and order is handelled by the J&K police in a community policing role. For this to materialise, apart from capacity building and police reforms, there is a need for the police to understand its responsibilities to the people by bearing the brunt of sacrifice in the face of adversity and threats to their kin. They are also to be waned away from high-handed, coercive and corrupt methods of booking first time small-time offenders and making them hardened criminals. Needs no gainsaying that positive perception management and training of Police personnel by trained Professionals would go a long way in establishing positive peace in the state.

SF. The security forces including Army and CAPF need to understand the need to show extreme restraint in the face of difficult situations. There is a need to carry out case study analyses to bring home the point of negative impact on positive peace due to small seemingly inconsequential actions.

Govt Machinery - the Bureaucracy. In order to bear the fruits of corruption-free good governance, the govt machinery has to be motivated to sacrifice their today for the bright tomorrow of their generations to follow. Status Quoist perceptions have to be moulded to an interactive state of mind.

The Judiciary. There is a need for the Judiciary to constantly be reminded about the difficult circumstances that the Security forces are operating in J&K and that the justice system within the SF will take care of the aberrations to the generally good and measured behaviour of the troops. In case the Judiciaries perceptions are not addressed in a timely manner, the morale of the troops could get affected in an adverse manner.

Youth Connect Self-Help Groups. The municipal and Panchayat elections have brought to the fore many youth connect self-help groups who believe in the cause of peace and prosperity and are daring to change the narrative of a dysfunctional and infiltrated polity to that of positive peace. They have given many candidates in the face of threats by militants. There is a churning of sorts that seem to be going on in Kashmir, a new wave which needs to be supported. If these groups stand up for progress, there will be no turning back for the upward graph of peace and prosperity.

Corporate Houses. Corporates have a perception that no industry can progress in the face of frequent shutdowns and adverse security situation. This perception needs to be amended. Jobs will get a new lease to life in the Valley. They also need to come forward with corporate social responsibility initiatives to support Deradicalization camps and youth connect models being planned out by youth Self-help groups.

Local Media. Vernacular newspaper houses need to churn out positive news and correct reporting. Their perceptions are influenced by threats from militants as well as negative influence of the OGWs and agents of ISI from across the LoC. This needs to change to avoid them giving out a constant dose of slow poison to the masses thereby vitiating the already charged environment.

National Media. National newspapers and TV channels need to temper the hatred that hey generate amongst the masses against the interests and wellbeing of a common citizen of Kashmir. The hysteria that they create in mainland India has a far-reaching negative impact on the minds of the youth of Kashmir further polarizing them.

Fringe Hindutva Elements. Fiery statements of fringe groups affect the psyche of a common man. Ensuring restraint through education of these elements and managing the perception of the media to temper down follow-up debates and headlines in national interest even for a couple of years could be beneficial.

Kashmiri Pandits. The syncretic culture of Kashmir can never be complete without the presence of the Kashmiri Pandits. The desire of the Awaam for their Pandit brothers and sisters is reducing day by day due to the disconnected lives that they live separated by the Pir Panjal. In the recent Survey, only 51% youth wanted them to come back to the Valley. It is a matter of time that the society will get completely polarised in the Valley. It is therefore necessary to manage the perceptions of the Kashmiri Pandits, to motivate them or some dare-devils amongst them to get back to the land of their forefathers. With adequate security and a liberal investment environment, this feat can be achieved. This could be the turning point in the Battle of Perceptions for Kashmir.

Teachers and Students of Colleges where (including) Kashmiri students join for Studying. Quite a large number of Kashmiri students pursue their dreams of education in institutes of excellence outside the state in rest of India. Of late, there have been disturbing newsmakers of Kashmiri youth ending up in clashes with their peers in these colleges due to difference of opinion where they are more often than not branded anti-national.[5] Though it is true that in many instances the Kashmiri youth are also to be blamed for links with anti-national and terror outfits,[6] but there is a need to bend the perceptions of the teachers and the students of these colleges to have a more humane touch towards a particular lot of students who have practically lived their entire lives in a conflict zone. A little accommodative spirit could go a long way of winning the hearts and minds of the students from J&K.

The Separatists. Continuous talks for changing the perceptions of the hardline separatists should be initiated in order to wean them towards the idea of a prosperous Kashmir in the state of J&K under the umbrella of a great and progressing nation India. Indian NGOs and Art of Living foundation celebrities like Sri Sri Ravishankar could be requested to head the effort so that no Agenda politics is seen by this group.

International News Channels. According to the recent Survey, 28.23% of the youth were seeing international news channels to form opinions and perceptions. There is no way in which the reach of these channels and their footprints reduced. A very workable solution is to make efforts to give them access to true news of current news stories as also commence diplomatic initiatives with the host countries for eradicating fake and needless sensationalization.

The People of Pakistan. Although the people-to-people contact between the two countries has suffered due to policies of no talks till terror is controlled, the concept of multi-track diplomacy suggests that people-to-people contact should continue. The change in perception of the people of Pakistan will finally be a harbinger for peace to prevail in the region.

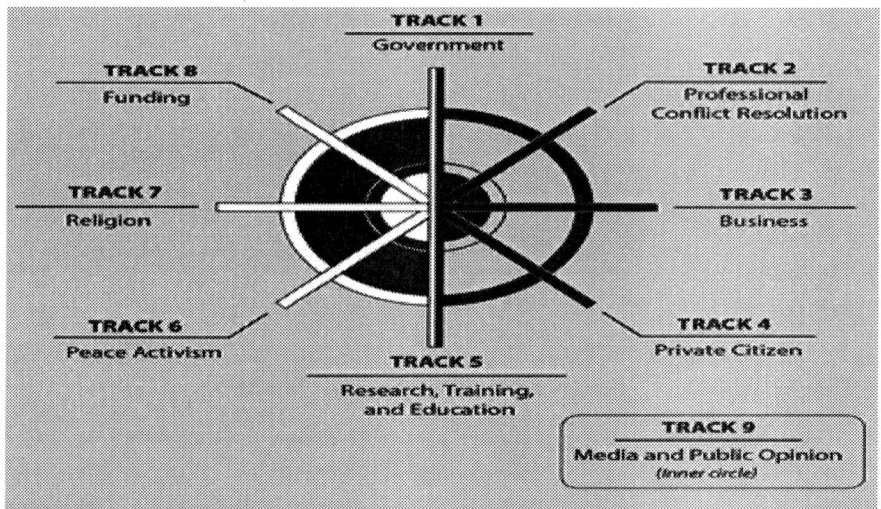

Source: Institute for Multi-Track Diplomacy (IMTD)

International Social Media Giants. Social media apps like Facebook, Twitter have to be reined in for allowing anti-India objectionable material on their sites. Their perception that these companies are invincible due to their global presence needs to be modified to our advantage.

The People of PoK including Gilgit-Baltistan. There are very few families who still have living relatives who got separated in the J&K war between India and Pakistan in 1948, yet there are many common things including the large number of Kashmiris who crossed the LoC into PoK in the early 1990s when militancy struck J&K. There is exchange of trade, ideas and brides across the LoC and there is a need to address the perceptions of locals on the other side of the LoC. Many parts of J&K are progressing exponentially in terms of infrastructure development which in turn is likely to get investments, development, peace and prosperity. There is a need to force the population across the LoC to constantly compare their standards of living with their counterparts this side so that a quiet revolution to bridge divides starts taking place within the next decade.

Pak Military and ISI. Hard nuts to crack as their perceptions are cast in stone but a constant effort needs to be placed on record in order to make them realise that it is a zero-sum game that there are playing, and there is only one loser in it, the one who does not have the wherewithal to sustain such activity economically and diplomatically.

Staff at Participants International Organizationsand Conferences. Diplomatic offensives to show to the world the collusive support to terrorism that Pak is providing should not be restricted to the UN and a few international agencies. The Perception offensive should be taken to all other relevant Organizations and Conferences in order to create a soft corner for the people of J&K and India's efforts to bring peace and prosperity to the state.

PERCEPTION IMPROVEMENT

Strategies

There are broadly eight principles for perceptionmanagement/improvement. These include:

- Centralized control. Employing entities such as propaganda/Perception Management Offices in the National Security Council.
- Preparation. Having clear goals and knowing the ideal position you want people to hold.
- Credibility. Make sure all of your information is consistent, often using prejudices or expectations to increase credibility.
- Multichannel Support. Have multiple arguments and fabricated facts to reinforce your information.
- Security. The nature of the perception improvement campaign is known by few.
- Flexibility. The deception campaign adapts and changes over time as needs change.
- Coordination. The organization or propaganda ministry is organized in a hierarchical pattern in order to maintain consistent and synchronized distribution of information.
- Concealment. Contradictory information is destroyed.

While the exercise of perception managementhas been carrying on in the Kashmir valley for years, by way of Sadhbhavna and other measures, there needs to be a more focused and concerted approach towards the same which is carried out at all levels over a sustained manner to get the desired end state of the state and people of J&K to seamlessly integrate with the nation with stable IS. In line with the tenets mentioned in the previous paragraph, it is suggested that the matter be dealt at three distinct levels. These would be:

- Strategic – Central govt and Army/SF HQ.
- Operational – State Govt, Command and Corps HQ.
- Tactical – Divisional HQ and below.

Strategic Level. At the strategic level, Central Govt should take measures to alleviate the sense of alienation of the people of J&K. Towards this, the following could be adopted:

- Form a nodal agency for the perception management, preferably under the aegis of MHA. The agency could be headed by a representative of MHA with members from concerned stakeholders like MEA, MOD, Ministry of I&B, Ministry of Commerce, Govt of J&K, representatives of the various SF (Army, CRPF, JKP), IB and others as deemed fit.
- The Central govt should take proactive and visible measures to ensure that there are no double standards being followed when dealing with the state, e.g. the handling of the Afzal Guru incident, vis-à-vis pardon for Rajiv Gandhi killers, reconsideration of sentence to Beant Singh's killers etc.
- I&B Ministry and other commercial channels to produce and telecast promotional films on J&K for the whole nation (including the state itself) to be telecast on all feasible occasions – before movies (in cinema halls), television, etc.
- I&B Ministry should also exercise control over various national print and vernacular media including television channels. With proliferation of internet and consequent networks like social media, it becomes all the more important that regular and positive updates about the state be provided and negative posts/tweets etc be rebutted.
- Ministry of Commerce in sync with Govt of J&K should discuss with industrial barons and encourage them to set up industries in J&K. This would facilitate employment for the youth and engage them positively. All these measures should be adequately publicized in the media both at the national and state levels and internet (govt sites, social networking sites etc).
- The Central govt also needs to facilitate NGOs to come to J&K as well and provide succor to the Awaam by way of providing education right till the grassroots level, bring out a neutral view of the country as against the biased views and education taught in religiously polarized schools and madrasas.
- Initiate national level discussions on Article 370. The need for it to be discussed in the context of obstacles to development has not been realised in Kashmir. It is to be understood that any state can only integrate with nation, jump on to the bandwagon of development and prosper when there are no restrictions of any kind between that state

and the rest of the country. Only then would people from the rest of the country and world would come in as tourists, set up industries/hospitality establishments etc.
- Measures to project the emerging normalcy in Kashmir need to be taken by opening J&K to visits by foreign delegations and international media personnel, proving that there is nothing to hide.
- Reach out to the religious teachers and Ulema not only in Kashmir but in other parts of the country too, so that delegations can be sent to Kashmir in order to change the harsh perceptions of the religious teachers of the state who indulge in spitting venom in Friday prayers and in Funerals.
- Get the teachers to attend camps in renowned schools in rest of India to give them an idea of strengthening the secular fabric amongst the children of the state.
- Run perception management campaigns for the people of PoK and Gilgit-Baltistan highlighting the peace and prosperity that the landscape of the state is achieving due to positive peace initiatives in the state. Compare their lives and standard of living.
- Give unrefusal packages to Kashmiri Pandit familes to return to their hearths in Kashmir in the next round of positive peace in the state.
- Prepare a national level monitoring and educating team to visit colleges where Kashmiri students take admissions to carry the message of peace and secularism.
- I&B Ministry should ask national media channels to rein in polarizing talk shows on their channels.
- Encourage people-to-people contact with Pak intelligentsia and commom citizens in order to change their perceptions about India which is propagated over generations since independence and through the Pak army.
- If India has to eliminate terrorism threat from social media, the government should create awareness about cyber terrorism and set up highly competitive and efficient cyber-security think tanks which will monitor and report suspected terrorism related activities. A database should be maintained on the accounts of users who frequently search these words online. Just merely by eliminating provocative video and text contents from YouTube, Twitter or Facebook will not be sufficient to stymie the growth of terrorist web. The symbiotic relationship of terrorist organizations that has taken root must be prevented. India, as

a country is fast evolving into one of the largest internet users in the world, and therefore is much more susceptible to the challenges posed against its national interest in the backdrop of growing misuse of social media by the hands of terrorist. It is only but need of the hour to congregate an agile foundation for cyber security, where the government agencies must work on a robust monitoring and filtering of anti-national activities conducted online.

- Working on leaders who have the potential to shift sides for money or power needs to be relentlessly pursued as the gains far outweigh the efforts of Counter-Terror operations.
- Check-mate the Radicalisation Campaigns in schools, religious institutions, educational institutes and Prisons through socio-scientific methods and assistance.
- Implement a detailed perception management strategy on prime-time channels; seeing is believing.
- Give detailed briefings on the current situation in J&K in international events and conferences in order to positively change the perception of international participants to support our cause.
- Create a central organisation with tens of content writers, artists, actors, cyber experts, social scientists, who can collectively and continuously prepare counter narratives to the ongoing radicalisation by the terrorists and Pak. Bombard the youth of Kashmir who are falling prey to damaging content on social media in the absence of any alternative.

Operational Level. The operational level should serve as a bridge between the strategic and tactical level and coordinate activities.

- During the study groups interaction in 2014 with the state media, it emerged that the media is hungry for inputs from the security forces, the state govt. In absence of these, the void is filled up by a more proactive stance from the separatists and their likes. Hence the SF is always on the backfoot and reactive in its approach. This trend needs to be reversed and the local media cultivated with adequate inputs and rapport. After a few apparent faux pas, the Army has limited its media and public outreach. It also fears criticism of interfering in administration when actually the people are happiest when it is proactive.[7]
- Nodal contact persons (akin to Comd Public Relations Officer) must be designated at each formation level, right down to the battalion level

towards this. The designated officers should have adequate maturity and undergo PR course.
- It also emerged that adequate and regular feedback must be taken for all the activities carried out under the aegis of Sadhbhavna. Accordingly, the efforts could be tempered in specific fields. Also, observations reveal that it does not make enough efforts for measuring and assessing the impact (impact assessment) and hardly investigates about the rapport amid all its welfare programmes. Undeniably, the education they deliver in the goodwill schools is a quality and according to the local sensitivities (proper infrastructure, with quality education, local participation, local teachers, local ethos, etc), but in the overall picture the Army seems to have failed (or never bothered) to measure the impact of this education service.
- Many activities which are being carried out as part of Sadhbhavna need to be gradually taken over by the State Govt.
- The Tourism Ministry of Govt of J&K needs to more proactive and come out with promotional clips, schemes like some other states and enhance the image of the well-known paradise of Kashmir.
- Target the OGWs and the ideology that they are propagating rather than only foot soldiers and poster boys.
- OGWIS, OGWRS and OGWR can be grouped together for the purpose of response strategies. These workers are omnipresent in all walks of life. They could be sympathisers, belong to families of killed militants, teachers, religious teachers, separatists, members of larger networks like Al Qaeda or off-shoots of ISIS ideology, Pakistani proxy war agents or even disgruntled elements of society. Though these workers look benign at the face of it, they are the most dangerous to society as well as the security forces. They make their presence felt in all walks of life including the funeral processions of killed militants. Merely picking them up in night raids will only alienate the society further. On the contrary, launching intelligence-based sting operations over a period of time, gathering proof of their damaging activities of recruiting, radicalising or merely pushing the youth into militancy by handing them over guns, will expose them in the eyes of the Awaam. This proof will not only be useful for convicting these elements but also form a tool for strategic communication with the Awaam, showing them how their children are being misled for an unjust cause. Long drawn out stake-outs will garner richer dividends as against perceived arbitrary arrests.

- Patronise the Youth connect Self-help groups who are daring to stand for Panchayat elections against all odds. Give them the required funds and where-withal to run deradicalization camps.

Tactical Level. At this level, it is very important for the concerned personnel to understand *Awaam* and their safety first. Towards this, the following could be practiced:

- The SF-civilian disconnect can only be abridged by working on the binding threads between the two, preparing a common platform where two can meet and discuss without any fear, increasing the interaction between the two, learn to listen against each other, understanding the local culture and sensitivities and above all checking any HR violations.
- The Force ethos being instructed at the Battle Schools needs to ensure that "cultural terrain" of J&K is as much a subject as the physical terrain.
- Concept of embedded journalists could be attempted during CI ops.
- Proactive interaction with media.
- Exercise utmost care about HR issues. The SF, especially CRPF and JKP be sensitized regarding the same.

Perception Improvement of Media (print, vernacular and social). The points regarding the same have been covered in the previous paragraphs under the levels as applicable. However, certain basic tenets which should be followed are as follows:

- Media has a great role in forming/shaping the opinion of the populace.
- Media is always hungry for news. If the govt agencies would not provide it with the news which is factual and needs to be come out, the void would be filled by somebody else, namely separatisits, disgruntled elements etc. Hence, they need to be dealth from a position of confidence.
- PROs need to be detailed for every formation, who should be in sync.
- Malicious/false propaganda/fake news needs to be aggressively countered, the medium of internet being very effective for the same.
- Instil creative thinking and proactiveness in media dealings by identifying positive stories and highlighting them keeping in mind psychological aspects and the psyche of the people.

Conclusion

Perception Management/Improvement of the state of J&K with the Awaam in particular has been carrying on for past two and half decades since the

Indian Army has made its presence felt for combating militancy. However, it has been restricted to the efforts of the Army and has been carried out in a disjointed manner, the actions by the Central Govt, actions of the state govt, the Army and other agencies not being in consonance. And this needs to be seen in the light of the perception of the local populace that they have always been persecuted, been at the receiving end. Hence, a sustained, concerted, coordinated whole of the govt approach should be followed which should be long term, with all stakeholders being in sync towards the greater good of the nation in general and the state of J&K in particular. The battle is for the minds of the people of Kashmir, rest of India and the rest of the world. It must be understood and accepted that the exercise of Perception Management/Improvement would be slow and arduous but has to be steady and consistent – decades of perception cannot be changed in minutes, hours or days. However, it is quite evident from the writings on the wall and the contents of this book that the battle for Jammu and Kashmir can only be won by winning the Battle of perceptions.

Jai Hind

NOTES

1. Jammu and Kashmir, Where Are We And Where Are We Going? *Lt Gen (Retd) Syed Ata Hasnain, PVSM, UYSM, AVSM, SM**, VSM**,* https://usiofindia.org/publication/cs3-strategic-perspectives/jammu-and-kashmir-where-are-we-and-where-are-we-going/.
2. https://courses.lumenlearning.com/boundless-management/chapter/individual-perceptions-and-behavior/, accessed on November 10, 2017.
3. https://www.linkedin.com/pulse/perception-management-how-steers-public-nazrul-khan, accessed on November 10, 2017.
4. https://www.rrg.sg/about-rrg/, op. cit.
5. https://scroll.in/article/805827/anti-nationals-and-terrorists-this-is-how-the-rest-of-india-views-kashmiri-students, accessed on November 18, 2018.
6. https://www.hindustantimes.com/punjab/two-kashmiri-students-among-three-arrested-with-weapons-in-jalandhar/story-i7USBlCzXLaFF4778FwWLM.html, accessed on November 18, 2018.
7. Jammu and Kashmir, Where Are We And Where Are We Going? op. cit.

APPENDIX A

Detailed Analysis of the Questionnaire J&K (2014)

In 2014, a survey was carried out for a net assessment study in which questions were asked to various groups as per the details given below. Depending on the applicability, some of the questions were common while others were specific to a particular group.

(a) Questions for Awaam.
(b) Questions for Surrendered Militants.
(c) Questions for Kashmiri Pandits.
(d) Questions for J&K Police (JKP) personnel.
(e) Questions for various levels of Service Officers (presently not posted in valley but served there earlier).

Questionnaire Analysis. The data collected from various strata was analyzed with the help of "Statistical Package for Social Sciences" software. Detailed analysis of the questionnaires is given in paragraph 4 onwards. Summary of analysis is given below:

(a) *Methodology of Counter-Terrorist (CT) ops.* There is a need for review of the methodologies for conduct of CT ops. Army should gradually move from hinterland to LoC and start operating from large bases.
(b) *AFSPA.* All sections of the society understand the importance and necessity of immunity provided by AFSPA; however, Awaam had mixed opinions about its continuation. The call for review of AFSPA by politicians is more of a gimmick.
(c) *External support.* 46.9% Awaam, 68.8% Surrendered Militants, 82.9% Kashmiri Pandits and 92% of JKP soldiers felt that PAK/ISI is responsible for continuation of militancy in J&K.
(d) *Present State of Militancy.* Militancy is under control and erection of LoC fence has been the major contributor towards reducing infiltration. Hurriyat still enjoys the support of Awaam though majority of people feel that young boys join the militant cadres for lack of employment and not for reasons of Jihad.

(e) *Sadhbhavna.* People had mixed opinions about Sadhbhavna. Some sections believe in its continuation while others feel that this aspect should better be left to the state government agencies.

(f) *Rehabilitation of Surrendered Militants.* It was found that a large number of militants have surrendered because of good rehabilitation policy of the government and they were further contributing significantly towards CT ops.

(g) *Kashmiri Pandits.* All sections of the society unanimously voted for their rehabilitation back to valley.

(h) *Article 370.* 36.6% Awaam (majority) opted for continuation of present status for J&K while 92.7% of Kashmiri Pandits and 68.8% Surrendered Militants have opted for J&K status similar to other states of Indian Union.

(i) *Fundamentalism.* Officials at various levels felt that fundamentalism is on the rise and there is no policy to counter it. Awaam however still believes in the concept of Kashmiriyat.

(j) *Governance.* People felt that corruption is rampant in the various state departments and there is lack of employment for the youth. Some expert feel that 99-year lease clause should be exploited to attract investments from businessmen who are not domicile of J&K. More than 60% of Awaam had access to internet in 2014 and e-governance should be exploited to increase transparency as well as efficacy of government schemes.

(k) *Surgical Strikes.* Interestingly, majority of the Officers (82.76%) in 2014 agreed that surgical strikes should be undertaken, well before they were actually undertaken in 2016.

(l) *Perception Management.* Majority of officers were of the opinion that Perception Management is not being done correctly.

(m) *Capacity Building of J&K Police and Para Military Police.* An overwhelming majority (93.6%) were of the opinion this was dire need of the day in 2014.

Responses of Awaam

1. What is your dream about J&K?

		Independent J&K	Autonomous Province	Federal Republic like other states of India	Special Status in Indian Union (present status)	Total
Govt Employees	Count	16	13	7	18	54
	% of Total	11.0%	9.0%	4.8%	12.4%	37.2%
Non-Govt Employees	Count	2	2	0	4	8
	% of Total	1.4%	1.4%	.0%	2.8%	5.5%
Businessmen	Count	7	4	0	1	12
	% of Total	4.8%	2.8%	.0%	.7%	8.3%
Shia Students	Count	2	3	7	20	32
	% of Total	1.4%	2.1%	4.8%	13.8%	22.1%
Others	Count	7	15	7	10	39
	% of Total	4.8%	10.3%	4.8%	6.9%	26.9%
Total	Count	34	37	21	53	145
	% of Total	23.4%	25.5%	14.5%	36.6%	100.0%

2. Who do you think is responsible for continuation of militancy in J&K?

		Pak/ISI	State Govt	Central Govt	Security Forces	Total
Govt Employees	Count	35	6	9	4	54
	% of Total	24.1%	4.1%	6.2%	2.8%	37.2%
Non-Govt Employees	Count	3	5	0	0	8
	% of Total	2.1%	3.4%	.0%	.0%	5.5%
Businessmen	Count	3	6	3	0	12
	% of Total	2.1%	4.1%	2.1%	.0%	8.3%
Shia Students	Count	18	3	11	0	32
	% of Total	12.4%	2.1%	7.6%	.0%	22.1%
Others	Count	9	28	1	1	39
	% of Total	6.2%	19.3%	.7%	.7%	26.9%
Total	Count	68	48	24	5	145
	% of Total	46.9%	33.1%	16.6%	3.4%	100.0%

The following table shows the percentage of Awaam that has access to internet in J&K.

3. e-Governance can help improve the state of affairs in J&K in a big way. Do you have access to Internet?

		Yes	No	No Response	Total
Govt Employees	Count	42	11	1	54
	% of Total	29.0%	7.6%	.7%	37.2%
Non-Govt Employees	Count	8	0	0	8
	% of Total	5.5%	.0%	.0%	5.5%
Businessmen	Count	4	8	0	12
	% of Total	2.8%	5.5%	.0%	8.3%
Shia Students	Count	16	16	0	32
	% of Total	11.0%	11.0%	.0%	22.1%
Others	Count	23	16	0	39
	% of Total	15.9%	11.0%	.0%	26.9%
Total	Count	93	51	1	145
	% of Total	64.1%	35.2%	.7%	100.0%

4. What in your view is the road map to prosperity in J&K?

		Promote Kashmiriyat	Improve State Governance	Resolve Indo-Pak Conflicts	Promote Islam	Total
Govt Employees	Count	1	22	19	12	54
	% of Total	.7%	15.2%	13.1%	8.3%	37.2%
Non-Govt Employees	Count	0	3	3	2	8
	% of Total	.0%	2.1%	2.1%	1.4%	5.5%
Businessmen	Count	1	1	6	4	12
	% of Total	.7%	.7%	4.1%	2.8%	8.3%
Shia Students	Count	1	1	29	1	32
	% of Total	.7%	.7%	20.0%	.7%	22.1%
Others	Count	1	7	10	21	39
	% of Total	.7%	4.8%	6.9%	14.5%	26.9%
Total	Count	4	34	67	40	145
	% of Total	2.8%	23.4%	46.2%	27.6%	100.0%

Response of Surrendered Militants

5. What is your dream about J&K?

		Independent J&K	Autonomous Province	Federal Republic like other states of India	Total
Employed with TA	Count	0	4	22	26
	% of Total	.0%	12.5%	68.8%	81.3%
Others	Count	3	3	0	6
	% of Total	9.4%	9.4%	.0%	18.8%
Total	Count	3	7	22	32
	% of Total	9.4%	21.9%	68.8%	100.0%

Appendix A: Detailed Analysis of the Questionnaire J&K

6. Who do you think is responsible for continuation of militancy in J&K?

			Pak/ISI	State Govt	Central Govt	Total
Emp	Employed with TA	Count	22	4	0	26
		% of Total	68.8%	12.5%	.0%	81.3%
	Others	Count		0	5	16
		% of Total	.0%	15.6%	3.1%	18.8%
Total		Count	22	9	1	32
		% of Total	68.8%	28.1%	3.1%	100.0%

7. Reason for your joining Tanjeem

			Disillusion-ment	Money	Freedom/Religion	Total
Emp	Employed with TA	Count	22	4	0	26
		% of Total	68.8%	12.5%	.0%	81.3%
	Others	Count	2	3	1	6
		% of Total	6.3%	9.4%	3.1%	18.8%
Total		Count	24	7	1	32
		% of Total	75.0%	21.9%	3.1%	100.0%

8. What in your view is the road map to prosperity in J&K?

			Improve State Governance	Resolve Indo-Pak Conflicts	Total
Emp	Employed with TA	Count	20	6	26
		% of Total	62.5%	18.8%	81.3%
	Others	Count	5	1	6
		% of Total	15.6%	3.1%	18.8%
Total		Count	25	7	32
		% of Total	78.1%	21.9%	100.0%

9. Reason for your joining Tanjeem

			Disillusion-ment	Money	Freedom/Religion	Total
Emp	Employed with TA	Count	22	4	0	26
		% of Total	68.8%	12.5%	.0%	81.3%
	Others	Count	2	3	1	6
		% of Total	6.3%	9.4%	3.1%	18.8%
Total		Count	24	7	1	32
		% of Total	75.0%	21.9%	3.1%	100.0%

10. What in your view is the road map to prosperity in J&K?

			Improve State Governance	Resolve Indo-Pak Conflicts	Total
Emp	Employed with TA	Count	20	6	26
		% of Total	62.5%	18.8%	81.3%
	Others	Count	5	1	6
		% of Total	15.6%	3.1%	18.8%
Total		Count	25	7	32
		% of Total	78.1%	21.9%	100.0%

Kashmiri Pandits from Jammu

11. What is your dream about J&K?

		Autonomous Province	Federal state like other states of India	Special Status in Indian Union (present status)	Total
Private Job	Count	1	20	0	21
	% of Total	2.4%	48.8%	.0%	51.2%
Business	Count	1	7	1	9
	% of Total	2.4%	17.1%	2.4%	22.0%
Govt Job	Count	0	9	0	9
	% of Total	.0%	22.0%	.0%	22.0%
Student	Count	0	1	0	1
	% of Total	.0%	2.4%	.0%	2.4%
Ex-servicemen	Count	0	1	0	1
	% of Total	.0%	2.4%	.0%	2.4%
Total	Count	2	38	1	41
	% of Total	4.9%	92.7%	2.4%	100.0%

12. Who do you think is responsible for continuation of militancy in J&K?

		Pak/ISI	State Govt	Central Govt	Total
Private Job	Count	16	3	2	21
	% of Total	39.0%	7.3%	4.9%	51.2%
Business	Count	8	0	1	9
	% of Total	19.5%	.0%	2.4%	22.0%
Govt Job	Count	8	1	0	9
	% of Total	19.5%	2.4%	.0%	22.0%
Student	Count	1	0	0	1
	% of Total	2.4%	.0%	.0%	2.4%
Ex-servicemen	Count	1	0	0	1
	% of Total	2.4%	.0%	.0%	2.4%
Total	Count	34	4	3	41
	% of Total	82.9%	9.8%	7.3%	100.0%

Appendix A: Detailed Analysis of the Questionnaire J&K

13. I have easy access to the Internet

		Yes	No	Total
Private Job	Count	13	8	21
	% of Total	31.7%	19.5%	51.2%
Business	Count	6	3	9
	% of Total	14.6%	7.3%	22.0%
Govt Job	Count	6	3	9
	% of Total	14.6%	7.3%	22.0%
Student	Count	0	1	1
	% of Total	.0%	2.4%	2.4%
Ex-servicemen	Count	0	1	1
	% of Total	.0%	2.4%	2.4%
Total	Count	25	16	41
	% of Total	61.0%	39.0%	100.0%

JKP

14. Who do you think is responsible for continuation of militancy in J&K?

			Pak/ISI	State Govt	Security Forces	Total
Region	Jammu	Count	19	1	1	21
		% of Total	38.0%	2.0%	2.0%	42.0%
	Valley	Count	26	1	1	28
		% of Total	52.0%	2.0%	2.0%	56.0%
	Ladakh	Count	1	0	0	1
		% of Total	2.0%	.0%	.0%	2.0%
Total		Count	46	2	2	50
		% of Total	92.0%	4.0%	4.0%	100.0%

15. What in your view is the road map to prosperity in J&K?

			Promote Kashmiriyat	Improve State Governance	Resolve Indo-Pak Conflicts	Promote Islam	Total
Region	Jammu	Count	2	8	11	0	21
		% of Total	4.0%	16.0%	22.0%	.0%	42.0%
	Valley	Count	1	12	14	1	28
		% of Total	2.0%	24.0%	28.0%	2.0%	56.0%
	Ladakh	Count	0	0	1	0	1
		% of Total	.0%	.0%	2.0%	.0%	2.0%
	Total	Count	3	20	26	1	50
		% of Total	6.0%	40.0%	52.0%	2.0%	100.0%

Junior (Battalion Support Weapons, Junior Command Course, Defence Services Staff College), Mid Level (Higher Command) and Senior (National Defence College)

Course * 1. There is a scope of reduction of troops in Valley due to reduced levels of violence

		Disagree	Neutral	Agree	Total
Higher Command Course	Count	29	11	6	12
	% within Course	100.0%	37.93%	20.69%	41.38%
JC Course (RR)	Count	38	21	1	16
	% within Course	100.0%	55.26%	2.63%	42.11%
JC Course (LC)	Count	41	25	5	11
	% within Course	100.0%	60.98%	12.20%	26.83%
Bn Sp Wpns Course	Count	31	12	6	13
	% within Course	100.0%	38.71%	19.35%	41.94%
DSSC	Count	50	19	16	15
	% within Course	100.0%	38.00%	32.00%	30.00%
NDC	Count	14	1	0	13
	% within Course	100.0%	7.14%	0.00%	92.86%
Total	Count	203	89	34	80
	% within Course	100.0%	43.84%	16.75%	39.41%

Course * 2. Army should focus more on Counter-infilt strat than operating in hinterland in the valley

		Disagree	Neutral	Agree	Total
Higher Command Course	Count	29	11	1	17
	% within Course	100.0%	37.93%	3.45%	58.62%
JC Course (RR)	Count	38	14	5	19
	% within Course	100.0%	36.84%	13.16%	50.00%
JC Course (LC)	Count	41	10	8	23
	% within Course	100.0%	24.39%	19.51%	56.10%
Bn Sp Wpns Course	Count	31	4	8	19
	% within Course	100.0%	12.90%	25.81%	61.29%
DSSC	Count	50	15	3	32
	% within Course	100.0%	30.00%	6.00%	64.00%
NDC	Count	14	1	0	13
	% within Course	100.0%	7.14%	0.00%	92.86%
Total	Count	203	55	25	123
	% within Course	100.0%	27.09%	12.32%	60.59%

Appendix A: Detailed Analysis of the Questionnaire J&K

Course * 3. Surgical ops would give better dividends in the present day environment in J&K Cross-tabulation

		Disagree	Neutral	Agree	Total
Higher Command Course	Count	29	3	0	26
	% within Course	100.0%	10.34%	0.00%	89.66%
JC Course (RR)	Count	38	2	9	27
	% within Course	100.0%	5.26%	23.68%	71.05%
JC Course (LC)	Count	41	3	9	29
	% within Course	100.0%	7.32%	21.95%	70.73%
Bn Sp Wpns Course	Count	31	0	5	26
	% within Course	100.0%	0.00%	16.13%	83.87%
DSSC	Count	50	3	1	46
	% within Course	100.0%	6.00%	2.00%	92.00%
NDC	Count	14	0	0	14
	% within Course	100.0%	0.00%	0.00%	100.00%
Total	Count	203	11	24	168
	% within Course	100.0%	5.42%	11.82%	82.76%

Course * 4. Perception Mgt and Media handling is being done effectively by the Army

		Disagree	Neutral	Agree	Total
Higher Command Course	Count	29	19	4	6
	% within Course	100.0%	65.52%	13.79%	20.69%
JC Course (RR)	Count	38	17	5	16
	% within Course	100.0%	44.74%	13.16%	42.11%
JC Course (LC)	Count	41	26	5	10
	% within Course	100.0%	63.41%	12.20%	24.39%
Bn Sp Wpns Course	Count	31	12	6	13
	% within Course	100.0%	38.71%	19.35%	41.94%
DSSC	Count	50	26	8	16
	% within Course	100.0%	52.00%	16.00%	32.00%
NDC	Count	14	7	1	6
	% within Course	100.0%	50.00%	7.14%	42.86%
Total	Count	203	107	29	67
	% within Course	100.0%	52.71%	14.29%	33.00%

Course * 5. Op Sadbhavna is achieving the desired outcome of Winning Hearts and Minds of Awaam Cross-tabulation

		Disagree	Neutral	Agree	Total
Higher Command Course	Count	29	17	5	7
	% within Course	100.0%	58.62%	17.24%	24.14%
JC Course (RR)	Count	38	18	7	13
	% within Course	100.0%	47.37%	18.42%	34.21%
JC Course (LC)	Count	41	12	9	20
	% within Course	100.0%	29.27%	21.95%	48.78%
Bn Sp Wpns Course	Count	31	13	8	10
	% within Course	100.0%	41.94%	25.81%	32.26%
DSSC	Count	50	20	2	28
	% within Course	100.0%	40.00%	4.00%	56.00%
NDC	Count	14	7	0	7
	% within Course	100.0%	50.00%	0.00%	50.00%
Total	Count	203	87	31	85
	% within Course	100.0%	42.86%	15.27%	41.87%

Course * 6. There is a dire need for capacity building for the Para Military Forces (PMF) and Police operating in J&K Crosstabulation

		Disagree	Neutral	Agree	Total
Higher Command Course	Count	29	1	1	27
	% within Course	100.0%	3.45%	3.45%	93.10%
JC Course (RR)	Count	38	0	1	37
	% within Course	100.0%	0.00%	2.63%	97.37%
JC Course (LC)	Count	41	0	1	40
	% within Course	100.0%	0.00%	2.44%	97.56%
Bn Sp Wpns Course	Count	31	0	5	26
	% within Course	100.0%	0.00%	16.13%	83.87%
DSSC	Count	50	3	0	47
	% within Course	100.0%	6.00%	0.00%	94.00%
NDC	Count	14	1	0	13
	% within Course	100.0%	7.14%	0.00%	92.86%
Total	Count	203	5	8	190
	% within Course	100.0%	2.46%	3.94%	93.60%

APPENDIX B

Questionnaire Analysis by Tata Institute of Social Sciences as well as in-House Resources

General

A simple analysis of the demography of Kashmir region brings to fore two salient aspects: Firstly, the Youth Bulge, with 62% population being below 30 years of age, which is above the national average, even though youthful population profile is a pan-India reality, and secondly, Unitary Nature of Religious Faith and Ethnicity is a peculiar phenomenon, specific to Kashmir region of State of J&K in India (with the exception of Lakshadweep). Out of seven million population of Kashmir region, an overwhelming 98% are Muslims (88% Sunnis). Similarly, 84% of the population are ethnic Kashmiris.

The alienation in varying degrees among a large cross-section of Kashmiri population, especially the youth, is an accepted fact. However, no realistic assessment of the same has been carried out in recent years. Many experts attribute the agitation dynamics and stone-pelting phenomenon to this perceived alienation, apart from the role played by Pakistan.

To assess the mood of youth credibly, it was therefore imperative to obtain a feedback from them in a manner that reflects their true beliefs, feelings and opinions. Accordingly, a questionnaire, comprising 50 questions, was scientifically designed by Tata Institute of Social Sciences (TISS). A survey was then conducted among the most relevant section of youth, i.e. those studying in degree colleges located across the Kashmir region. Approximately, 550 students from Degree Colleges in all ten districts of Kashmir region were approached for the survey, through random sampling method, which is a fairly large Sample. The guidelines for selecting this Sample had come from TISS.

Methodology of Conduct of Survey

The survey was conducted by engaging the trustworthy civil society members having unquestionable acceptability among the youth with no footprints of

Army or any other government agencies. The principals and professors were taken into confidence by explaining that TISS is conducting this survey like it does in various parts of the country, especially troubled zones, in a routine manner. It was also told that TISS is undertaking this survey independently to ascertain the feelings of the youth as also what their aspirations are. An effort was made to ensure that group dynamics do not play out. However, some influence of group dynamics or inherent desire to maintain secrecy for certain questions of the survey, e.g. "Do you consider yourself to be an Indian?", "Radicalisation", "Affiliation to religious organisation", and so on cannot be ruled out.

ANALYSIS BY TISS

Age of participants

Age (years)	Participants (%)
18-20	19.48
21-25	70.57
26-29	8.34
30+	1.59

Home-town of the participants

Home-town	Participants (%)
Baramulla	28.42
Pulwama	15.10
Anantnag	10.93
Ganderbal	10.73
Shopian	10.53
Kupwara	6.16
Budgam	5.96
Srinagar	5.96
Kulgam	5.56
Banihal	0.59

Course pursued

Course	Participants (%)
High school	0.79
Diploma	0.79
Graduation	89.86
Professional course	1.39
Post graduation	5.56
MPhil/PhD	0.59
None	0.99

Mostly students were undergoing a general graduation course (BA, BSc, BCom), and very few were doing professional courses like BEd, BTech, etc. It's very significant to note that a general graduation doesn't help very much in directly getting a job after the course.

Place of study

Place	Participants (%)
Bandipora	0.19
Bijbehara	0.19
Delhi	0.19
Islamic College	0.19
Jammu Medical College	0.19
Kargil	0.19
Nagpur	0.19
SKIMS	0.19
Hazratbal	0.39
Govt Degree College	0.59
Women's College	0.59
Handwara	1.78
Kupwara	2.18
Pattan	2.78
Tangmarg	2.78
-	3.18
Uri	3.97
Budgam	4.77
University of Kashmir	4.97
Kulgam	5.16
Anantnag	7.15
Srinagar	7.15
Sopore	8.15
Baramulla	8.94
Shopian	8.94
Ganderbal	9.74
Pulwama	15.10

Reasons for joining the course

Reason	Participants (%)
Parents' advice	52.28
It is the only course I got admission into	24.85
My friends are joining the same course/college	17.89
Other reasons	4.97

The influence of parents is very marked. Parents seem to be a very important motivating factor.

Father's occupation

Occupation	Participants (%)
Artisan	2.78
Business	17.29
Doctor	4.37
Employee	3.37
Employer	4.57
Engineer	0.59
Farmer	26.83
Fruit trader	4.17
Govt employee	12.72
Labour	1.59
Lawyer	1.39
Lecturer/Professor	0.59
Shopkeeper	4.97
Teacher	11.92
Transporter	1.98
No response	0.79

Mother's occupation

Occupation	Participants (%)
No response	10.13
Artisan	0.19
Employee	0.39
Employer	3.57
Govt employee	4.97
Home-maker	66.60
Healthcare worker	1.39
Teacher	12.72

Mothers being home-makers is very normal in an area like Kashmir.

Satisfaction with the course

Option	Participants (%)
Somewhat satisfied	47.51
Somewhat dissatisfied	24.45
Very satisfied	17.89
Very dissatisfied	6.75
Prefer not to say	3.37

The level of satisfaction is, surprisingly, not bad.

Appendix B: Questionnaire Analysis by Tata Institute of Social Sciences

Reasons for dissatisfaction

Option	Participants (%)
Infrequent classes due to strikes and *bandhs*	59.24
Bad infrastructure	22.46
Uncertainty about exams	10.53
Poorly trained faculty	4.57
Not enough books and reference material	3.18

Infrequent classes is the significant reason for dissatisfaction. Extension of classes and inability to graduate are also factors. Infrastructure issues are not significant.

What will you do after completing the course?

Option	Participants (%)
Look for a job	58.64
Prepare for entrance exams for higher studies	23.45
Don't know as yet	17.89

Optimism about the future

Option	Participants (%)
I can only hope for the best	43.53
Things are bad, jobs are difficult to get	31.01
Yes, I am very optimistic	25.44

Most are very optimistic about the future. The cautious optimism in terms of "I can only hope for the best" is useful to look at.

Things to consider while looking for a job

Option	Male (%)	Female (%)
A job which provides security and stability	26.85	28.49
Good salary	24.38	25.69
Job satisfaction	23.14	19.55
Can't say	15.12	15.08
A job which allows me to be close to family	10.49	11.17

Security and stability is a useful thing to look at. Both men and women show this preference.

Where would you like to work?

Option	Participants (%)
Central government job	61.03
Don't know as yet	18.68
State government job	11.92
Armed Forces	4.77
Private Sector	3.37
Others	0.19

Nobody wants to go into farming as a profession despite coming from that background. Most prefer a central government job, not even a state government job. It links well with their preference for security and stability in job.

Will you look for a job in Kashmir

Option	Male (%)	Female (%)
Yes	60.80	54.18
Can't say	30.55	38.54
No	8.64	7.26

A central government job in Kashmir would make them the happiest. They want to stay in Kashmir and the feeling of being Kashmiri is very strong.

DIVERSITY IN FRIENDSHIPS

Friends from other parts of India

Option	Male (%)	Female (%)
Yes	55.55	37.98
No	44.44	62.01

Friends from other religions

Option	Male (%)	Female (%)
Yes	68.51	68.15
No	31.48	31.84

Friends of opposite gender

Option	Male (%)	Female (%)
Yes	63.88	49.72
No	36.11	50.27

Males have more exposure in terms of friends from other parts, religion, and gender. This suggests that families tend to keep daughters more protected.

THE KASHMIRI IDENTITY

How important is the identity of being Kashmiri?

Option	Male (%)	Female (%)
Very important to a great extent	62.03	61.45
Important to some extent	24.69	25.69
Can't say	12.65	10.05
Not important at all	0.61	2.79

Meaning of being Kashmiri

Option	Male (%)	Female (%)
Source of pride	75.30	76.53
Oppressed people	11.72	8.93
Second-class human beings	6.79	7.26
No solution in sight	6.17	7.26

Though the people are very proud to be Kashmiris, the way they define being Kashmiri is problematic, even though the number of such people is less.

The return of Kashmiri Pandits

Option	Male (%)	Female (%)
They should be encouraged to come back	50.30	49.16
No, they chose to leave, and should not be allowed to come back	32.09	28.49
I don't know	17.59	22.34

The people who give "I don't know" as the answer are the problematic ones as they aren't saying anything clearly right now, but given a chance, may not welcome the Pandits back.

What do you do in your spare time?

	Often (%)	Sometimes (%)	Never (%)	Can't Say (%)
Go out with friends	25.84	68.19	4.37	1.59
Spend time with family	83.49	14.71	0.39	1.39
Read books and magazines	29.22	57.05	9.74	3.97
Play outdoor games/sports	16.10	63.02	17.49	3.37
Watch movies/TV	18.48	66.60	9.94	4.97
Go to a religious institution	39.76	44.33	12.52	3.37
Go for political meetings	3.97	23.65	52.28	20.07
Pursue a hobby	25.84	38.36	20.07	15.70

Family is very important, with people spending a lot of time with their families, so is going to religious institutions. Sports is not that important. The importance of religion cannot be overlooked. It's a crutch that they use and we have to look at how religion can be used in terms of developing "Vichaardhaara".

As for going to political institutions, they show disenchantment with the government.

INTERNET

Use of internet

	Male (%)	Female (%)
Yes	81.17	84.91
Sometimes when the internet works	13.27	10.05
No	5.55	5.02

Reasons for use of internet

Social media	-41.74%
Information related to jobs	-33.79%
Information on Kashmir	-10.93%
Games	-8.94%
Others	-4.57%

SOCIAL MEDIA

Use of social media

	Male (%)	Female (%)
Yes	81.48	79.88
No	18.51	20.11

Reasons for use of social media

	Male (%)	Female (%)
To connect with friends	64.81	58.10
To express opinion on an issue	25	28.49
To follow a celebrity	2.46	4.46
To join groups	4.32	7.82
Others	3.39	5.02

Appendix B: Questionnaire Analysis by Tata Institute of Social Sciences 323

Radicalisation by social media

Response	Participants (%)
Yes	28
No	29
Can't say	43

The "can't say" group is important to look at because they are a group who prefer not say anything right then, but they have their own ideas and the ideas are probably not something which we would like to hear; in this group, 63% are males.

Ease of influence by social media

	Male (%)	Female (%)
Yes	34.56	27.93
No	20.67	16.75
Can't say	44.75	55.30

How truthful is information on social media?

Response	Participants (%)
Very truthful	5.16
Sometimes truthful	34.19
Not very truthful	28.42
Can't say	32.20

Combing the "very truthful" and "sometimes truthful" would constitute a significant number. It's important to look at if one is looking to use social media to modify perceptions.

Are you a part of any youth organization?

Response	Participants (%)
Yes	3
No	97

The speaker thinks the response could be different if the question were framed differently.

Of the 3%, 9 respondents were part of a religious organization; 7 were part of a cultural organization.

NEWSPAPERS

Do you read newspapers?

Response	Participants (%)
Yes	32.40
No	24.05
Sometimes	43.53

Of the total number of respondents who read newspaper daily or often, 89.36% are male.

Which newspapers do you read?

Response	Participants (%)
Local newspaper	41.88
National daily	33.50
Whatever I can get	24.60

Can newspapers report accurately on Kashmir?

Options	Response (%)
A newspaper in Urdu that is published in Kashmir	40.35
No newspaper can report accurately about what is happening in Kashmir	31.21
An English or Hindi newspaper that has its headquarters in Delhi	15.70
A newspaper that is published in Pakistan	12.72

Urdu newspaper published in Kashmir is the most trusted. People have very little trust in newspapers published in Pakistan.

Which are the most watched TV channels in Kashmir?

Options	Response (%)
International channels	28.23
Pvt Hindi news channels	22.86
Pvt English news channels	21.86
Doordarshan	15.30
Local channels	9.14
Pakistan TV	2.58

Perhaps they think that the reporting is much more nuanced in international channels.

Whose interests does the government take care of?

Options	Response (%)
It doesn't take care of anybody's interests	42.74
It takes care of the interests of people from outside Kashmir	20.47
It takes care of the interests of Kashmiris	20.87
It takes care of mine and my family's interests	15.90

This statistic shows their alienation. They feel no one except their family. They don't know whom to rely on in times of trouble. They government does not care. They're left with their family and religion.

UNHCR REPORT ON KASHMIR

Awareness about the UNHCR report

	Male (%)	Female (%)
Aware	50	37.43
Not aware	50	62.56

Accuracy of the UNHCR report

Options	Response (%)
Accurate	67.24
Not accurate	24.89
Can't say	7.86

DISCRIMINATION

Discrimination faced

Options	Response (%)
Yes	33.99
No	33.20
Can't say	32.80

Reasons for discrimination

Options	Response (%)
The state you belong to	83.04
Religion	5.26
Social class	5.26
Others	4.09
Caste	1.16
Gender	1.16

Life Satisfaction

Satisfaction Level	Male (%)	Female (%)
Very satisfied	13.88	15.08
Fairly satisfied	35.18	32.96
Can't say	31.17	37.98
Not satisfied	17.28	12.29
Not at all satisfied	1.85	2.79

Life Satisfaction and Gender

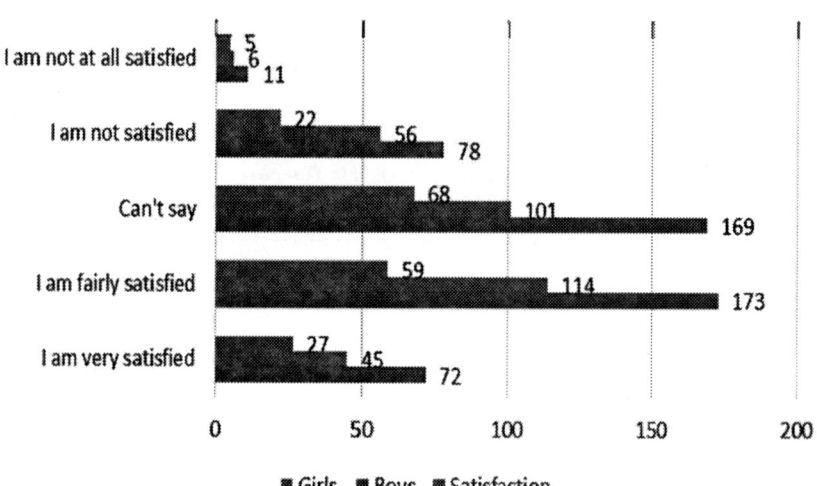

Satisfaction of friends

Satisfaction Level	Male (%)	Female (%)
Very satisfied	12.34	12.84
Fairly satisfied	29.01	24.02
Don't know/Can't say	26.23	30.72
Not satisfied	29.01	30.72
Not at all satisfied	3.39	1.76

Satisfaction of Friends and Gender

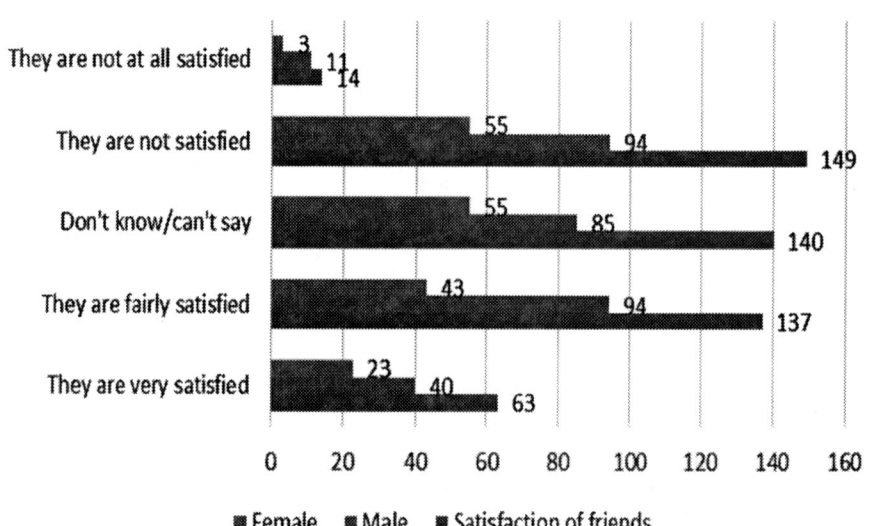

Appendix B: Questionnaire Analysis by Tata Institute of Social Sciences

Satisfaction of self and friends

Satisfaction Level	Self (%)	Friends (%)
Very satisfied	14.31	12.52
Fairly satisfied	34.39	27.23
Can't say	33.59	27.83
Not satisfied	15.50	29.62
Not at all satisfied	2.18	2.78

The levels of satisfaction are okay, not bad. But the important part is that they rate the dissatisfaction level of their friends higher. This is important because it is very easy to attribute things to others than to oneself. So the actual levels of dissatisfaction for self are likely to be much higher, closer to the one given for friends.

Reasons for dissatisfaction

Reason	Male (%)	Female (%)
No jobs	40.74	28.49
Uncertainty about future	18.20	19.55
Being forced to live under the rule of the Indian govt	21.60	24.02
Life disrupted due to curfews and *bandhs*	6.48	12.29
Others	10.49	13.96
No dissatisfaction	2.46	1.67

Important things in life

	Very important (%)	Somewhat important (%)	Somewhat unimportant (%)	Not important at all (%)
Getting higher education	58.05	8.94	1.39	31.61
Getting a job	56.85	7.95	1.59	33.59
Having a peaceful life without disruption	56.26	6.16	3.57	33.99
Being assured human rights	42.54	12.32	10.93	34.19
Being provided basic amenities	40.55	19.28	5.96	34.19
Getting married	40.35	16.30	8.54	34.79
Having a stable govt	38.96	13.12	11.33	36.58

Almost as many say it's important as the ones saying it's not important for "having a stable government" and "being assured human rights". This is reflective of a strong sense of alienation.

Trust in social institutions

	Great degree of trust (%)	Some trust (%)	No trust at all (%)	Can't say (%)
Family members	90.05	7.55	0.39	1.98
Friends	55.26	36.58	2.98	5.16
Teachers	41.15	50.29	4.37	4.17
Religious institution	21.27	43.93	25.04	9.74
Local state govt	15.10	38.76	39.56	6.56
NGOs	12.92	0	73.16	13.91
Army	11.72	30.41	48.70	9.14
Central govt	10.93	30.01	45.12	13.91
Local admin	10.53	31.21	40.15	18.09
Court	9.14	53.28	25.84	11.72
Local police	7.15	30.41	51.49	10.93
Central police	4.17	20.67	54.87	20.27

Family, friends, teachers, and religious institutions are very important. They trust the judiciary, but not entirely.

Feeling of being Indian

Options	Response (%)
Yes	33.99
No	32.80
Can't say	33.20

The "can't say" group is again worrying.

One thing that can bring about a change

	Male (%)	Female (%)
Change of govt	32.71	36.31
Better education/employment	25	23.46
Withdrawal of army	20.06	21.22
Better life	20.06	18.43
Improvement of drug policy	2.16	0.55

IN-HOUSE DATA ANALYSIS

Critical Findings

Though the comprehensive analysis of the results of survey can only be done by the competent agency, i.e. TISS, an in-house effort has been made to bring out certain critical findings of the survey employing available analytics tool and intimate knowledge of the ground reality. The salient aspects of survey responses are as follows:

Appendix B: Questionnaire Analysis by Tata Institute of Social Sciences   329

- **Being Kashmiri.** Whereas more than 75% respondents stated that they were proud of being a Kashmiri, around 25% saw no solution in sight or felt oppressed or second-class citizen.
- **Return of Pandits.** Around 50% favoured return of Kashmiri Pandits, whereas 30% were against their return and 20% preferred not to express their view. Those favouring return comprised 57% of the female and 63% of male "Yes" respondents
- **Religious Places and Political Meetings.** 84% said that they visited Religious Institutions in spare time with 40% doing so frequently. However, only 28% participated in Political Meetings (4% often).
- **Social Media and Radicalisation.** More than 80% youth of Kashmir region use Social Media (SM). Around 75% said the contents were "Not Very Truthful" (28%) or "Sometimes Truthful" (34%). Around 32% affirmed getting influenced by SM and 28% had heard people getting radicalised through SM.
- **Trust Factor with Establishment.** While 15% expressed a great deal of trust and 39% had some trust on State Government, the corresponding figures for Central Government were 11% and 30%. Compared to around 42% respondents, who had a great deal of trust (12%) or some trust (30%) on Army and Local Administration, only 7% + 31% = 38% trusted Police. The figures for PMFs were even lower (4% + 21% = 25%). Trust on Religious Institutions and Leaders appeared to be far more as around 65% respondents expressed a great deal of trust (21%) or some trust (44%). Only 25% had no trust at all in them. Youth also reposed more faith in Teachers as 91.9% of respondents trusted them.
- **Youth Aspirations.** An overwhelming 61% of youth wanted to take up Central Government jobs, whereas 12% showed preference for State Government jobs and only 5% wanted to join the Armed Forces.
- **Nationality.** By far, the most important and direct question asked in the questionnaire was "Do you consider yourself to be an Indian?" Around 35.6% said "Yes", 35.8% said "No" and 27.6% preferred not to take a position. A majority of respondents from Kupwara (71%), Shopian (66%) and Pulwama (51%) districts opted for "No", whereas those from Kulgam (71%), Budgam (63%), Gandarbal (53.7%), Anantnag (49%) and Srinagar (40%) districts chose "Yes". Compared to males, a larger percentage of female respondents said "Yes".
- **Satisfaction with Present Situation.** Around 34% of respondents felt that they or their family members were discriminated against for which

30% ascribed the reasons to being Kashmiri, 3.6% cited religion and 62% assigned other reasons.
- **Changes in Current Situation.** Approximately 50% respondents were happy with their present state of life, 30% were dissatisfied and 20% said "Can't Say/Don't Know"; 34% wanted a change of government, 21% were in favour of withdrawal of Army and around 45% clamoured for better jobs and education opportunities and 2% wanted better anti-drug abuse policy in the State.

Comments

The comments on the findings of the survey are as follows:
- The **sample of survey represents the most volatile section** of the society and apparently most alienated as well. Hence, extrapolating it to the entire population could see the moderation in anti-India sentiments.
- There are **pockets in both North and South Kashmir** where **anti-India feelings are at higher levels.** Some impact of incidents in the run-up to the date of survey or at the time of survey also needs to be factored in.
- There is quite a sizeable percentage of population even in areas greatly affected by the ongoing turmoil who have **opted to be called Indian** and hence **if harnessed well, the situation could further improve.**
- Preference for Central Government jobs corroborates the aspect of hope for a better future within Indian framework. However, **most youth want to see a change** and a lasting solution for Kashmir.
- **Social Media influence in the society is clearly discernible** and its role as a catalyst to lend momentum to the radicalisation process in the Valley is undeniable. A very large percentage of youth are inclined towards religion in their spare time, which **may reflect the current trend of youth tilting towards radicalisation.**
- An interesting finding was that only 50% of youth wanted Kashmiri Pandits to return, which could be an indicator to the **widening divide between Pandit Community and Muslims of the Valley. This does not augur well for future** and efforts must be made to facilitate dialogue between Pandits and prominent mainstream Muslim leaders from the Valley.
- **Army remains the most trusted agency amongst all the Security Forces** operating in the Valley despite years of conflict, but **overall trust figures are not flattering.** It would therefore prudent to **consider what best practices could be co-opted** to improve the acceptability.

- The survey quite closely validates the description of the situation in the Valley as "**stable, but fragile**". Hence, if all the agencies including the civil administration work closely and in unison (synergy has improved, but a lot of it still remains compartmentalised) to wrest the initiative from **Separatist-Terrorist-Pakistan troika**, there is a great probability of the goal materialising.
- A road map of **well thought out initiatives in the field of education, sports and entertainment** could counter growing radicalisation footprints.

Conclusion

Overall, the **survey reveals that the situation in the Valley is not as bad as it is often painted by the national electronic media.** Apart from various affirmative actions, if Kashmir-centric polarised debate in national TV channels could be curtailed, it would do a world of good towards improving the perception of situation in the Valley. Conducting such surveys in a more comprehensive manner may throw up **"Hints or Clues"** as to what could be the **"Way Forward"**.

Software used for Data Analytics

- KNIME Analytics Platform is the open source software for creating data science applications and services. Intuitive, open, and continuously integrating new developments, KNIME makes understanding data and designing data science workflows and reusable components accessible to everyone.
- Builds end-to-end data science workflows – Creates visual workloads with an intuitive, drag and drop type graphical interface, without the need for coding.
- Shapes data – Derives statistics, including mean, quantiles, and standard deviation, applies statistical tests to validate a hypothesis, integrates dimension reduction, correlation analysis, and more into the workflow.
- Aggregates, sorts, filters, and joins data either on local machine, in-database, or in distributed big data environments.
- Cleans data through normalisation, data type conversion, and missing value handling. Detects out-of-range values with outlier and anomaly detection algorithms.
- Extracts and selects features (or construct new ones) to prepare dataset for machine learning.

Age profile

The age profile of the participants is **18 to 27 years** with the majority between 21 and 23 years of age.

RowID	Count
18	12
19	39
20	63
21	116
22	92
23	82
24	51
25	39
26	30
27	4

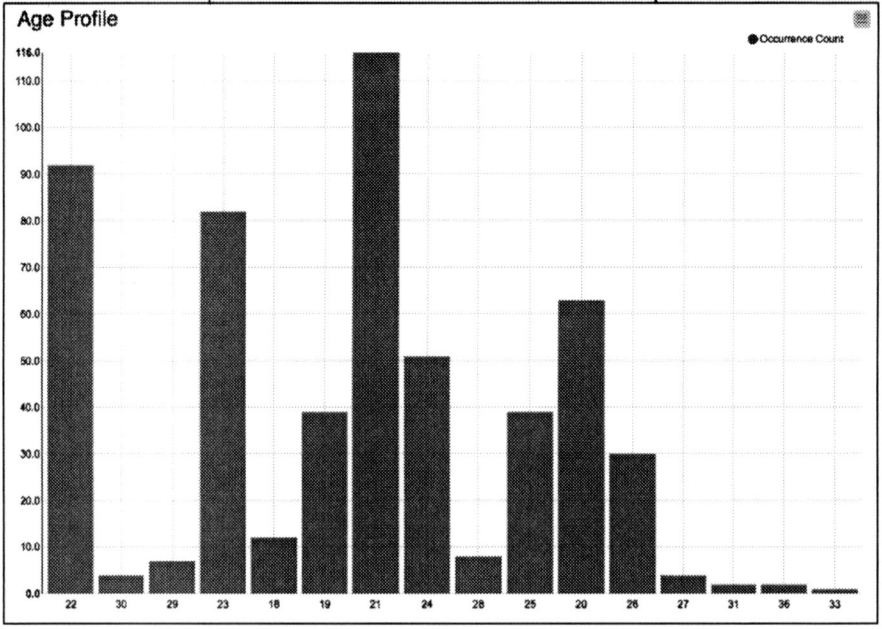

Gender profile

Out of 502 participants, there are 324 Male participants and 179 Female participants.

RowID	Count
Female	195
Male	357

Appendix B: Questionnaire Analysis by Tata Institute of Social Sciences 333

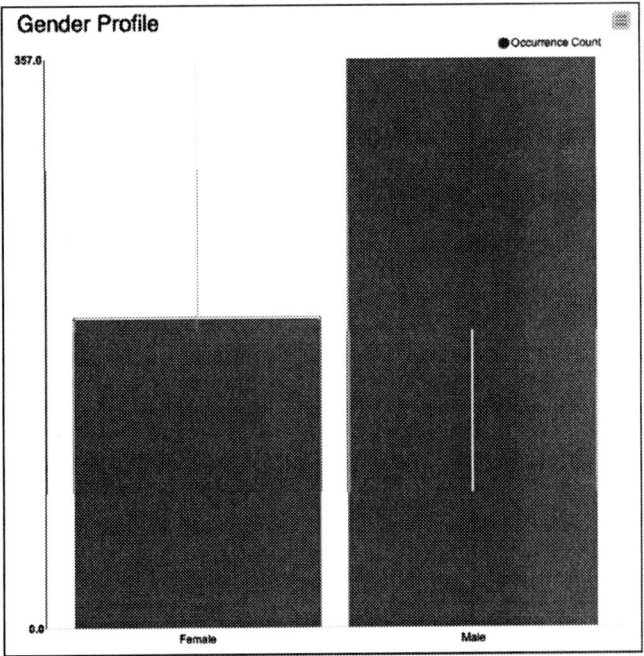

52% of them have friends from other gender.

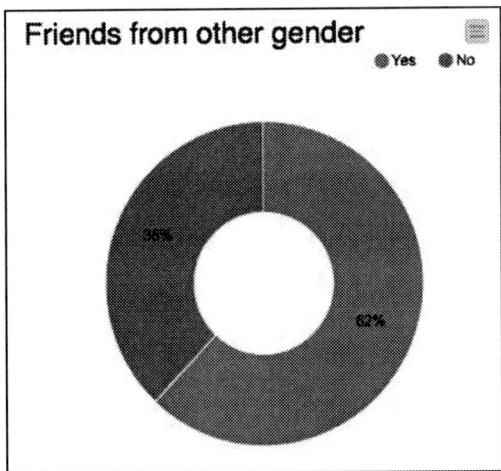

Demographics

- **Region wise**

The survey has been divided into three regions, i.e. Central Kashmir, North Kashmir and South Kashmir. Analysis of the demographics shows that there is equal participation from every region of Kashmir thus covering the perception of youth from each part of the valley in a balanced manner.

RowID	Count
Central Kashmir	114
North Kashmir	221
South Kashmir	217

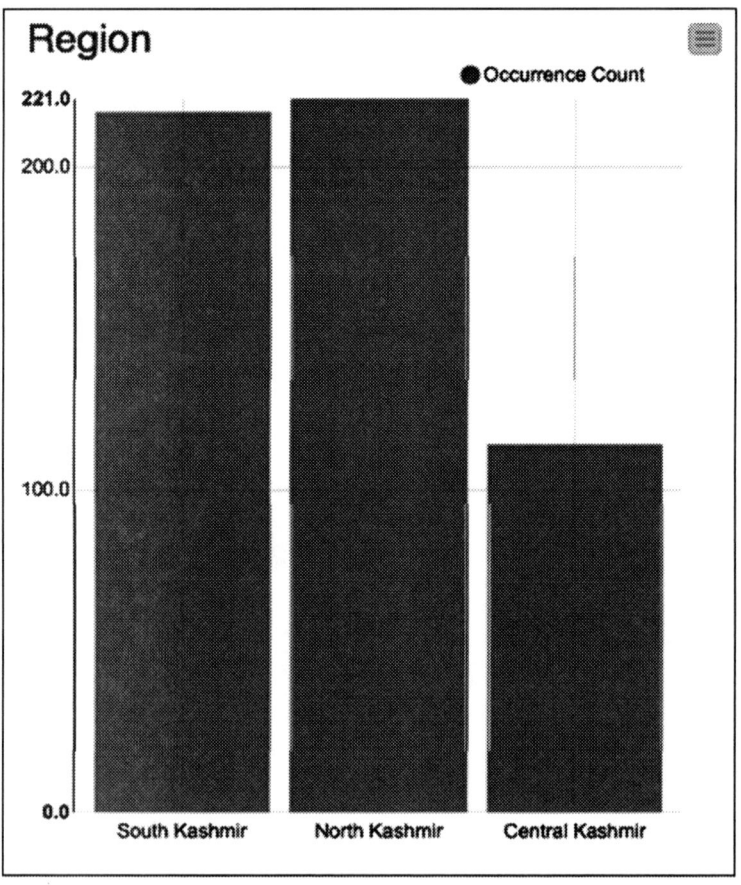

- **District-wise**

The figure shows the district-wise count of the participants. The maximum

Appendix B: Questionnaire Analysis by Tata Institute of Social Sciences   335

number of participants are from Baramulla district followed by Pulwama, Anantnag, Bandipora, Ganderbal and Shopian.

RowID	Count
Anantnag	55
Bandipora	50
Baramulla	145
Budgam	30
Ganderbal	54
Kulgam	28
Kupwara	31
Pulwama	76
Shopian	53
Srinagar	30

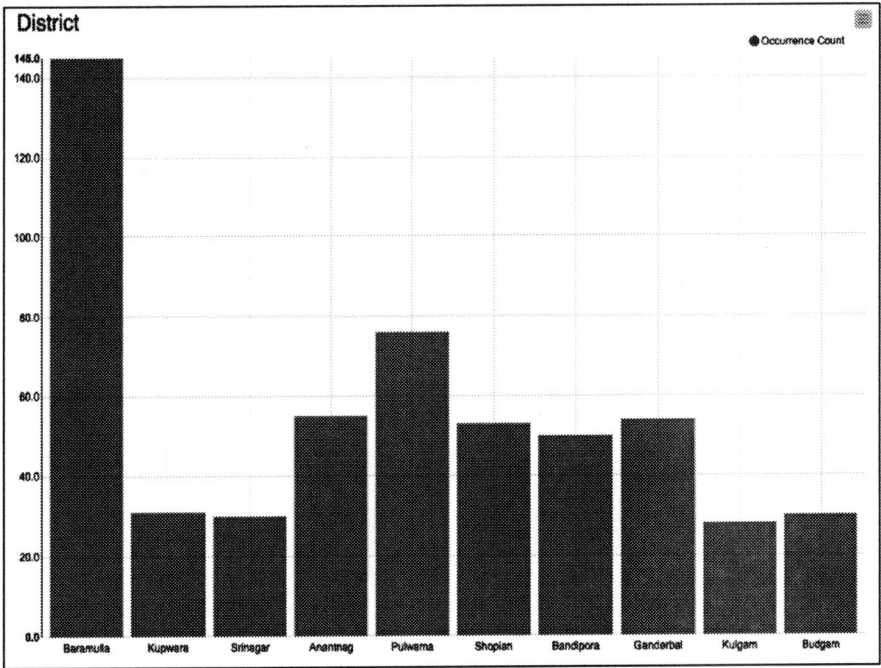

Religion

A total of 99% of the participants are followers of Islam with only 19 out of 552 belonging to Sikh community. There is no representation from any other community in the survey.

RowID	Count
Islam	533
Sikh	19

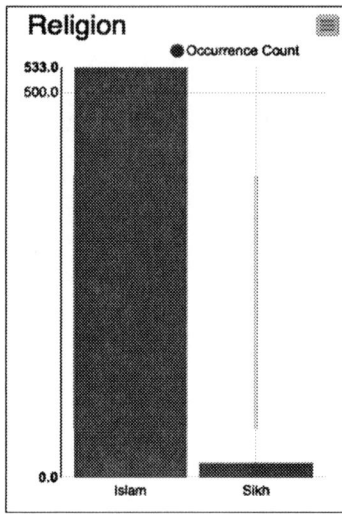
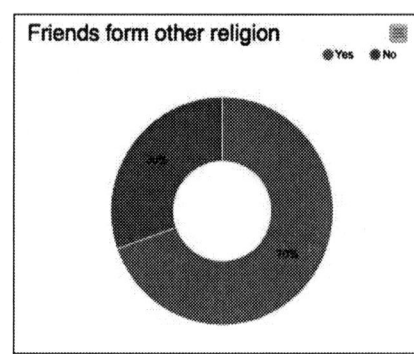

Thoughts on being a Kashmiri

Participants were asked "What does being a Kashmiri mean to you?" The response shows that 75% of them are proud of being a Kashmiri. The rest 25% feel that they are being discriminated and are suffering.

RowID	Count
No solution in sight	34
Oppressed	62
Proud	413
Second class human being	43

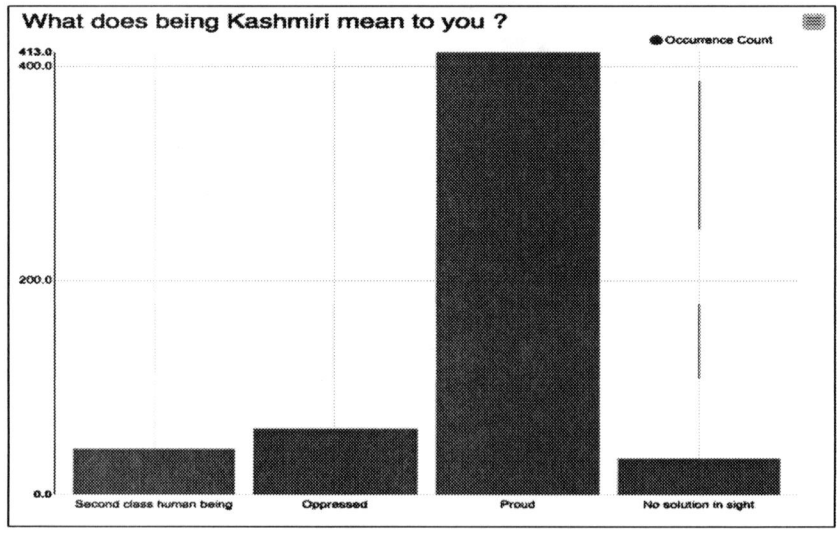

Aspirations

The data shows that more than 60% students of Kashmir aspire for a Central Govt. job followed by State Govt. with 11.93%, and then Army with only 4.77%.

Sl. No	Organisation	Percentage
1	Central Government job	61.59
2	Army	4.89
3	State Government Job	13.04
4	Private sector service job	3.26
5	Others	0.18
6	Don't know as yet	17.03

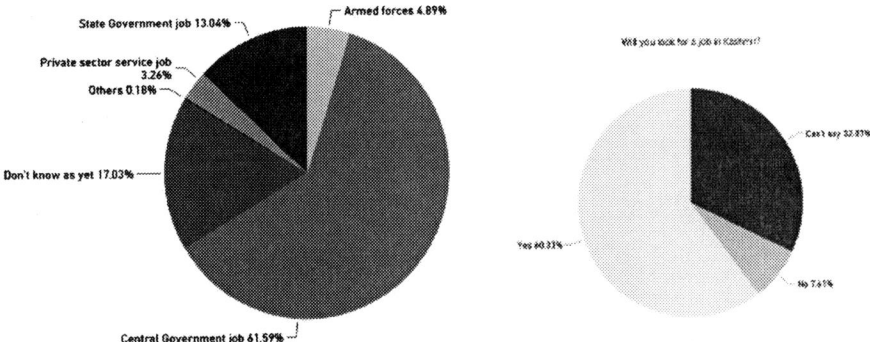

60.33% of the participants want to work in Kashmir and the rest are not sure.

Change you want to bring about in Kashmir?

The survey shows the maximum resentment among the youth of Kashmir is against the Govt. with 34% wanting to change the government rule of the region; 19.5% youth looks for a better life and 24.5% want education/employment opportunities in Kashmir and want to bring about structural changes in the way people are living their life in the valley. In the survey, it is also seen that 20.5% have shown resentment towards the presence of Army in the valley and want it to be withdrawn from the region.

RowID	Count
Change Government	192
Bring Education/Employment	131
Withdraw Army	112
Better life	109
Improve Drug Policy	8

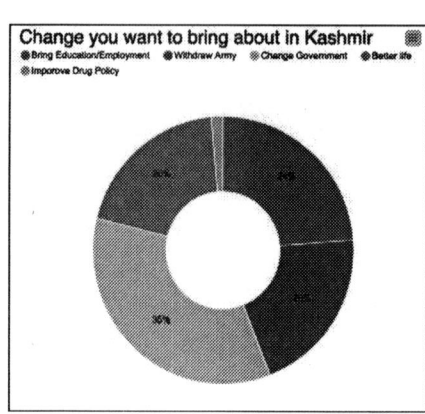

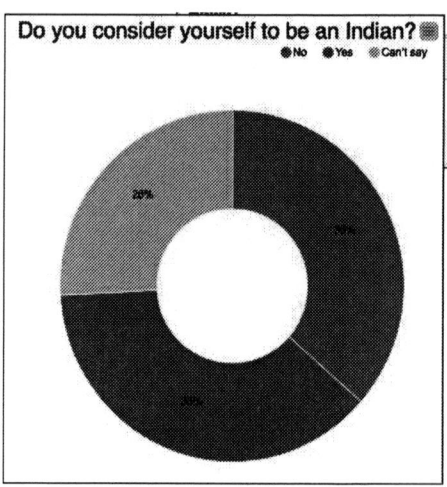

Only 63% of the population identify themselves as a Kashmiri

50% of the participants have friends from other parts of the country

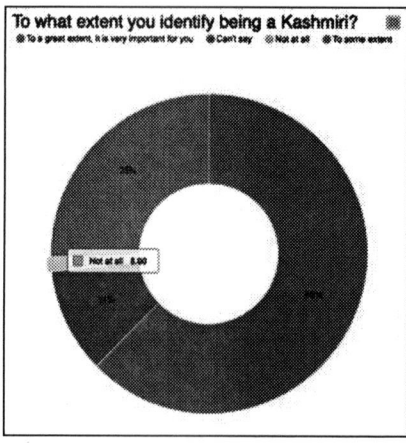

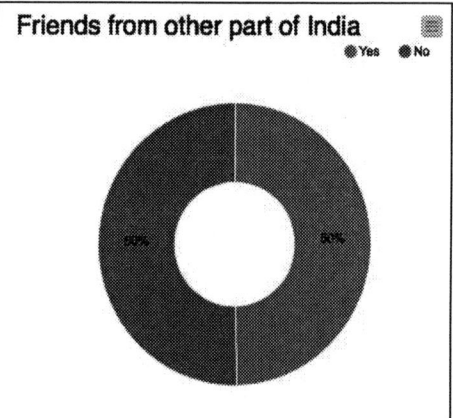

Indian or Not?

In the survey, the participants were asked to give their identification as Indian or Not? The result came out to be interesting as it was 50% on both the sides. Half of the people said they recognise themselves as Indian and the rest did not; 27% of the youth showcased confusion among them in recognizing themselves as Indian citizens.

RowID	Count
Yes	208
No	201
Can't say	143

UN Report on Kashmir

- According to the data, 48.0% of the participants have heard of the UNHRC report on Kashmir.
- Of the people who said "Yes", 98.9% people believe it is an accurate report.
- Of the people who said "No", 50.0% people believe it is an accurate report and 50.0% people feel it is an inaccurate report representing the Kashmir issue.
- The figure given below gives the relation between the answers given by the participants in the form of a tree.

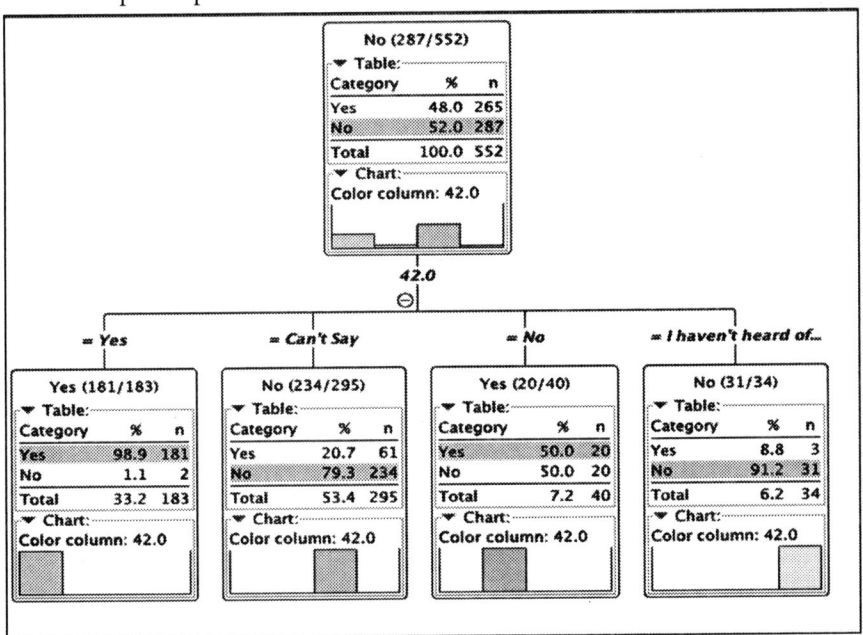

Social Media Interaction

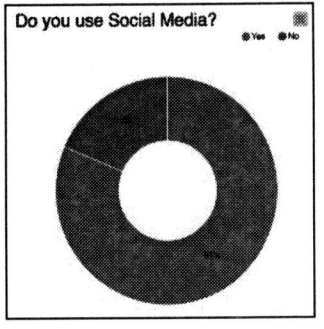

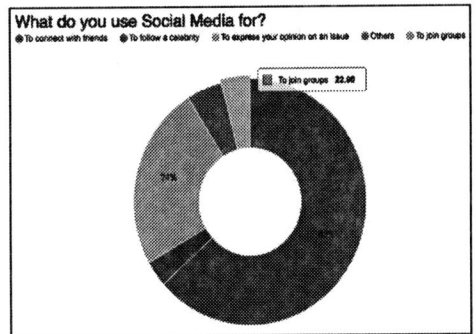

Around 81% of the people in valley are using social media in their daily life. According to the statistics, 63% of them are using it for the purpose it serves, that is to connect with friends; 24% are using it to express their opinions.

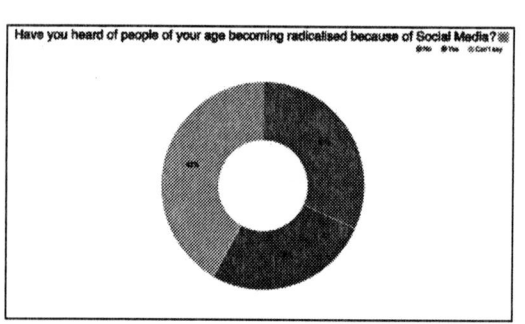

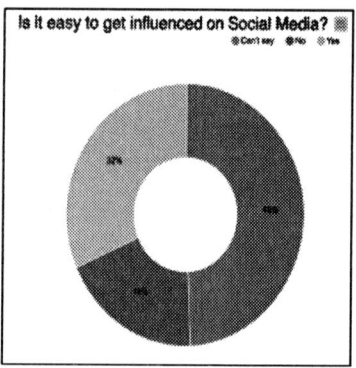

According to the findings, 26% students have agreed to know a person becoming radicalised on social media, which directly indicates that the influence of social media on the youth of Kashmir is detrimental in terms of the content and narrative they are coming across; 32% of them believe that it is very easy to get influenced by the narrative that is being provided on the social media and 49% of them are not sure, which is lending them into the category of vulnerable users.

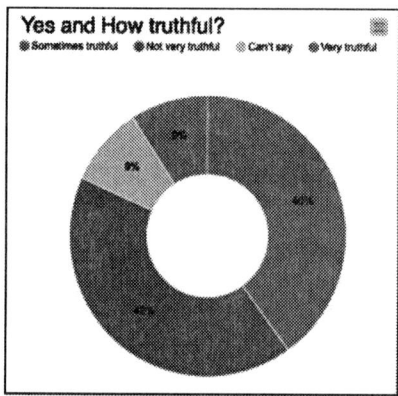

Amongst the people who claim to know someone who has been radicalised because of social media, 40% think that the information there is sometimes truthful and 43% think it's not truthful. It clearly shows that the half the generation is inclined towards the narrative shown on the social media and half is using their head to analyse and evaluate. The situation is critical and there is an urgent need to provide a correct narrative to the people of Kashmir and efforts should be focused on banning of the malicious content from the various online platforms.

Satisfaction

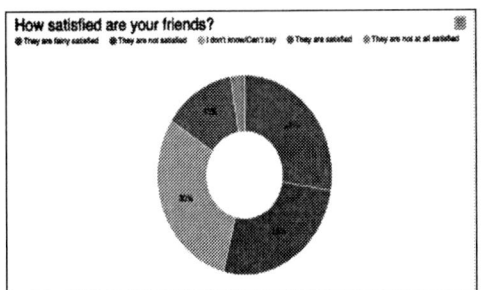 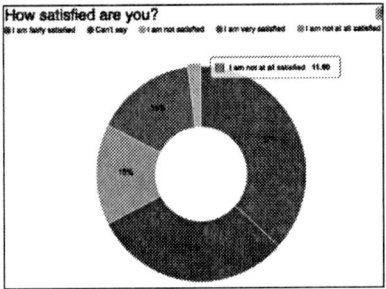

Evaluation of the data on the questions asked for the level of satisfaction they have, 52% people seem to be content with their life with 15% being very satisfied and 37% being fairly satisfied. Only 16% seem to be dissatisfied with their life with 1% being not at all satisfied and 15% being not satisfied. They were also asked to evaluate the satisfaction level among their friends, and the results have similar characteristics to their own satisfaction level. On the cause of dissatisfaction, as per the chart given below, 24% feel that being forced to live under the rule of the Indian government is their major reason of dissatisfaction but maximum number of them feel that uncertainty of better life and lack of job opportunities is the biggest reason for their dissatisfaction.

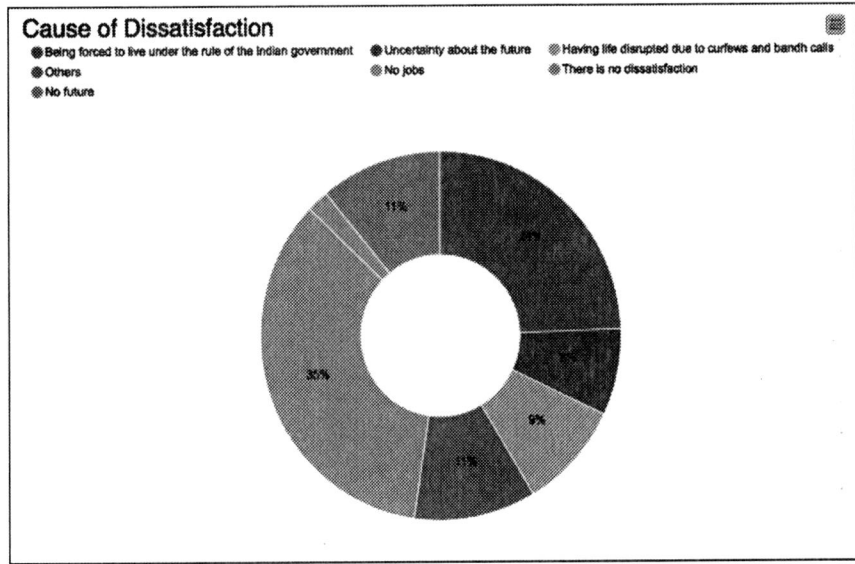

Activities in spare time

Participants were asked to give details about their activities in their spare time. The responses on the scale of how often they do these activities are given below:

S.No.	Question	Percentage (Often)
1	Go to a religious institutions	38.6
2	Go for a political meeting	0.03
3	Play outdoor games or sports	19.5
4	Watch movies or TV programs	17.5
5	Pursue a hobby	27.3
6	Read books/magazines	28.3
7	Spend time with family	80.3
8	Go out with friends	28.8

The results show that the youth of Kashmir is very actively going to the religious institutions. According to another question asked to them about their trust in the religious institutions and leaders, 24.28% have shown a great deal of trust and 41.67% have shown some trust. The analysis is given in the form of pie chart below.

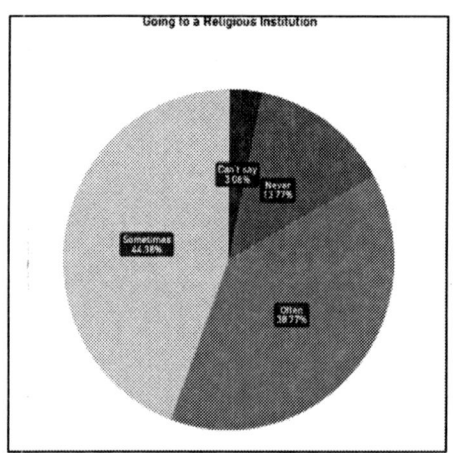
Level of trust in the organisations

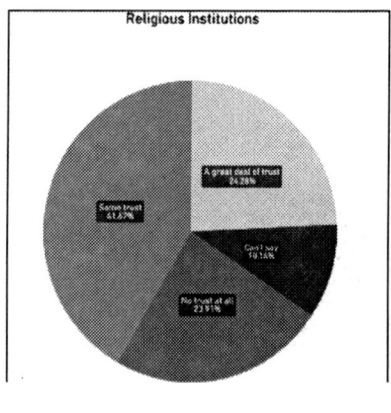
Level of trust in religious institutions and leaders

Participants were asked to give their level of trust on the different organisations present in the state of J&K. The results are given below:

Appendix B: Questionnaire Analysis by Tata Institute of Social Sciences 343

S. No.	Organisation	Great deal of trust	Some trust	No trust at all	Can't say
1	State government	13.95%	39.67%	40.22%	6.16%
2	Army	11.41%	30.62%	48.91%	9.06%
3	Local administration	9.78%	33.15%	40.22%	16.85%
4	Local police	6.7%	31.34%	51.09%	10.87%
5	Central government	10.14%	30.43%	45.83%	13.59%
6	Paramilitary	4.17%	20.11%	55.98%	19.75%
7	Judiciary	8.88%	53.62%	26.63%	10.87%
8	Religious institutions and leaders	24.28%	41.67%	23.91%	10.14%
9	Teachers in school/colleges	45.11%	46.74%	4.35%	3.8%
10	Family	90.58%	7.07%	0.54%	1.81%

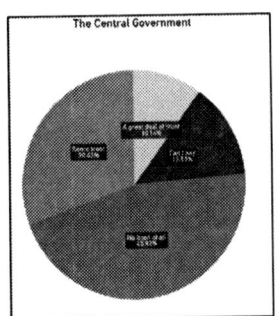
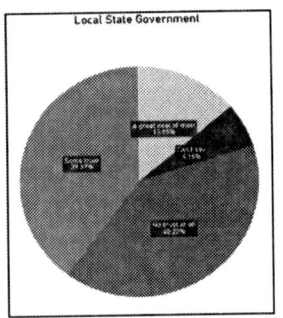
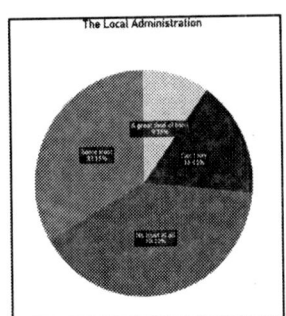
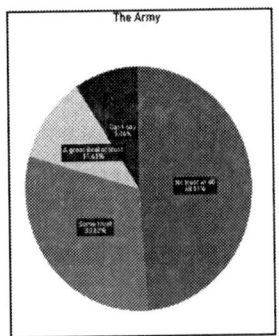
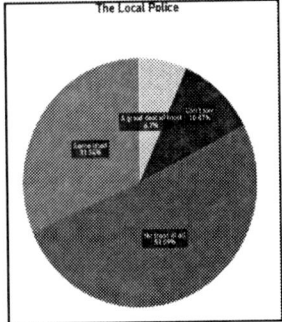
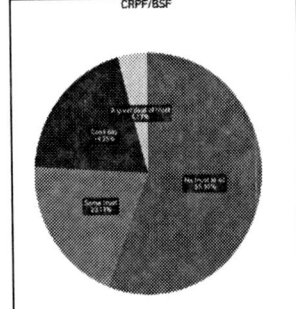

ANNEXURE TO APPENDIX B

Trust, Perceptions and Effects of News Sources and Social Media: A data-driven study of the recent unrest in Kashmir
Auton Lab, Carnegie Mellon University and CLAWS, New Delhi

ABSTRACT

In recent times, the Kashmir Valley in India has seen a resurgence of mass protests and separatist violence. Experts believe that the new wave of separatism has its roots in social media which provides a fertile platform to catalyze mass protests. While the penetration of Internet is fairly even throughout the Kashmir Valley, certain regions and subdivisions have been affected more adversely by the recent unrests. We seek to model these dichotomies in both the demographic factors along with regional effects, and external factors like the influence of both Social and Traditional Media in the form of Television Broadcasting and Print. To this end, we describe a data-driven approach to model the propensity of Kashmiri youth to secessionism based on an extensive survey that includes basic demographic data and its use, belief in social and news media, and uncover some interesting patterns of activity with regards to the Kashmir Valley.

Introduction

The Indian state of Jammu and Kashmir has remained relatively peaceful since the 2005. Inhabitants of the region have been participating in elections, both at the local level and in the national elections. In recent times, however, this has changed, with renewed support of violent separatism especially from the youth in Kashmir. The recent unrests during the period of 2015-17 have resulted in 4799 "Stone-Pelting"[1] incidents and also in deaths of 273 individuals,[2] which includes security forces and the civilian population in militant violence, which is a spike from previous years.

While there is no clear consensus as to what led to the situation deteriorate in the recent times, experts generally attribute it to a combination of factors including the lost opportunity by successive governments at the centre and the state level to provide a semblance of positive peace when there was a near rejection of external insurgency by the people of Kashmir, the inability of the state to provide meaningful Governance at a very critical time between 2004

Copyright © 2019, Association for the Advancement of Artificial Intelligence (www.aaai.org). All rights reserved.
[1]https://en.wikipedia.org/wiki/Stone_pelting_in_Kashmir.
[2]Indian Parliament, Rajya Sabha, Unstarred Question 556.

Appendix B: Questionnaire Analysis by Tata Institute of Social Sciences 345

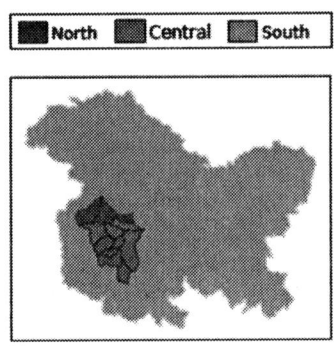 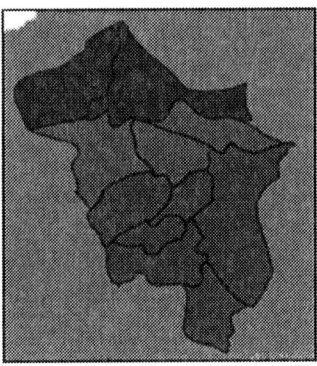

Figure 1: The Kashmir Valley (Coloured Regions), within the larger state of J&K. This study primarily focused on the regions in the Valley, most affected by separatist violence.

and 2010, and finally the elimination of a poster boy of separatist militancy in 2016. While such incidents are not unusual to Kashmir, owing to its long history of dealing with violence, in the recent surge, Social Media is believed to have played a big role in the organization of such protests and violent strikes. This hypothesis is further strengthened by the fact that the militant in question was a popular face on many social media platforms, with the individuals videos and pictures organizing and inciting the Kashmiri masses being shared across platforms like Facebook, Twitter and Whatsapp.

It is interesting to note that while the Valley is somewhat homogeneous with respect to factors like culture, language and other demography, certain regions especially in the Southern and Central parts of Kashmir seem to be more adversely affected by the recent violence. This also stands to contrast with the fact that other social indicators, including levels of literacy, Internet penetration etc. also seem fairly homogeneous across various different regions of Kashmir.

In the light of such unobvious dichotomies, we conducted a large survey amongst the youth population of Kashmir enrolled in Higher education programs from ten districts in the Kashmir valley, a region of the state of Jammu and Kashmir depicted in colour in Figure 1. The respondents were asked certain basic questions representative of their predisposition to the Republic of India along with demographic information and certain questions reflective of their propensity to be influenced by social and traditional media. Our contributions in this paper can be summarized as follows:

- We present results of the f Anonymous g survey [**AQ: Please check** "f

Anonymous g"] in Kashmir, and determine the relationship between the disposition of the Kashmiri population towards India and various Instruments of the Indian State.
- We further propose a Latent Variable model to incorporate regional dissimilarities and isolate effects of Social Media and Traditional News Sources including Electronic and Print Media on the respondents' predispositions.
- We determine relations between these Latent Effects and determine if such effects are correlated across individuals, as well as other basic demographic variables in the different regions of the valley.

Through this study, we aim to model these propensities in order to understand the reasons for rising separatism, to better support decision making by policymakers.

Related Work

There has been considerable research effort in detection of rumour and events from social media. Shao et al. (2017), Vosoughi (2015), Shu et al. (2017) and Zubiaga et al. (2018) describe Machine Learning–based approaches along with relevant Feature Extraction pipelines in order to detect Microblogs suggestive of Rumours and Fake News. Most of these directions have employed the use of Supervised Learning models in order to train their models.

Quantifying the effect of Social Media on mass political movements and uprisings and natural calamities is another popular research area. The community has attempted to research social media posts and its impact on events like the Boston Marathon Bombings (Starbird et al. 2014), Hurricane Sandy (Kogan, Palen, and Anderson 2015) and the BP Oil Spill (Starbird et al. 2015).

The use of Latent Variable models for Computational Social Science is gaining popularity and widespread acceptability. Abebe et al. (2018) describe topic-modelling of search queries for modelling healthcare needs in Africa, while Jo et al. (2017) describe a Graphical Model to model Human Dialogue and Discourse. De-Arteaga and Dubrawski (2017) describe an anomaly detection approach to extract patterns of Sexual Violence in El Salvador.

The research of religious extremism and its political ramifications in other parts of the subcontinent has also been studied in the social science literature. In a series of papers, Blair et al. (2013), Shapiro and Fair (2010), and Fair, Malhotra, and Shapiro (2012) explored the impact of religion and poverty on extremist tendencies in Pakistan. Their analysis was however limited to linear models, and they did not consider the effect of Social and Traditional Media as a possible confounders.

Pandita described various print media houses in Kashmir, while Gul and others (2013) described how traditional Kashmiri print and electronic media have embraced social media. Towards the best of our knowledge, this is the first study that combines Hierarchical Bayesian modelling in order to explicitly understand the impact of social media and traditional media along with regional idiosyncrasies specifically in the case of the Indian administered Kashmir Valley.

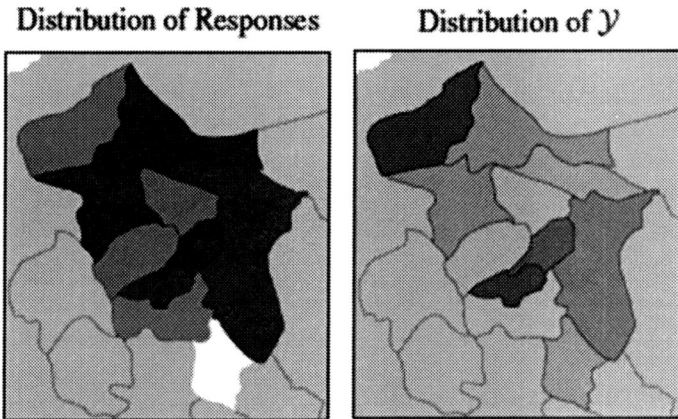

Figure 2: Heatmaps depicting the number of responsders and the extent of separatism, y, across various districts of the valley.

Survey Description

A large survey of the Kashmiri youth enrolled in higher educational institutes was conducted across ten Districts in the valley. The responders were asked questions about their level of education, age and some other questions indicative of their preferences of use of Social Media and Traditional News Sources. Tables 1 and 2 present some basic statistics about the responders and the questions that the responders were asked, respectively.

Table 1: Survey Statistics

No. of Participants	503
No. of Males	324
No. of Females	179
Age Group (Min, Max)	18-36
Age Group (25th-75th) percentile	21-24
Home Districts	10

Table 2: Questions that the responders were asked, alongwith the answer options. The questions were selected in order to get estimate the responders propensity to Separatism along with there preferences to Social Media and Traditional sources of News in the forms of Print and Electronic Media.

	Sense of Separatism and belonging to India
Q1	*Do you consider yourself Indian?* a) Yes, b) No, c) Can't Say
Q2	*Trust on Various Instruments of the State* We asked the responders to report their level of trust on the following Instruments of the Indian Union: (a) Local Government, (b) Central Government, (c) Local Law Enforcement, (d) Local Administration, (e) Armed Forces, (f) Central Law Enforcement and the (g) Judiciary on a 4-Point Scale, ranging from No Trust (-2), Can't Say (0), Some [AQ: Score is missing]
	Use of Social Media
Q S1	*Do you actively use Social Networks?* a) Yes, b) No
Q S2	*If Yes, what do you use it primarily for?* a) Connecting with Friends, b) Joining Groups, c) Following Celebrities, d) Expressing Political Opinion, e) Others, f) Never use it
Q S3	*Do you trust what you see on Social Media?* a) Yes, b) Sometimes, c) Can't Say, d) Not Very Truthful
	Use of Traditional Media
Q T1	*Do you read newspapers daily?* The responders were asked to choose between (a) Daily, (b) Sometimes or (c) Never
Q T2	*If Yes, What Kind?* a) National Daily, b) Local Newspaper, c) NoPreference or d) Don't Read
Q T3	*What kind of newspapers reports Kashmirinews most accurately?* a) Delhi and Other Indian Newspapers, b) LocalNewspapers from Kashmir, c) Newspapers from Pakistan, d) Other
Q T4	*What News Channels do you watch on TV?* a) Private English News Channels, b) Private Hindi News Channels, c) Government Funded News Channels d) Local News Channels e) Pakistani News

Determining Separatism, the variable *y*

It is true that alienation and separatism amongst the Kashmiri population lies on a spectrum rather than a strict binary. Separatist sympathies tend to increase around certain times and events. In times of peace, a large number of the people take part in democratic elections and seek employment in both the local and federal government, while this is not the case, in the event of a recent public outrage. Under such circumstances, it is arguable as to what a correct definition of separatism is. For the purposes of this experiment, we used a combination of responses to the following three questions on the survey in order to determine a proxy label for separatism.

We assigned all individuals who responded with Yes as Positive (+ve) for the variable y, and the ones who responded with a No as a Negative (-ve) for y. A large number of respondents responded with Can't Say for whom we resorted to the next question in order to determine a label. Table 3 presents Spearman's Rank Correlation for each individual to Q1 versus their response to Q2. Most responders who responded with a No to Q1 also had low mean scores for this question, although the distribution for the Can't Say and Yes was fairly more even.

Table 3: Spearman's Rank Correlation (ρ) between the Response to Q1 and Score Assigned to each instrument in Q2. **Indicates p-value<0.05.

Instrument	All Regions	Central	South	North
Armed Forces	0.50**	0.40**	0.53**	0.58**
Central Govt	0.43**	0.34**	0.50**	0.41**
Central Police	0.42**	0.37**	0.42**	0.39**
Local Admin	0.40**	0.28**	0.53**	0.32**
Local Govt	0.35**	0.17	0.39**	0.39**
Judiciary	0.32**	0.24**	0.35**	0.24**
Local Police	0.23**	0.11	0.42**	0.08

Trust on the Indian Armed Forces, deployed in Kashmir, seems to be most highly positively correlated with the sense of being Indian, across all the three major geographical regions of the Kashmir Valley. This is expected, since the Indian Army has played an active role in fighting armed militancy and also undertaken numerous civic actionprograms aimed at Human Development in the region through the "Sadbhavana" (Goodwill) program. This campaign has included setting up of co-educational Junior and High Schools, Vocational training centres and Healthcare and Medical Camps.[3]

Interestingly, Trust on the Local Governments in these regions also seems to be positively correlated with belonging to India, for both North and South Kashmir, whereas that is not so in the Central Region. We also found that Trust on Local and Police agencies seems to not be correlated with this sense, suggesting an opportunity for the Local Police to take up similar civic action programs to reach out and play a more active role in creating a nationalistic and democratic sense of belonging to the Union of India.

Based on these scores, we proceeded to train a Logistic Regression with an '2 penalty [**AQ: Please check highlighted text.**] in order to predict their

---

[3] https://economictimes.indiatimes.com/news/defence/operationsadbhavana-7800-jammu-and-kashmir-youths-went-oneducational-trips-in-three-years/articleshow/50271238.cms

responses to Q1 based on responses to Q2. We tuned the strength of the regularization parameter by performing grid search and cross-validation. For all the responders who responded with "Can't Say" to Q1, we deferred to this classifier in order to obtain a label, by deploying it at a fixed threshold of False Positive and False Negative Rates. Thus, for all the following experiments, with this combination of the responses, y was used as a label determining separatism for each responder.

Effects of Social Media, the variable S

Table 4 presents the statistically significant correlations between responses to QS1-3 and our definition of separatism, y. Interestingly, we found that a large number of participants who responded that their primary purpose of using Social Media was to express opinions and engaging in political dialogues also had a positive disposition towards the Indian Union. This suggests that Social Media, although infamous for its deleterious effects in the Valley, does provide a platform for the youth to engage in political discourse, encouraging state instruments to play a more active role on Social Media in positively engaging the population through these media.

Table 4: Spearman's Rank Correlation (ρ) between the Response to Q2 and Score Assigned to each instrument in Q2. **Indicates p-value<0.05.

	Response	All	Central	South	North
S2	Connect with friends	0.21**	0.08	-0.40**	-0.13
S2	Express opinions	0.23**	-0.02	0.34**	0.24**
S3	Trust Score	0.11**	0.03	0.25**	0.12

Effects of Print and Electronic News, T

We would further like to quantify the impact and relationship the International, National and Local press has to this alienation. This includes both the Print Media in the form of the Newspapers as well as Electronic Media like Television News Channels. Table 5 lists some significant correlations between responses to QT1-4. Notice that from the responses, it is clear that individuals actively engaging in reading newspapers have positive correlations with y. On the contrary, individuals not actively reading or having strong preferences for Newspapers tend to be negatively correlated with y, suggesting a more negative disposition towards the Indian State. This suggests an interesting similarity of the use of Print Media with that of Social Media.

Appendix B: Questionnaire Analysis by Tata Institute of Social Sciences

Table 5: Spearman rank correlation (ρ) between the response to Q2 and score assigned to each instrument in Q2. ** Indicates p-value <0.05

	Response	All	Central	South	North
T1	tm_use	-0.18**	0.23**	-0.38**	-0.05
T2	Don't Read	0.12**	-0.03	0.19**	0.1
T2	No Preference	-0.22**	-0.04	-0.2**	-0.27**
T3	Eng./Hindi (Delhi)	0.22**	0.18	0.26**	0.18**
T3	Local Urdu	0.14**	0.02	0.16**	0.1
T3	No newspaper	-0.26**	-0.11	-0.32**	-0.19**
T4	International	-0.16**	-0.0	-0.21**	-0.07
T4	Pakistani	-0.15**	-0.14	-0.09	-0.25**
T4	Private Hindi	0.22**	0.21**	0.15**	0.22**

For Electronic Media, the results were somewhat less surprising; consumption of India-based Hindi News is positively correlated with y, while consumption of Pakistani and International News is negatively correlated with y. We thus hypothesize that amongst the population with a general lack of trust in the Indian State and its instruments, such mistrust extends to even other Non-State Instruments, including the Private Electronic Media.

Demographic Covariates, X

Apart from just the responses to the Questions involving use of Print Electronic and Social Media, we also include additional covariates, suggestive of certain basic Demographic information. We hypothesize that the addition of these covariates would help better adjust our models for confounding. The variables include the responders Gender, their Home District, Place of Study, Age and Educational Level, that is whether they are enrolled in Undergraduate, Masters or Graduate Programs in the Science or Humanities. In the case of the proposed model, these factors are represented as an observed variable x in Figure 3.

Modelling Effects with Latent Variables

We propose a Latent Variable Hierarchical Model (Figure 3) in order to model our dataset and better understand how Social Media impact and regional differences impact the propensity to separatism.

Regional Differences

We hypothesize that in general owing to similar circumstances, Kashmiri youth have similar reasons for predisposition towards separatism. It is however clear from survey responses (Tables 4 and 5), as well as commonly believed by domain experts and policymakers, that their important regional differences

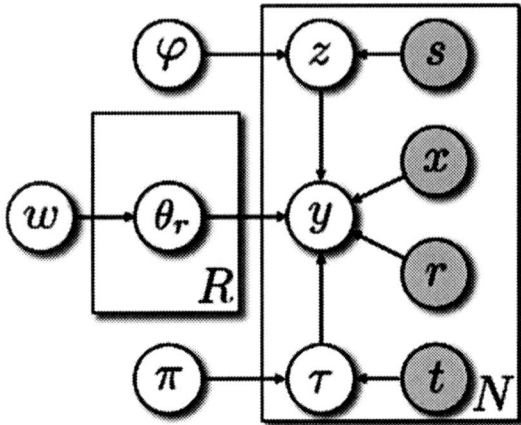

Figure 3: The Proposed Latent Variable Model. x represents observed Demographic Features, r represents the region the individual is drawn from, s and t are the responses to questions about use of social and traditional media, while z and τ are the Latent Effects of the mediums. θ is the set of parameters that determine the outcome y.

cannot be ignored. In order to incorporate these regional differences into our model, we adopt a Hierarchical Graphical model. Not only does the use of the hierarchical model help better model the regional differences, but it also helps alleviate the challenges of working with the relatively small dataset we are working with ($n < 500$).

Latent News and Social Media Effects, s and τ

We further hypothesize that the impact or influence of Social Media on an individual can be thought of as a Binary Variable that indicates whether the user is negatively influenced, or motivated by separatist ideologies. We further assume that this binary variable can be characterized by a log linear parameterization of the individuals' responses to **QS1-S3 and QT1-T4**.

The Generative Story

1. We first draw the set of parameters, ω, φ, π
   (This corresponds to an $\ell 2$ penalty)
   $\omega \sim \text{Norm}(\omega_0, \lambda_0)$, $\varphi \sim \text{Norm}(\varphi_0, \lambda_0)$, $\pi \sim \text{Norm}(\pi_0, \lambda_0)$
   $\omega_0 = 0$, $\varphi_0 = 0$.

2. For each region $r \in R$, we draw the parameters, θ_r,
   $\theta_r \mid (\omega, \lambda) \sim \text{Normal}(\omega, \lambda)$

3. We draw the latent z_i, conditioned on φ and s_i as
   $z_i \mid (\varphi, s_i) \sim \text{Bernoulli}(\sigma(\varphi^T s_i))$
   and the latent T_i, conditioned on π and t_i as
   $T_i \mid (\pi, t_i) \sim \text{Bernoulli}(\sigma(\pi^T t_i))$
4. The final output, y_i conditioned on r, θ and x_i, z_i is
   $y \mid (x_i, \theta, r_i, z_i, T_i) \sim \text{Bernoulli}(\sigma(\theta_r^T [x_i, z_i, T_i]))$

Here, $\sigma(\cdot)$ is the sigmoid function

Inference

Let the observed data $\{x_i, s_i, t_i, r_i, y_i\}_{i=1}^N$ be represented by $\mathcal{D}$. We denote the set of all parameters, $\{w, \varphi, \{\theta_r, \pi_r, \varphi_r\}_{r=1}^R,\}$ as Θ. We would like to maximize the joint probability of the dataset under our model.

Our first attempt at performing inference was using a Markov chain Monte Carlo sampling method. To this end, we experimented with both a Metropolis–Hastings–based sampler with a Multivariate Gaussian Proposal Distribution, and Hamiltonian Monte Carlo NUTS–based sampler (Hoffman and Gelman, 2014; Salvatier, Wiecki, and Fonnesbeck, 2016). Unfortunately, since most of the features we work with are categorical, this results in a large parameter space. Thus, this did not allow us to have high acceptance rates for the samplers. We instead proceeded to model the point estimates of the parameters by using a maximum a posteriori estimator of the log-likelihood, given by

$$p(\mathcal{D}|\Theta) = \prod_{i=1}^{N} p(x_i, s_i, t_i, y_i, r_i, \Theta)$$

$$= \left(\prod_{i=1}^{N} \int_{z_i, \tau_i} p(y_i|x_i, \theta, \pi, r_i, z_i) p(z_i|s_i, \varphi) p(\tau_i|t_i, \pi) dz_i d\tau_i \right) \prod_{i=1}^{R} p(\theta_r, \pi_r | w)$$

Note that we ignore the parameter prior to simplify notation. For inference, we perform Stochastic Gradient Descent on the objective, with Mini-Batching for 10,000 epochs.

Experiments

We experiment with the following models:

1. Parametric Max Entropy Classifier (MAX-ENT)

This amounts to learning a logistic regression model for the outcome variable y_i given x_i. This model assumes that the output y_i is a linear function of the inputs xi on the log-odds scale.

2. Region-Specific Max Entropy Classifier (R-MAX-ENT)

It is similar to the previous baseline approach but involves separate models for each region. This allows learning more Non-Linear hypotheses by allowing for the model to linear separate functions for each region. However, the lack of data does not let the model to benefit from sharing knowledge about similarity of the regions.

3. Hierarchical Graphical Model (HGM)

The HGM is similar to the Proposed Figure 3, but the observed covariates (s, t) corresponding to the responses to the Questions are grouped together with other demographic covariate, x, instead of reducing to latent variables.

4. Hierarchical Latent Variable Model (H-LV-GM)

Finally, we experiment with the proposed Latent Variable model. The advantage of incorporating Latent Variables is that it reduces the adverse effects of Social and Traditional Media on single variables, helping interpretability and analysis.

Experimental Setup

For both our model and the baselines, we perform 5-fold cross-validation over the dataset. We compute the Area under the ROC Curve, the Mean Average Precision, and the Accuracy over the held out fold and report the mean of each metric over each of the 5 folds. Before training the model, we standardize each column of our data matrix X by subtracting the column mean and dividing by the column sample variance, to ensure all the features are on a relatively same scale.

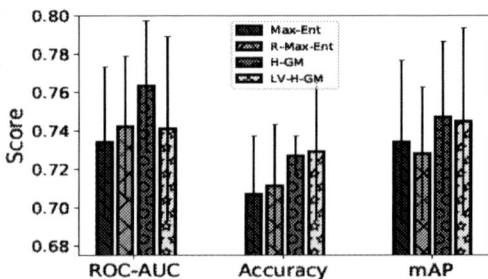

	AuROC	Accuracy	mAP
H-GM	0:763 ± 0:04	0:727 ± 0:01	0:747 ± 0:05
LV-H-GM	0:741 ± 0:05	0:729 ± 0:04	0:745 ± 0:06

Figure 4: Performance comparison of the proposed graphical

Results

Figure 4 compares the performance of the proposed approaches (HGM, H-LV-GM) against baseline linear models. Note that the HGM has larger number of parameters than H-LV-GM, which justifies better performance on classification metrics. H-LV-GM however while having lower performance allows collapsing effects of media into a single variable allowing for a single variable of comparison for analysis, and outperforms the other two baselines.

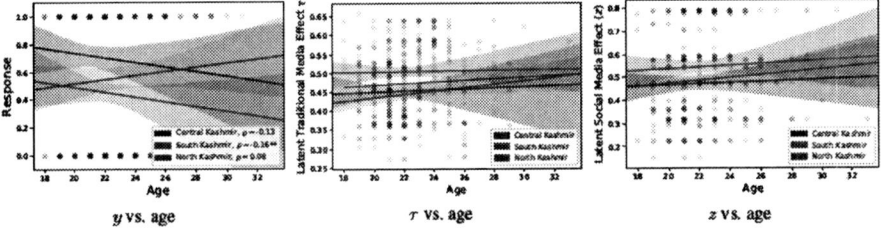

Figure 5: The Response Variable (y), and the Latent Effects of Media with age of the responders. Interestingly, we found that as opposed to common belief, our definition of separatism tends to be weakly positively correlated with Age, suggesting that younger responders seem to have a more positive disposition towards the Indian Union. The effects of both Traditional and Social Media seem to be positively correlated with the responders' age too, which is contrary to public opinion about social media being more popular with the younger population.

Figure 6 compares the distribution of the Latent Variables τ and z, representing the effects of Traditional News Sources and Social Media respectively. Notice that for both North and Central Kashmir, the effects seem to be mostly uncorrelated, while for South Kashmir, there seems to be some weak positive correlation. This suggests that for the most part, cohorts of individuals who are likely to be adversely influenced into separatism from social media and traditional news sources respectively are disparate.

We also establish that as opposed to popular belief, there seems to be an overall increasing trend in separatism with age, as evidenced from Figure 5. Also notice that the effects of Social Media and Traditional News sources, as captured by the latent variables, z and τ, seem to increase with age across all regions of the valley. While one would expect this to be the case for electronic and print media, the fact that social media's influence on separatism seems to increase with age is an interesting discovery.

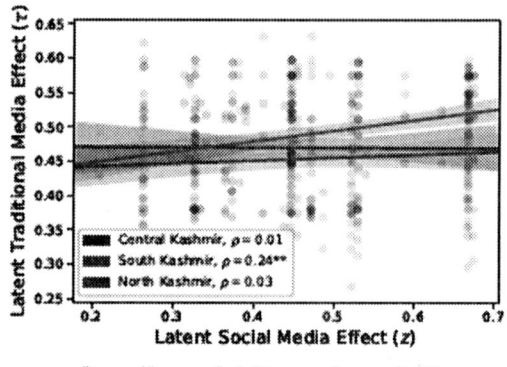

Overall $\rho = 0.147$, p-value≈ 0.00

Figure 6: Correlation between the Latent Social Media Effect, z, and the Traditional Media, τ. Notice that the effects seem to be mostly uncorrelated, across the regions except for South Kashmir where the effects have a weak correlation.

Limitations and Future Work

While we discovered some interesting trends and patterns in the Kashmiri youth populations support for separatism, we would like to caution that this study is limited by its comparatively smaller sample size and sample selection representative of mostly students enrolled in higher education programs. These factors may disallow the interpretation of these results in the context of other demographic groups in the Kashmir Valley. We further caution the readers of the temporal nature of Kashmiri separatism, which tends to have a cyclical pattern of periods with mass unrests, followed by relative peace with high participation in electoral politics. Given these realities, in the future we aim to extend this study to larger sample sizes, representative of all heterogeneities of the Kashmiri Demographic, sampled over fixed time intervals. In the future, we also aim to incorporate other demographic factors in order to better model all confounding evidence to make stronger causal claims.

Conclusion

In this paper, we aimed to study the recent rise of separatist unrest in the Kashmir Valley in India, especially in the youth population. Towards this end, we conducted a survey of the youth population in the Valley, to understand the nature of separatism with regard to trust in various instruments of the Indian state. We further tried to model the impact of Social Media and Traditional Sources of News towards rising separatist movement based on this definition and exploited a Hierarchical Latent Variable Model, in order to better understand how these effects vary with the demography and determine separatism.

ACKNOWLEDGMENTS

We would like to thank the reviewers for there valuable suggestions

REFERENCES

[Abebe et al. 2018] Abebe, R.; Hill, S.; Vaughan, J. W.; Small, P. M.; and Schwartz, H. A. 2018. Using search queries to understand health information needs in Africa. arXiv preprint arXiv:1806.05740.

[Blair et al. 2013] Blair, G.; Christine Fair, C.; Malhotra, N.; and Shapiro, J. N. 2013. Poverty and support for militant politics: Evidence from Pakistan. *American Journal of Political Science* 57(1):30–48.

[De-Arteaga and Dubrawski 2017] De-Arteaga, M., and Dubrawski, A. 2017. Discovery of complex anomalous patterns of sexual violence in El Salvador. In Data for Policy. Zenodo.

[Fair, Malhotra, and Shapiro 2012] Fair, C. C.; Malhotra, N.; and Shapiro, J. N. 2012. Faith or doctrine? Religion and support for political violence in Pakistan. *Public Opinion Quarterly* 76(4):688–720.

[Gul and others 2013] Gul, S., et al. 2013. Adoption of social media by online newspapers of kashmir. *Annals of Library and Information Studies* (ALIS) 60(1):56–63.

[Hoffman and Gelman 2014] Hoffman, M. D., and Gelman, A. 2014. The no-U-turn sampler: Adaptively setting path lengths in Hamiltonian Monte Carlo. *Journal of Machine Learning Research* 15(1):1593–1623.

[Jo et al. 2017] Jo, Y.; Yoder, M. M.; Jang, H.; and Ros'e, C. P. 2017. Modeling dialogue acts with content word filtering and speaker preferences. In *Proceedings of the Conference on Empirical Methods in Natural Language Processing. Conference on Empirical Methods in Natural Language Processing*, Volume 2017, 2169. NIH Public Access.

[Kogan, Palen, and Anderson 2015] Kogan, M.; Palen, L.; and Anderson, K. M. 2015. Think local, retweet global: Retweeting by the geographically-vulnerable during hurricane sandy. In *Proceedings of the 18th ACM Conference on Computer Supported Cooperative Work & Social Computing*, 981–993. ACM.

[Pandita 2013] Pandita, R. 2013. Scenario of print media in Jammu & Kashmir (India): An analytical study. *Journal of Mass Communication & Journalism* 4(170):2.

[Salvatier, Wiecki, and Fonnesbeck 2016] Salvatier, J.; Wiecki, T. V.; and Fonnesbeck, C. 2016. Probabilistic programming in python using PyMC3. Peer J Computer Science 2:e55.

[Shao et al. 2017] Shao, C.; Ciampaglia, G. L.; Varol, O.; Flammini, A.; and Menczer, F. 2017. The spread of fake news by social bots. arXiv preprint arXiv:1707.07592.

[Shapiro and Fair 2010] Shapiro, J. N., and Fair, C. C. 2010. Understanding support for Islamist militancy in Pakistan. *International Security* 34(3):79–118.

[Shu et al. 2017] Shu, K.; Sliva, A.; Wang, S.; Tang, J.; and Liu, H. 2017. Fake news detection on social media: A data mining perspective. ACM SIGKDD Explorations Newsletter.

Bibliography

Amnesty International. *Disappearances in Jammu and Kashmir*, https://amnesty.org.in, accessed on 15 December 2016.

Bazaz, Prem Nath. *Democracy through Intimidation and Terror*, Srinagar, India: Gulshan Books, 2007.

Bazaz, Prem Nath. *Struggle for Freedom in Kashmir*, Srinagar, India: Gulshan Books, 2003.

Byman, Daniel. *Deadly Connections: States That Sponsor Terrorism*, Cambridge: Cambridge University Press, 2005.

Byman, Daniel; Chalk, Peter; Hoffman, Bruce; Rosenau, William; and Brannan, David, *Trends in Outside Support for Insurgent Movement*, Washington, D.C.: RAND, 2001.

Devadas, David. *In Search of a Future: The Story of Kashmir*, New Delhi, India: Penguin Books India, 2007.

Devadas, David. *The Generation of Rage in Kashmir*, New Delhi: Oxford University Press, 2018.

Economic Survey of India, 2015/2016.

Economic Survey of J&K, 2015/2016.

Army Field Manual, FM 3-24/MCWP 3-33.5, "Counterinsurgency" December 2006, US Department of the Army.

Galula, David. Counterinsurgency Warfare. Theory and Practice, Westport, CT: Praeger, 1964.

Human Rights Watch. *India's Secret Army In Kashmir*, May 1996 Vol. 8, No. 4 (C).

Johnston, Patrick. "The Geography of Insurgent Organization and Its Consequences for Civil Wars: Evidence from Liberia and Sierra Leone", *Security Studies,* Vol. 17, No. 1 (January 2008).

Lamb, Alastair. Kashmir: A Disputed Legacy 1846-1990, Karachi, Pakistan: Oxford University Press, 1994.

Lawrence, Sir Walter Roper. *The Valley of Kashmir*, London: Henry Frowde, 1895.

Luttwak, Edward N. "Give War a Chance", *Foreign Affairs*, 78-4: 36 – 45 (July/August 1999).

Lyall, Jason; and Wilson III, Isaiah. "Rage against the Machines: Explaining Outcomes in Counterinsurgency Wars", *International Organization, Vol. 63, No. 1 (Winter 2009)*.

Maldonado, Ferdinand, Captain, USAF. The Hybrid Counterinsurgency Strategy: System Dynamics Employed to Develop A Behavioural Model of Joint Strategy, *AFIT/GEM/ENV/09-M10, March 2009*.

Nagl, John A. *Learning to Eat Soup with a Knife: Counterinsurgency Lessons from Malaya and Vietnam*, University of Chicago Press, 2002.

Peters, Ralph. "The hearts-and-minds myth – Sorry, but winning means killing." *Armed Forces Journal (September 2006)*.

Puri, Balraj. *Kashmir: Towards Insurgency*, New Delhi: Orient Longman, 1993.

Raina, A.N. "Geography of Jammu and Kashmir", Radha Krishan Anand & Co., *Jammu, India, 1978*.

Schofield, Victoria. *Kashmir in Conflict - India, Pakistan and the Unending War*, Diane Pub, 2003.

Singh, R.L. (ed.). *India: A Regional Geography*, Varanasi, India: National Geographical Society of India, 1971.

Singh, Tavleen. *Kashmir: A Tragedy of Errors*, New Delhi: Penguin Books, 1996.

Staniland, Paul. "Organizing Insurgency Networks, Resources, and Rebellion in South Asia, International Security", *International Security, Vol. 37, No. 1 (Summer 2012)*.

Swami, Praveen. *The Kargil War*, New Delhi: LeftWord Books, 2000.

Senge, Peter. *The Fifth Discipline: The Art and Practice of the Learning Organization*, New York: Doubleday/Currency, 1990.

Index

Abdul Ghani Lone, 21
Abdullah, Farooq, 18-19
Abdullah, Sheikh, 15-17
Afghanistan, 2, 18, 61-62, 69, 73, 76, 84-87, 92, 94, 182, 204, 206, 208
Agriculture, 43
Al Qaeda Connection, 63
All Parties Hurriyat Conference (APHC), 19-20, 40-41, 230, 232
    Formation, 40
    Ideology and Role, 41
    Pakistan's Role, 42
    People's Perception, 42
    Split, 41
    Right to Self-determination, Views on, 41
Animal Husbandry, 44
Armed Forces Special Powers Act (AFSPA), 54-56, 106, 112, 199, 204, 231, 259-60, 284
    Repeal/Retain, 55
Artificial Intelligence (AI), 5, 8, 110, 153, 286
Assuage Feelings through Greater Autonomy, 155
Autonomy, 111

British Experience, 147

Capacity Building of J&K Police and Para-Military Police, 107
Capacity Building of Police and PMF, 270
Categorisation of OGWs, 125
CATWOE Analysis, 103
Causal Loop Diagrams (CLD), 105
Centre-State Relations, 49, 224
Chasm-Baraah, 242
China's Influences in IOR, 83
China's Position on Kashmir, 77
China-Pak Partnership, 83
Climate, 24
    Cold, 171
Constitutional Framework, 47
Contingency Strategy Options, 271
Corporate Houses, 295
Corruption, 176
Crawling Kashmir, 226

Daagh-Daar, 235, 248
Decline in Infiltration, 198

Democratic Govt Setup, 167
Demographic Base, 26
Demography, 161
Dependence on Central Aid, 183
Deployment of SF and CAPF, 106
Drugs, 183

Economic Development, 42-43, 113, 166, 209, 212, 215, 218, 221, 223
Economic Strategies, 278
Education Higher, 30
Education, 28, 179, 211, 213
Alienation/Isolation, Effect of Sense, 125
Ejaaz-e-Maseehaaee, 236
Electronic Media, 57
Empower, 157
Energy, 46
Engage, 155
Environmental Forces, 200
Environment-Shaping Strategy Options, 279
External support, 105

Floriculture, 44
Forest, 44
Fringe Hindutva Elements, 295
Fruit Sector, 43
Funding of Groups, 63
    Direct Funding, 63
    Hawala, 63
    Remittances from Abroad, 64
    Pakistan High Commission, 64
    Nepal Route, 64
    J&K Bank, 64
    Narcotics, 64

Geography, 160
Geology, 177
Geo-Strategic Location, 165
Global Influence, 90
Gordian knot, 2
Governance, 106, 224
Govt. Machinery, 294
Greater Autonomy/Self-Rule, 53

Handicraft Industry, 45, 167
Harakat ul-Mujahideen (HuM), 61

Index

Hawala Money, 183
Hedging Strategy, 287
Historical Baggage, 171
Hizb-ul-Mujahideen (HM), 18, 39, 61
Horticulture, 43
Human Behaviour, 143
Human Development Index, 34, 170
Hurriyat Agenda, 225
Hurriyat Sp, 106
Hydro-power potential, 166

India State of Forest Report (ISFR), 167
Indo-China Relations, 179
Indonesian Response, 147
Indo-Pak Trade, 74, 179
Industrial Policy, 44
Information Technology, 45
Infrastructure, 46
    Development, 107
Insurgencies, 83
Integrate the Power of Technology, 153
International News Channels, 296
ISIS, 87-88, 121, 146, 182, 206, 276
    Migration, 112
Islamic State in Khorasan (ISKP), 87

J&K
    Article 370, 49
    Comparison with PoK, 106, 198
    Governs Centre-State Relations, 50
    Interlocutors Report on Review of AFSPA, 55
    Militancy, 105, 198
    Police, 294
    Threats for, 74
Jaish-e-Mohammed (JeM), 61-62
Jamaat-e-Islami, 58
Jammu and Kashmir Liberation Front (JKLF), 18
Jammu and Kashmir State Women Development Corporation (JKWDC), 32
Job Opportunities, 179
Judiciary, 294

Kashmir Problem, Born, 15
Kashmir Valley, Seasons of, 24
Kashmiri Pandits Rehab, 107, 295
Kashmiri Psyche, 113, 145, 216, 219, 221, 223
Kashmiriyat, 35-37, 130-31, 143, 151, 168-69, 211, 213
Kashyap-Mar, 11
Khan, Amanullah, 18

Lalitaditya, 12
Lashkar-e-Jhangvi (LeJ), 62
Lashkar-e-Toiba (LeT), 19, 62
Line of Control (LC), 17

Trade, 107
Literacy, 170
Local Media, 106, 295
Low Population Density, 169

Manage Perceptions Internationally, 154
Mandatory Strategies, 192
Media Management, 112
Media, 56
Militancy/Terrorism, 60
Militants Dynamics, 204, 206, 208
Minerals, 166
Misuse of Media, 183
Mothers of Slain Militants, 293
Muslim United Front (MUF), 18

Naadir-e-Rozgaar, 254
Narcotics Trade, 66
National Democratic Alliance (NDA), 53
National Investigative Agency (NIA), 126
National Media, 295
Natural/Local Resources, 166
Nepal, 89
Networks Can Only Beat a Network, 156
New Great Game, 76
New Tradecraft, 158

OGFWLS, 126
OGWs, 178, 293
Op Sadhbhavana, 66-67, 107, 112
Operation Gibraltar, 17
Opportunities, 164, 178

Pakistan, 71, 91
    Aspirations of Ethnic Groups, 72
    Civilian Governance with Military 'Pre-eminence', 72
    Connection, 62-63
    ISI, 73
    Nuclear Capability, 71
    People , 296
    Propaganda and OGWs, Name & Shame, 157
    Proxy War, 182, 204-05, 208
    Rise of Religious Extremists, 72-73
    Role of Islam and Fundamentalism, 72
    Socio-economic Divide, 76
    Support, 198
    Weak Economy, 75
Pak-Taliban Relations, 182
Pan-Islamic Wave, 182
People of the State, 292
People's Republic of China (PRC), 76, 89, 91
    Foreign Policy and Diplomacy, 79
    Industry and Technology, 79-80

Opportunities and Threats, 80-84
Perception Management, 107, 112
Philosophy, 36
Physiography, 24
Political Deadlock, 48
Political Importance, 47
Political Strategies, 274
Poor Governance, 176
Private Investment, 177
Proactive Strategy, 288
Prof Sujata Sriram, 107
Prospering Kashmir, 228
Public Safety Act (PSA), 56, 124, 261, 284-85

Radicalisation, Society, 181
Radicalisation, Youth, 215, 220, 222
Regional Autonomy Committee (RAC), 20
Regional Disparity, 47, 209
Relevance of Awaam, 100
Religious Fundamentalism, 106, 210, 212
Religious Teachers/Ulema, 293
Respond Full spectrum, 152
Rising Fundamentalism, 176
Role of Army, 113
Role of Local Media, 106

Security Environment, 267
Security Forces (SF), 57, 86, 106, 109, 118, 169, 190, 203, 205, 207, 263, 294
Security Strategies, 275
Self-Destructing Kashmir, 231
Separatists, 296
Singaporean Concept, 147
Sipah-e-Sahaba Pakistan (SSP), 62
Social and Religious/Cultural Strategies, 277
Social Divide, 209, 212
Social Media, 57, 112, 270
Social Welfare Department, 32
Soft Systems Methodology (SSM), 99
Special Status & Alienation, 53, 107
Spread of Fundamentalism, 38, 144
State Autonomy Committee (SAC), 20, 51
Strategic Location, 69
Strategies, 298
Strength, 164-65
Strength-Opportunity (SO) Strategies, 190
Strength-Threat (ST) Strategies, 191
Sufism, 37, 114
Surgical Strikes, 107
Surrendered Militants, 106
Swayam Sidha, 32
SWOT Analysis, 164
    Rank-Ordered, 187

Teachers, 293
Terrorism, Agitational, 177
Terrorist Activities, 183
Terrorists, Operational Tools, 119
    Agitational Space, 121
    Command and Control, 119
    Cyber Space, 121
    OGWs, 121
    Operational Security, 120
    Operational Space, 120
    Weapons and Equipment, 120
Terrorists, Organisational Tools, 116
    Alienation through Radicalisation, 117
    Finance, 118
    Ideology, 116
    Leadership, 117
    Publicity, 118
    Recruitment, 117
Terrorists/Militants, 114
Threat, 164, 181
Tourism, 46, 170
Trader Community, 294
Trans-LC Indo-Pak Trade, 76
Trends, 156
Troubled History, 171
Turmoiled History, 144

Udaan, 33
Unemployment, 177
United Jehadi Council (UJC), 19
United Nations, 95
United Nations Security Council, 15
United Nations Commission for India and Pakistan (UNCIP), 15
Unsettled borders with Pak & China, 182
USA, 90
US-Af-Pak, 92
US-China, 91
US-Pak, 92
US-Saudi Arabia, 91

Vernacular Press, 56

Water Resources, 166
Weakness Opportunity (WO) Strategies, 190
Weakness, 164, 171
Weakness-Threat (WT) Strategies, 192
Women Empowerment, 31-32, 172, 210-11, 213
Working Groups, 51

Youth Bulge, 27, 170
Youth Connect Self-Help Groups, 295
Youth Empowerment, 32-33, 210, 213